MW01615344

HIS NAME IS RON

HIS NAME IS RON

The Family of Ron Goldman
with William and Marilyn Hoffer

Published by Graymalkin Media

www.graymalkin.com

Copyright © 1997 by RLG Family Corporation

Originally published by William Morrow and Company Inc.

This edition published in 2016 by Graymalkin Media

Book design by Timothy Shaner

ISBN: 978-1-63168-076-2

Printed in the United States of America

1   3   5   7   9   10   8   6   4   2

In loving memory and in honor of Ron

Ron,

We can no longer hold your hand,
Embrace you in a hug,
Or share in your dreams,
But you are with us every day.

Our minds are filled with the sounds of your voice,
Our hearts . . . with your love,
Our souls . . . with your warmth,
We are forever connected.

You brought us pride, love, joy, and happiness,
We hope we have brought you honor.

Missing you now,
Loving you always

—Dad, Patti, Kim, Michael, and Lauren

We dedicate this book . . .

To the hundreds of thousands of victims of violent crime and to their families. We hope that by expressing the pain that we share, a nation will better understand the total devastation caused by the violence that has become a part of all of our daily lives.

On behalf of our loved ones,
we need, we demand, we deserve change.

A Letter from Ron's Family

A bout 5:20 P.M. on June 13, 1994, we received the phone call that is every family's worst nightmare, and our lives were changed forever. Within minutes of that call, a photograph of our beautiful twenty-five-year-old son and brother, Ronald Lyle Goldman, filled the television screen. From that moment on, our quiet family was caught in the eye of a legal and emotional hurricane. Part of our heart and soul had disappeared forever, but we had no chance to grieve in private for the son and brother whom we loved so dearly. Our loss was so profound, our pain so deep, that it was almost impossible to function.

Many people had suggested that we write a book about our experiences. Originally we had no interest in such a project, but subsequent events proved to be so bizarre that now we are compelled to speak.

Our primary purpose is to give Ron an identity. So much attention, publicity, and even sympathy swirled around the defendant that Ron's death seemed to become a mere postscript to the "trial of the century." Ron was a real person, with talents and faults, promises and disappointments, hopes and dreams. We cannot allow him to remain the forgotten victim.

For clarity, we have chosen to tell much of this story in Fred's voice, but the reader should note that this book is a collective family effort. We have all shared our memories, our experiences, our heartbreak, and our search for healing.

For his own reasons, Ron's brother Brian chose not to participate. We respect his wishes.

We have received thousands of letters of support from all over the world. People invariably ask us to keep speaking out about the excruciating pain of our loss and our frustration over the inequities in a system that frequently seems to care more about the rights of criminals than of victims. When you speak out, these people said, you are speaking for us. Their letters, and our increased involvement in victims' rights issues, convinced us that sharing our experiences with the public might serve a worthy purpose. Ours is a very personal story, but one that far too many people in this country have lived as well. If we can help just one family deal with its own agony, Ron's memory will be well served.

—Fred, Patti, and Kim Goldman
—Michael and Lauren Glass

HIS NAME IS RON

ONE

❧

Messages left on Ron Goldman's answering machine:

Sunday, June 12, 1994.

. . . Ron, Ron, Ron, Ron, Ron, Ron, Ron, Ron. Hey bonehead, it's almost ten. I'm debating whether I'm just going to head over to your house or not. I want to get movin' here. I'll probably give it about ten . . . fifteen minutes. Call me. Later.

. . . Hey Ron, what's up? It's Eric. It's twenty after ten. Wake up, Ron, you bum. What are you doing? Ahh man. I'm just going to finish watching this show then I'll probably head over. Call me. Later.

. . . Ron where are you at, boy? It is eleven. Oh man. Call me. Page me as soon as you get up. Think I'm gonna start headin' over there in a little bit. All right? Later.

Monday, June 13, 1994.

. . . Hey Ron, this is Stuart. It's about ten-forty-five, I just was curious if you wanted to come to work today? So, talk to you later. Bye.

. . . Hi Ron, it's Patty. I know you're at work so I'll just leave a message, and it's twelve and I know it's probably really busy . . . but don't forget to come visit . . . that would be great. Thanks, bye.

. . . Hi Ron, this is Shawna. I'm just calling from the bank. Just give me a call here if you get a chance, it's no big rush. Just wanted to talk with you, or you can stop by. So, um, hope everything is okay and going well, just give me a call when you get a chance. Bye.

. . . Ron, it's Patty. I just talked to Jeff, um, I-I-I-I-I-I, um, need to talk to you and I'm not sure if what I'm hearing is right. So, um, Andrea is coming home tomorrow, um, I don't know if they're playing a joke 'cause you have the car and the keys and everything. But, call me, I'm gonna try paging you.

. . . Ron, this is Jeffrey. If you're dead, man, you'll hear from me up above. I love you, man. I just heard on the news right now. My fingers are crossed and I'm hopin' it's not you. Rumor went around town like fast, wildfire. Tryin' to get ahold of your parents. Love you, man, take care.

. . . Hey Ron, this is Todd callin', how you doin'? Hope you're doin' well because I was watchin' the news and they said they found, found somebody dead named Ron Goldman over in Brentwood on Bundy and I'm just like, fuck, I hope that's not you. So I hope it's not you. And if you feel like calling me back; let me know you're okay. I hope you're still alive and doin' well, man. Later.

. . . Hey Ronnie, this is Dave, um, I don't know if you're ever gonna get this or not, oh man. Please call me, let me know what's goin' on, if the name is a coincidence or if it's not, obviously.

. . . Ron, it's Trish. I was just calling you back and just wanted to see if you're okay. Okay, bye.

. . . Ron, this is Todd calling again and, uh, I just talked to your boss and he's confirming what we all hoped not to be true and, uh, I'm still praying that something is wrong with the information. But if it's true I'm sure you're hearing this and we all love you very much and we just hope that everything for the better or whatever and, uh, if anybody gets this message tonight which is, uh, what is tonight, uh, it'd be Monday night if you could call and let me know exactly what might be happening. Talk to you later. Bye.

. . . Hi Ron, this is Kelly, can you call me? We heard something on the news I just want to make sure it's not you. Call me, bye. As soon as possible, anytime tonight, okay? Bye.

. . . Ron, this is Kymberly, it's Monday night, I haven't talked to you in a while. Heather Burk just called me and said something happened to you. If something didn't happen to you, call me back . . . I need to talk to you. Bye.

. . . Hey Ron, just wanted to hear your voice one more time and, uh, hope everything works out for you. Goodbye, Ron.

TWO

~

As she prepared to leave work, Patti scrawled a brief shopping list: salad greens, pasta, cottage cheese, sliced deli turkey, and bananas. Bananas were always on her list.

Rather than plan menus and shop once a week, Patti often waits until the last minute, picking and choosing as the mood strikes. Our family was beginning to turn up its collective nose at red meat, but everyone was tired of chicken. And Patti needed something that would hold until Lauren arrived home; this was the big day of her class trip to Disneyland.

Patti's part-time position at the Right Start catalog company in Westlake Village kept her busy only three days a week, leaving plenty of time for what she liked best—being a mom—with a few extra hours for tennis. Orchestrating a dinnertime ritual was one of the benefits of her schedule. Dinner was a special event for our family, a chance for each of us to catch up on the events of the day. We continued the custom, even as the numbers around the table had dwindled from seven to four. My son Ron, now just a few weeks shy of his twenty-sixth birthday, was living in an apartment in the Brentwood section of Los Angeles. My twenty-two-year-old daughter, Kim, was in college in San Francisco, majoring in psychology and working part time at a branch of Wells Fargo Bank. Patti's eldest son, Brian, was a freshman at the University of Hartford, in Connecticut. Her two younger children were still at home with us. Michael was a sophomore at Oak Park High School, and Lauren was two days away from her junior high graduation. Children grow up so fast. We savored our time with them.

It was 4:30 P.M. on Monday, June 13, 1994, when Patti left her office and squinted at the bright blue, cloudless sky. She climbed into her 1991 antique white Toyota Previa bearing the license plate that described her so well: RUNGODO.

Our family moved to the San Fernando Valley only three days after Patti and I were married. That was seven years earlier, but Patti still missed Chicago sometimes. On the plus side, the gentle California climate allowed her to play tennis year round. But she worried about earthquakes and brushfires. The crime rate in and around L.A. was always a concern. Patti had decided that one either falls in love with California or never quite gets used to it.

She selected the groceries quickly and, making sure that she did not have too many items, breezed through the express checkout line. Tossing her shopping list inside the bag, she headed back to her car.

From Vons grocery store it is an easy five-minute drive to our home in a quiet, meticulously cared-for section of Agoura. Smooth green lawns with built-in sprinkler systems were manicured to perfection. Flowers of every variety and color were in bloom. Patti made the left turn onto our street and saw Michael's black Jeep Wrangler parked in front of the house. As she entered the house from the garage, she noticed that the security system was not turned on, so she assumed that Michael was inside.

From the foyer Patti called out, "Michael, are you home?" There was no response, and she thought that he might be upstairs, talking on his phone—or perhaps he had gone out with a friend and forgotten to set the alarm, which sometimes happened.

She set the bag of groceries on the kitchen counter and greeted the pets. Riley, the cat, brushed against her leg. Lucy, a black Labrador mix, wagged her tail and bounded around the room. Pitzel, our aging West Highland terrier, growled with her customary displeasure at Lucy's very existence, but allowed herself to be petted. Patti scooted the dogs outside to their run and then returned to the kitchen to put the perishables into the refrigerator. Then she headed upstairs to check the answering machine in our bedroom.

The light was flashing, informing her that several messages awaited. She pushed the PLAY button and heard a man's voice announce, "Hi. This is John DuBello from Mezzaluna. As soon as someone gets home, would you please call us? It's very important." His tone conveyed a sense of urgency. Alarmed, Patti quickly jotted down the telephone number.

Mezzaluna? she thought. That's the restaurant where Ron works. Why are they calling here? Her pulse quickened. Mothers do not like mysterious phone messages. The upstairs phone had not been working properly, so, ignoring the other messages on the machine, she went back downstairs to the wall phone in the kitchen and punched in the number. It was just after 5:00 P.M.

"Is John DuBello there?" Patti asked.

"This is John DuBello."

"This is Patti Goldman. You called?"

"Do you know where Ron is?"

Patti was confused and a little bit annoyed. Why didn't the man just leave a message on Ron's machine? She demanded, "Why are you asking *me* where Ron is?"

"Because he was supposed to call in for his schedule and he didn't call in," DuBello explained.

"But why are you calling here? Ron doesn't live here. He lives in Brentwood in his own apartment."

"Well, this is the phone number he had on his application," DuBello responded.

There was a catch in the man's voice that deepened Patti's anxiety. "I have no idea where Ron is, and how dare you call our house and leave such a pressing, urgent message. I thought something had, God forbid, happened to Ron. Don't ever do that to us again!"

DuBello apologized. "I'm really sorry. I just thought maybe you knew where he was."

Patti hung up the telephone, aware that her hands were shaking.

She stared through the glass patio doors at the sight of a backyard that was vintage California. A built-in barbecue stood just outside, with the swimming pool behind. A tall privacy wall surrounded the yard, with lush, trailing, pink and red ivy geraniums festooning the perimeter. Directly to her right, an atrium with a huge cactus housed a humming-bird feeder that the tiny birds frequently enjoyed. Wind chimes rang softly in the breeze, but at the moment Patti did not find them soothing. Something was going on. She could feel it.

A scant thirty seconds passed before the phone rang. The caller was a woman whom Patti did not know but would never forget.

"Hello, is this Mrs. Goldman?"

"Yes."

"I'm Claudia Ratcliff from the coroner's office."

Patti knew what a coroner's office was, of course, but the import of this information did not immediately register.

The woman added quickly, "If you don't believe that this is who I am, I'll give you a phone number and you can call me back."

"What are you talking about?" Patti responded.

"Did you hear that Nicole Brown, O. J. Simpson's ex-wife, was murdered?"

"No, I don't know what you are talking about." Patti's voice rose in pitch and volume as she repeated, "I have no idea what you're talking about!"

Patti thought: O. J. Simpson? Who the *hell* is O. J. Simpson?

Monday was just like any other workday. I was a salesman for Reliable Container, a company that manufactures corrugated displays and packaging. Sometime during the day, as I visited customers and made my phone calls, I heard on the radio that Nicole Brown Simpson, ex-wife of O. J. Simpson, had been found murdered, along with someone else. I like football, but I am not an avid fan, so the news meant little to me. Unfortunately, such crimes are not that uncommon, especially in large cities, and L.A. is no exception. There was no reason to pay particular attention to the story, other than to note that the victim had been married to someone I considered a has-been sports star.

I rarely arrive home before 6:00 P.M., but on this day I seized the opportunity to leave the office early. My mood was good as I drove the Ventura Freeway north, keeping a heavy foot on the accelerator. The week ahead was a busy one, a good one, highlighted by Lauren's junior high graduation ceremony on Wednesday evening. Our family always used every holiday or special occasion to come together and celebrate. Kim was flying down from San Francisco, and when we had spoken with Ron on the phone a few days earlier, he assured us that he would find a ride or bum a car from someone. Nothing would keep him from

"Squirt's" big evening. Squirt was a nickname he had always used for his sister Kim, and he had bestowed it on Lauren as well.

Idly I turned off the freeway onto Lindero Canyon Road, and only a few minutes later I pulled into our garage, noting that both Patti's and Michael's cars were there.

As I walked through the door from the garage into the family room, Patti looked up in surprise at my early arrival. At that very moment Claudia Ratcliff from the coroner's office said to her, "Well, I hate to tell you this, but your son Ron was the other victim."

Patti looked stricken. She yelled at me, "Fred! Hurry up! Pick up the phone! You have to talk to someone. Something has happened to Ron!"

I did not understand what she was talking about, but I ran into the kitchen and grabbed the receiver. Someone, either Patti or the woman on the phone, told me that the call was from the coroner's office.

The woman asked, "Did you hear today that Nicole Brown Simpson has been murdered?"

"Yes."

"Your son was the other person."

The instant I heard those words I fell into shock, stunned by a blast of disbelief and pain so great that the only thing I could do was push it down and bury it somewhere deep inside. I could not face this reality.

"How do you know?" I asked quickly. "Oh my God! Are you sure? Are you absolutely sure?"

"Yes, we're sure."

"How do you know? Maybe it isn't him."

"No, we're sure."

"How?"

"Because of his driver's license."

Patti gripped my shoulder and held her other arm around my waist. She was leaning against me, shaking. I felt the blood rush from my face and my body go rigid. A question stumbled out of my mouth: "Do I need to be there? Do you need me there?"

"No."

The moment blurred. I was numb. Everything was going blank. Suddenly the receiver was back in its place on the kitchen wall. Patti and I held on to one another, quivering. Muffled screams came from places deep inside of us, places that were totally alien and uncomprehending.

"What happened?" Patti asked.

"Ron's been killed," I said, the words choking in my throat.

"Are they sure? Oh my God. I can't believe it. What happened?"

"They're sure," I said.

It was final exam week, so when Michael had come home from school about 12:30, he was tired and had taken a long nap. It was about five o'clock when he woke up and hopped into the shower.

He had just gotten back to his room, wrapped in a towel, when he heard a knock on the door. He thought that he heard weird, hysterical laughter coming from the hallway.

The door opened. Patti stood there, her face ashen. Tear-drenched mascara tracked down her cheeks. Michael had never, ever, seen his mother look so shaken.

"Mom, what's the matter?" he asked.

Patti put her arms around her son and worked hard to get the words out. "Ron was murdered," she said.

Michael's face stiffened. His brain could not accept the words that his ears had just heard. "Ron who?" he asked.

"Ron! Your brother!"

A car accident? Michael wondered. No, Mom had said he was "murdered." Michael could not comprehend that. Who would want to kill his brother? No one. "There's no way Ron was murdered!" he yelled.

But Patti just sobbed on Michael's shoulder and nodded her head.

Michael lost control. He pulled away and threw himself onto his bed and began to weep. Patti tried to embrace him, but he pushed her aside. He leaped from the bed and ran from the room. He found himself in the bedroom immediately at the top of the curving staircase, the room that had once belonged to Ron. He slammed the door and sat on the edge of Ron's bed. All he could do was cry. And cry. And cry.

Patti decided, for the moment, to leave Michael alone. Grasping the railing, she stumbled down the stairs to rejoin me.

I was in the family room, pacing. Patti noticed that my face was as stone, cold white as the shirt I was wearing. She pulled me down onto the large, beige sectional sofa, and we held tightly to one another. Both of us were suspended in a state of total horror and disbelief.

I had turned on the television. A still photograph of my son filled the screen. It was taken from his photo ID. Ron? Murdered? The words screamed, then echoed and reverberated in my head.

We could not be sure, but Patti mentally scrambled to put together the sequence of events. Obviously the media had been waiting for word that we had been notified. The authorities could have been trying to contact us all day, but did not know how. Had they asked John DuBello at Mezzaluna to leave a message for us? After speaking with Patti, DuBello must have reported to the coroner's office that someone was home because now, only moments after the cold, cursory notification was made, an onslaught of media attention began.

"Oh my God," Patti whispered suddenly, "Kim! How are we ever going to tell Kim?"

I was afraid that if I let myself fall apart, I would never be able to put the pieces back together again. I had to be there for everyone, and I willed myself to stay in control. There were Patti, Lauren, Michael, and Brian to consider. And Kim.

Kim was at the core of it all.

Ron and Kim were truly a pair, closer than I could have imagined my two children would ever be. From the day Kim was born, Ron looked at her like he had been waiting for her all his life. In the snapshots of my mind I saw them as children, holding hands, hugging, whispering, laughing. And, as the years passed, that had never changed.

My marriage to Ron and Kim's biological mother, Sharon, had ended when Ron was only five and Kim barely two. Over the course of the next few years, I had obtained full custody of the kids and Sharon drifted from their lives. As the years passed, Ron became not only Kim's big brother, but her protector, her confidant, her second father, and her best friend. They shared a bond that was unique in its depth—a "you and me against the world" resolve.

Now Patti and I were terrified that Kim might see or hear something on the news before we could contact her. At the same time, I knew that informing Kim of her brother's death would be the most excruciating task I had faced in my fifty-three years.

Quickly, deliberately, Patti and I moved back into the kitchen. I reached for the wall phone and dialed Kim's number in San Francisco. Patti picked up the extension on the kitchen desk.

Each unanswered ring of the phone increased our anxiety. Finally, on the fourth or fifth ring, just as the answering machine kicked in, Kim's boyfriend, Joe Casciana, picked up. "Joe, it's Fred, have you been listening to the news? Is Kim home?"

"No, not yet. She's on her way," Joe replied.

I hoped desperately that she did not listen to the news on her car radio.

"What time is she going to be home?"

"I don't know. Maybe six-thirty or so."

I blurted out the words. "Ron's been killed. And we have to tell Kim. As soon as Kim gets home I want you to have her call me. Don't tell her anything. Just be by her side."

"Oh my God," Joe said.

The semester had just ended, so Kim was able to put in a few more hours at her job with Wells Fargo Bank. A recent promotion had her handling loans, accounts, and customer service.

Joe usually plays soccer on Monday nights, but Kim had called home earlier and was surprised to find him there. When he told her that he had decided not to play this night she was delighted. "That's great," she said. "We can go to the gym together!"

Kim's friend Amy Levine drove her home from work. The sun was shining as they sped along the coast and Amy had her usual R&B station blaring on the radio. The two young women laughed and joked about an eccentric customer they had dealt with during the day.

When Kim walked into the apartment, Joe had a strange expression on his face. Kim had always been attracted to his Mediterranean look— jet black curly hair, dark eyes, and olive skin. This evening his face was fixed in what Kim called his "nervous look," but she did not immediately sense tension. She was in too good a mood, preoccupied with her plans for a trip to the gym.

He greeted her with a terse "Kim, you've got to call your father."

We talked all the time. Getting a call from me was not at all unusual. "Okay," she said, "I'll call him in a bit."

Joe was persistent. "Kim, you've got to call your dad," he repeated.

"Okay, okay," Kim said. "I just got home. Give me a breather." She sat at the kitchen table and idly began to sort through the mail.

"Kim, call your father," Joe repeated.

Kim ignored him.

He leaned close and said firmly, "Kim, just call your dad." He was wearing a T-shirt with a low collar, and Kim noticed that his chest was flushed and his heart seemed to be beating fast.

A small light went on in her brain. She and Joe had been discussing the possibility of marriage. Ah-ha, she thought. The phone is in the bedroom. Maybe Joe's got a surprise waiting for me in there! She made a quick stop in the bathroom and then headed for the bedroom.

No surprises were apparent and Kim was a little disappointed, but she decided that as long as she was there, she would go ahead and call home. As she dialed, Joe came into the room and motioned for her to sit down on the bed. He sat very close, as if he wanted to listen in on the conversation.

Patti and I answered the phone on two extensions at the same time. The conversation went very, very fast.

"Kim, are you at home?" I asked.

"Yeah," she said.

"Is Joe with you?"

"Yeah."

"Did you watch the news today?"

This is totally weird, Kim thought. "No, I didn't. Why?"

"Did you hear about Nicole Brown Simpson?"

"I don't know who that is."

"She's O. J. Simpson's ex-wife."

"Who's that?"

Kim could tell that I was stalling. Get to the point, she thought. Who are these people he's talking about?

How could I tell her this? I had to do it. I said, "Well, she was killed with somebody else, with a friend. Did you hear that?"

"No."

There was another short pause.

"Kim," I said, my voice breaking, "Ron was killed."

Kim's mind raced erratically: I didn't call him back. Ron called me last week and I never called him back! Why didn't I call him back?

She could hear Patti and me crying on the other end of the line. She looked at Joe. He was crying too.

When you learn that someone has died, you think cancer. When you hear that someone was killed, you think car accident. Ron had a car accident? Kim thought. She threw the phone down and screamed, "How did Ron die? Did he die in a car accident?"

Joe picked up the phone and heard me crying. "Calm her down," I stammered. "Get her some Valium. Calm her down."

I told Joe that it was not a car accident. We did not know yet what had happened, just that he had been murdered.

Kim grabbed the phone out of Joe's hands. "Do we have to identify him?" she asked.

I told her that would not be necessary.

I kept crying and begging her to calm down, but Kim was falling backward into what she would later describe as a bottomless black tunnel. Ron was gone. Her brother was gone. Those were the only words she heard.

Before Kim had arrived home, Joe had called the airline and changed their reservations from Wednesday night to tonight. They would leave for the airport in a few hours and would be in L.A. later this evening.

Kim paced, dry-eyed, around the apartment. Adrenaline rushed through her like some kind of unknown, frightening narcotic.

Suddenly she was five years old again. She began to ramble: "I've got to pack. Do I have to go to a funeral? Is there a funeral? Do we bury? I have to pack."

Joe watched silently as she threw dozens of pieces of underwear, and nothing else, into a suitcase.

Michael did not know how long he sat on the edge of Ron's bed, crying. Finally he composed himself as much as he could and went downstairs. He heard me on the phone, repeating over and over again, "It'll be okay, honey. We'll make it through." He knew that I was talking to Kim. Patti was standing over me, watching carefully.

Michael knew how close Kim and Ron were. How will she ever be able to handle this? he wondered.

He turned and ran back upstairs to Ron's old room. He still needed to cry in private.

Patti phoned two of our close friends, Rob and Barbara Duben, and told them what had happened. Barb said that they would come over immediately. Then Patti called her mother, but had to leave a terse message on her answering machine, telling her to call as soon as possible. She placed a call to her father. When his wife, Alecia, answered, Patti said, in a cracking voice, "Have you been listening to the news?" Alecia said that she hadn't, and Patti simply blurted out, "Ron has been murdered." Immediately her dad was on the line and, in utter disbelief, asked, "How? Why? When? Who?"

Of course, Patti had no answers. Her dad said they would be there as soon as possible.

Within minutes, the Dubens were at our front door. They found me sitting in front of the television. My shoulders were slumped, tears sliding down my cheeks. My eyes were transfixed by the recurring image of my twenty-five-year-old son on the screen.

Once more, Michael came down the stairs. As he passed by the front door, he saw our neighbors and good friends Andrea and Jim Ziegler turn into our street on their way home. Quickly he ran into the front yard, followed by Patti, and motioned for them to stop. He screamed, "Ron's been murdered!"

Andrea misunderstood. "What do you mean your mom's been murdered?" Andrea snapped at him. "She's standing right behind you!" They quickly ascertained the awful truth, and came inside to help.

Barb called Rabbi Gary Johnson from our temple, and he hurried over to be with us. Then Barb and Andrea called several other friends, activating a support system.

Patti's mother phoned and, after receiving the news, broke into tears and said that she was on her way.

The house filled quickly. It was the beginning of what is, in the Jewish tradition, a *mitzvah* (a good deed) to care for the needs of a family that has suffered a loss.

The activity swirled about us. Patti and I sat on the sofa, clinging to one another, repeating the unanswerable question: "Why? Why? Why?"

There was a knock on the front door. Barb opened it and Patti saw our landscaper, Adán, standing there. We had a 6:00 P.M. appointment with him.

Patti rushed over. "We can't do this," she babbled. "Fred's son was just killed and this is a really bad time, we can't—you can't—you're just going to have to leave . . . " Patti simply shut the door, leaving Adán standing there.

It dawned on Michael that Lauren was not home yet. Then he remembered that this was the day of her class trip to Disneyland, and he thought: It's probably the only happy day she'll have for a long, long time. Rob offered to pick up Lauren, and Michael volunteered to go along. Michael was still crying as Rob's van pulled out of the driveway.

"Michael, you need to try to control yourself in front of Lauren," Rob reminded him.

It is only a short drive to Medea Creek Middle School. As they approached, Michael saw Lauren waiting outside, along with her friends, twin sisters Jamie and Julie Berke. Lauren had a wide, bright smile on her face. She was searching the crowd, looking for her mother, but she was not too surprised to see Rob and Michael there instead. Our families often shared chauffeuring duties. She figured that her mom probably had some things to take care of at home.

Along with Jamie and Julie, Lauren walked over to Rob's van. The three girls scrambled into the backseat and started talking about their day. Lauren had found Disneyland disappointing; perhaps she was just getting too old for it, or maybe because she had been there so many times, the day seemed to drag. Now she was anxious to get home.

Michael sat in the front seat, facing forward. He could not allow himself to speak. He could not look at his little sister. He knew that if he did, he would break down again. Lauren could tell that he was not acting like himself at all. Normally he would ask questions in his rapid-fire, enthusiastic style: What rides did they enjoy? Were there any new attractions? Did they pig out on junk food? Any cute boys? But Michael did not seem to want to talk at all. From what Lauren could see of his face, he appeared blank, almost stunned, and a strange, foreboding feeling came over her. She shivered involuntarily.

Rob had the radio on. During the short drive home, an announcer began to report: "Nicole Brown Simpson and—" Rob reached over and snapped off the radio.

When they reached Jamie and Julie's house, their mother, Sherri, was standing outside in the driveway. Her face was ghostly pale. She was usually very friendly and talkative, but this afternoon she ushered Jamie and Julie inside without a word.

Rob drove Michael and Lauren the short half-block home.

As they rounded the corner, Lauren saw her mom and some of our friends outside of our house. Cars filled the driveway and lined both sides of the street. When they got out of the van, Barb put her arms around Michael. Patti approached Lauren and asked, "How was your day?"

"Fine," Lauren answered, but she wondered what was going on.

"Was it really good?" Patti asked as big tears started to well up in her eyes.

"It was okay," Lauren said, "what's going on?"

Patti wrapped her arms around her daughter as warmly and securely as possible. The words seemed to lodge in her throat as she whispered, "Good. Because—Ron—was—Ron—was—murdered."

Lauren yelled, "No! No!" Her head spun and she lost her balance, falling to the ground. She thought: I'm not hearing this. It can't possibly be my Ronnie. There has to be some big mistake. A piercing, intensely painful shriek emerged from her throat. Lauren thought that if she just screamed loudly enough, someone would tell her that she was having a nightmare and she would wake up. Then everything would be okay.

Lauren's scream was so shrill and filled with such excruciating pain that Michael had to flee into the house. Never in his life had he heard such a mixture of anguish, disbelief, and horror come out of someone. It resounded in his ears as he bounded up the steps and headed for his room.

His best friend, Alexa, and Rob and Barb's daughter, Melanie, were waiting for him. Alexa put her arms around him and told him that everything would be okay. "If you need to talk, I'm here for you," she said.

Still in the driveway, standing between two parked cars, Patti kept trying to embrace her daughter. But Lauren pushed her away and ran into the house. She found me sitting alone at the bottom of the staircase. I wrapped my arms around her waist and gently pulled her onto my lap. I rocked her back and forth, and told her that everything would be okay. But all she could do was cry, and say the words "No, no, no" over and over again. Through my own tears, I told her that I loved her—and so did Ron.

Lauren wanted to be alone. She squirmed from my grasp and ran upstairs to her room. Even though it was still warm outside, she felt icy cold and could not stop shivering, so she put on a sweat suit.

Her friends Jamie, Julie, and Lindsay came upstairs to be with her. One of them asked, "Oh my God, are you okay?"

Lauren did not know how to respond. Did she want to be alone? Did she want her friends around? Did she want to be in her room? Did she want to walk about the house? Was she okay? No. How could she be?

The girls came downstairs and mingled briefly with our friends and neighbors. Many were in the family room, camped in front of the television, and Lauren kept hearing the name of a man, the one who had been married to the woman who was murdered alongside Ron. She had never heard of him before.

Finally she drew her friends back up to her room. She had decided that she did not want to watch TV. She said, "I don't want to know how it happened."

As Joe packed for the flight from San Francisco to L.A., Kim's mind was still spinning. Although she had a sometimes turbulent relationship with her maternal grandparents, it seemed necessary and important for her to call them. They now lived in Florida, but Kim had received a letter from them telling her that they planned to visit Kim's aunt and uncle in Chicago. She had not seen any of these people in at least ten years, but she called Information and succeeded in getting the number of her aunt Donna.

Donna answered the phone and started to make small talk, but Kim interrupted. "Have you been watching the news?" Donna said that she had, but had not paid any particular attention to it. When Kim told her what had happened, Donna started to cry.

"Are my grandparents there?" Kim asked.

"Yes, but you can't tell them this. Grandma has a heart condition."

A senseless, frustrating argument developed about when and how the elderly couple should be informed until, finally, Kim's grandfather got on the line.

"Grandpa, I have some bad news," Kim said.

"What's the matter?"

"Ron is gone."

"What are you talking about?"

Kim said it straight: "Ron died."

"What?"

"Ron was killed."

"What do you mean?"

Kim repeated the horrible news over and over again.

Finally her grandfather simply said, "Okay."

"*Hello!*" Kim screamed into the telephone. "Did you hear what I said? Can you hear me?"

The words simply did not make a connection.

His tepid reaction infuriated Kim and she screamed, "Ron! Your grandson, Ron. Your grandson was killed! He's *dead*!"

Finally her grandfather began to yell something to the others in the room. Kim heard sounds of bedlam. Frustrated, she hung up.

Moments later, her aunt Donna called back. "Are you going to call your mother?" she asked.

"I didn't even think about that," Kim admitted. "I guess I have to, but I don't even know what her last name is now, where she's living, anything. Do you have her number?"

Donna informed Kim that her mother's name was now Sharon Rufo, and gave her the number in St. Louis. Kim promised that she would call. But after she hung up the phone she had second thoughts. This Sharon Rufo person was someone Kim barely knew. So she called me instead and asked for my advice.

"Just bring the number with you," I suggested. "We'll handle it when you get home." I could not imagine how Kim and I were going to deal with this aspect of things. Sharon was a virtual stranger to us.

While we were talking, the call-waiting signal sounded on Kim's line. I held on while Kim took the call. It was Sharon. Donna had already taken it upon herself to notify her. Sharon was irate that Kim had not called her first.

"I just got your number," Kim stammered. "I . . . I was just about to . . . "

By now it was past time for Kim and Joe to leave for the airport. Both of them cried as the car sped down the highway, and Joe constantly checked his watch. When they finally reached the airport, they had to park in a lot that seemed miles away from the terminal. Grabbing their bags, they started running, dropping things, picking them up again and running, running, running. A security guard passing through the lot saw them and laughed at their plight. "Why don't you get a cart?" he hollered after them. His laughter made Kim furious.

When they finally reached the terminal, checked in, and headed for the gate, they were surprised to see the same security guard manning the metal detector. Kim rushed through, but the alarm sounded and she had to go back. Frantic that they would miss their flight, Kim ripped off her belt with its metal buckle and ran back through the detector, but it beeped once more. She yanked off her earrings, feeling as if she were doing some kind of ridiculous striptease. Tugging at her beltless jeans, trying to keep them up, tears streamed down her face as she finally made it through.

"Lighten up," the security guard said. "Are you having a bad day?"

They reached the gate with only a few minutes to spare. Kim spotted a pay phone and placed a hurried call, trying once again to reach Amy Levine. The phone rang several times before Amy picked up and Kim babbled, "Amy, something really horrible has happened. My brother was murdered and I have to go to L.A." Amy began to weep as Kim pleaded: "Please, Amy, please, just tell Rae, okay? Tell her I won't be at work. Tell her I'll call her as soon as I can." Through her tears, Amy said that she would do whatever she could to help.

The forty-five-minute flight seemed endless. Joe held Kim's hand, and they both let the silent tears flow. A flight attendant asked if she was okay, but Kim was unable to answer her.

Kim's mind floated back to something that happened in 1991. The Hastings family lived in Agoura, about five minutes from our home, and they were friends of ours. In a tragic incident, their son Craig became involved in a fight with another boy who was high on drugs. Craig was stabbed and killed. It was the first and only violent incident that we were aware of in our safe, peaceful neighborhood. Craig had been very close to his brother Scott, and because Ron and Kim were so close, her heart just broke for Scott. Scott once told Kim that he was going to kill the killer himself, or find someone who would. Back then Kim had counseled against such an act of vengeance, but she had thought: What if it were us? I couldn't bear it.

And now, it was us.

We had told Kim that Rob Duben would probably meet her plane, so she was surprised to see that Patti and I were with him at the gate. We all embraced, crying and clinging to one another for support.

I saw in my daughter's eyes a pain so great that it was almost incomprehensible. The walk through the LAX terminal seemed chillingly cold and dark. Hours of crying had left Kim numb and sweaty. She was shivering by the time we got to Rob's van.

Patti sat in the front seat next to Rob. Kim and I sat behind them, and Joe was in the far back. I put my arms around Kim and Joe held on to her shoulder. It was about 10:45 P.M. as we started the long drive home.

Rob had the radio tuned to KNX 1070. A newsman reported: "Nicole Brown Simpson and a man named Ronald Goldman were found slain . . . " The words sounded as empty and hollow as we all felt. It was the first news report that Kim had heard.

It was nearing midnight when we got home. Michael was waiting for us in the driveway. He ran to Kim, and she grabbed him and hung on. She just kept saying, "He loved you. He loved you." Lauren and Kim embraced also, and the endless supply of tears continued.

The house was still overflowing with people, but it was eerily quiet. Everyone was stunned and terribly sad. No one really knew what to say. What was there to say?

Even the animals were suffering. Lucy, our Labrador, usually leaps about, shadowing me. Now she was subdued and cowering, her big brown eyes downturned and sad. Pitzel, the feisty terrier, was hiding, keenly aware that something was very, very wrong. Riley, the cat, walked the perimeter of the rooms, confused and nervous.

Kim began crying as I had never seen her cry before—deep, body-wrenching sobs. The pain was profound. The tears could not be stopped.

Friends and neighbors finally prepared to go home for the night. One of them, Dr. Jon Matthew, gave me a Valium. I swallowed the pill and retreated to our bedroom. Eventually the tranquilizer took effect, and I drifted into a troubled netherworld—half awake, half asleep, caught in the middle of an unspeakable, surreal nightmare.

The others tried to get some rest, but it was impossible. As Lauren lay in her bed, vivid pictures of Ron flashed through her mind, like horrible dreams—except that she was awake. She stumbled into our room and tried to sleep on the floor, but that did not work either.

Unable to sleep herself, Patti got up and rubbed Lauren's back, but nothing could bring her comfort. Resigning themselves to the fact that sleep was impossible, Patti and Lauren went out to the landing at the top of the staircase and sat there in shock, talking and asking all those impossible "Why?" questions that neither of them could answer. Soon, Kim joined them.

Michael had no tears left, but he could not sleep either. When finally he stepped out of his room, he found his mother, Kim, and Lauren sitting on the floor, dazed and broken.

At about 2:00 A.M., Kim called her longtime friend Sarah Kupper. She wanted to be the one to inform her friends of the tragedy, and did not want them to hear about it on the news. Sarah, like Amy, dissolved into tears.

All night long Patti repeated, "Ron was murdered."

All night long Kim cried.

All night long Michael remembered the sound of Lauren's scream.

At about 4:30 A.M. Kim called a friend, Erika Johnson, in Chicago. Erika, half asleep and dazed, said that she had heard about the murders the night before, but would never have believed that one of the victims was the Ron Goldman she knew. She was devastated and offered to fly to L.A. immediately.

Kim could not wait for the sun to rise. Somehow she had convinced herself that when a new day dawned, the nightmare would be over.

THREE

B ut when the bright California sun finally rose, nothing had changed.

  An early phone call from the police underscored the hideous reality. Two men who identified themselves as Detectives Tippin and Carr of the Los Angeles Police Department asked me to meet them at Ron's apartment. For legal reasons they needed a family member present when they looked around the apartment. I did not want Kim to come along, but she insisted; she just needed to be there.

  Rob and Jim picked us up and drove us to 11663 Gorham, in Brentwood.

  We arrived at apartment 3 before the detectives. We did not have a key, so the four of us silently paced back and forth in front of the locked door.

  "It's like Ron's away on vacation," Kim said softly.

  I nodded through fresh tears. We sorted through a few pieces of junk mail that were in his mailbox.

  Soon the detectives arrived. They were polite and pleasant, sympathetic to our anguish.

  We had contacted the landlady, and she arrived to open the apartment for us. Tippin and Carr entered, but we held back, unsure that we wanted to be there. Finally I decided to go in. Kim, Rob, and Jim followed.

  When I stepped from the front door into the living room I felt an overwhelming sense of closeness to Ron. He was all around us; his food, his clothes, his furniture were here, but he was not. It was painful to realize that this was as close to him as I would ever get again.

The apartment was a still life. A glass of water and a half-eaten Mrs. Fields cookie sat on the coffee table. Is that the last thing he ate? Kim wondered. A list of foods, with their protein and carbohydrate contents, was taped to the refrigerator door. A meager supply of fat-free snacks were scattered on the countertop.

Kim picked up Ron's Rolodex and immediately checked the "S" section. She was surprised to find an entry that read: "Nicole Simp.," followed by a phone number.

One of the many rumors floating around was that Ron was barefoot when he died, and Kim was obsessed by this. For a time, it was all she could think about. Ron never went barefoot. Finally she asked, "Did my brother have his shoes on?"

Carr replied, "Yes."

A flashing light indicated that there were numerous messages on Ron's answering machine. The detectives took custody of the tape, and the Rolodex.

Ron's waiter's clothes—a pair of black slacks and a white shirt— were hung haphazardly on the bedroom door. Kim thought: This must have been the last thing he wore.

Wandering through the apartment, Kim felt like an intruder. It's so cold, empty, and lonely, she thought. It's as if life was stripped away in a flash.

In a drawer, Kim found a letter that she had once written to Ron. The sight of it brought some painful memories to mind, but she could not deal with them at this moment in time.

I felt as though I was sleepwalking and watching myself from some unknown place. As we prepared to leave, I glanced around the room. I simply could not accept that I would never see, hold, or touch my son again.

At home, no one knew quite what to do.

Our friends and neighbors were back in full force, bringing food, offering solace, taking care of details. The telephone rang incessantly. Barb and Andrea tried to field most of the calls.

Patti called one of my bosses at Reliable Container. "This is Patti Goldman," she said. "I just wanted to let you know that Fred is not going to be in. His son was killed."

"Okay," the man said. Patti was dumbstruck by his bland reception to the news. "Did you hear me?" she asked.

"Yeah, okay," he repeated.

"Okay, goodbye," Patti said, hanging up the phone.

A few minutes later my boss called back and issued a lukewarm apology. "I'm sorry I reacted that way," he said, "but I didn't really understand you. I'm so sorry." His voice was flat.

Needing to be with her friends, Lauren decided to go to school. Sherri Berke picked her up and drove her there, along with Jamie and Julie. Graduation practice was scheduled in the morning, and this would be followed by the traditional round of yearbook signing. All of Lauren's friends and teachers were very supportive, but she could not hold back her tears. After a short time, she arranged to come home.

Michael skipped his final exam in U.S. history. He stayed at home, trying to sleep, trying to block out everything. He knew that all our friends were trying to help, but he just wanted to be alone, so he remained in his room for a time. After a while, overcome by a suffocating feeling, he slipped downstairs and out the door. Moving quickly, he walked the familiar route along Lindero Canyon Boulevard to the small shopping center several blocks away. He and Ron had walked this way often. Maybe once a week, while Ron was living at home, he had suggested that they take a walk, just so that Michael would have a chance to tell him what was going on in his life. They would wander through Vons grocery store, or the drugstore, or have a slice of pizza. Their favorite place was the Donut Inn. They rarely bought much of anything; mostly they just talked.

Ron could give a great pep talk. "Michael," he would advise, "if you don't feel good about yourself, then no one else will feel good about you. You've got to walk with confidence to make people look at you with confidence." He encouraged Michael to do his best in everything he tried. "Don't make the same mistakes I made," he said once. "Finish college." He pointed out that Michael was a good problem solver and a people person. "You know how to deal with people," he said, "and that's going to take you far in life."

But Michael did not know how to deal with people right now. As he neared the Donut Inn, he realized that he could not face anyone he might meet inside. So he turned around and retraced his steps, knowing that about halfway home there was a quiet area with a stone bench. When he reached the bench, he sat there alone, crying.

He thought about the last time he had spoken with Ron. Over the phone, Ron had promised that he would come out to see Michael's last tennis match of the season. For Michael, Ron and tennis would always go together.

A strapping, well-built young man, Michael was one half of the top-seeded doubles team at Oak Park High School. Ron always called him "Sport" and praised his game, but in fact Michael knew that Ron was the superior tennis player. He remembered the first time he had played tennis with Ron. His older brother had made the game look easy. Sometimes Ron's serve hit with such force that Michael could not even see it.

During Michael's freshman year, when he learned that his school was looking for a tennis coach, he mentioned the fact to Ron. Ron interviewed for the job and was hired. Michael had been so proud that his big brother was going to coach his tennis team!

Michael was excited when the team assembled for the first day of practice. Ron was a good-looking, charismatic guy, and he was an ace tennis player. The school was just starting its tennis program and the kids were not expecting to work too hard, but Ron changed that attitude quickly. He turned out to be a tough coach who would not tolerate any whining or excuses. He made the boys work diligently at their game and then ordered them to run long and hard to develop stamina. He quickly earned their friendship, and their respect.

Another memory haunted Michael. He was the youngest brother, always looking up to Ron, Kim, and Brian. But Ron had moved out to a series of apartments. Kim had gone away to school, first in Santa Barbara and then in San Francisco. Brian was in college, back east. Michael recalled the moment when Ron had taken him aside and said, "Okay, Sport, you just went from the youngest brother to the oldest at home. You have to take care of Lauren now. It's your job. I'm leaving it to you. Don't disappoint me."

Michael suddenly remembered that Lauren's junior high graduation was tomorrow night, and he wondered how she was going to get through that.

* * *

On a normal day, I drive past Pierce Brothers Valley Oaks Memorial Park twice, going to and from work. It is on Lindero Canyon Boulevard, in Westlake Village just off the entrance to the Ventura Freeway. But this was not a normal day. Would there ever be another? I wondered. Rob drove Jim, Patti, Kim, and me to the cemetery, where we had a 2:00 P.M. appointment.

Nothing seemed real. Kim had always thought of me as being very strong—emotional, but strong—and now she witnessed me disintegrate before her eyes. It was as if all the oxygen had been siphoned from my body. I could not hold my head up. My shoulders melted into my chest. I kept repeating: "It's not right. It should be me. You're not supposed to bury your children."

Kim could not believe that we were making plans to bury her big brother. There was nothing anyone could say, nothing anyone could do, to lessen her grief.

The funeral director asked, "Does Ron have a mother?"

I replied, "Yes."

"What is her name?"

"Sharon Rufo."

"Where is she living? Does she live here?"

"No, in St. Louis."

The director then informed us that, according to California law, he needed the signatures of both parents to proceed with the burial plans.

That confused us. "She hasn't seen Ron in years," I commented. "I don't know if it's going to be that easy for me to get her signature."

Kim called home and asked Joe to get Sharon's telephone number. She wrote it down and handed it to one of the funeral directors. He immediately called, but was told that Sharon was unavailable and would call back later.

Another gentleman reminded us about Jewish burial practices. Traditionally, he said, Jewish people do not embalm and the deceased is wrapped in a sheet. The coffin is plain—as earthlike as possible. Kim thought: Forget tradition, I want it to be nice. I want it to be dignified. I want Ron buried in a suit, not a sheet.

Lifeless and limp, running on empty, I left the room for a few minutes to use the bathroom. While I was gone the mortician approached

Patti and Kim. He looked directly at Kim and explained, "I didn't want to say this in front of your father, but I have just spoken to the coroner. If you want Ron buried in a suit, the body will have to be embalmed. There is no way to keep him intact without embalming him. He is too badly cut up—the autopsy, you know—"

"—Go ahead, embalm him," both Patti and Kim said quickly.

When I returned, Patti and Kim told me of their decision and why it was necessary. We had been too immobilized even to think about asking the authorities for details of the crime, so this was our first inkling of its vicious nature. The images that ran through my mind were more than I could bear. My son was gone, and now the thought of what he had endured filled me with even more intense anguish.

We needed to choose a coffin, but it was just too painful to consider. We walked into the room, pointed at a simple oak casket, and fled.

Television sets were on all through the house, and every channel seemed to be running constant reports about the murders.

Officials were refusing to identify any suspect publicly, but there were reports that police had found a blood-soaked glove at O. J. Simpson's estate, and they believed that the glove may have been worn by the killer. Police were saying very little about the crime, declining to offer a possible motive or to say exactly when the attack was believed to have occurred. Officers said only that there were signs of a struggle and that there was no evidence that the attack occurred during a robbery or a burglary.

Police revealed that they had been called to Nicole's townhouse, in the 800 block of South Bundy Drive, several times in the recent past to deal with domestic disputes between Simpson and his former wife. "It's an ongoing problem," one officer said. We also learned that Simpson had pleaded no contest to a spousal-battery charge filed after he allegedly hit Nicole, kicked her, and threatened, "I'll kill you." None of this seemed to make any sense. What did it have to do with Ron?

Were Ron and Nicole lovers? Absolutely not. Ron never hid those things from his family, especially his sister. Kim had no doubt that if the two had been involved in a romantic relationship, or even a close friendship, he would have confided in her, in all of us. In fact, it was a standing joke between Ron and Kim. Ron used to tell his dates that they had to meet Kim, to "pass muster," and she told her dates the same thing about Ron.

Nicole was simply a friend who happened to come to Mezzaluna that Sunday night; her mother had left a pair of glasses there; Ron offered to return them.

Kim took a call from Jeff Keller and Mike Davis, who introduced themselves as two of Ron's friends from Brentwood. They informed Kim that they and some others from the area had been interviewed for a segment about Ron on one of the many tabloid TV shows, and they did not want our family to be surprised by the broadcast. We appreciated that. Kim told them about the funeral arrangements and they indicated their desire to attend.

In the television reports we continued to hear frequent references to "Nicole's friend Ron, an aspiring actor," or "sometime model," and these descriptions upset us. Ron had been searching for his niche, but he'd had ambitious plans for his life, and they never included acting or modeling. The reporters did not know Ron, so how could they characterize him so falsely and in such a cavalier way?

Every time Michael heard the phrase "Nicole Brown and a friend," it drove him crazy. Finally he shouted at the screen: "You know what? He's got a name. He's got a family. It's not just Nicole Brown and . . . a friend!"

Over the years Ron and Kim had made their own decisions about their relationship with their mother. I could picture them so clearly—two little tykes, standing on the balcony of our second-floor apartment, gazing at the street below, waiting for their mother to arrive for a planned visit. She rarely showed up, but she always had a good excuse. One day when the kids were still young, about nine and six, they came to me and asked: "Do we have to call Mom . . . Mom?"

Surprised, I asked, "Why?"

"Well, she doesn't act like a mom, so why do we have to call her Mom?"

Their matter-of-fact manner surprised me. They had clearly given this a great deal of thought.

I replied, "No, not if you don't want to, but what will you call her?"

"Sharon," they answered simultaneously.

"If that's what you want, it's okay. Are you sure?"

Again they answered in unison: "Yeah."

They never again referred to Sharon as "Mom."

And now Kim asked: "Why do we need Sharon's signature? She hasn't seen Ron in years. She wouldn't know him if she saw him. It's ridiculous."

"I don't know why," I answered. "But we have to do it. Let's be done with it."

A determined look appeared on Kim's face.

After all my years as primary caretaker, our roles suddenly reversed. While I sat, staring at the walls, Kim began trying to take care of me. She placed the call to St. Louis and told Sharon that we would fax her a paper to sign so that we could bury Ron.

Sharon answered, "No." She did not want Ron buried in California; she wanted him buried in Chicago, where, she said, his family was. It made no sense. She lived in St. Louis, and her parents now lived in Florida. In addition, Ron had not seen anyone from Sharon's side of the family in many, many years.

An emotional, tear-filled argument ensued. Kim begged, "Please, if you ever loved me at all, you will do this for me." But Sharon held firm.

I could not understand the mentality of this woman, and I sensed a premonition. This tragedy, horrible as it was, seemed destined to open old, deep, all-but-forgotten wounds. I could not deal with the memories now, but I knew that I would have to face them.

Kim called back several times, but could not get Sharon to change her mind.

Lauren did not know why the entire world was watching.

She continued to vacillate—she wanted to be alone, then she wanted to be with her friends. It did not matter, because they were going to be here anyway. Breann, Teresa, Vicky, Jenny, Jamie, Julie, Megan, and John—all of them—were determined to remain close.

All Lauren could think of was the way Ron loved to dance and joke around. She remembered the day when they were sitting in the family room watching a favorite music video. Ron suddenly swooped her up, spun her around, and danced with her while her legs dangled in the air. She also remembered how Ron—aided and abetted by Michael—would often hold her down on the floor and tickle her unmercifully. None of that was going to happen anymore.

This evening, Rabbi Johnson held a service at our home. When he asked Lauren to repeat some of the parts of the Torah that she had recited at her Bat Mitzvah, she was surprised that she remembered them after nearly a year. She knew that whenever she thought about her Bat Mitzvah, she would remember Ron and how much fun we all had at the party following the ceremony.

Ron's date that night was a lovely young woman named Lauren Cohen, whom we all liked a lot. She was not glamorous, as many of Ron's girlfriends had been, but she was very pretty and radiated a genuine warmth. She made an easy connection with everyone. I took Ron aside and, glancing at Lauren, told him I thought he had a real winner. He responded with an ear-to-ear grin.

At one point during the party, Ron and I picked up inflated rubber guitars and lip-synched to Bob Seger's "Old Time Rock 'n' Roll." Ron spent the entire evening dancing, singing, smiling, and laughing. It is a memory permanently etched in our minds.

That night, all of Lauren's girlfriends had told her how cute and how much fun Ron was. They were the same friends who remained close to her now, and some of them stayed as late as midnight. Several of them asked if she wanted to sleep at their houses, but she preferred to stay at home.

When Lauren was finally alone, trying to get some sleep, her eyes fell upon a poignant object. She remembered the time she caught the flu from Ron. She was lying on the couch with a 104 degree temperature when Ron walked in with a special present. He felt so guilty about bringing the flu bug into the house that he had bought "Squirt" a new teddy bear.

She clutched the bear close to her now.

FOUR

～

For some unfathomable reason, the sun continued to rise and set. Details still had to be attended to. Rob drove Joe, Kim, and me to Ron's apartment to pick out a suit for the funeral. Kim and I wandered aimlessly around the living room, incapable of any kind of decision making. Joe and Rob went to Ron's closet and selected a dark blue suit.

As we were about to leave, the phone rang. For a moment, we simply stared at it. Finally Kim picked it up.

A man's voice asked, "Is Ron there?"

Kim began to cry hysterically. "What?" she sobbed, "Why are you asking me this? Don't you know he's been killed?" She slammed the receiver back into its cradle.

Moments later, the phone rang again. When Kim picked it up, the same voice asked, "Is this Kim? His sister?"

"Yeah," Kim replied, still shaken. The poor man was nearly as upset as Kim. "I'm really sorry," he apologized. "I didn't know what to do, what to say. I just wanted to go to the funeral. I wanted to know where it would be. I used to work with your brother and he talked about you all the time. I'm really sorry."

The words "he talked about you all the time" pushed every emotional button Kim had. The comment devastated her, but it also made her feel cherished to know that her brother spoke of her to people whom she had never met.

The rest of us watched in silence as Kim wandered through Ron's apartment, opening cabinets, looking into sparsely stocked cupboards, checking the refrigerator's contents. There was very little to eat here. Kim commented about the likelihood of Ron starving to death. As soon as the words were out of her mouth, she regretted them. "How could I say something so stupid?" she muttered to no one in particular.

Seven years earlier, shortly after we moved to California, someone had suggested that Rob and Barb Duben should call us because they had children about the same age as ours, attended the same synagogue, and otherwise had a lot in common with us. Barb's response had been "I don't want to meet them. I've got too many friends already. I can't deal with any more friends." We had laughed about that comment over the years because when we did meet, the four of us hit it off immediately. We became the closest of friends, sharing vacations and other good times. Now we shared the worst of times. Rob and Barb were there for us, doing everything possible to help us through this horror, as were many more of our wonderful friends.

The phone rang constantly. Gifts of food and flowers covered every available table and countertop. People did everything for us, cooking or warming meals, answering the phone, running errands, responding to the doorbell. It was similar to what is called "sitting *shiva*," when people care for a bereaved family the week following a funeral, but it was much more than that. Our friends were here, not out of a sense of duty, but because they truly cared. They were the rocks that we held on to. We could not have made it without them.

By now an army of reporters, with their vans, cameras, and microphones, were camped outside, lining both sides of the street. We were under siege, but still unaware of the magnitude of what lay ahead.

The media were reporting that mounting evidence was linking Simpson to the murders, and projecting the possibility that he could be arrested within days. Sources said that bloodstains were found in Simpson's car and at his Brentwood mansion.

Neither the coroner's office nor the police would release further details about the time of death, the exact nature of the wounds, or the weapons used to inflict them. However, a source said that Nicole's throat was slashed and that Ron's wounds indicated that he put up a fierce struggle before he died.

The press said that investigators planned to move quickly and might rely on matching blood types, rather than waiting for full DNA test results. We learned that Assistant District Attorney Marcia Clark was assigned to the case.

Simpson's lawyer, Howard Weitzman, insisted that his client was not involved and that he was a victim of unfair and unfounded rumors.

That same day, Simpson retained the services of Robert L. Shapiro, a high-profile attorney who had previously represented a number of celebrities, including baseball player Darryl Strawberry and Frank Sinatra's daughter Tina. Although he said he would remain as an adviser, Weitzman stepped aside, saying, "I have decided because of my personal relationship with O. J. Simpson and my many other professional commitments, I can no longer give O. J. the attention he both deserves and needs."

Shapiro stepped quickly and eagerly into the spotlight. It was reported that he had solicited the services of a criminologist and a pathologist whom he refused to identify other than saying they were top professionals.

The *Los Angeles Times* ran a hastily prepared profile of Ron that bore little resemblance to the son and brother we knew. Ron sounded like some fast-track Brentwood "wannabe":

> Life for Ronald Lyle Goldman was a nonstop merry-go-round of working out at a trendy gym, serving dinner at a trendy restaurant and dancing at trendy nightclubs. . . . he had model good looks, a body sculpted by daily weight lifting sessions and tennis, and a magnetic personality that friends said made them want to hang around him, just to see what he would be up to next . . . .

In the article, Ron's best friend, Mike Pincus, confirmed what we already knew. "He definitely would have told me if he was seeing O. J. Simpson's ex-wife," Mike said. "That's just the kind of guy Ron was. Whenever he was dating someone, we all knew about it."

Kim's reaction to the friends and neighbors who filled our house was very much like Lauren and Michael's. When she was around people,

Kim wanted to be alone. When she was alone, she could not stand the isolation. She spent much of the day maniacally dialing the phone, ignoring time zones, calling a variety of old friends around the country, confirming the horrible news.

"I need to talk to Brian," Kim said. Brian Swislow had been Kim's first serious boyfriend. He and his sister Julie still lived in Chicago, and the four of them, Brian, Julie, Kim, and Ron, had remained close over the years. She called him and broke the news. He was crushed, as she knew he would be.

After they talked, Kim recalled a conversation they once had. Brian told her that he gave a sentimental speech at Julie's wedding, and what a wonderful experience it was. Kim told him how much she looked forward to the day when Ron and I would give her away at her own wedding.

"Sometimes looking at Brian and Julie was like looking at a mirror image of us," Kim said, "but now a piece of that reflection is gone forever."

The funeral was scheduled for tomorrow, but Sharon was still refusing to sign the wretched release form, still demanding that Ron be buried in Chicago. At this moment she was in control, and she knew it. Could she really stop us from burying Ron where and when we chose? That possibility frightened us. Deciding once more to take matters into her own hands, Kim called Sharon back and begged for cooperation.

Sharon responded by spouting how she had been shut out of Ron and Kim's lives—everything was my fault, Patti's fault, Patti's kids' fault, Ron's fault, or her second husband's fault. The fact that she had told Kim repeatedly that she wanted absolutely nothing to do with her, or her brother, apparently escaped her memory. Sharon complained to Kim that I should be grieving with her instead of with Patti. She was also angry that I had informed Kim about the tragedy before notifying her.

Kim has borne the brunt of this ludicrous relationship for much of her life. For the most part, Ron simply chose to absent himself from the reality of Sharon's rejection. However, several years earlier, for some reason Ron had tried to call her. She was out, but Ron spoke to her husband, Steve, who did not even know who Ron was. We assumed that Sharon had never told him that she had a son and daughter living in California. But now she wanted to claim that son.

Frustrated by Sharon's irrational, selfish tirade, Kim hung up.

I could put it off no longer. This time, I called Sharon. I sat at my desk near the front door and Kim sat close by, in the living room. Now Sharon was in a negotiating mode. She declared that she could not afford to fly to California for the funeral, and asked me for money.

"Absolutely not," I replied.

She demanded, "Who is the slut who got my son killed?"

"Get your head out of the gutter," I snapped. "Your son has been killed. Are you coming here or not?"

She would not give me a straight answer.

"You are making a horrible situation even more horrible," I raged.

We were still at an impasse.

Two of the many friends who were gathered at our home, Jeffery Zabner and Ernie Wish, are attorneys. Both of them told us not to worry—they would do something. One of them said, "Don't think about it. Put it out of your mind. It's done. We'll find a way to overcome this problem."

The whole matter was compounded when the mortuary asked us to write an obituary notice, and we were confronted with the question of whether or not to include Sharon's name. This issue made Kim hysterical. She ran about the room, screaming, "Why should we include her if she doesn't even want to be here? It's an honor to be included. She doesn't deserve it! I'll call the mortuary and make them leave her name off!" Kim was at the breaking point. "All these years," she sobbed, "Ron never dealt with her. I did! Now, here I am. I've lost Ron and I have to deal with Sharon. I can't take it. I can't stand it!"

Joe got a glass of water, and Patti and I physically forced a Valium down Kim's throat.

I tried to be the voice of reason. "Maybe Ron would want her name included," I said.

Kim had no lucid response to that. She was spent, exhausted. We reluctantly included Sharon's name in the notice.

Throughout its intense coverage, the press continued to refer to Ron as merely "Nicole Brown Simpson's friend."

We decided that the only way to alter the situation was to speak to the mass of reporters who had gathered in front of our house. "Let's go out there and say something," somebody suggested. One of our friends stepped into the front yard and announced that we would be coming out to give a brief statement; however, we would not answer questions.

We did not prepare. We simply stood in the middle of our driveway, a family grieving for its son and brother. As far as we could see, the yard and the street were filled with vans, cameras, lights, microphones, and hordes of people.

The reporters were extremely respectful. I told them that I had a statement to make and that was to be the extent of our appearance. I had no idea what I was going to say. I knew that my voice would crack and that I would ramble. I knew the tears would come, but none of that mattered. The words sputtered out, emanating directly from the heart.

"It's hard to imagine that your flesh and blood, a twenty-five-year-old, could touch so many people," I began. "Ron was a special human being who didn't deserve what's happened."

I told them that Ron was a carefree young man who quickly made friends wherever he went and added that I would not be surprised if he had struck up a friendship with Nicole. I said that my son was killed just as he was beginning to realize some of his dreams. "For a long time, Ron's aspirations have been multifold," I continued, "he was putting his life together. Even when things didn't go a hundred percent with the things he wanted to do, he seemed to have a way of bouncing back. The bottom line is that Ron was a good person from the top of his head to the bottom of his feet, inside and out."

Referring to Nicole, I said, "It was not uncommon for Ron to have friends who were ladies," but added that he had never spoken of a relationship with her. "We would have known," I assured them.

I said that it did not surprise me to find out that when Nicole called Mezzaluna to tell them that her mother had left her prescription glasses there, Ron would be the one to offer to take them to her. His answer was "I don't mind, she lives close by and I'll be glad to do it."

Responding to reports that Ron had put up a struggle with his attacker, I said, "If it's true that Ron put up quite a fight, maybe to help Nicole, that wouldn't surprise me either."

I explained that it was agonizing for us to hear our son referred to simply as Nicole Simpson's friend, and I concluded, "He has a name. His name is Ron."

* * *

The news broke that blood samples recovered from the murder scene matched Simpson's blood type. This was not rumor or speculation. This was the first concrete piece of evidence that we felt could and would link this man to the murders. What evidence could be more damning than a blood match? This was something that every prosecutor would wish for—blood that matches the suspect, found at the murder scene!

Patti was alone in our bedroom when she pushed the PLAY button on our answering machine, and a cold, ugly, male voice filled the room: "Mr. Goldman, sorry to hear about your son, but he deserved it and he should rot in hell and he had a lot of nerve driving Nicole's car and he got what was coming to him."

Patti was shaken, but she did not know what to do about this sinister call. She did not want to upset the rest of us. She endured several hours of private torment before she came to me and said, "Fred, I think you should listen to something." She took me upstairs and played the hate-filled message for me.

Patti was shaking. I could see the fear in her eyes. I tried to reassure her, telling her that it was just some nut, but inside I was frightened, too. When Kim heard the vile recording, she felt violated and vulnerable. Someone, somewhere out there, knew who we were, where we lived, and had our telephone number.

We tried to save the message, but there were so many others on the tape that we were unsuccessful. We erased it from the machine, but not from our memories.

It should have been a night of celebration. Lauren's dad and her brother Brian had arrived, as they had planned, to attend her eighth-grade graduation.

School officials let us come into the gymnasium through a back door, so that we could go to our seats quietly and privately.

Lauren, of course, sat with her classmates. She was exhausted.

It was impossible for any of us to pay attention to what was going on. For me, the speakers appeared to be standing at the end of a long tunnel, and their meaningless words echoed and faded away.

Finally the class stood up and the principal began to call out names.

It is a small school and everyone knew that Lauren was Ron Goldman's sister. When the principal intoned, "Lauren Glass," the auditorium suddenly grew very quiet.

Wearing her black Bat Mitzvah dress, Lauren marched forward. She kept glancing toward the ceiling, thinking that maybe Ron was somewhere up there watching her. Ron had called her just a week earlier to ask what time the ceremony started. The last thing he said to Lauren on the telephone that night was "I love you, Squirt."

Both Kim and I planned to speak at Ron's funeral. I tried to write down what I wanted to say, but the words would not come out right. I did not believe that my son was in a "better" place. He belonged here, with me, with his family. I could not express, in mere language, how much I loved him. The words did not exist. I could not bring myself to say that I missed him. To do that was to acknowledge that he was gone.

Kim had not eaten or slept for two days. At 2:00 A.M. she began to write her thoughts about Ron. How can I be eulogizing my brother, my best friend? she wondered. Do I use the past tense? Do I use the present tense? What can I say? How can I say it?

It's got to be right. It can't possibly be right.

Suddenly the words began to fill the page in a rambling stream of consciousness.

FIVE

〜

Early Thursday morning, Michael sat in his room thinking: I can't believe I am going to my brother's funeral. I just can't believe it.

He took his suit out of the closet and noticed that it was badly wrinkled. This would not do. He could not go to Ron's funeral in a wrinkled suit. He grabbed the suit, ran out to his car, and sped off to the Clubhouse Dry Cleaner.

"I need this suit pressed right away," he told the man behind the counter.

The clerk replied that they were very busy and he did not know when he could get to this job.

"But I have to go to a funeral," Michael persisted.

Still the clerk was uncertain.

Michael did not want to tell the man who he was, but finally he realized that he had to. "Look," Michael said, his voice rising in volume, "my brother is—was—Ron Goldman. I have to have it for the funeral."

A short time later Michael was sitting in his room, staring at his freshly pressed suit, when Patti, Kim, and I came in and asked if he wanted to view Ron's body before the service.

"No," Michael said. "I want to remember him with a smile on his face."

Lauren agreed with Michael. She was fearful of how Ron might look.

Sharon appeared on *Inside Edition*, in an interview from Los Angeles, so we knew that she was in town. But we did not learn until 9:30 A.M. that a deal had finally been struck with her the very morning of the

39

funeral. Sharon would sign the release form in return for an opportunity to spend some time with Ron before the burial.

When we arrived at the funeral parlor, Kim excused herself to use the ladies' room. Her friend Leslie Wilcox accompanied her. Once inside the restroom, Kim came face-to-face with Sharon, Sharon's sister-in-law Mary, and Mary's daughter Cindy. It appeared to Kim that the three women were hiding out here.

Sharon immediately approached Kim, hugged her, and prattled, "Oh, you're so beautiful. You look just like me."

Kim was cold and emotionless. Internally she screamed: I am nothing like you. Nothing like you at all!

"Aren't you going to say hello to your cousin?" Sharon asked.

Kim felt trapped and angry. It was a suffocating experience to be caught in this room with these people. Finally she said to Cindy, "I'm sorry, I didn't recognize you." Then she turned on her heels and walked out.

Sharon was in the chapel, viewing Ron. We waited our turn.

Someone told us that Sharon had an attorney with her, a local man named Michael Brewer. Why would she have an attorney? I wondered. It did not matter. She had signed the papers, and that was all that we cared about.

Finally one of the funeral directors asked, "Do you want to see Ron?"

"Yes," I replied softly.

Patti, Kim, and I walked down what seemed like a black, endless hallway. We turned to the left, entered the chapel, and saw the coffin at the front of the room, after rows of pews. We stood at the back for a moment, frozen in place.

Slowly we walked forward. Kim felt the narrow aisle grow longer and longer, as if we would never arrive at the front. She needed to see Ron because if she did not, she would never, ever, accept the fact that he was gone. However, she was petrified. Her entire body shook. She tried to peer ahead, so as to see Ron before we were actually beside him.

Ron's left side faced the wall.

He's so beautiful, Kim thought, and reached out to touch his hand. He was so very cold. "Why is he so cold?" she asked.

"Ron looks so good," Patti said. "So good."

It was hard for me to look at Ron. He had no business being here. There was no smile, no sparkle. I kept whispering his name, "Ronny, Ronny." I had not called him that in years. I bent over the oak coffin and kissed my son. He *was* cold. I laid my hand on his chest. It was so hard. One of my tears landed on Ron's eyelid.

"Look! he's crying," Kim whispered to Patti. Her own tears made it difficult to speak.

My hand reached forward to brush the tear away, but Kim stopped me. She whispered, "I want him to have something of us with him."

We could not pull ourselves away. There seemed a slight grin on Ron's face, but it was unnatural, unreal, mannequin-like. Then, in an instant, he appeared angry or sad. Kim thought: He's angry because he's gone and he just doesn't understand. She touched his hand again. Cold. Hard.

The casket was closed.

We sat quietly in the chapel, amazed at how many people had assembled to pay their respects and share our grief. Our close friends were here, and a crowd of people both inside and outside the chapel bore testimony to Ron's incredible ability to make friends.

The service was delayed for about ten minutes as everyone waited for Sharon to make her appearance. Finally someone told me that she was sitting in the front row, across the aisle from us. I did not recognize her, and we did not speak.

The rabbi spoke and offered prayers.

Then Ron's best friend, Mike Pincus, made a beautiful speech. "Where do I begin?" he asked.

Well, Ron and I met 19 years ago in Buffalo Grove. We were the best of friends although Ron was the best of friends with a lot of people. He was the class clown and we were always getting in trouble. I blamed it on him and he blamed it on me. I must say that growing up with Ron was a dream come true. . . . Ron and I were inseparable—we went everywhere together. . . . We often went to Ed Debevic's for burgers and to dance on the table. There isn't a better dancer around—Ron had the moves.

Ron and I grew up in the 70s and 80s but we loved the music of the 50s. If you can all remember for a minute a song written by Dion: "The Wanderer." It is about having different people around you all the time and roaming from town to town. That song was Ron and me.

Mike recalled that what he and Ron did best was to shop for clothes:

One day Ron and I found the most obnoxious-looking jacket you could ever imagine. We had to have it but there was only one so we decided to share it. We brought it home and Ron's dad looked at it and said, *"No way!"* But we wore it anyway.

The friends were separated when our family moved to California, but Mike recalled:

In May of 1989 Ron said, "Let's be together forever. Get your butt out here and live with me." I was the straitlaced kid from Chicago and of course said no way. Needless to say, Ron talked me into it and I packed everything up and drove to California by myself. I unloaded the car and we went to Gladstone's for the 4th of July fireworks. From that day on, life began all over again. We were finally together forever.

A few years earlier Ron had introduced Mike to a lovely young woman named Lisa. Two years later Mike and Lisa were married and were now expecting their first child. Mike's voice cracked as he said:

I think the hardest part of all this is that Ron won't be able to see my baby in three months. He would have made a great Uncle Ron.

On June 13th my life with Ron was over. We were separated one last time. I will miss him more than he will ever know. A part of Ron still lives inside me. I will always love you and one day we will dance again—forever.

Lauren was crying so hard that she could not hear the words. It was difficult for her to believe that Ron was actually inside the casket in front of us.

Kim spoke next:

Ron, my dear, sweet, innocent Ron. Not in my worst nightmare did I imagine that I would be standing here in front of Dad, Patti, and the kids and all our family and friends, expressing how much I will miss you. I don't want to be, but I wanted you to know how much I love you and what you mean to me.

From the bottom of my heart, you were my hero. You were my protector, my support, my laughter, my drive to be the best. You are my best friend. I don't know, Ron, that we could ever explain to anyone the close bond we shared. I can't even explain it. I can only feel it. We will have that closeness forever.

No matter what, it was always you and I standing together, through all of the bad and the good. To be honest, I wouldn't change the negative for anything because that just made us a stronger team.

You and Dad were such a pair. You both bombarded me with so much love, so protective of me and making sure I was safe and happy and loved. Dad raised a beautiful young man. He raised you to be strong and honest and caring and loving. The two of you took on quite a challenge to raise a little girl on your own and I want to thank you, because I would not be half the woman I am now if it were not for you.

Ron, I admire everything about you, your magnetic personality always amazed me. The way you were with kids and other people delighted me. I don't know if I ever told you, but I am so proud of the man you have become. I am honored to be a part of your life. You touched so many people in your young life and they are here today to give you some of that back.

Ron, your kind and gentle soul is a gift that we now all share and will be a part of our lives forever. Thank you for giving us your gift.

I cherish you and all our wonderful memories. Wherever you are now, I hope you can feel all the love in this room. It is all because of who you are!

I loved that you were so protective even though at the time I may not have appreciated or realized your intentions, but as I got older I knew it was only because you loved me so much.

Ron, I want to thank you for being my rock and my anchor

when things were tough for us. You always held your head high and managed to find something positive to make the bad things go away. In a weird way I'm grateful for the troubles we had growing up. I think that if it did not happen we would not be this close. Dad did an excellent job raising you to be so strong and so good hearted and enabling you to share that with me. We made an excellent threesome!

Ron, you developed into such a beautiful person. You had such energy and zest. I admire your strength and desire to go on when things got bad and always making out like a champ. You have a good soul and wherever you are now, I want to say I love you and I am very proud of you.

I also want to say that both Dad and I knew what a great person you were. However, we had no idea to what extent. You led a full life and touched many people and influenced them all. And that shows here today. I hope that wherever you are you realize how much people loved, admired, and respected you.

For everyone that is here today, I can't tell you enough how honored my family and I am to have such support and love from all of you. You know, this is a very tough time for everybody but if Ron were to tell us anything, he'd say, "It will be okay. We'll get through it. Tomorrow's another day. Be strong."

I know this sounds crazy to say but please don't ever let Ron leave your memories. Please keep him close to your hearts, because you are close to his.

Ron, thank you for being my brother, my best friend. I love you with every fiber that I have. Wherever you are, please put your arms around yourself and squeeze because I am giving you a hug and I need one too! Ronny, I love you.

It was my turn. But I was stunned, overwhelmed by Kim's words and my own grief. I felt paralyzed. Kim read the message that I had hand-printed onto a single sheet of paper:

Ron,
    My love. My son.

I've adored you since the day you were born. I have been
proud of you and who you had become. You touched deeply
every one whom you met.
A good, kind, considerate person always there for others.
I will miss being with you—but you will be in my heart and
thoughts every day.
God will watch over you.
Some day we will hug and kiss again.
Love, Dad

I was upset that I was unable to say these words myself, and disappointed that I had not written more. I hoped that somehow I could
make it up to Ron.

After the chapel had cleared, we were asked if we would like a few additional minutes to say our last goodbyes.

The casket had remained closed during the service, but they opened
it for us now. Kim plucked a few roses from one of the flower arrangements and placed them on Ron's chest, but she wanted to give him
something more. She took the notes from her speech and mine and laid
them carefully at Ron's side. Then she leaned down, kissed his cheek,
and whispered, "Goodbye."

I heard someone crying, whispering, "Ronny, Ronny . . . " Then I
realized that it was me.

We had planned to ask Ron's friends from Brentwood, Jeff Keller and
Mike Davis, to be pallbearers. Neither of them showed up for the funeral,
so we had to quickly designate two others. Rob Duben walked in front.
Michael and Brian, along with Jeff Tierstein, Pete Argyris, Mike Pincus,
and John Baskett carried the coffin, and Jim Ziegler walked behind.
Long afterward, I would swear that I had helped them carry the casket,
but I did not.

The walk to the grave site was surreal. I was engulfed in a fog of
pain, mixed with an eerie floating sensation. I kept mumbling, "You're
not supposed to bury your kids. It should be me. It should be me."

I was amazed to see the gently sloping hill behind the grave site covered with hundreds of people who had been unable to fit into the tiny chapel. I saw a blur of faces—young people—people whom Ron had touched in the seven years he had lived in California.

Tears streamed down Michael's face as he forced his legs to keep moving up the hill, staring at the hole in the ground where Ron would be buried. In his mind he saw Ron serving a tennis ball, running on the beach, dancing with Grandma at Lauren's Bat Mitzvah.

Brian, Michael, and Lauren were crying inconsolably.

Kim stared straight ahead and saw her friend Jana Robertson in the crowd. She began to focus on Jana's weeping face.

The rabbi spoke, but Kim could not listen. She just focused on Jana.

We were handed black mourning ribbons. Kim just focused on Jana.

She thought: I'm five years old again. I don't understand what death is. I don't understand any of this.

Patti, Kim, and I held in our fists a portion of the dirt that had been dug from the grave site. We were to sprinkle it on top of the casket as it was lowered into the ground.

Kim clenched the grains of soil in her hand, refusing to let them go. I took her hand in mine and tried to shake the dirt free, but she still would not release it. Finally, her fist opened and she let it go.

The earth was ready to receive her brother, but Kim was not ready to let him go. As the casket was lowered, Kim thought she saw it slip and feared that it would fall. She lunged forward and hung over the side of the grave, her arms stretched, grasping toward her brother. She just wanted to be close to him, to make him safe. She felt my arms, pulling at her.

The pallbearers quietly filed by and dropped their white carnations into the open grave. As Michael approached, he saw Kim on her knees, lunging for the coffin, as if she wanted to join her brother in eternity. He saw a part of Kim disappear that day, and he doubted that it would ever return.

SIX

~

After the funeral, Michael drove Brian and his dad back to their room at the Radisson Hotel.

Brian wanted to drive, but Michael insisted. He thought: For days I've felt my life spinning out of control. I've lost my brother. I've carried his casket. I've seen my family in the worst kind of pain imaginable and there is nothing I can do about it. I just need to be in control of something, even if it is only the wheel of my car.

What seemed like hundreds of people filled our house.

While I was cold and dead inside, Patti, as always, was there for everyone else. She struggled with her obvious pain, but still managed to be available for each of us. I will never understand her strength, but I knew then, perhaps more than ever, just how much I loved her.

Kim continued to cry. Well-meaning words of comfort did nothing for her. She and Ron had often talked about family and religion. Ron believed in God, whereas Kim was always filled with doubts, questions, and skepticism. Although Ron did not keep kosher, or attend services regularly, he enjoyed the traditions of our Jewish faith. They held a special meaning for him. Kim analyzed. Ron accepted. Now Kim thought: I am not an existential person. If I am here, sitting in this chair, that is exactly where I am. Don't tell me I'm floating in some third dimension somewhere. I saw my brother in that casket, and I saw that casket go into the ground, and that's where Ron is.

Jeff Keller and Mike Davis, whom we had not seen at the funeral, now stopped by to pay their respects. They were accompanied by another young man from Brentwood, who drew Kim aside and said, in a cryptic tone, "I'm not like that. I'm not like the rest of them." Kim had no idea what he was talking about.

As we watched the taped coverage of Nicole Simpson's funeral, which was held at about the same time as Ron's, we were surprised to see Jeff and Mike there. Why had they gone to Nicole's funeral when they were supposedly Ron's friends?

Others from Brentwood seemed more caring. Andrea Scott, a young woman Ron had been dating, came to the house to pay her respects and asked if she might have a moment alone with Kim. Kim was sitting in the living room, crying. Andrea reached into her pocket and pulled out a ring. "I think Ron would want you to have this," she said, handing the ring to Kim.

The ring had three intertwined circles. Andrea told Kim that when Ron had given it to her he had told her that one circle represented their first date, the second, their engagement, and the third, their wedding.

"I know he was only kidding around," Andrea confided, "but I thought his comments were so endearing—I just want you to have this."

Kim was touched beyond measure. She placed the ring on her finger, silently changing the meaning of the three intertwined circles to represent Ron, Dad, and Kim—always connected and bound to each other.

On Thursday evening we were told that Simpson was going to be arrested for the murders. We knew that this meant that the police had "probable cause" to believe that Simpson had committed the murders. In the midst of our grief, it was tempting to accept this as a judgment, and to vent our rage. But throughout this nightmare we had been too distraught to pay close attention to the details of the police investigation, and we did not wish to disrupt the process.

"Let the system work," I counseled. "We'll go through the system. We'll hear all the evidence."

We did think it was absurd that Simpson would be allowed to turn himself in the following morning at ten o'clock. That was a joke. Only if you are a celebrity or wealthy do you get to "turn yourself in." We asked ourselves: Why don't they just arrest him? Who is this person who gets the kid-glove treatment and makes these decisions for himself? No one suspected of with double murder should get special treatment.

Throughout the week we had heard reports of people saying, "He's O. J. Simpson, the sports hero, he couldn't have done it."

Michael, as the family's resident sports fan, had his own perspective on that. He loves to play sports and loves to watch events on TV, especially basketball, but he has never been one to put a sports figure on a pedestal. To Michael, a hero is someone who does a good deed, someone who gives to charities, someone who cares about other people. A hero risks his life to save another. A hero pulls a kid out of a burning building. A hero is a teacher who turns a kid's life around. A hero is not someone who scores four touchdowns in a football game.

On Friday morning, like much of America, we gathered anxiously in front of the television to watch the official arrest. The live coverage bounced between scenes at the courthouse and Parker Center Police Headquarters. Because the crime was a double homicide, the charge included "special circumstances," and reporters discussed the impact of that. The only possible sentences for a person convicted of homicide with "special circumstances" would be life without parole—or death.

Our frustration grew as the deadline was extended from 10:00 A.M. to 11:00 A.M. Then it was extended again, to 11:45. What was going on? we wondered.

Finally, an extraordinarily tense-looking Commander David J. Gascon appeared on the screen and began to speak:

"This morning, detectives from the Los Angeles Police Department, after an exhaustive investigation, which included interviews of dozens of witnesses, a thorough examination and analysis of the physical evidence both here and in Chicago, sought and obtained a warrant for the arrest of O. J. Simpson, charging him with the murders of Nicole Brown Simpson and Ronald Lyle Goldman.

"Mr. Simpson, in agreement with his attorneys, was scheduled to surrender this morning to the Los Angeles Police Department. Initially that was eleven. It then became eleven-forty-five. Mr. Simpson has not appeared."

There were audible gasps from those assembled as Commander Gascon continued: "The Los Angeles Police Department, right now, is actively searching for Mr. Simpson. The Los Angeles Police Department is also very unhappy with the activities surrounding his failure to surrender, and we will be further looking into those activities, including anyone who may have intervened on his behalf. . . . Mr. Simpson is a wanted murder suspect. Two counts of murder, a terrible crime. We need to find him. We need to apprehend him. We need to bring him to justice. And we need to make sure that we find him as quickly as possible."

And so the supposedly great O. J. Simpson, the sports hero who "couldn't have done it," was now a fugitive from justice.

I thought: If you're not guilty, you don't have to flee. You have nothing to fear if you're not guilty. Why do you flee if you're an innocent man?

If I were in his shoes and I were innocent, they would have to tape my mouth shut, put a muzzle on me, and tie my hands down to keep me from ripping the tape and muzzle off and screaming "I'm not guilty!" I would demand a lie detector test. I would invite every expert in the land to witness it and want to take the test on national television in front of the world. I would never stop crying out, "I am an innocent man!"

But I would not run away.

Simpson's long-time friend Robert Kardashian appeared on the screen, reading what was described by some reporters as a suicide note. It did not sound like a suicide note to us, and suicide was the last thing that we wanted to happen. All of us desperately wanted this man to stand trial; we were certain that the American justice system would find the truth.

The phone rang. One of our neighbors informed us that Channel 2 had spotted the fugitive on the freeway. He was being driven by a friend, A. C. Cowlings, in a white Ford Bronco. Reporters said that Simpson was hidden in the back. They said that he had a gun.

Kim began to pace.

We watched intently. The vision of people lining the overpasses, holding signs, urging him on, nauseated us. They were rooting for an accused murderer! I said, "These people are warped."

Michael raged, "Wait a minute! What is this? It's not normal. He's a fugitive. He ran from the cops. Catch him and haul him to the police station!"

Kim thought: Just get him in jail. Lock him up. If it were anyone else, they would have blown him away by now.

Instead, twenty police cars surrounded the white Bronco, following it at a methodical pace. Time seemed suspended. We sat immobilized in front of the TV screen. We had planned on going to Friday night services at our temple, but none of us was going to move until this man was in custody.

As word of this unbelievable drama spread, our house once again filled with friends and neighbors. Nobody left the room.

Melanie Duben held Lauren's hand. Lauren thought: Oh my God, what is going to happen? If he shoots himself, we'll never find out exactly what happened. He might be the only person who knows.

Kim realized that she had chewed through the skin of her lower lip.

I paced like a caged animal.

Someone in the room yelled, "He's such a coward he can't even shoot himself."

"No," Kim said quickly, "then we'll never know."

The chase continued until the macabre caravan reached Simpson's Brentwood estate. By now it was dark. Helicopter news teams provided live coverage from overhead. The white Bronco sat in the driveway. Hundreds of supporters gathered outside the gate chanting "Free O. J." and rocking police cars. The LAPD Special Weapons and Tactics team surrounded the house. Cowlings spoke to hostage negotiators. For nearly an hour the fugitive sat in the Bronco, cradling a blue steel revolver and demanding to speak to his mother. He finally put his gun down and emerged about 8:50 P.M., carrying a framed family photo. He entered the house, used the bathroom, drank a glass of orange juice, and called his mother before finally being transported by police motorcade to Parker Center for booking.

Sunday was Father's Day. Over the years, Ron and Kim always pooled their money on a gift for me and went together to pick out a card. As they got older, the cards became more personal and meaningful, and were always a special treat for me.

This Father's Day was very different. Kim walked into a drugstore and began to peruse the card selection. "I was mortified," she said. "Most of the verses spoke of the impact a father has on a son, dreams for the future, passing on the lessons of life, and gratitude for the years gone by. How could there be a Father's Day card to fit this empty, sad, grief-stricken reality? I was immobilized. I didn't know what to do."

She finally settled on the card that she would give me. Then she found one that she felt Ron would have chosen. She bought them both.

"Shock does funny things to you," she said later. "A part of me was convinced that Ron would thank me for buying the card and sign it himself. A part of me knew that was insane."

Later, at home, she signed her card. Then she wrote Ron's name on the one she had selected for him. She had only three letters to scrawl, but it seemed to take forever.

Shortly after we had moved to Los Angeles, Ron and Kim had bought us a lemon tree as a wedding present. We planted it in the backyard.

For seven years it had never bloomed.

This year it did.

SEVEN

Four of us—Patti, Kim, Lauren, and I—drove to 11663 Gorham, in Brentwood. Michael could not bring himself to come along. He had been there before during happy times. He did not want to walk into apartment 3 ever again.

We felt very strange being there, and purposely left the door ajar.

Ron's dark slacks and white shirt, the clothes he had worn during his last evening of work, were still hanging on the bedroom door. Kim and I put them on hangers.

The work "uniform" of simple black slacks and a plain white shirt was perfect for Ron; he was color-blind. On mornings long ago, back in Chicago, when Ron was ready to head off for high school, he sometimes appeared dressed in what Kim called "the most godawful combinations." She would shake her head and command, "Ron, go back upstairs," and then tell him what shirt and sweater would go well with a particular pair of pants. Ron always took the razzing with a good-natured grin.

We made arrangements with the landlady to leave the water bed and a few other things, because none of us felt up to moving large pieces of furniture. Patti spotted a few pop-open water-bottle caps. She carries water with her constantly; she quietly slipped them into her pocket. Working quickly, we shoved everything into cardboard boxes, crying as we packed up kitchen utensils, clothes, and all the minutiae of Ron's existence.

There were a thousand little details to attend to, small fragments of Ron left dangling in the wind. We found a dry cleaner's receipt and realized that we would have to stop there to see if Ron had left clothes to pick up. His checkbook reminded us that we had to close out his account.

Lauren mentioned to Kim that she would like to have a baseball cap that Ron had worn frequently. It had a "Stüssy" logo on it, and it evoked many memories. Lauren had owned two Stüssy caps, and it had become a long-running prank for Ron to swipe them. Lauren used to pretend to be mad at him, but he knew that she was not, and the mock confrontations often ended in tickling sessions. Finally Ron had bought one of his own, and now Lauren wanted to keep it. She would always picture Ron wearing it in the style of the day, with the brim turned to the back.

Little decisions became monumental. Do we wash the clothes in the laundry basket or pack them the way they are? Kim finally decided that washing them would be like washing away a part of Ron. She could not bear that. She took his down comforter, noticing that it too was soiled, and had a small rip that needed to be sewn. However, she folded it gently and placed it in one of the boxes.

I spotted one of those big, plastic coin cups such as slot machine junkies use in the Las Vegas casinos. It was full of change, probably tips from Mezzaluna. There was also about $60 in cash. I knew that Ron owed Kim some money, so I tried to get her to take it. It was an irrational, emotional gesture and although Kim understood my intentions, she recoiled. There was no way that she could take any of Ron's money.

I spotted a bracelet that Ron wore frequently and tried to slip it on my wrist, but it was too tight. I decided to have it enlarged so that I could wear it.

When we were finished at Ron's apartment, we drove to Mezzaluna. The staff had told us that many people, not knowing any other way to reach us, had sent us mail in care of the restaurant. We told them we would come by to pick it up after we left Ron's apartment.

None of us had ever been to Mezzaluna before. We arrived during the quiet time, between the lunch and dinner crowds, and the restaurant was almost deserted. Manager John DuBello was there, along with the owner, Kareem Suki, and Stuart Tanner, a waiter and friend of Ron's. They were very gracious and wanted to serve us lunch. Lauren accepted a slice of pizza, but the rest of us declined; we were very uncomfortable there.

As Lauren picked at her food, a heavyset man, sitting next to the window, continued to stare at us. Finally he rose and walked over to our table. He said that he lived in Texas and was in Los Angeles on a business trip. He had come to Mezzaluna because he felt a need to be connected in some way. We were not really sure what he meant. "It's really weird that on the day I chose to come, you are here," he said. He was pleasant and courteous, and while we were sure that he meant well, the encounter was unsettling and a little creepy. It was the first time we sensed that people we did not know somehow felt they knew us, and it left us feeling vulnerable.

At the dry cleaner's we learned that Ron had put in a claim for a pair of damaged pants. When they realized who we were, the clerks came from behind the counter, hugged us, and began to cry. They mumbled something about wanting to help with funeral costs, and gave us the money that was due Ron.

At Union Bank I explained to an official that we needed to close Ron's account. Checking the files, the banker noted that Ron had designated me as his beneficiary. Just hearing this simple business detail brought the weight of the emotional day crashing down upon me. Tears flowed down my cheeks. I thought: This isn't right. It should have been the other way around. Ron should have been my beneficiary.

As I struggled to complete the paperwork, Patti, Kim, and Lauren walked across the street to a restaurant known as the Cheesecake Factory—another place where Ron had worked. A men's clothing store called Z 90049 that billed itself as "Only 127 Steps West of the Cheesecake Factory" ran a full-page ad in the restaurant's menu. The clothing store manager, spotting Ron in the restaurant, had asked him if he would model for the ad in exchange for free clothing. Ron said, "Sure." It was a one-time thing, but it explained why the press referred to him as a "sometime model."

Kim asked the manager of the Cheesecake Factory if she could have one of the menus. The woman did not understand her request and asked why. Kim pointed to the picture of Ron, and sobbed, "That's my brother."

The menu was a slick, quarter-inch-thick package of ring-bound, laminated pages. On page 9, across from the listing of exotic pastas, was the beige-tinted "Z 90049" ad. Ron was one of two men in the photo standing on either side of a woman. He wore a trendy, double-breasted suit with a tennis shirt underneath, buttoned up to the neck, with no tie. He looked very handsome. The woman in the middle, wearing a man's blazer, had long blond hair that was eerily reminiscent of Nicole's.

Patti, Kim, and Lauren cried as they examined the photo. The entire staff of the Cheesecake Factory gathered around. Soon everyone was weeping.

When two families merge, the transition inevitably produces some rough edges. Once, shortly after Patti and I were married, we all visited a family counselor. During the session both Ron and Kim broke down as they told the therapist how, years ago, Sharon had just walked out of their lives. Until that day, Michael had not realized how much both of them had been hurt by their mother's rejection.

This was the one issue, more than any other, that bound Ron and Kim together. During their childhood it was still fairly unusual for a father to have custody. They jokingly called me "Mr. Mom," but in fact, each tried to fill that role for the other.

As far back as I can remember, when we lived in Chicago, and later in the suburb of Buffalo Grove, Ron was Kim's other caretaker. As youngsters, they walked to school together. Later, when they began riding a bus, Ron always made sure that he sat with Kim. After school, before I came home from work, they kept close tabs on one another.

When I close my eyes I can see Kim, the tomboy, tagging after Ron and his friends. I see them playing Wiffle ball in the cul-de-sac and I see her trying to be brave during all the inevitable times that she took a ball in the face. I picture them playing catch and Frisbee, and laughing— always laughing.

When she grew a little older, Kim would follow Ron to the baseball diamond and watch him play. She stood with her nose to the fence, cheering him on. After the games, he and his friends would take her for ice cream. She was always shadowing him, and he never seemed to mind.

Often, during those early years, Ron and Kim had dinner ready for me when I came home from work. I have a sneaking suspicion that Kim did most of the actual cooking, but the meal was always presented as a joint effort.

Dinnertime frequently brought on giggle attacks. One evening they annoyed me so much that I separated them, sending Ron to the upstairs bathroom and confining Kim to the downstairs bathroom. Instead of settling down, they tapped out coded messages on the plumbing pipes.

It was impossible for Kim to stay mad at Ron. He would come after her with a silly grin on his face, jab her in the ribs with both of his index fingers, and chide her: "Oh, Kimmy, you know you can't be mad at me. You love me, you know you do!" And she did. She always will.

When Kim was old enough to show an interest in boys, Ron claimed the right to pass judgment. "Don't hang around with him," he advised. Or "He's a good kid. He's okay."

In fact, both Ron and Kim insisted on approving *my* dates. Whenever I introduced them to someone new, the instant she turned her back, Ron and Kim would flash me a thumbs-up or thumbs-down.

I did a lot of dating in those days, looking for the right woman who would complete our family and fulfill the role that Sharon had abdicated. In 1978 I married for a second time. Joan had not been married before and had no children of her own. By that time, Ron, Kim, and I had formed such a tight circle that it was difficult for Joan to break into it. She felt like the proverbial fifth wheel, and I still had a lot to learn about sharing my love and attention. After only a few years, Joan and I decided, amicably, to go our separate ways, and I was once more on the dating scene.

Ron and Kim were teenagers when one day I brought home a cute, petite, blond woman named Patti Glass. She received an immediate double thumbs-up. Patti's eldest son, Brian, was six years younger than Ron and three years younger than Kim. Michael was her middle child and Lauren was the baby. I had always sworn that I would not get involved with a woman who had children, but Patti and her kids were irresistible and I quickly changed my mind. After our first date, we were inseparable.

At first the five children did not spend much time together. Then one day Patti's father suffered a heart attack during a flight to San Diego. The plane made an emergency landing in Michigan in order to get him to a hospital, and Patti and I traveled there to see him. Ron and Kim were old enough to take care of themselves, but Patti arranged for a babysitter for her children. Lauren thought that the sitter was mean to her, and she wanted to call her mom to complain. Instead, Patti's children called Ron and Kim, since we lived only twenty minutes away. Even though it was snowing, Ron and Kim went over to Patti's house and immediately assumed the roles of big brother and sister. They fired the babysitter on the spot and brought Brian, Michael, and Lauren home with them. After putting Lauren to bed, they invited a few friends over and included Michael and Brian in a huge snowball battle in the front yard. Afterward, they stayed up way past midnight, eating and talking and having fun. Looking back on the incident, we realized that it was the beginning of becoming a real family.

Ron was a skinny, gawky teenager, but always popular. The same traits that could sometimes drive us crazy were what drew people to him and made him so much fun to be with. Ron was born with a laid-back, "What, me worry?" attitude. Many of life's petty irritations simply did not bother him. He was more concerned with living life than worrying about it. He had a good mind, and was very quick, but that did not always translate into topflight grades.

In our family, when you graduate from high school, it is assumed that you will go on to college, and that is what Ron did in 1986. Kim and Patti fashioned numerically coded labels for his clothes so that he could match the colors correctly. We all laughed because it reminded us of the ad for toddlers' clothes when they are first trying to dress themselves. The labels on the shirts and the pants featured animals that could be matched. Only this time it was Grranimals Go to College! We drove him to the campus of Illinois State University, and helped him settle in.

But Ron simply was not ready. Like many eighteen- or nineteen-year-olds, he had no idea what career he wanted to pursue and had no real focus on the future. College is tough enough when you are driven by a goal you want to achieve, but when the goal is missing, it is hard to attend to classwork. Add in Ron's zest for life and his engaging personality and you have a recipe for academic disaster.

During that semester at college, Ron majored in "fraternity." Although he was never a heavy drinker, we guessed that he partied pretty hard. Predictably his grades suffered and, at the end of the semester, he was back home in Chicago. I was very disappointed, but Kim was thrilled to have her big brother back. For Kim, Ron's reappearance came just in time because we were ready to make major changes in our lives.

Patti and I were married on February 21, 1987. Three days later we were all on a plane to California, where I had a new job waiting.

Kim had desperately wanted to stay in Chicago. She was "in love" with Brian Swislow. Also, she had just completed her first semester of high school. Her school in Chicago was huge, and she loved it. In contrast, the high school in California had only three hundred students, most of whom had grown up together. Kim was the new kid on the block, and she was miserable. She elevated self-pity to an art form. Now, more than ever, she depended upon her best friend—her brother.

My new employer supplied me with a company car, so I passed my white Nissan 200SX on to Ron. The license plate was perfect for him—UFORIC—incredibly happy. Ron drove Kim to school every morning. He pretended that it was a burden to get up so early and chauffeur her, but with the top open, and the stereo blasting the music of one of his favorite groups—The B-52s, Violent Femmes, Fine Young Cannibals, or Tears for Fears—he actually enjoyed the attention he got from the high school girls who giggled and stared at the new guy in town. When those same girls found out that he was Kim's brother, and not her boyfriend, her popularity took a giant leap forward.

Patti's parents were already in California when we arrived. Her mother lived in Rancho Mirage, and her father and his second wife resided in La Jolla. Her sister, Joyce, lived in Menlo Park with her two boys. As a result there were lots of family gatherings on holidays and other special occasions. These celebrations were second nature to Brian, Michael, and Lauren, but Ron and Kim had never been surrounded by a large, extended family. During these events Ron and Kim often shied away, clinging emotionally to each other. Sometimes they took a walk together; other times they sat off to one side and talked. Once again, it was Ron and Kim against the world.

Kim was the bookworm, the good student, the serious, responsible person. Ron was the free spirit. He would tease Kim, "You're Daddy's little angel. Little angels never do anything wrong, do they?" At times Kim worried that he really thought that and was resentful of her. Kim could not abide the thought of Ron being mad at her, so she would try to list for him every little mistake she had ever made. In fact Ron was incredibly proud of his sister, and said so, frequently.

In typical sibling chats that always had a goofy overtone, they used to plan their future based upon their differing personality traits. Ron would see to the religious upbringing of the kids in their respective families. Kim would graduate from college and make lots of money. In the distant future when it came time to place me in a nursing home, Kim would pay for it and Ron would visit me.

Ron's personality and affinity for children enabled him to step into the role of Brian, Michael, and Lauren's big brother with energy and ease. They shared a very special bond, different yet deep. He was funny and very affectionate. He listened to them and made everything they said seem important. They sought his attention at every opportunity. At first Kim was resentful, wanting her brother all to herself. However, after a time she realized that there was enough of Ron to go around; his affection for the others took nothing away from her.

Michael likes to tell a story that happened when he was eight or nine years old: "Ron took me to the beach one day. I remember how dorky I looked, with my pants pulled up about ten feet above my belly button. I was all legs and arms. First he tugged my pants down to where they should be and then he said, 'Okay, Michael, I want you to go up to that girl over there and tell her you have this really cute older brother who really wants to talk to her. Do you think you can do that?' Of course I did what he asked, and this awesome girl just smiled at me and told me how cute I was. The next thing I knew she and Ron were deep in conversation. On the way home Ron said, 'You know what, Michael? You're not so bad. Good work!' I think I was smiling for a week."

In a large family someone usually assumes the role of mediator and in our case, that was Patti. I tend to be high-strung, sometimes critical and strict with children, but Patti has a more relaxed approach.

Patti's goal was to be, first and foremost, a good friend to Ron and Kim; she never accentuated the stepmother role. And she succeeded. In some ways, Patti's relationship with Ron was even better than mine. Ron and I were both headstrong, sometimes stubborn. We could easily let an argument simmer for days without resolving it. Patti was able to view any difficulties that Ron and I had through a more detached eye. When Ron and I clashed over something, Patti would be in the middle, listening to both sides and striving for compromise. Ron and Patti spent countless hours just talking things over. Ron thought that he had disappointed me by dropping out of school; but she wanted him to understand that I was tough on him because I loved him so much. Patti cautioned me to back off, relax, and give Ron some time and space.

Had it not been for Patti, Ron and I would have had far more difficulty getting past some of the natural father-son squabbling. For that I will forever be deeply appreciative, and thankful to her.

Ron went through a lot of external changes during those years. Our new house in Agoura was only about twenty minutes from the ocean, and Ron fell in love with the scene. He gloried in the sunshine and the lure of the beautiful girls. His diet changed dramatically. He no longer ate much red meat. He started to work out in a gym and discovered the tanning booth. He wore his hair a little longer, a little spiked, causing me to grumble, "Is that really what you want to do to your hair?"

He was already a bit taller than I was, but now he seemed to grow even taller, and his body filled out. The difference in appearance was dramatic, but inside he was the same happy-go-lucky, caring, and protective person we had known. He made friends easily. I had often said, "When Ron came to California, it was as if he had died and gone to heaven." Now I regret those words.

He enrolled at Pierce Junior College and applied himself a bit more than before, but his grades still hovered around the average mark. I came to the realization that he was never going to be a dedicated student. His talents lay in other directions.

At college one day, Ron noticed a flyer advertising positions for camp counselors. Upon investigation he learned that the campers were all inner-city, minority children who came from really tough home situations. He was already working at a tanning salon, but he took this second job, which required him to spend nights at the camp in the mountains near Malibu. The pay was low, but he loved working with kids.

After his death, the woman who ran the camp contacted us and praised the work that Ron had done. Ron never pigeonholed people; he saw everyone as an individual. The woman explained that Ron was a role model who talked easily to these children, saying, "Let me tell you what you can do right, and let me explain to you what you can do wrong, 'cause I've made all the mistakes already." It was the same way he talked to Michael on their long walks to the shopping center.

In truth, Ron continued to make his share of mistakes. He was a young man speeding into his early adult years, often without bothering to look at a road map. For several years he bounced in and out of school, in and out of several apartments, and in and out of various jobs.

He worked for a time at the Westlake United Cerebral Palsy Residence Home. His job was to help patients get out of bed, bathe, get dressed, eat, and do all the other daily activities that most of us take for granted. Even though many of the patients were so physically challenged that they required help for the most fundamental tasks, Ron saw them as people who deserved respect and dignity. He never patronized them. To him, they were simply people who had an illness, and they were perfectly capable of controlling their lives and making their own decisions.

On an outing one day, Ron and several patients stopped at a fast-food restaurant. A patient named Jane attempted to place an order, but the counter clerk either could not understand her or simply grew frustrated. He turned to Ron and asked, "What does she want?"

"Why are you asking me?" Ron responded. "This is Jane. She can order for herself."

The director of the residence recalled for us a day when Ron put music on the public address system and set about dancing with patients in wheelchairs; it was almost like a Fred Astaire routine. The director said that she had never seen so many smiles on the patients' faces.

However, it was the restaurant business that seemed to captivate him. Over the years he worked at several establishments, and thoroughly enjoyed the constant interaction with people. Seeing him in waiter's clothes always bothered me a bit because I wanted him to do something more substantial with his life. But I had to admit that he was good. One evening, Patti and I stopped in for dinner at a place called Truly Yours, where Ron was working. It was a modest establishment, but Ron hammed it up for us, acting as if Truly Yours was a five-star restaurant. He placed a towel over his arm, deferred to our every whim, and called us "Ma'am" and "Sir." I was not surprised when the manager told me that customers often requested his tables.

Ron never expressed any interest in being an actor. That notion was raised when reporters learned of his one and only television appearance. Kim was in college in Santa Barbara when Ron called one day and teased, "Guess what I did!"

"Uh-oh," Kim said, her anxiety level rising.

"I got dared to go on *Studs*," he said. *Studs* was a low-budget version of *The Dating Game*.

At the time, the show was very popular in a campy sort of way, but Kim knew that it had a sleazy aura. She thought: Oh my God.

The show was supposed to pay for three dates with three different women, but Ron did not feel that the money they offered was sufficient, so he spent some of his own, just to make sure that the women were treated properly.

When the show was ready to air, Kim threw a small party for her friends. "I was so embarrassed," she remembers. "There he was, larger than life, hair slicked back, assuming the cocky, arrogant role he could slip on when he wanted to. I knew it was all a lark, and that he was blowing smoke, but half the time the show was on, I hid my eyes." We all got a kick out of it, though.

I watched the show at home, alternately laughing and cringing as he camped it up. I knew that he did not take it seriously; he was just having fun. But at one point I slunk down on the couch, hid my eyes, and muttered, "Oh my God! Where did that ego come from?"

Later, when we teased him about it, Ron just laughed. "It was a blast," he said. "Who cares?"

Sometime after that one of Kim's friends talked her into auditioning for the same show. When Ron found out, he informed his little sister: "You are *not* the kind of girl who goes on that show! No way! I won't allow it."

There were two Rons. The one that the world saw now, in abbreviated clips on the nightly news or the tabloid shows, was carefree, a little cocky, and could dismiss any problem with a shrug of his shoulder. With family and close, trusted friends, however, he was a warm, vulnerable, incurable romantic who loved to send flowers, create intimate dinners, write notes, and send cards. Kim knew far better than the rest of us that Ron, at age twenty-five, desperately craved stability. He had come to the point in his life when he was ready to start his own business. He wanted to put down roots. He was searching for the woman he would marry and who would bear his children. Whether a boy or a girl, he wanted to name his first child Dakota.

Ron was ready to settle down. All he needed was a little more time.

EIGHT

I have always been emotional. A Hallmark commercial or a Kodak moment invariably causes my eyes to fill and my throat to tighten. As emotion peaks in a sentimental movie, it is Patti who hands *me* a tissue. Those are tears of the bittersweet moments of life. Now, dealing with the intensity of this irrevocable loss was nearly impossible.

For the first time in my life I have nightmares on a regular basis. I never sleep through the night.

Only at night, in the privacy of my bedroom, when no one is watching and no one is listening, do I allow myself to break down. They say that a good cry can be cleansing, that it can make you feel better. That is not necessarily true. Nothing helps.

The sight of a child, photos of someone else's son, comments from a friend, overhearing other parents speak about dreams for their child's future, a familiar melody on the radio—any one of these things, and hundreds more—are capable of creating the lump in my throat that inevitably leads to tears. There is no way to expect it. There is no way to control it. When the pain becomes too great to bear, I push it down again. I shove it to some unknown place, knowing all the while that it will surface again very soon.

Jim Ziegler had seen one of his employees through a similar situation. It was the mother of Craig Hastings, the young man who had been stabbed to death in 1991, whom Kim had recalled during the frantic flight from San Francisco to L.A. Jim told us that the Hastings family had been aided by a state-run agency called the Victim-Witness Assistance Program, funded by property and money confiscated from convicted criminals rather than by tax dollars. We were immediately interested, knowing that we needed all the help we could get.

Susan Arguela from the program contacted us. She visited our home and took some time to explain to us, as the family of a murder victim, what to expect from the legal system. She detailed the process that would lead to a formal trial: The first step was an arraignment, wherein the defendant would hear the charges against him or her and would be allowed to enter his or her plea. The judge would determine whether the defendant would be held in the county jail or if he would be allowed out on bail. Susan explained that bail in this case was unlikely, since the defendant had already attempted to flee. After that, the prosecutors planned to present evidence in secret to a grand jury, which could then vote an indictment. Another option was to hold a preliminary hearing in public to determine whether there was sufficient evidence to bring the defendant to trial.

This was a new, and macabre, vocabulary for all of us, and it was a bit intimidating. What's more, it already seemed obvious that because of the high profile of the defendant and his ability to hire a high-priced legal team, the entire process would consume a great deal of time. All we wanted was justice for Ron, but it appeared that patience was paramount. Susan assured us that she, or someone else from the Victim-Witness Assistance Program, would be present in court to shepherd us through the unfamiliar proceedings.

Susan told us that if and when the defendant was convicted, California law granted each member of the victim's family an opportunity to speak to the court, prior to sentencing. We could say anything we wished.

My eyes met Kim's, and I knew that she was already beginning to formulate her words.

Like everyone else, we were shocked and saddened when authorities released tapes of Nicole's 911 calls. We heard the sound of Nicole's terrified voice on October 25, 1993, less than eight months before the murders, wailing, "He's fucking going nuts. . . . He's going to beat the shit out of me."

There was no dialogue on the tape of the 1989 incident that led Simpson to plead "no contest" to a misdemeanor charge of wife beating. There were only background sounds that the police log characterized as: "Female being beaten . . . could be heard over the phone."

The tapes worried and angered us. Why wasn't this man prosecuted more vigorously in the past? Why did Nicole have to live in constant fear? It seemed clear that Simpson was accustomed to receiving special treatment, not only from the community, but from the police and the courts as well. It was offensive to realize that he had received a mere slap on the wrist for terrorizing his wife.

We had all grown up believing in the concept of "innocent until proven guilty," and we tried to apply that standard now. But it was becoming more difficult to keep an open mind.

What would I have done if I ever suspected that this man had beaten my daughter?

God help him.

He and I would have a conversation, and it would go something like this: "If you ever lay a hand on my daughter again, you'll be in major trouble with me. I'm going to keep my eye on you real closely, and if—God forbid—it ever happens again, I will break every bone in your body."

As the days passed, we found it extremely difficult to turn our attention to the details of normal life. We had work to do, appointments to keep, airplanes to catch. But it was nearly impossible to attend to life's trivialities when every morning was preceded by a mere few hours of restless, nightmarish sleep, and every day was filled with increasingly bizarre and disturbing developments.

It was supposed to have been a busy, happy summer.

Kim and Joe had planned to fly to New York near the end of June to attend the wedding of one of Joe's friends. After the wedding they would fly to Chicago, where Kim was scheduled for surgery. Prior to our marriage, on a joint vacation to Florida, Patti, Kim, Ron, and I had been involved in an automobile accident. A drunk driver, speeding on the opposite side of the boulevard, lost control of the car and mowed down several trees in the median strip. His car battery flew through the air and through our windshield, spewing acid. Ron and I were spared. Patti was burned slightly, but Kim caught the brunt of it. When Ron pulled her from the wreckage, he saw that her face and eyes were badly burned.

Ron was at her side constantly in the hospital. For a time, her vision was gone and her face looked, as she put it, like barbecue. Ron fussed over her, catered to her, and assured her that she was still beautiful and that everything would be all right.

Over the years, a series of surgeries had corrected most of the damage, but Kim had timed this additional procedure to coincide with her New York trip.

Michael and Lauren had reservations to fly to Chicago for a two-and-a-half week visit with Brian and their dad.

Finally Patti and I were going to join everyone in Chicago for a few days' vacation.

Now we did not know what to do. Everyone's nerves were frayed, and an ongoing tension accompanied the roller coaster of emotions that we were riding. The horror was still too fresh, the emotions too raw. And there was another issue at hand. Evidence against Simpson would be presented in open court at a preliminary hearing on June 30. We wanted to be there.

Lauren was in no mood to go to Chicago. Ron's murder had left her frightened and feeling vulnerable around strangers. She cried constantly and had great difficulty sleeping. Most nights she brought a blanket or sleeping bag into our room and curled up on the floor next to Patti's side of the bed.

Lauren did not want to disappoint her dad, but she did not want to leave home, either. Yet she had a difficult time communicating her mixed feelings. Kim, sensing the dilemma, took Lauren for a long walk through our neighborhood and got her to open up. Kim explained that it was normal to feel the constant fear and encouraged her to do what she needed to make herself feel safe. She assured her that her father would understand if she wanted to stay close to home for a while longer. "Just be honest about your feelings," she counseled. "It's okay to do what's best for you." With the issue in the open, we were able to come up with a compromise. Michael would fly to Chicago by himself. Lauren and her friend Elise Main would join him later.

For her part, Kim really wanted to attend the preliminary hearing, but she did not want to miss the wedding in New York or the surgery in Chicago. She still thought she could "do it all."

We wanted to keep a low profile and let the system proceed without our interference. We believed that Ron's death would be dealt with in a fair way; we were sure that justice would ultimately prevail. We were still too consumed by our loss to be aware of the immensity of what was happening around us.

As Patti and I walked into the nineteen-story Downtown Criminal Courts Building on West Temple Street in Los Angeles for the first day of the preliminary hearing, we saw a thick cluster of satellite dishes outside. Every network and every major L.A. TV station would broadcast the proceedings live, from gavel to gavel. Howard Rosenberg of the *Los Angeles Times* commented, "Moses parting the Red Sea wouldn't get this coverage. . . ."

Vendors, like rodents, had multiplied overnight. Ron's now-famous photo ID was being hawked on T-shirts, trading cards, Pogs, mugs, and anything else that the entrepreneurial spirit could dream up. We saw placards proclaiming, FREE O. J.! We were offended and sickened by the display. Tragedy, it appeared, was good for business.

As she had promised, Susan Arguela met us at the courthouse and took us upstairs to the office of Patty Jo Fairbanks, the secretary for the prosecutors. Susan reminded us of the purpose of the preliminary hearing. The prosecution's task was simply to persuade the judge that there was a "strong suspicion" of Simpson's guilt.

As we waited for the proceedings to begin, we met the Brown family for the first time. I remember all of them being there—Juditha, Lou, Denise, Tanya, Dominique—we all hugged and expressed our sympathy. It was truly genuine and the pain was overwhelming. Some of them were wearing angel pins, replicas of one that Nicole frequently wore.

After a time, Susan took us to the elevators and guided us down and into the courtroom. The room was filled with reporters and excited spectators. Despite Susan's coaching, we were clueless as to how this was going to play out. This was a foreign world to us.

We were seated, awaiting the start of the proceedings, when a side door suddenly opened and we first laid eyes on the man accused of murdering Ron. To Patti, he seemed huge. "His hands are massive," she commented. When he turned and faced the spectators, Patti noted a carefree, arrogant smirk on his face. Who do you think you are? she wondered. Fake it if you have to, but show some remorse, some sadness. Your wife is gone, the mother of your children. And you walk in here like you have the world by the tail? You're disgusting.

I had expected him to be wearing orange prison overalls or whatever prisoners normally wear. I thought that he would be restrained by handcuffs and shackles. Instead, here was a man in an expensively tailored suit, smiling at what he seemed to consider an adoring crowd, sauntering toward the defense table. Idly he tossed his arm around the shoulder of his defense attorney, Robert Shapiro. I felt an overwhelming revulsion. This man was accused of murdering my son. What did he have to smile about?

Much of the morning was squandered by legal bickering between Robert Shapiro and Assistant District Attorney Marcia Clark, but slowly we began to learn about the evidence. Police had found blood on the driver's-door handle of Simpson's white Ford Bronco, parked outside of his Rockingham estate. Inside the Bronco, detectives found bloodstains on the driver's door, the instrument panel, the floor, the steering wheel, and the center console. In a search warrant affidavit, LAPD Detective Philip Vannatter stated, "Blood droplets were subsequently observed leading from the vehicle on the street to the front door of the residence." Vannatter's affidavit confirmed that police recovered a leather glove "containing human blood" on the south side of the Rockingham house. The glove "closely resembled" the glove that was found at the crime scene, near Ron's feet. Inside the house, police found bloodstains in the foyer and a bathroom.

The defense fought to have all of this evidence suppressed. Shapiro filed a motion charging that when Detective Mark Fuhrman scaled the fence at Simpson's estate, he had had no search warrant and had compromised the defendant's privacy; therefore, all evidence found as a result of this action should be thrown out. Judge Kathleen Kennedy-Powell said that she would rule on the motion next week.

"This is crazy," I said to Patti, who agreed. Evidence is evidence, we thought. Blood is blood.

So much of the day was consumed with procedural matters that very little was accomplished.

On Friday, the second day of the preliminary hearing, several of the witnesses' statements caused us to shudder, and we could sense that the prosecution was setting the stage for what we knew would be very difficult testimony to hear.

Pablo Fenjves, a neighbor of Nicole's, said that he heard the "plaintive wail" of a dog barking about 10:15 or 10:20 the night of the murders.

Steven Schwab, another neighbor of Nicole's, described how he came upon an agitated dog with bloody paws shortly before 11:00 P.M.

Sukru Boztepe, yet another neighbor, was the first to discover Nicole's body lying in front of her condominium. His wife, Bettina Rasmussen, testified that she saw the body for a moment, then turned away. "I never looked back again," she said.

"They will never get over this as long as they live," Patti whispered. "What a horrible and devastating experience."

Kim, still in New York, was glued to the television screen, watching their testimony. Seeing and hearing the genuine emotion in their voices was very hard for her as well.

Kim quickly realized that her decision to go to New York with Joe was a terrible mistake. She was supposed to share in the enjoyment of a friend's wedding, but her heart was back in L.A. She knew that she should be at the preliminary hearing and she wanted to be with us on Saturday. Saturday, July 2, would have been Ron's twenty-sixth birthday.

She cried constantly, making everyone around her uneasy. No one knew what to say to her, or how to bring her comfort.

They stayed at the home of Joe's mother, Janette, and Kim asked Joe to drive her from store to store, searching for the perfect candle that would burn for the entire twenty-four hours of Ron's birthday. They stayed up until midnight when, as they sat around the kitchen table, Kim solemnly lit the candle. Then she and Joe, together with his mother, wrote a few words of love and remembrance for Ron. Kim watched as the flickering flame burned.

The next day, as they were driving around New York with Rob, one of Joe's friends, they happened to pass a cemetery. Rob made an idle comment; he had read a newspaper story about grave robbers who were digging up bodies and stealing jewelry. Joe punched his friend in the arm and reminded him that the topic was not appropriate. Kim, in the backseat, was crying softly.

Back home, things were not much better. I was running some errands and Lauren was at a friend's house. Deciding to relax in the pool, Patti put on her bathing suit, grabbed a towel, and went into the backyard. She floated on a raft for only a few minutes before a panic attack struck. She had the sudden, eerie feeling that she was being watched, and she realized: I'm here all by myself. The whole world now knows who we are and where we live. Anybody could come over that privacy wall at any moment, with a camera or a knife. There are a lot of crazy people out there.

She did not see or hear anyone, but the fear was so real, so tangible, that she jumped out of the pool and raced back into the house.

Later, when she told me what had happened, I tried to calm her. "Relax, don't be silly," I said, "you're perfectly safe here." But my advice did not help. She simply could not shake the ominous feeling.

We decided that we were not up to traveling to Chicago. And as we talked further, we grew concerned about Kim. We wondered if she was under too much stress to undergo surgery right now. I phoned Kim in New York, and she agreed to postpone the operation. She and Joe would change their flight reservations and come directly home.

Prior to leaving New York, Kim spoke to her cousin Stacy in Chicago. Stacy told her that Sharon was planning to file a wrongful-death lawsuit against Simpson, asking for $1 million in damages.

"I went crazy, absolutely nuts," Kim told me. "I called Sharon and asked her what the hell was going on. She denied that she was going to file a suit and said that she didn't know a thing about it."

Michael was relieved to be away from the chaos in L.A. and to have a chance to think about something else for a while, but even in Chicago the media were hungry. A reporter tracked him down, but the doorman at his father's apartment house ran interference, telling the newsman that he had the wrong Glass family.

As a retired defense attorney, Michael's father tried to get him to look at things from both perspectives. Although he felt, as Michael did, that Simpson was probably guilty, he kept reminding him that it was possible that prosecutors would not be able to convict him. Michael bristled at this negativity, but knew that his dad was trying to keep him from being devastated if the worst happened.

For the first time in his life, Michael found himself truly scared. He did not want to be outside after dark. Ominous strangers seemed to lurk around every corner. If this horrible thing could have happened to Ron, it could happen to anyone. It could happen to him. While still in Chicago he bought an expandable metal billy club to keep in his car for protection. He dubbed it his "O. J. Beater."

In the midst of this chaos, I had a family to feed, a mortgage payment to make. My clients had problems, new projects and questions, and it was my job to deal with them. In the ghastly context of my life, these details were trivial, but attention to them was what put food on the table. The simple fact was that I could not afford to attend every courtroom hearing. Kim was on her way back from New York. She and Patti would attend the remaining sessions of the preliminary hearing; I would try to get some business done and slip into the courtroom if and when I could. In addition, nearly every TV station in L.A. was covering the hearing, so I would have plenty of opportunity to follow the course of events.

I could not keep my mind even remotely centered on my job. However, I quickly discovered that I was blessed with numerous clients who were unbelievably understanding. Many of them said, "We can talk on the phone if you can't make it over." Some of them even offered to come to my office.

When the preliminary hearing resumed on July 5, Kim had her first chance to attend, her first opportunity to view the defendant in person.

The moment he entered the courtroom, Kim's body began to shake. She was petrified.

He sat down at the defense table and placed his huge hands in front of him. Like Patti, Kim could not believe how large he was. She stared at his back, willing him to look in her direction, but he would not.

Patti and Kim listened to an array of witnesses, who now appeared before the world for the very first time. Each would take his or her place in the lore of this bizarre case.

Limousine driver Allan Park testified that Simpson did not respond to his repeated buzzing. He said that just before 11:00 P.M., he saw a shadowy figure—"six feet, two hundred pounds, black, wearing dark clothes"—move across the driveway and into Simpson's house. Moments later, the buzzer was finally answered.

Simpson's houseguest, Brian "Kato" Kaelin, testified that he heard thumping sounds outside his window, where a bloodstained glove was later discovered.

Detective Mark Fuhrman told how he spotted what he believed to be blood on the driver's door of Simpson's white Ford Bronco. Only then did he jump the fence to enter Simpson's property, concerned that there might be more victims inside the home. Once inside the property, after talking to Kaelin, it was Fuhrman who found the bloody glove that matched the one left at the crime scene.

Detective Phil Vannatter also contended that Simpson, at that point, was not considered a suspect.

We respected the detectives' long and dedicated service to the community, but Patti said, "I think they made a mistake by insisting that Simpson was not a suspect. I don't pretend to know the ins and outs of the law, search warrants, procedures, that sort of thing, but I do know that when someone is killed, the spouse or the ex-spouse is automatically suspected, and it seemed a little disingenuous to deny it."

We were scared. Would the judge rule that the search of Simpson's estate was illegal and, therefore, throw out the evidence? And if she did, would Simpson even be held over for trial?

But Judge Kennedy-Powell ruled that the detectives had reason to believe that an emergency situation existed when they scaled the wall of Simpson's estate. Thus the search was legal; the evidence could be used. We were tremendously relieved. "We just might get a fair trial," Patti said.

Day after day the evidence continued to mount. Day after day Simpson appeared uglier and smaller.

Vannatter testified that Simpson had a cut on the knuckle of the middle finger of his left hand. Prosecutors introduced a photo taken after he returned from Chicago, showing the cut.

Vannatter's partner, Detective Tom Lange, testified about a trail of bloody shoe prints that led away from the bodies. The shoe prints did not match the high-topped athletic shoes that Ron was wearing, and Nicole was barefoot.

LAPD Crime Lab supervisor Gregory Matheson said that the trail of spots and shoe prints was made by human blood. Concentrating on one particular sample taken from the cobblestone path leading away from the murder scene, he presented the results of blood-typing tests.

Marcia Clark asked, "Could Nicole Simpson have left the blood drop at 875 South Bundy?"

"No," Matheson responded.

"With respect to Ronald Goldman . . . could he have been a source of that blood drop on the trail?"

"No."

"With respect to the defendant, could he have been the source of the blood drop that was found on the trail at 875 South Bundy?"

"Yes," Matheson said. "He can be included in the group of possibles."

Additional testimony told us that the odds against someone having an identical match were more than 200 to 1.

On the final day of the hearing, Patti and Kim were forced to endure the testimony of Deputy Medical Examiner Irwin Golden. And what he said was ghastly.

Nicole died from a cut to her throat so deep that it nicked her spinal column. Dr. Golden described it as a "gaping" wound and pointed to a chart that highlighted the gash in deep red. Nicole's knife wounds were largely confined to her head and neck.

Ron suffered dozens of knife wounds up and down his body, several of which could have killed him—two punctures that entered through the rib cage and into his right lung, a pair of deep slashes across his throat, one of which had severed the jugular, a five-inch-deep wound to the left side of his abdomen, and a puncture of his left aorta. There was also a deep wound to the left thigh.

Dr. Golden said that both victims were cut on the hands, arms, and face. These were defensive wounds that indicated they attempted to fight off their attacker.

This was the first time we had been confronted with the exact nature of the attack. Kim could not shake the image of a knife going into her brother's chest, and she clutched at her stomach, fighting nausea. At the same time she was petrified and full of rage at the man accused of doing it.

Patti's mind reeled. Ron was not just murdered, she realized, he was butchered! Tears welled in her eyes as she thought of how scared he must have been. "He didn't have a chance," she whispered to Kim.

The image of the terror that Ron must have experienced was etched on our minds, forever.

The defense team raised questions about the medical examiner's work, noting that he had waited hours before performing tests that might have more closely pinpointed the time of death. Dr. Golden seemed to wither under the attack.

Golden's wife was seated behind us. During a sidebar, worried about the effects of his bumbling delivery, Kim leaned back and asked her, in a whisper, "Is he nervous?"

"No," Mrs. Golden said, gushing with pride, "he's always like this."

Judge Kennedy-Powell looked directly at the defendant and asked him to stand. She said simply, "The court feels that there is ample evidence to establish the strong suspicion of the guilt of the accused." She ordered that Simpson would be arraigned in Superior Court on July 22. Until then, he would continue to be held at the Men's Central Jail. There would be a trial. There would be no bail.

We were thrilled. Patti and Kim hugged each other and later congratulated Marcia Clark. "One down, one to go," Marcia said.

Kim returned to her job at Wells Fargo Bank in San Francisco, but her attention was focused on the upcoming trial.

Each morning she took a bus to work, and the trip became a daily half hour of terror. She was obsessed with an irrational fear that the bus would tip over, she would be killed, and I would have to bury her, too. She decided that she was no longer afraid of dying, but terrified about what would happen to those left behind. She checked and rechecked her wallet, making sure that everything was in order. Morbid questions flew though her head: Do I have my ID with me? Will they be able to identify me? Who's going to tell my dad?

Sometimes the panic caused her to hyperventilate.

She tried to calm herself by beginning to compose the victim's statement that she would deliver when the defendant was convicted. She asked herself: What will I say to the court? A list of rabid obscenities came to mind.

NINE

◡

Patti and I were back in the courtroom on July 22 for the formal arraignment. When Simpson was asked how he pled, he declared in a cocky, arrogant voice that he was "absolutely one hundred percent not guilty!" His demeanor, his complete failure to behave like a truly innocent man further persuaded us of his probable guilt. Why was he not pleading to take a lie-detector test? Why was he not screaming that there was a real murderer on the loose?

Patti shook her head. "There is no emotion there," she said, "no sense of loss, no grief. He seems concerned only about himself."

In San Francisco, Kim was at work, taking a coffee break, watching television in the employee lounge. When she saw the defendant respond to the formal charge, she felt physically ill. She ran downstairs to her co-workers, Amy, Rae, and Barbara, and shared with them what had happened. As always, they were in her corner, comforting and supporting her.

Meanwhile, two more players entered the arena. Judge Lance A. Ito was assigned to try the case and Johnnie L. Cochran, Jr., joined the team of defense lawyers. We had never heard of either man.

Contrary to what Sharon had told Kim over the phone, her Los Angeles-based attorney, Michael Brewer, filed a wrongful-death civil suit against Simpson. Sharon sought an unspecified amount of damages for the loss of Ron's "companionship, society, comfort, attention . . . and support." We thought that she had lost all that twenty years earlier. We were now, however, beginning to understand why she had appeared at Ron's funeral in the company of an attorney.

76

I was very angry. How could money be on her mind at this moment? I wondered. Ron had been dead for only five weeks and she had reduced his life to a search for dollars. Loss of comfort? Loss of companionship? She would not have known Ron if he had bumped into her.

Reached by a reporter, I commented, "I don't know anything about it other than what I've heard on the news. But it doesn't surprise me."

As part of her strategy, Sharon petitioned the court for power of attorney over Ron's estate. I felt boxed into a corner. I could not allow this absurdity to continue, but I did not want to dredge up past miseries. Once again, my attorney friends came to the rescue. They told me they would file executor papers on my behalf, and not to worry about it.

Nevertheless, Kim went on the attack, writing a letter to the judge. When I read it, I felt the pain begin to surface. Kim wrote:

Your Honor . . .

I will get right to the point:

Sharon Rufo, our birth mother, made a conscientious choice every day for 20 years, to have no relationship with her two children.

My father, Fred Goldman, took on the challenge as any loving parent would, to raise two babies from ages 6 and 3, single-handedly . . . .

The last time Ron spoke to Sharon, was 3 years ago and before that he had not seen or spoken to her in at least 15 or more years. I, on the other hand, have had slightly more contact, none of which was positive or resulting in any type of ongoing communication.

Without rehashing every incident to explain the lack of mothering on her behalf, my father NEVER once said an ill word of her to Ron and I, even until this day. The decision to write this was mine as I am also sure Ron would have done the same.

Sharon Rufo gave up her right to be in control of anything when she walked out on us 20 years ago and it is beyond my comprehension that she would take the death of my brother and use it to her advantage to be in control now.

I am pleading with the court to not allow Sharon Rufo to be executor. She has a history of lying, cheating and manipulating situations to her best interest, which never included Ron and I, even until this day. She is continuing to be selfish as well as self-serving, having no regard for others or the pain she may be causing, especially at a time as tragic as this one. Please do not grant her the opportunity to subject myself and my family to any more pain and grievance than we are already suffering.

My father is a caring, supportive, sincere and fair man. The three of us were/are very close, and are very honored, proud and fortunate to have been raised by such a wonderful and dedicated father. He sacrificed his life for the benefit of his children. Please, don't take away all he has done, especially at a time when he is so vulnerable. My brother has already been taken from him, please don't take away the last chances he has to be close to Ron and continue the wonderful job he has been doing for Ron and I our whole lives. My brother would want it this way. . . .

Immediately after our divorce, Sharon had custody of the children and I had full visitation rights. Then I learned from Ron's grammar school teacher that he was acting up in class and not doing as well as he had been. Knowing that divorce can be hard on kids, I pushed for all of us to get some counseling. Sharon balked at the idea, but eventually agreed to attend some of the sessions. In our early conversations with the counselor, Ron and Kim complained about Sharon's lack of attention. She bailed out, and refused to continue the process.

I offered to take over the day-to-day responsibility for the children. Realizing that she would have more time for herself, Sharon readily agreed. So that the children would not have to change schools, I moved into Sharon's apartment and she found another place.

We signed an informal agreement. Now our situations were reversed. I had custody, and she had full visitation rights. But she seldom utilized those rights. She often failed to show up for prearranged visits, and when the children tried to call her, she was seldom home. When they did speak to her, she offered lame excuses for not coming: She needed to do her laundry; she did not have money for gasoline. Sometimes, after she made these excuses, the kids would see her driving around the neighborhood.

After this scenario played out for one chaotic year, I decided that it was time to formalize the agreement and contacted my attorney to file the necessary papers.

On Friday evening, I arrived home from work, opened the door and called out, as I always did, "Hi, I'm home!" I was greeted with silence. The housekeeper was gone. The children were gone. Ron and Kim's closets were empty. Their toys had vanished, along with them.

Immediately, I picked up the phone and called Sharon. Her response was a terse "I don't know anything about it," and she hung up the phone. I called one of Sharon's sisters-in-law, Mary, and received a similar response. Then I called Sharon's other sister-in-law, Donna. She was as shocked and panicked as I and concluded that Sharon and Mary must be in this plot together.

I called my attorney. He told me to determine the children's location, but not to attempt to do anything over the weekend.

I drove to Mary's house. Sure enough, Ron and Kim were playing outside, but I hung back and followed my lawyer's advice. My children never knew I was there, but I kept a sharp eye on them the entire weekend.

On Monday morning, we were in court. I told the judge what had happened and showed him the written agreement Sharon and I had signed regarding the children's custody. In an angry, no-nonsense tone he slammed down the gavel and decreed that the kids were in my hands until the matter was fully resolved. Then I petitioned the court for full and complete custody.

From court, my fiancée, Joan, and I went immediately to Sharon's apartment to retrieve the kids, but her housekeeper resisted. She tried to restrain Ron and Kim as they yelled, "Daddy! Daddy!" Ron broke loose and ran to me, but the housekeeper pulled Kim back inside the apartment and locked the door.

Joan took Ron out to the car and I went back upstairs to get Kim.

The housekeeper screamed at me and threatened to call the police. I invited her to do so.

Soon, Sharon's boyfriend arrived. He was a police officer who promptly informed me that he would "throw my butt in jail" for causing all these problems. I thrust the court order at him and reminded him that as an officer of the court, he was obligated to obey it.

Kim cowered in a corner, scared and crying. Then Sharon arrived and demanded that her boyfriend arrest me. But I told him that if he did not restrain Sharon, I would have *her* arrested for attempting to defy the court. By that time, he had read the court order and told her to back off.

I swept Kim into my arms and kept her there while I gathered the clothes and toys that were strewn about. Then we went home.

Only later did I learn that Sharon had told Ron and Kim, "Your daddy doesn't want you anymore, so you're coming with me."

Ron and Kim had been with me ever since.

Kim received a small package in the mail. When she opened it, she found a note and a lovely necklace. They were from Ron's last girlfriend, Andrea Scott. "I found this necklace in my car," Andrea wrote, "and I know that Ron would want you to have it."

Kim examined the necklace. It had one simple pendant, in the shape of an Egyptian ankh—a symbol Ron had spoken of so often. What a lovely thing to do, Kim thought.

She fastened the necklace around her neck, and has not removed it since.

The strategy of Simpson's defense team became ever more obvious— delay, obstruct, object, confuse, entangle, confound, perplex. Judge Ito seemed to cater to them, conducting one interminable pretrial hearing after another.

Controversy began to swirl around Detective Mark Fuhrman. Defense lawyers accused him of being a racist, based on remarks he made in a 1983 pension case. Fuhrman filed a declaration explaining his remarks. "These statements attributed to me were misquoted and taken out of context," he stated. "Any other racially insensitive comments that I may have made . . . were in the context of a therapeutic session and were specifically intended to refer to my work with violent gangs and gang members and the emotion that this stressful, dangerous and diffi-cult type of police work engendered in me."

We had a lot of admiration for the way Detective Fuhrman car-ried himself, and we felt bad for him. Here was an obvious effort by the defense to attack the messenger. Why? Because he found a key piece of evidence—the bloody glove. Patti said nervously, "Now his reputation has been sullied. I don't like the way this feels."

I struggled to understand this. Racism repels me. But this case had nothing to do with racism.

We were still clinging to the delusion that everyone in the courtroom was ultimately after the same goal: the truth.

Jury selection was scheduled to begin on September 16, although that date would likely be pushed back because the defense continued to file motion after motion, tying up everyone's time. Just a few weeks before that date the postal service, which was forwarding Ron's mail to us, delivered an official-looking letter summoning Ronald Lyle Goldman to jury duty on the same date: September 16, 1994.

When we called Kim and told her about this bizarre coincidence, she, too, was incredulous. A part of her thought: Don't they know he's dead? And another part wondered if this was some kind of message or omen. For a moment she was speechless, then she echoed our thoughts. "Unbelievable," she said.

There is an element of the American press that seems to delight in rumors and innuendo and, since the media knew so little about Ron and apparently did not check their facts carefully, they seemed eager to speculate on everything, from Ron's so-called relationship with Nicole to his sexuality. Tabloid headlines routinely shouted that he was Nicole's lover, that he was gay, that he was a would-be this or a wannabe-that, and that he lived his life in California's fastest lane. Apparently the fact that he was a young man blessed with a gregarious and caring personality, who devoted hours of his time to working with cerebral palsy sufferers, who cherished his family and friends, who always viewed life with a "the glass is half full rather than half empty" mentality simply would not sell tabloids. We were angered and hurt by the sloppy and irresponsible reporting, and determined to introduce the Ron whom we knew and loved to anyone who would listen.

Speaking in public comes relatively easily to me, as it does to Kim. Patti, Michael, and Lauren much prefer to remain in the background, but we decided to approach this task as a family.

We considered calling a press conference, but Kim wanted to do more than that, for Ron's sake, so we decided to grant a single, selective interview. Patti and Kim had always admired Barbara Walters, and wondered if she would help us give Ron an identity. At a serendipitous moment, just as we were discussing how to get in touch with her, Barbara Walters called us.

She told us that she would be in L.A. on a certain date and asked if Patti and I would meet for dinner at Adriano's, off Mulholland Drive. That way we could get to know one another, and we could decide whether to tape an interview.

As the evening approached, we became apprehensive. Just before we were to meet Barbara for dinner, we called her at the hotel and told her we had decided against the interview.

She was very understanding. She did not push us, but encouraged us to meet her for dinner anyway. We felt bad that she had flown all the way to L.A. for this meeting, and realized that it would be rude to cancel it altogether. So we decided to go ahead with the dinner, but not the interview.

When we arrived at the restaurant, we spotted Barbara immediately, sitting at a corner table with one of her producers, Shelley Ross. After a few minutes of conversation, we felt as if we had known her for years. The entire evening was relaxed and enjoyable. We told her that we were quiet people, and were apprehensive about appearing on national television. She assured us that if we decided to go ahead with the interview, she would see to it that the taping would be as easy and comfortable as this dinner meeting.

As Patti and I drove out of the parking lot, we looked at each another and said in unison, "I think we should do it."

Kim flew home from San Francisco immediately, and the interview was taped the next day at the Peninsula Hotel. We reserved comment on the guilt or innocence of the man who would be tried for Ron's murder. It was Ron whom we wanted to discuss. There were no pre-set guidelines for the interview, but Kim made it clear that she wanted it known that Sharon had no relationship with Ron.

Barbara began by asking me why we had agreed to the interview. I responded, "I think it's probably because so much time has gone by that we as a family have begun to feel that Ron is a bit forgotten. And we'd like for people to know who the real Ron was, and where he came from."

When Barbara asked Kim what kind of brother Ron was, the tears began slide down her cheek. "My brother was very protective," Kim said. "He was like a second father to me."

Patti said that it was unbelievable how well the various members of our family came together.

Michael agreed. Ron, he said, "was just like another brother to me . . . anytime there was a problem I went to him, probably first, because he understood all my problems because he went through them all, too."

Lauren remembered how much fun Ron had been at her Bat Mitzvah.

To counter one of the press's hackneyed images of Ron as a party animal, Kim disclosed a "little secret" that she had shared with her brother. I knew that Ron had expressed interest in opening a restaurant but, according to Kim, he was much farther along in his plans than I had ever realized. When Kim had asked Ron why he did not tell me of this, he answered, "'Cause I want to put it all together so I can present it to him, 'cause I want him to be a part of it."

Turning her attention to the upcoming trial, Barbara noted that it is a common defense tactic to attempt to put the victim on trial. She asked, "Are you prepared for that?"

I answered, "I think that I expect almost anything to occur."

After the interview was taped, Kim flew back to San Francisco. Joe saw her slipping increasingly into despair, and he enlisted Kim's friend Amy in a plot to bring some cheer into Kim's life. On their way back from a soccer game, they stopped at an animal shelter. A short time later, Amy burst through the door of Kim's apartment. Kim looked up as Amy skipped across the room, followed by what looked like a little black rat. Kim chased after the animal and picked up what she said was "the cutest little kitten I have ever seen."

"Dakota" became an instant member of the family.

Lauren was ready to start high school. It was a painful time for her because she associated Ron with so many of the "firsts" in her life. One year, when she toddled off to her first day at a new school, she looked about her at all the strange sights and unfamiliar faces and realized that she was very scared. Then she flipped open her brand-new notebook and discovered a warm and friendly message:

Have a good day, you'll do great!
    Love, Ron

We had created a supply of buttons with Ron's picture on them. Now, as she dressed for her first day of high school, she pinned one of them to her blouse. It was the only way her big brother could be there for her.

If ever a murder case involved "special circumstances," this was it. Punishment was a key question. The district attorney's office had to decide whether or not to seek the death penalty, and D.A. Gil Garcetti was pressured for a decision from all sides.

Gloria Allred, a prominent attorney and activist for women's issues, urged Garcetti to seek the death penalty, arguing that to do otherwise would be unfair to battered women.

Various groups of African-American leaders complained that the decision would be in the hands of the all-white, all-male Special Circumstances Committee.

Michael was angry. He argued, "Had these gruesome murders been committed by some average person, there wouldn't have been any question about the death penalty."

On September 8, Garcetti phoned to alert us that at a press conference the following day he would announce that the prosecution would not seek the death penalty. He explained that the defendant's celebrity status would make it difficult for a jury to sentence him to death and that we stood a better chance of conviction if the penalty was life in prison without the possibility of parole. We understood the logic, but thought it disgusting that, if this was indeed the man who murdered Ron and Nicole, he should be given any special treatment whatsoever. However, the decision was not up to us, and we knew it.

My problem was that Garcetti felt he had to include *any* portion of the community in his decision.

Being in jail did not seem like adequate punishment for this man. He could still get up and wash his face, eat breakfast, work out, read his mail, visit with his friends—things that Ron could never do again. However, we kept our thoughts private. Questioned by a reporter outside our home, I declared, "That's not an issue I want to comment on publicly."

Patti and I have always been firm believers in the death penalty, feeling that people who are genuine hazards to society should be eliminated, not placed in the revolving doors of our overcrowded prisons or sitting on death row for decades at taxpayers' expense.

Kim, on the other hand, had always been an advocate of rehabilitation theories. Her psychology courses had convinced her that everyone deserves a "second chance." But this was no longer an abstract concept, and her feelings took a 180-degree turn. She declared with venom in her voice, "I want to be there to see it. I want to see the murderer suffer and choke and I want to be the last face he sees before he dies."

The Barbara Walters interview aired on *20-20* the evening of September 16. In addition to her discussion with us, Barbara had also spoken with many of Ron's friends. She used photographs and videos to help paint a picture of Ron that was far more accurate than had previously been shown. That night, Ronald Lyle Goldman finally stepped from the shadows. We were pleased and grateful.

Kim watched the show in San Francisco with Joe. "I cried from the moment it started," she told us. "I couldn't believe that I was watching myself and my family on national television. It didn't seem real that I was talking about my brother to Barbara Walters."

We responded with both warm feelings and bitter tears when the show replayed the tape of Ron and me at Lauren's Bat Mitzvah, lip-synching to "Old Time Rock 'n' Roll."

Then we all broke down as Ron, wearing a goofy headband, looked directly into the camera and said to Lauren, "Okay, obviously this is your older brother. We are not going to get to spend very much time together, so I am very glad I was able to be here and spend this time with you because—God knows where I'll be in a year."

TEN

~

Mike and Lisa Pincus had a baby girl, whom they named Savannah. We went to visit them, and were delighted for them, but I had a hard time looking at this happy, vital young wife and husband as they cradled their beautiful baby girl in their arms. I could not stop thinking about things that would never be. I would never see Ron married. I would never see him enjoy the miracle that Mike and Lisa experienced. Most painful of all, I would never see Ron.

I love Mike like a son, so I did not want to be impolite. I did not want to hurt his feelings, but it was painful being there.

It was all becoming too crazy. We could not watch television, pick up a newspaper, pass a magazine rack, or turn on the car radio without hearing some comment about the case. The onslaught continued, day after day, night after night.

Saturday Night Live aired a skit about Ron and Nicole and the defendant. Their position was clear—Simpson did it—but Kim found the routine offensive. She ran to the phone and tried to find out who was responsible for this trash, but she could not get through to the studio. Even an episode of Kim's favorite soap opera, *Another World*, made an oblique reference to the upcoming trial.

Kim's moods took her from periods of weeping despair to manic activity. At times she was almost immobile and unable to function. At other times she became hyper and obsessed about the future. She worried constantly about losing me. She loved Patti, Brian, Michael, and Lauren, but she had always counted on Ron being around once I was gone. She felt out of control and desperate for structure in her life. She wanted something to plan for, something to look forward to, and she began to push Joe in the direction of marriage.

On the second anniversary of their relationship, Joe took Kim out to dinner to celebrate.

But the magic of the romantic evening was quickly broken. Dinner had just been served when Kim overheard a conversation at an adjoining table. "He must have done it like this," the man said and proceeded to pantomime his version of the murders. Kim's stomach tightened and a wave of nausea swept over her. Damn it, she thought. I can't even go out to dinner in peace. "I've got to say something," she said to Joe.

Kim walked over to the table, where two men and a woman were seated. "I'm Kim," she stammered nervously. "I'm Ron's brother—I mean—Ron is my sister—I mean—." The words simply would not come out right. She tried again. "I don't mean to be rude, but I'm trying to have a nice evening. Could you please just tone it down?"

The woman took Kim's hand and began to cry. Her companions were also shaken. "We're all behind you," they reassured.

On another occasion, Kim tuned in to one of the frequent awards shows on TV. Kim thought: A few hours of mindless escape, that's all I ask. But it was not to be. Almost everyone who took the stage had some tasteless joke to tell, some observation to share. Kim turned off the TV and called home, distraught. "Patti," she complained, "I can't even watch a stupid awards show."

Patti empathized, but she reminded her, "Kim, we're in the middle of this monumental thing—the so-called 'Trial of the Century'!"

There was nowhere to hide.

Two columns caught our attention.

Jeffrey Hart wrote in *The Valley Times-News*: "So much attention has been focused upon the monstrous O. J. Simpson that little notice has been taken of young Ron Goldman, who was the genuine hero of the despicable affair.

"Goldman probably could have fled the scene and saved his own life. Instead, he stood and fought, and from the evidence, put up a terrific battle against a muscular man twice his size . . . .

"Simpson's glory is gone. Simpson's occupations are gone. He stands naked, a killer, a bully, a coward and a fool.

"Goldman is the hero now."

And in the *Los Angeles Times*, columnist Andrea Dworkin wrote: "Surrounded by family, friends, and a community of affluent acquaintances, Nicole Simpson was alone. Having turned to police, prosecutors, victim's aid, therapists and a woman's shelter, she was still alone. Ronald L. Goldman may have been the only person in 17 years with the courage to try to intervene physically in an attack on her; and he's dead, killed by the same hand that killed her, an expensively gloved, extra-large hand."

The columns both comforted and disturbed us. It felt good to see Ron lauded as a hero, but it also brought back memories. One day, when he was about six years old, he came home from school crying, complaining that another boy was picking on him. I said, "You know, you gotta fight back." He did not like the idea, so I added, "You don't have to look at it as fighting. It's protecting yourself. If somebody hits you, you can hit back, but I don't want you to be the one who starts the hitting." As he grew older, he did learn to stand up for himself and others, but Ron was never a fighter.

"It's so sad," Patti commented, "you worry so much about your kids. I used to caution Ron about getting too much sun, driving too fast, things like that. It never occurred to me to warn him about helping a friend."

Faye Resnick's book, *The Private Diary of a Life Interrupted*, was an exposé that damned the defendant, but also painted a sometimes sordid portrait of Nicole.

Kim commented angrily: "I don't know the first thing about Faye Resnick, but I resent what she's doing. If she has information to impart, it should be in the courtroom, not between the pages of a trashy book. I think it is sad that she used her friendship with Nicole to tell tales out of school and chronicle lurid escapades, whether true or not. The woman was murdered. Let her rest with dignity."

Resnick was not the only one cashing in on the tragedy. By now, Kim had come to understand the comment that one of Ron's Brentwood friends had made on the day of the funeral: "I'm not like the rest of them."

The fact that Ron's supposed "close friends," Jeff Keller and Mike Davis, had opted to attend Nicole's funeral instead of Ron's was of no consequence to us, but the fact that they told us they had not attended Nicole's funeral was.

When I had a chance to confront them, I pointed out, "We saw you on the news at Nicole's funeral."

One of them attempted to respond: "We were just dropping off some flowers—"

"—Why did you lie to me?" I asked.

They had no convincing response.

Jeff sold his story to one of the tabloids, stating that he was present when Nicole, Ron, and a few other people were having coffee together at Starbucks. According to Jeff, the defendant had approached their table and stated in a menacing fashion that Nicole was still his wife. The defendant now claimed that he had never seen or heard of Ron. Jeff's testimony might have been helpful to the prosecution, had he been willing to cooperate with them. In any event, by selling his story his credibility was negated.

How could these people call themselves Ron's friends? Did they just care about money and their fifteen minutes of fame?

Every member of this family is possessed of a strong, often emotional, and sometimes volatile personality. We laugh when we are happy, cry when we are sad, and fight when we are angry. Tempers flare and feelings often simmer near the surface. Voices are raised. Doors are slammed. Ron's murder and the strain of seeking justice certainly exacerbated that.

Slowly we began to notice that Michael was away from home a lot. When Patti confronted him, Michael tried to explain that his friends were a great source of support for him, and it seemed that only at their homes could he escape the constant focus on the upcoming trial. Patti knew that this was true. At home, the trial was all we talked about. We analyzed every new shred of evidence that came to light. We discussed every pretrial motion and Judge Ito's rulings. From a distance, we followed the jury-selection process as best we could. We listened intently to every pundit on every talk show.

Michael said that if he wanted to talk about the case, his friends were always willing, but they also sensed whenever he had enough and would change the subject.

Patti understood this up to a point, but she also believed that Michael's place, right now, was with his family. Shortly before the Homecoming festivities in Michael's junior year, the issue exploded into a huge fight. Once more Michael tried to explain that different people handle things in different ways. Patti countered with the charge that he was insensitive and had developed a bad attitude. When the dust settled, they were able to reach a mutual understanding, but we all sensed that this was the tip of the tension iceberg. At times it seemed that not only had Ron been taken from us, but his murder might blow the rest of us apart as well.

The callousness of some people truly astounded us. Halloween masks bearing the likeness of the defendant were a hot item that year.

Kim was still working part time at the bank. Her off time was spent alone in her apartment, depressed and crying.

She maintained the fantasy that she would be able to fly back and forth between San Francisco and Los Angeles in order to attend the trial. She wanted to know every piece of information concerning every development in the case, but it was difficult. She felt disjointed and disconnected from us, the trial proceedings, and, most especially, from Ron.

Her mood darkened further when she received a call from a friend in Chicago who told her a chilling story. Kim's friend was at a Halloween party in a bar and noticed a young man with brown hair, slicked back, wearing glasses, black pants, and a white T-shirt. The shirt was stained with mock blood splatters, and he carried a white envelope in his hand. Kim's friend was distressed and asked, "Who are you supposed to be?"

Coolly, he replied, "Ron Goldman."

Assistant District Attorney Bill Hodgman called one evening to update us on the jury-selection process. His assessment of the jury pool was lukewarm; he worried that their level of education and sophistication was lower than we might have wished, and that this was generally considered a plus for the defense. "We have to deal with what we have," he explained. The prosecution was running out of peremptory challenges, and the group of potential jurors that was coming up was not much different from the group they had already been through.

We really did not know what to think, but the hint of disappointment in Bill's voice scared us. We felt like outsiders, with our noses pressed to the window, trying to see inside.

We could no longer bring ourselves to refer to the defendant by name, or by his infamous initials. And so we found ourselves calling him simply "the defendant" or "you-know-who." In private we often spit out more colorful language.

From the beginning of his incarceration in the Men's Central Jail, the defendant—through his lawyers—had badgered the county for special privileges. As a result, the star prisoner showered more often, slept later, and enjoyed ten more hours of free time per week than other inmates. He had an exercise bike for his personal use. He spoke on the telephone frequently and seemed to be allowed to watch television whenever he liked.

On days when he appeared in court for jury selection, or for procedural hearings, he arrived back at the jail after dinnertime. Following normal procedures, guards provided him with a cold sandwich. However, after his lead attorney, Robert Shapiro, complained about what he referred to as "mystery meat," the prison kitchen began to keep a late dinner warm for him.

He complained that his bed was uncomfortable, so he was provided with a special cervical pillow.

Under California law, anyone designated as a "material witness" may visit an inmate—if accompanied by an attorney. No physical contact is allowed between the inmate and the visitor, but, unlike normal visits, no time limit is enforced. So the defense team submitted a huge list of material witnesses that included family members, friends, and acquaintances who would otherwise be allowed only limited—or no—access. One of them was the prisoner's current girlfriend, Paula Barbieri. Other frequent visitors were former Los Angeles Rams defensive lineman Rosey Grier and NBC president Don Ohlmyer.

Kim entertained the fantasy of somehow tricking the authorities and masquerading as one of the visitors, but all the words she longed to say to the defendant seemed impotent and harmless compared to her internal rage. She knew that nothing she could ever do, or say, would affect him. He is incapable of remorse, she realized.

"Perhaps," Kim said, "I will send him a photograph of Ron every year on Ron's birthday—to remind him of what he took from us."

Most prisoners in his classification were allowed one hour per week in the jail's regular visiting room, an area where as many as 240 inmates and relatives were crammed together. To accommodate this prisoner's needs, however, the county was obliged to widen a private glass booth and install a telephone system that allowed for conference calls.

Defending the special perks, Shapiro fussed, "If we had a man who was allowed bail, we'd be able to meet with him seven days a week . . . some of the issues may involve character, may involve reputation, may involve life history. . . . "

Silly us. We thought the whole thing involved a double homicide.

The L.A. County District Attorney's office announced on November 7 that A. C. Cowlings would not be prosecuted for his role in helping the defendant flee from arrest. This was a positive development for the prosecution, because the deputy district attorney who had been working on the Cowlings case now became the sixth member of the government team. He was thirty-eight-year-old Christopher A. Darden.

The same day, during a hearing before Judge Ito concerning the possibility of sequestering the jury, Defense Attorney Johnnie Cochran, who more and more seemed to be taking center stage away from Robert Shapiro, made a statement. Arguing against sequestering the jury, Cochran declared, "We perceive them as people of good faith who want to dedicate their time, who to a person said, 'The reason we are here is because we believe in our oaths as jurors and we will not defile or defame that oath.' I think they take this task as a higher calling."

We hoped that was true, but were haunted by Bill Hodgman's earlier assessment.

Our decision to maintain a low profile was becoming increasingly difficult. Daily, the defense team preened before the cameras outside the courthouse, making ludicrous statements on behalf of their star defendant. I began to grumble publicly, and the defense immediately accused me of working with the prosecutors in an orchestrated campaign to deny their client a fair trial. This was blatantly untrue. I had never discussed with the prosecutors what I should or should not say in public.

On Wednesday, November 30, I spoke out, declaring, "I think what you're seeing is the culmination of months of frustration. For six months now we've watched as the defense attorneys have engaged in posturing and manipulation of public opinion. Why is it okay for them to speak and not us? I just felt that it was high time the playing field got leveled."

It was developing into a feud. Shapiro had the gall to respond by saying that he and the defense team were inclined to "forgive" the families for prejudging the case because we were so emotionally involved. This condescending pap outraged us. I called KABC-TV, saying, "Mr. Shapiro, I don't need your forgiveness. It is my right, as it is everyone's, to form, to have, an opinion."

This added fuel to the fire. The defense again accused the district attorney's office of orchestrating a media campaign and using the families as part of that effort. "All of a sudden, the D.A. speaks out, the chief of police speaks out, both families speak out," Cochran complained. "It's clearly orchestrated."

Marcia Clark countered, pointing out that they had only themselves to blame. She said that the families were angry at the manner in which the defense had painted all the evidence and the witnesses as tainted and unreliable. "They are outraged at the way you've turned this into a circus. If Mr. Cochran does not like the response, then don't make the first salvo. If you can't take the heat, get out of the kitchen."

On December 1, Shapiro cried uncle. Arriving for court, he told reporters, "In the spirit of trying to accomplish what we all want, we will take the high road. We no longer will be talking to the press on a daily basis. We will comment when we think it's necessary. We hope everyone else will take the high road with us." I said nothing, but I already had a pretty good idea of what a Shapiro-Cochran promise was worth.

On December 9, carrying a Bible in his huge hands, Rosey Grier took the witness stand at a pretrial hearing. In 1986, well after ending his football career, Grier had been ordained a minister. Deputy Sheriff Jeff Stuart claimed to have overheard an explosive private conversation between Grier and the defendant on November 13. Stuart's report had been filed with Judge Ito and was now held under seal. Neither the prosecutors nor the defense team had seen the material, but the rumor was that Stuart had overheard him confess his guilt to Grier.

Naturally the prosecution wanted to introduce Stuart's testimony. Of course the defense argued against this, contending that the statement had been made during a privileged conversation with clergy. Bill Hodgman tried to pry any information he could from Grier, but the witness remained stone-faced, aided and abetted by Johnnie Cochran.

Bill asked Grier what he and the defendant talked about during their frequent visits.

"We go over Scriptures," Grier replied. "We pray. We discuss various people in the Bible, problems they had, talk about who God is . . . what is sin. We talk about all kinds of things in the Bible."

During a later session of the hearing, Deputy Sheriff Jeff Stuart took the stand. Carefully warned not to divulge the actual statement that he said he overheard, Stuart testified that he was in a control booth about ten feet away from the two men, filling out paperwork, when a loud bang caused him to look up. The defendant had slammed down a phone. Then he slammed his fist against a table. He "appeared to be crying," Stuart testified. "He appeared to be very upset."

Asked to describe the defendant's tone of voice, Stuart replied, "He was yelling . . . it was very loud, in a raised voice."

Throughout the testimony on this issue, the defendant seemed almost bemused. He frequently smiled and arched his eyebrows.

Finally Judge Ito ruled that the statement should remain confidential.

That was an outrage. In my mind, the situation was analogous to a church full of parishioners overhearing something in a confessional. No, the priest could not be compelled to testify, but the members of the congregation certainly could.

We thought truth was the issue. If this man had confessed, we wanted the entire world to know about it.

For all of us, sleep was still an elusive commodity, and when it did come, it was often distorted by haunting imagery. "They say you don't dream in color, but they're wrong," Kim declared. Bright yellow was the color she had seen. The restaurant was very dark, and the bright yellow shirt that Ron was wearing almost glowed. Kim walked over to him. Just as Ron started to speak to her, he disappeared into the darkness.

In another of her dreams, we were back in Buffalo Grove, Illinois, where Ron and Kim grew up. I was pestering her to hurry up and Ron was waiting outside. The three of us got into the car and Ron drove us off to the coroner's office. We were going there to identify Ron's body—but Ron was driving the car! Suddenly Ron disappeared and Kim found herself alone in a huge, antiseptic room. She pulled open a metal door to find Ron's and Nicole's bodies lying on the slab, covered with blood.

Normally, when one awakes from a nightmare, reality is welcome. But not for Kim. Not for any of us.

The pain in Kim was so deep that I tried to hide my own anguish from her. But my strategy did not always work. When we spoke on the phone, tears welled up. My voice choked. I knew that I was adding to her pain, but I could not stop.

What I was not aware of was that Kim had some unfinished, painful business that she had not yet faced. In the spring of 1994, a few months prior to Ron's death, she was assigned to write a paper for her sociology course. Her task was to analyze an ongoing, interpersonal conflict. Her first thought was to focus on her relationship with Sharon, but a series of events had occurred over the past couple of years that changed her mind. Her relationship with Sharon was beyond repair. Instead, she focused on some troubling aspects of her relationship with Ron.

Ron had looked after Kim all through their childhood, but of course, once he reached adulthood he left home in pursuit of his own goals. Not only did he leave Kim physically, but it sometimes felt, to her, as if he became increasingly disinterested in her—unless he wanted something. The feeling opened old and very deep wounds in Kim that could be summed up in a single word: abandonment.

In the paper, Kim had revisited a specific pain that arose in 1993, when she was in school in Santa Barbara. Ron had a heavy foot when it came to driving the California freeways, and he had managed to accumulate his share of speeding tickets. Kim and I have also put in our time at traffic school, so we never came down on him too hard.

But this time, since he was driving a friend's Jeep and had several outstanding tickets, the police had thrown him in jail. Ron was reluctant to call me. Instead, he called Kim. Kim had made the drive from Santa Barbara, and loaned him the necessary cash.

Ron thanked her profusely, but as time passed he never mentioned the incident and seemed to forget his obligation to pay her back.

"My feelings were hurt," she confided, "and it began to gnaw at me. I saw him spending money on his apartment, and his girlfriend, without ever apologizing for not paying me back. I got madder and madder, but I kept it all inside. It was never about the actual money, I just wanted him to acknowledge what I'd done for him. I was always bad with confrontation and I didn't want anybody mad at me. I especially didn't want my big brother mad at me."

In December of 1993, during the holidays, Kim finally wrote Ron a bitter letter—the only gift she gave him that year. She vented some of her feelings about the things she had done for him over the years, and how she thought that Ron took her for granted. A single line in Kim's letter summed up how she felt that Ron had treated her: "You do for me and maybe I will do for you."

Ron called her and said that the letter bothered him a lot. "Kim," he said, "you're my sister. I don't take you for granted. You have to know how I feel. You're my sister. I love you and I don't feel like I have to call every week to tell you that. God, you're my best friend."

The phone call helped, but Kim had still retained a measure of anger, and she addressed it in her conflict paper. The assignment helped her to understand that she may have transferred—unfairly—some of her resentment from Sharon to Ron.

Kim wrote: "I have talked about this with other people and they cannot quite capture the bond that Ron and I share. They see me as being so strong and then to watch my brother hurt me, they wonder how I could be so stupid? How can they say that? Ron and I raised each other, only we know the dynamics of our connection. I do feel genuine love from him and part of me returning that love is accepting him for the whole person that he is, the same way I ask him to love me . . . unconditionally."

Both Kim the sister and Kim the psychology major knew that everything was muddled inside. Kim the psychology major knew that she and Ron would work through the rough spots and remain close, perhaps in a more adult manner than before. But it was Kim the sister who declared the bottom line: "My mother and I are not alike at all. I will not walk away when things get bad like she did."

We live our lives assuming that there is always tomorrow to say "I'm sorry" or "I love you." What was especially painful for Kim now was to look at the date on the paper, May 10, 1994. It was Mother's Day, the last time she had spoken with Ron.

We received a letter from Steve Rufo, who was now separated from Sharon. He expressed sorrow over our loss and told us that he wanted us to know that the things that Sharon was saying to the press were untrue. She continually stated how much she missed Ron, what a tremendous relationship they enjoyed, and how often they talked to one another. He told us what we already knew: Sharon had seldom mentioned Ron or Kim and that when she did, it was to complain that the pregnancies had left her fat. He said that her conduct had been outrageous and that he was embarrassed ever to have been associated with her.

I forwarded the letter to Kim in San Francisco.

With Joe listening on the extension, Kim called Sharon. They spoke for about an hour, and the conversation was ugly. Sharon maligned me, repeated her litany of lies, and in general continued to rant and rave. She complained that Kim was a selfish and uncaring person. Sharon would never admit that she was the one who disowned them. Kim tried to point out that a six-year-old boy and a three-year-old girl were not capable of making the decision to sever a relationship with their mother. She tried in vain to reassert her view that I had absolutely nothing to do with her and Ron's feelings toward Sharon.

The bitter conversation accomplished nothing, and when Kim hung up the phone she felt more isolated than ever.

Things got worse. Over the years Sharon had convinced Kim's maternal grandparents that it was the three of us—Ron, Kim, and me—who refused to have anything to do with her. Many letters flew back and forth between Kim and her grandparents, but they were never able to accept the reality of the situation. Now Kim received a letter from her grandfather telling her that he hoped God would forgive her for her sins and announcing that he was removing all of Ron's and Kim's pictures from his house. They were severing all ties.

Kim responded to the letter tersely: "If you can't treat me with respect and talk to me the way I deserve, I don't want to have anything to do with you." And it was clear they didn't want to either.

* * *

As the holidays approached, Kim tried to remember happier times. "Ron and I were always the youngest in our temple," she recalled, "and we would sit in the balcony, lean over the side, and giggle while we counted all the bald heads on the men and the pearl necklaces on the women. We would use the bathroom as an excuse, and sneak downstairs and chase each other around. As we got older, religion took on different meanings for all of us. We still went to temple, but mostly out of deference to our dad. It was important for him to have us there, so we went. Still, it took us back in time and often Ron and I resorted to our childish behavior."

Now, instead of bringing peace, she knew that the holidays would make her sad and lonely.

Supremely frustrated—as she put it, "Everything pissed me off"—Kim quit her job and took a leave from college. We drove to San Francisco to pick her up. Leaving her new kitten, Dakota, with Joe, she returned home.

It was, quite simply, where she had to be.

ELEVEN

The legal system staggered slowly forward.

The defendant's deep pockets allowed him to assemble a gaggle of attorneys that the media began to characterize as the "Dream Team." Johnnie Cochran was clearly elbowing his way into the starring role, pushing aside Robert Shapiro. Gerald Uelman handled the intricacies of constitutional law. DNA experts Barry Scheck and Peter Neufeld were brought in from New York. The defendant's longtime friend Robert Kardashian was technically assigned to the team; this appeared to be a ploy to activate the attorney-client privilege so that Kardashian could not be compelled to testify about his interaction with the defendant in the week following the murders. Attorney F. Lee Bailey was there for show. We were not quite sure why Carl Douglas was part of the team.

But the strategy was clear. Throw a thousand issues—like darts—at Judge Ito, to see if any of them found the target. This resulted in one pretrial hearing after another, and a series of rulings, some of which were vital and some picayune.

Judge Ito ruled that a single television camera would be allowed in the courtroom. And he ordered that the jurors and alternates would be sequestered for the duration of the trial. Handing the defense a clear victory, the judge decreed that, under California law, the prosecution could not introduce material from Nicole's diary because it was hearsay and because the defense lawyers could not cross-examine Nicole. The press speculated *ad nauseam* whether or not the defendant would testify. But Judge Ito, by his ruling, made it clear that one of his victims would not.

The defense tried to prohibit any of our or Nicole's family members from being present in the courtroom on the absurd pretext that some of us might be called as witnesses. Had it been entirely up to them, Ron's and Nicole's names would never have been mentioned at all. Judge Ito rejected that motion, and the issue then became a matter of degree. At first the judge decreed that our family could have five seats in the courtroom and the Brown family could have five seats. However, when we learned that the defendant's family would be assigned seven or eight seats, we raised a heated objection. Marcia Clark reported our dissatisfaction to Judge Ito, who grudgingly assigned the victims' families seven seats each. But there was a catch. If we were to be allowed seven seats, we had to fill them regularly or we would lose the privilege.

I had to work, but whenever I could get some time off, I would attend. However, Patti and Kim made a commitment to be present each and every day—for me, for Ron, for each other, to support the prosecution, and to witness the process of justice. Patti's employer, Right Start, responded wonderfully. From the beginning of our ordeal her bosses and co-workers had sent cards, flowers—even pastries—and lots of warm wishes. Now they told Patti not to worry about taking a leave of absence; her job would be waiting for her when she was ready to return. She quit the tennis league that gave her so much pleasure.

Wells Fargo Bank in San Francisco also gave Kim a special form of temporary absence and left her position intact.

Michael and Lauren would be able to attend a few times, but they would be busy with their schoolwork. Our victims' advocate would occupy one of our seats, but in order to comply with the judge's nitpicking attendance requirement, we would have to scramble every day. Patti's parents and our friends would accompany us when they could, but a lengthy trial seemed likely. Some of the pressure was relieved when the people from the D.A.'s office assured us that they would find men and women to sit in our section whenever necessary.

Many members of the prosecution team went out of their way to make us feel comfortable. We would be welcome in the D.A.'s suite of offices before and after all court sessions. A small room was assigned where we could take breaks and eat lunch. At the hub of this wheel was Patty Jo Fairbanks, an extremely competent woman with a booming voice. Her job description may have read "secretary," but in reality she was the lifeblood of the place. We came to rely upon her a great deal.

Next, the judge issued a strict set of behavioral rules: no talking, no gum chewing, no sucking on candy, no reading, no eye rolling, no hand gestures, no loud outbursts, no displays of emotion. Keep your face forward. No Kleenex boxes. No drinking cups or bottles of liquid. No beepers or cellular phones going off. The order that really infuriated me was a prohibition against wearing our lapel buttons with Ron's picture on them. What right did Judge Ito have to tell me I could not have a picture of my son with me? In sum, the judge's mind seemed to concentrate on trivia, whereas the question at hand was whether or not the defendant murdered his ex-wife and our son.

Nevertheless, we resolved to present ourselves with dignity and maintain a sense of decorum in the courtroom. We would do everything by the book—or almost everything. Patti wanted to have her beeper with her in case Lauren or Michael needed to get in touch with her, but she would disconnect the ringer and put it in a VIBRATE mode so that it would not disrupt the courtroom. She also routinely carries a bottle of water in her purse wherever she goes. She would continue to do so, but would never take it out while court was in session.

Our determination to play by the rules was, in retrospect, a clear symptom of our naiveté.

Alan Dershowitz was the most remote member of the "Dream Team." This Harvard Law School professor was the appellate attorney. He would watch the case carefully to detect whatever minutiae might present grounds for appeal, if and when the defendant was convicted. Dershowitz's status as an author allowed the defense team to circumvent its numerous hollow statements about not granting interviews. He was a frequent talk-show guest, appearing under the guise of promoting his latest book, and then freely discussing the case.

A producer from the Oprah Winfrey show called and asked us to appear with Dershowitz to discuss victims' issues. We were both interested and apprehensive. Here was a chance to counter the oft-seen, oft-heard "Dream Team" member, but we did not relish the idea of going one-on-one with the Harvard law professor. The producer assured us that family members of other murder victims would also be on the show. We were told that we would not be spotlighted or singled out in any way; rather, the conversation would be more of a general forum. I could not attend, due to work responsibilities. Patti, as always, was reticent but felt it might be a good opportunity for Brian to have a voice. So Patti, Kim, and Brian decided to go for it.

Patti and Kim flew to Chicago, where Brian joined them for the taping of the show. Kim specifically requested that she not be seated anywhere near Dershowitz. She detested the man, and she did not want to be put in a position of dealing with him in close quarters.

The show was taped on January 18, only about a week before opening statements were scheduled to begin.

In the green room, prior to the show, Patti, Kim, and Brian made small talk with several other families. A woman approached and tried to fuss with Kim's hair and makeup. Kim asked to be left alone. Those kinds of details have always made Kim uncomfortable. "I am who I am," she says. "All that extra stuff makes me feel altered." Soon, the other families were ushered out of the room. Then the producer came in and announced, "These are the seating arrangements. There will be five seats onstage, the three of you, Dershowitz, and George Fletcher." Fletcher is a Columbia University law professor, an author, and a victims' rights advocate.

Everything moved so fast. Before anyone had a chance to protest, they were swept into the studio and ushered onstage. Brian, Patti, and Kim sat in three chairs arranged in a diagonal line. Dershowitz was seated across from them. The other victims' families, instead of being a direct part of the discussion, were peppered throughout the audience. Kim was furious about the seating arrangements, and she glared at Dershowitz.

They were so new to this sort of thing and did not have the gumption to protest or refuse to proceed.

Patti had asked to be introduced to Oprah prior to taping, and the producer assured her that would happen, but it never did.

The tape started to roll.

During the opening moments Oprah introduced Dershowitz and mentioned that he was promoting his new book, a novel entitled *The Advocate's Devil.* She noted, "During his long career of defending high-profile clients, Alan Dershowitz admits that he sometimes knows when they are guilty."

Kim had the first chance to speak, and she commented, "I just don't understand how defense lawyers . . . if they are defending someone that is guilty, then how do they go home at night and sleep comfortably?"

Dershowitz conceded, "I much prefer to defend somebody who is innocent." Then he immediately plugged his book. He looked at Kim and said, "In *Advocate's Devil*, Emma, the young girl, really reflects your point of view."

In the first few minutes of the show, Dershowitz mentioned his book three more times.

Thus far, the show appeared to be an infomercial for the pompous lawyer's book.

Oprah attempted to regain control. She turned to Patti and asked, "So, what are you feeling as family members?"

Patti replied: "Our life is an open book as far as I am concerned. There isn't a day that goes by that we don't come home and find numerous messages on our answering machine from media and newspaper reporters, after changing our number three times. They come knocking on our door at dinner time, at eleven at night and if we're not home, they wait for us outside."

When Oprah wondered if there was any way to reduce the media attention, Dershowitz jumped in. The defense would like to try the case in court, he proclaimed, but they had been forced to speak to the media because the prosecution started it. "We have to level the playing field," he contended.

"Where does it stop?" Kim asked bitterly. "You level, we level, you level, we level."

Dershowitz promised that the defense would stop speaking out if the prosecution stopped first. It sounded like little boys scrapping in the schoolyard.

Although Dershowitz tried to interrupt, Brian jumped in with a key point: "You are trying to level the playing field through manipulation and false facts."

With this, Oprah called for a commercial break, and Patti and Kim had their first real opportunity to protest the format of the show. "We're not comfortable doing this," they said. But their concerns were ignored. Patti and Kim felt that they had been "gaslighted."

After the break, Oprah introduced George Fletcher, who immediately came to our defense, declaring, "It is imperative that you speak out. There is absolutely no way that you are going to keep Bob Shapiro and Alan Dershowitz quiet. . . . They are going to use the media for every advantage that they can see."

Dershowitz and Fletcher flew at one another, arguing the fine points of the law's attempts to balance the rights of the defendant with the rights of the victim. Oprah finally had to interrupt because, she said, Patti "can't get a word in edgewise."

Patti said: "We have basically been asked in one way or another to keep a very low profile, and we, for a while, were very quiet, and then we decided that we could not sit back and keep our mouths shut anymore because Ron is not here to speak. We need to represent his rights, and who better—who better than the victim's family?"

Dershowitz continued to plug his book until a frustrated Oprah interrupted. "—If you mention that book one more time I'm going to start screaming!"

This brought wild applause from the audience. Dershowitz was forced to let it subside before he responded, "I'm going to mention George's book next, but it makes—"

"IT'S *ADVOCATE'S DEVIL*, OKAY?!!" Oprah screamed. "Goodness gracious!"

Undaunted, Dershowitz managed to mention the book's title two more times in quick succession.

Near the end of the show, Kim once more responded to Dershowitz's criticism that the prosecution should not be speaking out. She addressed the issue in personal terms: "I have every right that anybody does to speak out about their family members. So if you are going to talk about him, you will know what the facts are. And the fact is that he was extremely loved by our family and we miss him dearly, and that is the bottom line."

Oprah asked Kim, "Are you dreading these coming days?"

"Yes."

Patti had the final word, saying, "We'll be there. It's very important that everybody remember there are victims here."

TWELVE

～

Who would have thought that a double homicide would inspire a theme song? Every time CNN commenced its coverage of the trial, the inane music drove us nuts. The defendant's face was prominently featured. Then an ethereal picture of Nicole filtered onto the screen. Ron was ignored.

Patti changed that. By now we were on a first-name basis with numerous reporters and news editors, and she called one of our contacts at CNN. She told him how disturbing it was to our family that, once again, Ron was not considered to be as important as Nicole. "Why isn't he pictured?" she demanded to know. The very next day CNN added Ron's image to its opening spot.

Still, the predominant face was that of the accused murderer. The victims faded to the background.

And that is precisely how the trial went.

A hush fell across the courtroom as the jury entered. Patti did not want to do anything that might anger or annoy them. She tried to sit very still, facing forward, with her hands folded in her lap. She did not want to stare at the jurors, so she watched them out of the corner of her eye. It was a bit bizarre to look at these strangers and realize that they were the ones who would make the ultimate decision.

In a shy and unassuming manner, Chris Darden opened the trial. Speaking directly to the jury, he said, "We're here today, obviously, to resolve an issue, to settle a question . . . Did O. J. Simpson really kill

Nicole Brown and Ronald Goldman? . . . The evidence will show that the answer to the question is yes."

Chris attacked head-on the problem of the defendant's fame. "Like many men in public, there is a public image, a public side, a public life," he said, characterizing that image as "the smiling face you saw in the Hertz commercial." But, Chris declared, "He may also have a private side, a private face. And that is the face we will expose to you in this trial, the other side of O. J. Simpson—the other face that Nicole Brown encountered almost every day of her adult life, the face she encountered at the last moment of her adult life, the face that encountered Ronald Goldman during the last moments of his life."

The prosecution had decided to lead with a one-two punch. Chris outlined the evidence of the defendant's systematic abuse of Nicole, thereby providing a motive. Then it was Marcia Clark's turn to discuss the physical evidence.

Methodically she listed the blood and hair samples connecting the defendant to the crime. She displayed photographs of five separate drops of blood, collected from the crime scene. As each photo was displayed on a screen in front of the jury, she intoned, "Matches the defendant." She declared that hair samples found on a cap at the crime scene appeared to match the defendant's hair. Fibers on the cap resembled fibers from the carpet of the defendant's car. A hair found on Ron's shirt resembled the defendant's hair. On and on it went. We were amazed at the sheer volume of physical evidence.

Then came the first of what we knew would be many difficult moments. The prosecution team projected two large photographs of the murder scene, which were not shown on TV but were very visible to us. Although we were warned not to look, we did. One photograph showed Nicole's body, wearing the same black cocktail dress that she had worn to Mezzaluna earlier that evening.

The other showed Ron's body, slumped around a tree stump. His shirt was pulled up, and there was blood all over the place. Weeping and holding on to one another, we were overcome by a barrage of feelings: shock, hurt, nausea, sorrow, and helplessness. How could anyone commit such brutality? Patti found herself hoping that Ron had died quickly. She could not bear the thought of him being scared and in agony. None of us could.

Up until this day, we could only speculate as to what had happened. Now there was nothing left to wonder about.

We continued to cry and embrace one another until the image was gone. But it was gone only from the screen. It was etched so deeply into our minds that it will never disappear.

Patti did not know a thing about Johnnie Cochran, but when he strutted into the courtroom the following day, glad-handing and blowing kisses, she decided that she detested him. The entire team of defense attorneys, with the defendant in their center, laughed and joked with one another as they awaited Cochran's opening statement. There was no sense from them that two young lives had been lost and that we were all there to search for the truth.

Court convened, and Judge Ito gave the floor to the defense. Moving meticulously, Cochran pushed his chair in, straightened his suit jacket, tugged at his tie, and walked slowly toward the podium. He glanced at Judge Ito, smiled, and nodded his head. Judge Ito returned the smile.

In silky tones, Cochran wasted no time in tugging at the sympathies of the black jurors. "You've heard a lot about this talk of justice," he said. "I guess Dr. Martin Luther King said it best when he said that 'injustice anywhere is a threat to justice everywhere.' So we are now embarked upon a search for justice, this search for truth, this search for the facts. . . . You, as jurors, are the conscience of this community."

At the mention of Dr. King, Patti's stomach tightened. Why would he bring that name into this trial? she wondered. Will this turn into some kind of racial test? No, she decided, they couldn't stoop that low.

Kim stared carefully at "the conscience of this community." To her, these men and women generally appeared to be attuned to what was going on, and serious about their task.

Cochran continued. "It seems to me that this case, the prosecution's case, is about a rush to judgment, an obsession to win at any cost and by any means necessary." He then promised the jury that the defense would call several witnesses whose testimony would prove the defendant's innocence. Other expert witnesses would attack the credibility of the physical evidence and the professionalism of the investigators.

Referring to Detective Mark Fuhrman, he said in a foreboding tone, "He's very much a part of this case."

Cochran said, "We expect there will be testimony that on the date of June 12 Mr. Simpson was involved in the acute phase of his rheumatoid arthritis. And on that date, after he had played golf, the problems with his hands were so severe he could not shuffle the cards when he played gin rummy at the country club thereafter."

W-a-a-a . . . give him a tissue, Kim thought.

The smoother Cochran attempted to be, the more reptilian he became. He seemed to slither from sentence to sentence.

Calling for a demonstration of how "Mother Nature and Father Time have taken their toll," he invited the defendant to come over to the jury box. To Patti and Kim's disgust, the defendant, feigning embarrassment, loped awkwardly across the room, flanked by two deputies. Jurors stood up to get a better view as the defendant rolled up his left pant leg to reveal a knee scarred by football injuries and surgeries.

Patti engaged in a mental dialogue: Why is he allowed to get so close to the jurors? So they could and would feel sorry for him? Are they implying that he has difficulty walking or standing? He manages to play golf—all the time. Big deal, he has a scar from an old football injury. Well, I have a scar on my lower lip from falling off a playground slide—from the very top—it was so high! I had a lot of stitches. Does that mean I can't talk now? What is this?

Cochran continued to ramble on at length before Judge Ito finally called a halt. The jury was dismissed for the day so that the court could rule on procedural matters. Cochran would have to finish his statement tomorrow.

Before long, the court was embroiled in a new fight. Under California law, both sides are required to share evidence in a timely manner. But now the defense team suddenly handed over statements from more than a dozen witnesses who had been interviewed months earlier. Carl Douglas assumed responsibility for the omission, declaring apologetically, "Both sides have made mistakes. We are human."

This was not good enough for Bill Hodgman. He accused the defense team of deliberately hiding evidence from the prosecution, only revealing it after Chris and Marcia had presented their opening statements. His face red, his voice filled with rage, Hodgman sputtered, "I don't think in the history of jurisprudence have we ever had anything occurring like what happened today in this courtroom."

* * *

Exhausted by the day's activities, Kim walked into the house at 5:50 P.M. and found a message on her answering machine. Her cousin Stacy had called from Chicago, reporting that Sharon was going to be a guest on CNN's *Larry King Live* that very evening at 9:00 P.M. It did not immediately register in Kim's mind that Stacy was referring to Eastern time. When we realized that the show aired in California at 6:00 P.M., we rushed into the family room and gathered around the television.

There was Sharon, with permed, shoulder-length, auburn hair. She wore a red and black jacket, bright red lipstick, and heavy black eyeliner. Larry King asked her why, as Ron's natural mother, she had not been more visible. Sharon complained that the press coverage had focused on Ron's California family. She said, "I just want everyone to know that Ronnie has family, you know, back in Chicago . . . "

Kim was practically on top of the set, growing more agitated by the minute. "I'm gonna call, I'm gonna call," she said.

I tried to calm her down. "Wait and see what she says, Kim," I advised.

Larry then asked, "Were you and Ron close?"

Sharon looked as if she might find the appropriate words printed on the ceiling of the TV studio. Speaking haltingly, she claimed, "Ron and I were very close. And I resent the fact that I have been called the estranged mother. I'm not the estranged mother."

This was more than Kim could take. "I'm gonna call, I'm gonna call," she repeated. Patti went upstairs and got the special CNN number. Kim soon had the phone to her ear. She paced back and forth in front of the television set, waiting for the connection to go through.

On the screen in front of us, Sharon continued to play the role of the bereaved mother, commenting on her warm and wonderful relationship with Ron. I thought: She wouldn't have recognized Ron if he'd been standing right next to her.

"You spoke to him frequently?" Larry asked.

Sharon's response was that her parents received a letter from "Ronny" one week before he was murdered.

Suddenly Larry was alerted that a call had come in on the special line. He said to Sharon, "I'm told that your daughter Kim is on the phone." He punched the proper button and asked, "Kim, are you there?"

Kim said, "Surprise!"

"Good," Larry responded.

"I just have one thing to say and that might lead to a few things," Kim said, speaking directly to Sharon. "Part of the reason that you have not been included is because you have not included yourself in Ron's or my life from the beginning. You feel like the estranged mother because you are the estranged mother. Okay? And, by the way, close? You were not close with me, and you don't have a right to sit here on national TV and claim your fame to Ron's death. You have only surfaced since Ron's death. You didn't even choose to come to the funeral until the day before."

Not a tear fell from Sharon's eyes as her daughter attacked her.

Larry's voice dripped with irony as he asked Sharon, "This is your daughter?" Sharon did not respond, so he asked Kim, "It is your mother . . . why do you have such anger?"

"Excuse me," Kim snapped. "She is my biological mother. She walked out on me when I was three years old. I did not live with her after my father and she got divorced. My father raised Ron and me from the beginning and if she doesn't know that, then she needs to go back to wherever—"

"So you have no feelings for your mother?"

"No, I have put up with enough baloney from her," Kim said.

Larry asked if Kim believed that Sharon was truly grieving.

"No, I don't take away from her grief at all," Kim said. "Because she has a lot of guilt which leads to her grief. Okay? I see her smirking and you know what? You would not have recognized my brother at all. You didn't see him for at least fifteen years."

Sharon finally found her voice. "Kim," she said, "there are two sides to a story. . . . I am sick and tired of hearing all this brainwashing that your father has done."

Kim snapped, "I'm sick and tired of you, honey."

After the call Kim was upset, angry, hurt—wired. The confrontation brought old wounds to the surface—all the maneuverings, all the lies, all the shuffling of blame. Her mind spun upon painful scenes:

We're little kids. We want to spend time with her but she tells us that she can't afford to do the things that our dad does for us . . . didn't understand . . . only four and seven . . . just wanted hugs and someone to play with . . . didn't care what she could or couldn't buy for us.

I can still hear the words: "I love you more than Ron . . . mommies and daughters belong together and boys belong with their father."

I am eleven. Ron and I are getting ready to go to a six-week wilderness camp. I hadn't seen her in a long, long time but I see her right before we leave. She tells me that she can't handle Ron and doesn't want him, but I am more important and more special and she wants me to come live with her when we get back. I have to promise not to tell Ron and Daddy what she had said. But Ron and Daddy are my world. I spend the next six weeks with this on my shoulders, worrying and wondering what I should do. I finally tell Ron what she said, and he doesn't seem to care. I think he already knows how she feels about him and hearing her words just verifies it. I finally tell my dad. He doesn't say much.

Never a kind word about anybody . . . always filled with venom about my dad, the women he dated, and eventually Patti and her children. Never, in all those years, did my dad badmouth her or try to mold our opinions against her. She did that all by herself. She didn't need any help from him.

I'm thirteen. I call her . . . upset . . . crying about something. Her response? "Stop crying. Call me when you can talk without crying. Like when you're nineteen!"

Years pass. I try again. I call her. She sounds pleased to hear from me, but she never calls back.

October 1992. I call her and tell her that I have forgiven her for all the choices she made over the years. "I'm finished expending energy on our relationship or our past," I say. I just wanted her to know that I felt I'd resolved the problems within myself.

How does she respond? With words that chill me now: "The next time we talk will probably be when someone dies. . . ."

Kim was not the only one who was distressed that evening. We called Patty Jo Fairbanks to get an update on the prosecution's plans to deal with the defense team's blatant misconduct in withholding evidence. But Patty Jo was uncharacteristically vague, saying only that something had happened and she could not talk to us.

Something had happened? What?

After worrying about this for some time, we called Patty Jo again and pressed her for information. This time she told us that something had happened to Bill Hodgman, but she did not give us any details.

At 11:30 that night, Gil Garcetti held a press conference at California Medical Center. He disclosed that, during an early-evening meeting of the prosecution team, Bill had been "quite subdued." Then Garcetti said, "He told me that he was not feeling well. He said he was disoriented and felt chest pains." Paramedics had brought him to the medical center. Tests did not reveal any evidence of a heart attack, but he was going to be held overnight for observation.

Garcetti said, "It is very likely we are going to ask that the case be postponed for a period of time."

The trial had only been under way for two days. Sometimes I wondered if it would kill us all.

THIRTEEN

Amid all this insanity, the defendant had the audacity to publish a book. *I Want to Tell You* was his response to letters he had received while he was in jail.

Kim declined a reporter's request to comment, but her mental response was: I haven't read the book and have no intention of ever reading the book. I think it is self-serving garbage and it bothers me that he is making money and autographing copies during breaks in the trial.

That is what Kim wanted to tell *him.*

Finally the first witness took the stand. She was Sharyn Gilbert, the dispatcher who answered Nicole's 911 call at 3:58 A.M. on New Year's Day, 1989. Her testimony laid the groundwork for the introduction of People's Exhibit 1.

We had heard the tape on the news, but when Patti and Kim listened to it being played in the courtroom, with the Brown family sitting so close by, they ached for the family as they heard the fear in their daughter's voice. A sad silence hung throughout the courtroom.

This was followed by the testimony of the police officer who responded to the call, Detective John Edwards, who had found Nicole outside of the Brentwood estate, hiding in the bushes. He said that she ran to him and collapsed into his arms, hysterically crying that her husband was going to kill her.

This was the episode that resulted in the defendant's "no contest" plea to spousal abuse, and we could see why. Photographs of Nicole were displayed on the screen and copies were handed to the jurors for their perusal. They showed a bruised and haggard-looking young woman with hollow, frightened eyes.

Patti and Kim met witness Ron Shipp and his wife, Nina, upstairs in the D.A.'s office, and liked them immediately. In court Nina sat next to Kim as her husband testified. Under her breath, Nina continually muttered, "There's more . . . why don't they ask him about the rest of it?"

Throughout the testimony the defendant avoided eye contact with Shipp. He busied himself by jotting notes or whispering to his attorneys. Once, when one of the defense lawyers made an absurd comment, Shipp looked over and said, "This is sad, O.J. . . . really sad."

Since Shipp happens to be a distant cousin of Johnnie Cochran, Defense Attorney Carl Douglas handled the cross-examination. It was Douglas's day in the sun, his chance at the limelight. His lispy voice echoed through the courtroom as he accused Shipp of being a drunk, a womanizer, and especially a liar. The litany rang in our ears: "Did ya *lie* about that, Mr. Shipp? Do ya *lie* about a lot of things, Mr. Shipp?"

Near the end of two days of testimony, Douglas sank to new depths. He asked Shipp, "Isn't it true, sir, that you have in the past told Mr. Simpson's friends that if Mr. Simpson were not around, you might have a shot at Nicole Brown Simpson yourself?"

"No, I did not," Shipp replied.

"You've never said that to any of Mr. Simpson's friends?"

"Excuse me for smiling," Shipp said. "But, no, I did not."

We felt very bad for the Shipps. Ron had put his reputation on the line, told the truth, and was attacked without mercy. And Nina had to listen to it. At the conclusion of the testimony, when the jurors were getting up to leave, Patti gave Shipp a thumbs-up for doing such a good job.

The following day, Marcia informed Patti that her thumbs-up gesture had been a "boo-boo." The defense had thrown what Patti characterized as "a hissy fit" and complained to Judge Ito. The judge addressed the issue in open court, reminding everyone not to make gestures to any of the witnesses. As the judge lectured, Patti felt his eyes trained directly on her, and she was sure that everyone knew he was talking about her.

Patti's so-called boo-boo became so infamous that it even made the ten o'clock news. "Can you believe this?" she said. "Another day at the circus." She wrote a brief note of apology to Judge Ito, but was never given the courtesy of a reply.

The prosecution continued to paint a portrait of the defendant as a wife beater and a stalker. Nicole's sister Denise testified, tearfully recalling how the defendant had humiliated Nicole in public, slammed her around, and berated her. At one point in her testimony, Denise described the defendant as having a "huge ego." From what we had seen, that was a massive understatement. Even during this testimony, he sat in court with his chin in the air, rolling his eyes.

"He really believes he's above it all," Patti commented. "So he was a big shot in his football days, so what? He thinks he can get away with anything."

Kim echoed her sentiments: "He is a narcissistic beast; it is so obvious that he only thinks of himself."

The trial became a daily ritual. Patti and Kim—and whoever else was attending that day—needed to be at the courthouse by 8:00 A.M., so they rose early, showered, packed a lunch, and grabbed a bagel or a banana and coffee. They were in the car and on the road by 6:30. Often I could join them later; often I could not.

It was about an hour's drive to our designated parking spot at Parker Center Police Headquarters. The parking-lot guard, Ron Zito, was always helpful and friendly and scurried to move the parking cones that reserved our place. D.A. investigators met Patti and Kim there and escorted them to the courthouse. Their policelike jargon was amusing. "We are picking up the package," they would say into a walkie-talkie, or "We are now delivering the package." It took us a while to realize that they were there to do more than act as simple escorts; they were there to protect as well. We all shared a fantasy—that just once we would get a chance to see the defendant being led out of the prison van in shackles.

Before the day's session began, everyone waited upstairs in Patty Jo's office, where there was always time for friendly and very down-to-earth small talk. Chris Darden always made time for us. The lead detectives, Tom Lange and Phil Vannatter, answered our questions patiently and thoroughly.

Susan Arguela was replaced by Mark Arenas as our Victim-Witness Assistance advocate. All of us warmed to him immediately. Mark was a compact, dark-haired young man of Hispanic descent, honest and clean-cut, who effectively shepherded us through some of the roughest times imaginable. The judicial system in this country is complicated for the initiated. For neophytes like us, it was nearly impossible to navigate. Mark not only saw to our needs, he often anticipated them, and we will be forever grateful to him.

When it was time for the day's session to begin, Mark accompanied Patti and Kim to the elevator that would take them downstairs to the courtroom. They often arrived in the hallway outside the courtroom at the same time as the defense lawyers, and this inevitably produced a mad dash to see which side could get through the metal detector first. Members of what we now referred to as the "Scheme Team," especially Johnnie Cochran, would elbow their way past, preparing to strut for the camera. To be fair, Robert Shapiro occasionally stepped back, allowing Patti and Kim to enter first, but those times were infrequent.

Kim preferred sitting in the first row so that she could be closer to Marcia and Chris. Occasionally our family sat in the second row, and when that happened Kim was usually on the end. That placed her closer to the defendant, with the result that she found herself focusing on him instead of the trial. This bothered her. She did not want the defendant to drain any more energy from her than he already had.

We understood the rules against eating and drinking in the courtroom. Judge Ito did not want the camera to record a sea of spectators in picnic mode, but it was also annoying to watch the prosecutors and the defense attorneys drinking coffee, eating pretzels and candy, and sipping Diet Coke while the families of the deceased were not allowed a sip of water or a cough drop.

The arrogance that permeated the courtroom was suffocating. You could smell it, taste it. Every member of the "Scheme Team" was an individual whom we would have instinctively avoided in everyday life. We never saw a shred of humanity or decency. It was a cockfight, plain and simple. And it was calculated and orchestrated.

We decided that Defense Attorney Robert Shapiro needed a third eye. As the camera panned, he and Carl Douglas constantly monitored it, so that they could alert the defendant to stop joking and grinning and tapping out a tempo with his fingers. *Lights! Camera! Action! Time to wipe the eye. Time to bite the lower lip.*

Often, during prosecution testimony, some of the defense lawyers would position themselves within earshot of the jury. Barry Scheck was a master at this. As Marcia questioned a witness, Scheck made certain that the jury heard him say to an associate, his voice laden with sarcasm, "That's bullshit," or "This is total crap." Simultaneously he shook his head in mock disbelief. Judge Ito let him get away with it. We worried about the effect these theatrics were having on the jury.

Johnnie Cochran was clearly the worst offender. He was the consummate showman, a fake, constantly playing to the crowd. He snickered at the witnesses and mocked the prosecutors. If we could hear his stage whispers—"What bull," "Oh my God," and "That's crap"—we knew that Judge Ito could hear him and that the jury could hear him as well. As with Scheck, we were concerned that by not reprimanding Cochran, the judge was sending the jury a message of tacit agreement and it bothered us tremendously. The prosecution remained professional and did not resort to this kind of trickery, but we constantly wondered how the jury was internalizing these messages.

Judge Ito was never in charge of that courtroom, Cochran was. His movements were choreographed and predictable. Whenever he rose from the defense table, we knew exactly what he was going to do. He pushed his chair in, straightened his shiny, colorful suit jacket, tugged at his African-motif tie (with matching pocket handkerchief), and strutted across the courtroom with the air of a bantam rooster. He glanced at Judge Ito, smiled, nodded his head, and waited for the judge to return the smile. The judge always did. The unspoken conversation said, "Hey, buddy, how ya doing?" Every time we saw this performance, we cringed, knowing instinctively that Judge Ito was sending a message to the jury: This guy is just peachy. Cochran also had a tendency to schmooze with Marcia and Chris, a tactic that drove Kim crazy.

After these nauseating niceties, Cochran stationed himself near the jury, at the podium, and made blatant eye contact with the jurors.

We did not know if Judge Ito was inept or stupid or starstruck, or if he was concerned because the trial was televised around the world, but he coddled the defense and Cochran played against this judicial weakness. Cochran objected. Judge Ito overruled. Five or ten minutes later,

Cochran argued the same issue again and the judge called for a sidebar conference. Cochran would walk toward the bench, turn his shoulders, thrust his chin in the air, and again gaze at each and every jury member with what Patti called "that Cheshire cat grin" on his face.

In sum, we began to realize that we were up against the most conniving, slimy, deceitful, unethical, immoral lawyers in the country. Perhaps they will take that as a compliment.

After the long, long days, Patti and Kim faced the drive home, often through rush-hour traffic, listening to the never-ending trial recaps on the car radio. Depending upon what had happened during the day, they would scream and otherwise vent their anger or ride in depressing silence. Often one of them would call me during the drive home and request that a bottle of wine and two straws be waiting for them when they arrived. Then, there was the obligatory stop at the grocery store, and dinner to prepare. If I had not been able to attend court that day, I wanted to know everything that had happened. Our dinner-table conversation would center on a blow-by-blow description of the day's events.

Patti was acutely aware that Michael and Lauren, although they too were vitally interested in the trial, had other needs. They were teenagers, one a freshman and one a senior, experiencing the normal, daily triumphs and frustrations. Patti felt that she should be spending more time with them, and guilt began to gnaw at her. Patti and I also knew that we should try to find some private, quiet time for each other, but it was nearly impossible. There were still only twenty-four hours in a day, and we had no energy left to deal with the usual issues of life.

We had always been such an open and talkative family, never wanting things to simmer and go unresolved. Now it seemed that we had all become closemouthed and afraid of stepping on one another's toes. All our feelings were raw, as if our nerve endings were exposed to a frigid blast of air.

Early in the trial we discovered that Judge Ito had incited jealousy among the pool of reporters by assigning the seat next to us to a man who introduced himself as Dominick Dunne. He explained that for the past eighteen months he had been writing articles about the murder case of Lyle and Eric Menendez, and was working on a fictionalized book about it. Now he had been assigned by both *Vanity Fair* magazine and CBS news to cover this trial.

Neither Patti nor Kim were familiar with his work, but he seemed like a gentleman.

In one of his pieces for *Vanity Fair*, he wrote that the case "is like a great trash novel come to life, a mammoth fireworks display of interracial marriage, love, lust, lies, hate, fame, wealth, beauty, obsession, spousal abuse, stalking, brokenhearted children, the bloodiest of bloody knife-slashing homicides, and all the justice money can buy."

This man who sat beside us was in a state of perpetual motion, always in a hurry. We did not understand his passion until he gave Kim a copy of one of his first books, *People Like Us,* and it explained a lot. It was the story of his daughter Dominique, an actress best known for her role in *Poltergeist*, whose boyfriend, John Sweeney, strangled her to death in 1982. After learning that he understood the indescribable depths of our pain, we warmed to him very quickly.

Unlike many of the other reporters covering the case, Dominick was not required to be impartial or neutral. In fact, he was quite outspoken about the way he felt. One morning later in the trial, as the door to our left opened, he wrote us a note: "Here comes the 'killer.'"

The term worked for us. So did "murderer."

After establishing the killer's penchant for beating up his wife, prosecutors began to document the events of June 12, 1994.

Marcia Clark asked Kim to bring in the clothes that Ron had worn to work on the last day of his life. Kim did not understand the reason for the request, but she complied.

The morning of February 7, Kim grabbed a brown grocery bag from a kitchen cupboard and went through Ron's personal effects, which we had stored, untouched, in our garage. The fact that she was finally able to *do* something gave her a positive feeling. Thus far, none of us had been able to provide any help whatsoever to the prosecution. But as she looked through the items in the boxes and realized once again that this was all that was left of her brother, an overwhelming melancholy took over. Her hand rested on a pen that was still in the pocket of the vest he had worn to work, and she drifted into a kind of dreamlike state, picturing Ron as she had last seen him, laughing and very much alive. She had to will herself back to the present.

She took the requested items to court. When she handed over the paper bag, she was surprised that Marcia asked her to testify as to where she had found the slacks and shirt in Ron's apartment. Kim agreed, and theorized that Marcia either wanted to humanize Ron to the jury or perhaps show that he had changed clothes quickly that evening, leaving his work clothes hanging haphazardly on the bathroom door.

Kim knew that all she had to do was tell the truth. She was nervous but happy to contribute, and was especially pleased when she learned that Cochran did not want her to testify. Perhaps he was worried that she would play upon the jury's sympathies.

We were sure that Kim's testimony would be little more than a footnote to the trial. Nevertheless, nothing was simple in this case.

First, we heard the testimony of the other witnesses describing the events of the evening of June 12. Karen Crawford, the former Mezzaluna manager, said that she saw Ron leave the restaurant about 9:50 P.M. Reaching into the paper bag, now marked "People's 30," Marcia displayed Ron's slacks and shirt, and asked if they appeared to be what Ron had worn to work that night. The witness broke into tears.

Ron's friend and co-worker Stewart Tanner testified that he and Ron had had plans to go to a Mexican restaurant in Marina del Rey later that night.

After a break, Kim was called. But as she walked toward the witness stand, a bailiff suddenly held up his hand and commanded, "Hold up." She realized that she was standing directly behind the defense table. She was only inches away from the defendant. F. Lee Bailey brushed against her as he took his seat. Gross, Kim thought. Where's the bug spray?

Marcia conducted a simple, straightforward direct examination. Exhibiting the bag, the white shirt, and black pants, she asked Kim, "Can you tell us where you found them?"

Kim answered, "They were draped over his bedroom door, the shirt and the pants . . . He obviously had taken them off and just swung them over the door."

"Not on hangers?"

"No. My father and I put them on the hangers."

Marcia asked, "Did you see any other white dress shirt or black pants like that in the apartment?"

"No, I did not."

That was all the information that Marcia wanted to get into the record.

Judge Ito turned to the defense table and said, "Mr. Cochran."

Johnnie Cochran replied, as usual, "Just a second, Your Honor."

What would come next? Thus far the defense had found some reason to cross-examine every witness. Often the attacks were lengthy, vigorous, and vicious.

Kim hoped that Cochran would find some picayune reason to doubt her simple story. She did not know how she would respond. She might say something unreasonable and counterproductive, but she just wanted to "let him have it."

Perhaps Cochran sensed this. Perhaps he read the message in Kim's eyes or body language. After a brief pause, Cochran declared, "No questions of this witness, Your Honor."

Before leaving the stand, Kim stared directly at the killer. He turned his head away quickly, refusing to return her gaze.

FOURTEEN

〜

Nicole's sister Tanya had purchased several small angel pins and distributed them to us and members of the prosecution team to wear in remembrance of the victims. Kim wore hers when she testified, but her long hair covered it from the jury's view.

Now Cochran complained about Marcia wearing hers in open court because it showed obvious sympathy with the victims' families. "She shouldn't have it on," he said. "And she knows she shouldn't have it on."

Judge Ito commented, "Jewelry is not my forte, as one who wears plastic watches." However, he ordered Marcia not to wear the pin anymore. We were livid. Isn't Marcia supposed to be on the side of the victims? we asked ourselves. We were incensed that the same logic did not apply to Cochran and the rest of the "Scheme Team" sporting their ties, pocket handkerchiefs, and pins with African motifs. Also, members of the defendant's family had their own pins demonstrating their support of him.

Bill Hodgman finally returned to work. He would remain part of the prosecution team, but he would generally stay out of the courtroom. Bill said to Patti, "The thing that upsets me most is that I feel I have let you down."

Patti was deeply touched by his sincerity. "Don't be ridiculous, Bill," she said, "your health is more important than this case. Just worry about taking care of yourself. We know you're here for us, working behind the scenes."

Patti and Kim were still in the D.A.'s office, waiting for court to convene, when Chris Darden entered. We had not met him yet. Patti walked over, reached up, and tapped him on the shoulder. "Hi," she said, "I'm Patti and this is Kim." Patti told him that we desperately wanted to be involved in whatever way we could.

Chris seemed quite shy. He nodded his head slightly, smiled, mumbled, "Nice to meet you," and quickly left the room.

Patti and Kim wondered if they had offended him or if there were some other problem. Later we learned why he had appeared a bit standoffish. Kim found out that she made Chris uncomfortable because she looked so much like Ron.

After hearing from a succession of brief witnesses who testified about the "plaintive" wailing of Nicole's Akita about 10:15 the night of the murders, and the dramatic testimony of Sukru Boztepe, who found the bodies, the prosecution called Officer Robert Riske, the first police officer on the scene.

I was able to come to court with Patti and Kim that day. We were accompanied by Erika Johnson. She had been one of Kim's closest friends when we lived in Chicago, and Ron had always thought of her as a little sister.

Officer Riske would provide necessary testimony, but we knew that it would be extremely difficult to listen to. What's more, the prosecution team warned us that several crime scene photographs would be displayed. We had seen two photos during Marcia Clark's opening statement; they were brutal. We had discussed this at length and came to the conclusion that if Ron had gone through this terrifying experience, the very least we could do was to be there for him now. As we took our seats in the front row of the spectators section, we placed a small box of Kleenex on the railing in front of us, knowing that we would need it. Very shortly one of the bailiffs came over and said, "Excuse me, Judge Ito wants you to take the box of Kleenex off the railing—the camera is picking it up." Unbelievable, I thought. With all that is happening, Ito is concerned that the courtroom ambience would be ruined by a box of Kleenex? How bizarre. The judge is supposed to be tuned in to the testimony, and he's looking around the courtroom to make sure that everything is in order. God forbid the TV camera should reveal a Kleenex package in front of us.

However, we had no choice, and pulled the offending tissues out of camera range.

Officer Riske testified that at 12:09 A.M. on June 13, 1994, he responded to an emergency call and discovered Ron's and Nicole's bodies. The most important part of his testimony was his description of the evidence that he found—a bloody glove, a watch cap, shoe prints, and a row of blood drops. He had noted all of this long before Detective Mark Fuhrman appeared on the scene. This was meaningful because the defense had already accused Fuhrman of being a racist. From this starting point they had taken a giant leap, suggesting that there were two gloves at the crime scene and that Fuhrman—acting out of dastardly and bigoted motives—had planted one of them at the killer's Brentwood estate. But Riske held firm; he asserted that there was only one glove at the crime scene.

During Riske's testimony the horrible crime scene photographs were projected on a screen above the witness box. When the first photo of Nicole appeared, Juditha Brown walked out of the room. Lou Brown stayed a bit longer, with his head bowed; then he left also.

We forced ourselves to remain as photos of Ron were displayed. Kim kept her eyes downcast. She opened her purse and focused her eyes on an photo of Ron, alive and smiling. Erika, who is usually stoic, broke down completely. Patti and I clung to one another and dabbed our eyes with the forbidden Kleenex.

It was a gross oversimplification to refer to what had happened to Ron as his "death." He was the victim of a brutally vicious murder.

Kim called a friend who lives in Brentwood. The young woman complained, "Kim, the streets are all closed off, helicopters are everywhere. I can't even get to work." It was Sunday, February 12, eight months to the day after the murders, and the jury was being treated to a field trip. We were not allowed to go along, and we had no desire to.

Motorcycle police closed down freeway ramps as a caravan of fourteen vehicles made its way to Brentwood. The twelve jurors and nine remaining alternates rode in a sheriff's department bus. They were casually dressed; one of the men was wearing a San Francisco 49ers cap. The murderer, who played most of his career with the Buffalo

Bills but finished as a 49er, rode in an unmarked car with darkly tinted windows.

A security force of some 250 police officers had already scoured the Brentwood area with bomb-sniffing dogs.

The caravan stopped first at Ron's apartment, pausing briefly outside, then drove on to Mezzaluna. Hundreds of sightseers lined the grassy median strip of San Vicente Boulevard. Others watched, sipping coffee and eating a light brunch in front of a nearby Mrs. Fields cookie store.

Next, the jurors toured Nicole's condominium, which was empty and up for sale. Marcia and Chris hoped to impress upon the jury how tiny the area was where the bodies were found, making it plausible that one person could have committed these murders. As Chris put it, "I think that Ronald Goldman, having confronted a suspect with a knife, was essentially caged."

The jurors toured the crime scene in groups of four or five, flanked by deputies and attorneys. They took notes, but were not allowed to ask questions or make comments. The killer himself waived his right to enter Nicole's condo. News reports indicated that he remained outside in a car, crying. But we had seen that act before, and knew that it was feigned.

Finally the group wound up at the Rockingham estate. For about two hours the jurors toured in small groups, taking a break to return to the bus to eat boxed lunches. Watching and listening to the news coverage, Kim grew furious. Although they were not supposed to alter the scene, the killer's minions had set up a tableau of pious domesticity. There was a Bible on the table. Pictures of children and mementos of family bliss abounded. Kim thought that she could almost smell the chocolate chip cookies baking in the oven and the apple cider simmering on the stove. It was disgusting and deceptive. And it was a dramatic contrast to Nicole's now stark and barren condominium.

The defendant stood outside beneath a clump of trees, chatting animatedly with his lawyers and others, acting as if he were the host of some kind of perverse garden party.

"What's going on here?" Kim raged. "He's charged with double homicide, he's a prisoner, he should be treated like one and look like one. He should be in handcuffs and leg irons." We half expected Robin

Leach to pop out of the bushes and introduce a special segment of *Lifestyles of the Rich and Famous*.

The *Los Angeles Times* reported, "As he [Simpson] and others stood near a children's play area . . . he looked wistfully about an estate that, if convicted, he might never see again."

I ached to tell him the true meaning of the words "never see again."

Events had reached the point where nothing surprised us anymore.

By now it was abundantly clear that the "Scheme Team," despite its many earlier denials, planned to play the so-called race card with a vengeance, seeking to portray the killer as a victim of a huge conspiracy on the part of dozens of investigators. This, of course, was pulp fiction.

Four detectives were on the scene that night, and each of the four would have had to decide, on the spot, to risk his career—indeed, risk a long prison sentence—in order to frame the "beloved" football has-been. To soften the impact of the expected attack on Fuhrman, the prosecution decided to call some of the other detectives first. Fuhrman's partner, Ron Phillips, testified for three days in a highly professional manner. Marcia used his appearance as an opportunity to introduce the bloody glove to the jurors.

Up in the D.A.'s office, before and after his testimony, Phillips befriended Kim. He nicknamed her "Kitten" and she, in friendly retaliation, called him "Puppy." Kim was especially grateful for his honesty. Whether the news was good or bad, Ron Phillips could be counted on to give it to you straight.

We were becoming ever more aware that this was a case of the State of California versus the defendant, rather than the Goldmans and the Browns versus the killer. The prosecutors were not obligated by law to keep us informed of their strategies and tactics, but we wanted to be included in the process. We would hear bits and pieces about what was going to happen, but we were not in the decision-making loop. We were babes in the woods.

Bill Hodgman, Chris Darden, and others were generally available when we had questions or simply needed to talk. Marcia Clark, on the other hand, was more aloof and difficult to reach. We understood the pressure that she was under and tried to be patient. She promised us a regular Friday-afternoon update session, but often it was canceled or ignored. It was difficult not to feel a little resentment. There were many days in court when she never acknowledged our existence. Even if we were in the front row, she sometimes looked by or through us.

This upset Patti so much that she finally confronted Marcia. "I understand that you are busy," Patti said, "and you have a lot of things on your mind. But we're here, not only for Ron, but for you also, to support you. Even if you can't talk to us, at least make eye contact and acknowledge that we are sitting here."

Marcia apologized, and for a time things were better.

Tom Lange was a veteran detective who had investigated more than 250 homicides. He was remarkably composed and polite both during his direct testimony and subsequent cross-examination by Johnnie Cochran.

Cochran tried to attack on all sides, attempting to discredit Tom's evidence-gathering ability, as well as point to sloppiness on the part of the investigators. He also pointed out that Tom lives in Simi Valley, the largely white community where LAPD officers were found not guilty of charges resulting from the 1991 beating of Rodney King.

Tom responded sharply to Cochran's assertion that the police should have investigated the possibility that Nicole had been raped. Tom replied, "In my observations and my experience, sex was the last thing on the mind of this attacker." Cochran tried to object, but Tom continued, "It was an overkill, a brutal overkill."

The graphic words devastated Kim. Later she said, "I guess you have to hear those words to understand the brutality of the murders, but it hurts so much. The killer just kept at it and Ron could do nothing. The killer was relentless."

Cochran persisted, searching for any scrap of information that could divert the jurors from the real issue of the trial. Digging into the paper bag that held Ron's slacks and shirt, he thought he found something of import that Tom had overlooked. He removed a small green piece of paper with a dramatic flourish worthy of Perry Mason, as if to say, "Aha! Detective Lange, and *what* do we have here?" One might have thought that he had suddenly discovered the murder weapon. He brandished the paper in Tom's face, demanding to know why the police had not booked it as evidence.

Patti squinted at the ominous green slip of paper in Cochran's hand and realized that it was her own grocery list! It dawned on her that when Kim had retrieved Ron's clothes from a storage box in our garage, she had simply, logically, stuffed them into a brown grocery bag. Patti, constitutionally unable to litter, always threw her shopping list into the grocery bag.

Patti was incredulous. She leaned over to Kim and whispered, "Kim, that's my grocery list!"

"You're kidding," Kim replied.

Both of them started to laugh. Trying desperately not to make any noise, they clamped their hands over their mouths in a futile attempt to stifle their laughter. During one of the interminable sidebars, Patti caught Marcia's eye and mouthed the words, "It's mine."

Chris saw their bodies shaking and raised an eyebrow. Through their giggles, Patti and Kim were able to tell him what Cochran had "discovered"—a "secret document" with the code words: "low-fat cheese," "pretzels," "chicken," and "fat-free ice cream." Patti was sure that the paper also listed "bananas," "turkey," and "lettuce."

Chris then asked Patti and Kim to leave the courtroom, which they did. At least in the hallway, they were able to laugh out loud.

This critical piece of "evidence" was treated with precision. It was placed into a white envelope, labeled "One piece of green paper with writing," and returned to the shopping bag.

Humor turned to panic when Marcia informed Patti that she might be called as a witness to testify that the mysterious piece of green paper was, indeed, nothing more than her grocery list. Patti thought: This is so bizarre. I have to testify about bananas and lettuce?

Michael found it difficult to concentrate in school. His thoughts constantly revolved around Ron, and he never knew what would set them off. To combat this he developed a strategy of immersing himself in class discussions, constantly asking questions, taking notes, and trying to focus on what was going on around him instead of in downtown Los Angeles. If he let his mind wander for only a second or two, he was off somewhere in a world of his own, lost in his memories of Ron.

Realizing that he had to turn this nightmare into something positive, he decided to do his main research project on the media's effect on the judicial process. It was a yearlong endeavor that would culminate in a forty-five-minute presentation and an eighty-page report. His research went all the way back to the Lindbergh kidnapping case.

Plus, he had some special contacts.

By now we had close relationships with some members of the press horde that covered the trial on a daily basis. These reporters had to walk a very fine line. Their job was to remain objective, and not to take sides, so sometimes it was difficult to switch from talking to a friend to listening to their reports as professional journalists.

Reporters Shoreen Maghame, Dan Abrams, and Cynthia McFadden fell into this category as well as Jane Kaplan, the booker for *Good Morning America*, and producer Shelley Ross, and of course Dominick Dunne and Barbara Walters. The press often gets a bad rap, but we found these individuals to be sensitive and honest. They were prisoners to this case, leaving family and friends to cover it. It was Cynthia McFadden who offered to help Michael with his research. One day she took him and his friend Alexa on a tour of "Camp O. J.," the massive gathering of news vans stationed outside the courthouse. All around, vendors hawked buttons, T-shirts, hats, and pins—the tackier, the better. The daily assortment of "crazies" was in attendance, some dressed in outrageous costumes, many exhibiting placards promoting all manner of religious, political, and socioeconomic viewpoints. It was overwhelming to Michael that this chaotic circus was a result of his brother being slain.

Michael tried to step outside himself as he viewed the scene. Finally, he smiled as he thought: If Ron had to go out, this is the way he would have wanted to go out. He went fighting. He went as a hero. No one here will ever forget his name, and a part of him would have liked that.

There was a great deal of tension in our household the evening of March 8. Kim, Patti, and I were in the family room. The defense, searching desperately for any minutiae that would divert the court's attention from the macabre truth, speculated that the "One piece of green paper with writing" indicated that Ron had gone grocery shopping after leaving work on June 12, thus casting doubt on the timeline that the prosecution had established. So Patti was indeed going to have to testify the next day. She was extremely nervous.

Patti is not comfortable in large groups. She does not like to speak in public, and we had to coax and cajole her to participate in the few interviews we had given. She definitely did not want to answer some arrogant defense attorney's questions in front of millions of viewers. While it would be foolish of the defense to try give her a rough time on the witness stand, she was still very anxious about having to testify.

"You have nothing to worry about," I encouraged Patti. "All you are going to do is tell the truth, speak from your heart. You are not someone making up a story. You're not in a position where you have to worry about anything."

This counsel did not help. The question that absorbed Patti's mind was: Which member of the "Scheme Team" was going to cross-examine her? We had grown to hate these men vehemently, and we assigned them nicknames and drew caricatures of them in our minds.

It was Kim who found a way to break the tension. She suddenly giggled and suggested that, for such an important witness, the defense team would obviously call on the abilities of the world-famous F. Lee "Flea" Bailey. Patti grimaced. Bailey, with his red face and bloodshot eyes, was always chewing on something. Kim thought it was Altoids, a curiously strong mint breath freshener. Every few minutes, another handful of them went into his mouth. He was never without a thermos, and we wondered if it was loaded with booze. Kim rose to confront the witness. She stuck out her chest, puffed up her cheeks, and scratched the back of her head the way Bailey did. She popped a handful of imaginary Altoids into her mouth. With shaking hands she muttered, "Where's my thermos? Where's my thermos?"

"Get that poor guy a drink," I said.

We were all laughing.

"But what if it's Cochran?" Patti asked.

"Ah," Kim said. "Johnnie Cockroach." With meticulous precision she pushed an imaginary chair back into place at an imaginary defense table. She smoothed an imaginary suit jacket, walked across the courtroom in a perfect imitation of the Cochran strut that we had learned to detest, and made a great show of smiling toward the bench. "Thank you very kindly, Your Honor," she crooned. Then she turned toward the jury box, waving and blowing kisses. Only when she was assured that every eye in the imaginary courtroom was upon her, Kim pointed her finger at

Patti and drawled, "Thank you very kindly, Mrs. Goldman, but did you really buy that *low-fat turkey*? Do you know what it *says about a person* to buy *low-fat turkey*?!"

I jumped to my feet and demanded, "Your Honor, we need a sidebar."

After our laughter subsided, I suggested, "What about Barry 'Schmuck'?"

Kim asked, "Remember in the movie *Big*, at the very end when Tom Hanks is walking home and he's in this big man's suit, and he starts to shrink back into a little boy?"

Patti nodded. "That's exactly what he looks like!" she agreed.

Kim tried to shrink down inside her clothes, to imitate Scheck's baggy, ill-fitting suit. She smirked and rolled her eyes condescendingly. Waving her hands in mock disbelief, staring through Patti as if she did not exist, she asked, "Did you or did you not testify, *Miss-us Goldman,* that you *always* put bananas on your grocery list? Is it your testimony that this is standard procedure in your household, *Miss-us Goldman*? Is that what you testified to on direct, *Miss-us Goldman*?"

Patti slunk down in her seat, as if she were properly chastised.

"Maybe it'll be 'Ugly-Dougly,'" Patti said. She was referring to Carl Douglas, who had gained attention primarily from his cross-examination of Ron Shipp, and Kim now mimicked his ramrod posture beautifully. In a hissing voice, she demanded to know: "Did ya *lie* about the pretzels, Mrs. Goldman? Did ya *lie* about the fat-free ice cream, Mrs. Goldman? Did ya *lie* about the bananas, Mrs. Goldman? Don't ya always *lie* about those foodstuffs, Mrs. Goldman?!"

We found welcome relief in our laughter. At least for a few moments, the life force was back in our house.

Ron would have loved it.

FIFTEEN

Patti was very much aware that the entire world was watching this trial. She knew, too, that everyone was watching with special attention that day, March 9, awaiting the appearance of (except for the killer himself) the most controversial character in the "trial of the century." However, just prior to Detective Mark Fuhrman taking the witness stand, private little Patti Goldman had to testify.

Her hands were sweating and her legs were shaking as she approached the witness stand. She did not even have the comfort of Kim's presence; as a witness herself who might for some unknown reason be recalled, Kim was not allowed to listen to Patti's "critical" testimony.

Patti sat, staring straight ahead. She made no eye contact with the jury. She risked only the briefest of glances at Judge Ito.

Marcia Clark produced the paper bag marked "People's 30" and asked, "First of all, do you recognize the shopping bag?"

"Yes, I do," Patti answered.

"And was it your daughter, Kim Goldman, who placed the clothing inside this bag into the bag?"

Patti replied, "I didn't see her put them in there, but she told me that she put them—"

Cochran once more brought the proceedings to a halt by objecting to Patti's testimony as hearsay. It was a minor technical point about a nonsensical piece of "evidence," but Judge Ito tolerated it and sided with the defense. Meanwhile, since objections were limited to the particular defense lawyer who would handle cross-examination, Patti was now on notice that it was Johnnie Cochran who would confront her.

Marcia moved on, noting for the record, "I have removed from that bag a white envelope on which is written, 'One piece of green paper with writing.' Taking out the piece of green paper with writing on it, I'm going to ask if you recognize what that is?"

"Yes," Patti said. "It is my grocery list." Patti thought she heard some laughter in the courtroom.

Marcia asked, "Can you tell us how it came to be inside the brown paper bag that you recognize?"

Patti explained. "When I get through grocery shopping, when I leave the supermarket, I always throw the list in my bag."

"And so this is the shopping list that you made?"

"Yes, it is."

Marcia was finished. Cochran commenced his normal ritual, rising, straightening his suit jacket, smiling at Judge Ito, and acknowledging the judge's returned greeting. He slithered over to the podium, wearing a fake, serpentine smile, as if he thought he could charm this particular witness.

Patti thought: I absolutely detest this man. I want to spit at him.

"Mrs. Goldman," Cochran began, "as I understand your testimony, this was brought to court from your home?"

"Yes, it was."

"So that I'm clear, Detectives Tippin and Carr did not bring that bag to court, you brought it along with your daughter, is that right?"

"Kim brought it. Kim Goldman brought it," Patti clarified.

"Do you know who Detectives Tippin and Carr are?"

"I have never met them."

Having established to his satisfaction that Patti's grocery list did not contain any racist statements and was apparently not a component of a conspiracy on the part of the LAPD detectives, Cochran smiled and said, "Thank you very kindly. Nothing further, Your Honor."

Thus did the court waste its time and the taxpayers' resources, and further obscure the one and only critical question: Did Cochran's client murder Ron and Nicole?

We met Detective Mark Fuhrman in the D.A.'s office prior to the court session. We wished him good luck and were supportive of him, and he was very pleasant to us in return.

Calmly and confidently, over several days of testimony, Fuhrman confirmed the accounts of Ron Phillips and Tom Lange, explaining their actions at the crime scene and then at the Brentwood estate. In unemotional tones he told of how he found the bloody glove at the defendant's house.

A few days later the cross-examination took an ominous turn when F. Lee Bailey asked Fuhrman if, at any time during the past ten years, he had ever used the infamous "N-word," and Fuhrman denied that he had. Patti felt a huge knot in her stomach. It was difficult to believe that a police officer, in a high-pressure job, fighting gangs and all other forms of horror on the streets of Los Angeles, would never, ever have uttered the epithet, perhaps as a quote, in a tasteless joke, or in a moment of fear or anger. Patti thought: Does admitting using the word justify it? No. Is it a despicable slur? Yes. But just tell the truth, and be done with it.

I had to agree that Bailey's questioning of Fuhrman was one of the most offensive things I have ever heard or seen. He repeatedly asked Fuhrman about the N-word, and each time growled it so loudly that it literally bounced off the walls and echoed throughout the courtroom. He did it for one purpose and one purpose only: to garner a reaction from a predominantly black jury.

Kim thought that he was an effective witness, calm, unflappable, and truthful. But Patti's anger at Fuhrman began to fester. In the D.A.'s office she told Patty Jo, "Don't let him anywhere in my sight. I don't want to see him. I don't want to talk to him. Just keep him away from me." She felt that he had done the case irreparable damage.

Over the dinner table she explained to the rest of us, "Even though I have never used that word in a derogatory manner, I certainly couldn't say, under oath, that it has never come out of my mouth. How many of us can? We may have read it aloud or quoted someone who said it. He's lying, and he's screwing up the case. He found a key piece of evidence and now everything will be tainted. No one will believe him. How dare he lie! How dare he jeopardize our case! Who in the hell does he think he is?"

When Judge Ito allowed the issue of race to come into this trial, he truly opened the floodgates. He had no legal reason to allow it. There was no connection whatsoever shown between a comment made ten years earlier and any kind of illegal behavior on the part of the police in general or Mark Fuhrman in particular. The defense simply argued that it showed that Fuhrman was not a very nice guy, ergo, he was capable of planting evidence. How Judge Ito could make that leap is beyond my comprehension. I think there needs to be a connection between common sense and the law.

There were only about a half-dozen black students in Michael's school and he had always gotten along well with them, just like he does with almost everybody else. Michael asked one of them, a boy named Billy, if he thought that the killer was guilty.

"Yes," Billy replied without hesitation.

"Do you think he will be found guilty?"

"No."

"Why not?" Michael asked.

"You know why," Billy said, "because of the jury." So there it was. Billy knew that a predominantly black jury would never convict this murderer because of the mistaken belief that such an action would set back the entire black community.

Michael wondered: Didn't they see that setting him free would set them back so much further? Shaking his head, Michael asked, "Do *you* think he should be found guilty?"

Billy would not answer.

The two boys never spoke to each other again.

The newspaper was delivered, the gardener tended the lawn, hummingbirds fed just outside the patio door. Lucy sought every opportunity to get loose in the backyard so that she could jump into the pool; Pitzel sought every opportunity to growl at her. Riley prowled and napped. It seemed that the world should have stopped. But it had not. It had simply tipped on its axis, throwing all of us off-balance.

One afternoon on her way home from the trial, Patti stopped at Vons, as usual, to pick up some last-minute dinner items. As she stood in the checkout line, she realized that a customer in front of her had recognized her. Very subtly, he began to turn all the tabloid covers facedown. We had gotten used to seeing the lies and innuendoes on the headlines of these rags, but Patti thought it was very thoughtful of this stranger to try to protect her. Some of the stores in our neighborhood took them off the shelves completely.

Friends and strangers told us that we were celebrities. Books and movies would be made out of this tragic story. We would always be recognized. Patti lost count of the number of times she said aloud, "Can you believe that we are in the middle of this monumental worldwide thing?" One day we were an average, quiet family from Chicago, minding our own business and the next—

The term "celebrity" was especially troubling to us, because we had no choice in the matter. A true celebrity seeks fame and notoriety, and all this was simply thrust into our laps. There was nothing we could do to escape it.

Although Kim and Joe had discussed marriage, Kim wondered if the pressure she was feeling was tied to her fear of being alone. She came to the conclusion that neither of them was ready to make such a decision during this turbulent time, and she decided that although Joe was a wonderful man, he was not the one for her. Kim told Joe, "I'll always be grateful for having you in my life and for the support that you have given me." They parted friends.

Kim's friend Jana was saddened by the news of the breakup. She told Kim that she had thought the romance had a "fairy-tale" quality and she remembered how well Ron and Joe had gotten along. "Ron thought he knew who his little sister would marry," Jana said, "and now he never will." Hearing this, Kim was saddened and wondered, for a time, if she had done the right thing.

But now it was over. Kim's cat Dakota came to live with us.

Michael's seventeenth birthday brought back memories of the previous year. Armed with a learner's permit, Michael had been driving around our neighborhood for several months and, of course, wanted to take his driver's test the very day he turned sixteen. Before Patti would allow him to take the test, she wanted him to prove that he could handle more difficult driving conditions. So Michael drove us south along the Ventura Freeway to Brentwood. We had met Ron at a Japanese restaurant for Michael's birthday dinner.

Now that he was a year older and holding a regular job at the deli, Michael was ready for a newer car, a Mitsubishi. As soon as he picked it up in Ventura, he drove straight to the Department of Motor Vehicles to order license plates that declared: RMBR RON.

Lauren was only able to attend the trial on a few occasions. One day she was with us as we sat in the courtroom waiting for the proceedings to begin. Robert Shapiro was talking to someone from the media. Lauren stared at him with bitterness in her eyes until someone said, "That little girl is giving you a dirty look." Shapiro walked away.

Most of the time, however, Lauren viewed the trial from a distance. When she came home from school she switched on the TV to see what was happening. Her interest depended on which side was being covered. She despised the defense team, and did not care to hear what they had to say. If the events of the day were too offensive, she turned off the TV, retreated to her room, and listened to her favorite CD, the Beastie Boys. Or she wrote in her journal.

Time is said to be the great healer, but in our experience that is an over-rated concept. How does one heal a gaping wound in the soul when it is on full view for the entire world to see?

Patti was stretching herself to the limit: attending the trial every day; caring for me and the kids; juggling schedules; housekeeping, shopping, cooking; still dealing with her grief over losing Ron; and trying to live with the anger and frustration that the "Scheme Team" engendered. It seemed that her whole world had spun out of control. Patti needed to do something for Patti. "I need a change," she announced. "I've had blond frosted hair forever. It's the time to live life as a redhead."

I simply shook my head. "You look great the way you are."

"I just want to do it," Patti said. "I need to do it."

Except for Kim, the rest of us voted against the idea, but that did not slow her down for a moment. Her stubborn streak had kicked in. Here was something about her life that she could control. She could change her hair color more easily than she could change other circumstances.

Once it was done, I thought she looked great. But Michael and Lauren were not at all pleased. They complained, "You don't look like our mom anymore. You look more like Kim's mom now."

Lauren was in tears over it. Patti tried to assure her that she had always been, was now, and would always be *her* mother, but nothing she said made any difference. Lauren and Michael's reaction went deeper than a simple hair-color change. Whether they realized it at the time or not, it seemed they were saying, "You spend so much time with Kim—and now you look like her—what about us?"

On March 18, Patti, Kim, Lauren, Michael, and I all went to select the headstone for Ron's grave. Kim had said repeatedly that she wanted an inscription that would make her "feel" every time she visited him. For weeks she had searched for the right words. One day she came across a greeting card with a verse that touched that place in her heart. She bought the card, brought it home for us to read, and we all agreed that with a few personal changes, it would be perfect.

At the mortuary, we had a long and emotional discussion over whether we wanted Ron's picture on the headstone. Finally we decided against it. Little decisions became monumental as we tried to pick the style of lettering we wanted and the layout of the design.

We decided to have the unveiling service on Memorial Day. On the day when the entire nation honored men and women who had lost their lives defending America, we would honor a man who had lost his life coming to the defense of a friend.

In court the parade continued. Phil Vannatter was the fourth and final detective to testify, and he appeared cool and unflappable. He supported the story of the other three detectives that they had not considered the defendant to be a suspect when they went to his Rockingham estate. Vannatter said that they had instructed Fuhrman to jump the wall and let them in, because they had found blood on the door of the defendant's Bronco and were concerned that there might be other victims. They did not consider that the defendant was a suspect, he said, until they discovered the bloody glove.

On cross-examination, Robert Shapiro attacked the story, claiming that the search of the Brentwood estate was illegal. The defense was building its characterization of Phil as being one of "the twin devils of deception," once more diverting attention away from the murderer.

Kim knew that Phil Vannatter had twenty-five years of distinguished service behind him, and that had to count for something. Although she never actually discussed the issue of the search with the detectives, she thought that they were hedging their testimony a bit. She knew, as Patti had voiced earlier, that rightly or wrongly the ex-spouse of a murder victim is always a suspect. But she said, "Phil, whatever you choose to do, just know that we support you."

What was important was that the killer had left a trail of blood around and in his home. And some of it was Ron's.

The police were not on trial here, but one would never have known that from the actions of the defense team. Peering out from a window of his ivory tower at Harvard Law School, Alan Dershowitz declared— without offering any evidence—that police officers are actually trained to lie on the witness stand. He called it "testilying."

LAPD Chief Willie Williams and the California Organization of Police and Sheriffs took issue with Dershowitz's pronouncement. The organization released a statement that declared: "A civilized, law-abiding society should no longer accept the unprofessional, counterproductive conduct of individuals such as Alan Dershowitz. One has to wonder why any credible university would allow Mr. Dershowitz the opportunity to spew his anti-law enforcement venom under the guise of freedom of speech. Speech lacking responsibility is nothing more than the ranting and ravings of a hate-filled, anti-social fool."

We say: Amen.

Patti and Kim spent a lot of time studying the jury. I had raised Ron and Kim never to base their opinions on stereotypes, but when you are in a room full of strangers, that is about all you have to go on.

Since we were unaware of the jurors' identities, we made up names for some of them. We nicknamed one of the alternates "Jeannie," because she had a blond ponytail that reminded us of the actress Barbara Eden, who played the title role in the old TV series *I Dream of Jeannie*. She was about Kim's age, quite attractive, well dressed, and carefully made up. She and Kim made occasional eye contact and exchanged subtle nods indicating a friendly "good morning." Kim knew that we were not allowed any communication with the jury, and it was a little weird, but it was just a pleasantry between the two young women.

What began as a positive reaction to the jury slowly eroded as time went by. We watched the jurors take notes, stare at the wall, gloat over Cochran, look Marcia up and down, snub her, and fawn over Judge Ito. Whenever the testimony grew long and tedious, the reactions of some of the jurors were alarming. Some of them simply closed their eyes; others were clearly zoned out.

Over and over again, Kim caught Cochran making overt eye contact with some of the jurors, even winking at them. Patti and Kim longed to be able to raise their hands, speak up, and say, "Excuse me, Your Honor, but did you see that?"

One of the jurors, a woman we called "Poodle" because of her curly hairstyle, sometimes wore an outfit made out of fabric similar to Cochran's African-American motif ties. We wondered if she was making a silent statement, and it bothered us.

What many considered to be the comic relief of the trial entered the courtroom on the afternoon of Tuesday, March 21. As Brian "Kato" Kaelin bounded to the witness stand, he nearly ran into Chris Darden. When Marcia asked him if he was nervous, Kaelin responded: "Feel great." Laughter trickled through the courtroom, and then he added, "A little nervous."

Dressed in black jeans and a blazer, Kaelin was a demonstrative witness. He gestured expansively, sipped water, licked his lips, brushed back his shaggy hair, and shifted his posture back and forth. As questions were posed to him, he nodded vigorously and arched his eyebrows.

Marcia led Kaelin through a methodical recitation of his actions the night of the murders. He testified that he and the defendant had returned from McDonald's at 9:40 P.M. He said that he took his food to his room and did not see the defendant again until 11:15 P.M.

He was on the phone to his friend Rachel Ferrara about 10:40 or 10:45 P.M., when he heard a thumping nose.

"How many thumps did you hear?" Marcia asked.

Kaelin said that he heard three thumps so loud that he feared that an earthquake had struck. He demonstrated the sound of the thumps by balling up his right fist and pounding three times on the witness stand.

We believed, as the prosecution did, that the noises occurred when the defendant vaulted the fence and bumped into the air-conditioning unit. This was where Detective Fuhrman had found the bloody glove.

A short time later Kaelin encountered the defendant in the driveway, ready to leave for the airport to catch his flight to Chicago. Kaelin testified that he helped load luggage into the limousine, but when he offered to pick up one small bag, the defendant stopped him, preferring to handle that piece himself.

Kaelin testified that he never noticed a cut or injury to the defendant's hand, either during the trip to McDonald's or later, as they loaded the limousine, but he did say that he noticed blood drops in the foyer early Monday morning. We knew that would be important because the defense was already posturing about police conspiracy and planted blood. At the time Kaelin noticed the blood spots, the defendant had not yet returned from Chicago and his blood sample had not yet been drawn.

Throughout Kaelin's testimony, Simpson was a picture of frustration. He gestured repeatedly with his hands, throwing them up in the air when he heard something that displeased him. He scowled. He rolled his eyes in a show of disbelief. It was very frustrating to see Judge Ito allow this behavior in front of the jury.

Limousine driver Allan Park was a welcome relief from the hyperkinetic Kato Kaelin. Poised and articulate, he reiterated the information he gave during the preliminary hearing: that he had been ringing the intercom buzzer at the gate of the defendant's home for several minutes, but no one had answered. About 10:55 P.M. he saw a black person, about six feet tall and weighing about 200 pounds, stride toward the front door. Once the person went inside, Park said, he tried the buzzer again, and this time the defendant answered, apologized for having overslept, and promised to be out in a few minutes.

Marcia asked the defendant to stand. Without waiting for direction from Judge Ito, the killer quickly scooted his chair back and rose to his feet. He grinned slightly and tugged the buttons of his olive-green suit jacket. Marcia asked whether the defendant resembled the shadowy figure who entered the house and Park replied, "Yes, around that size."

Michael believes that tennis probably saved his sanity. During his one season as the high school coach, Ron had taught Michael and the other boys that tennis was a mental as well as a physical game. He stressed the importance of keeping one's concentration, and Michael had developed a special routine. Prior to each match he went off by himself, knelt in a corner of the court, and silently dedicated the match to Ron. Every serve, every volley was for Ron. He told a friend, "I feel like he's right there with me, watching me with that trademark smile on his face." Michael and his doubles partner, David Newman, were nearly unbeatable that year.

One afternoon as he prepared for a home match, Michael said aloud, "Jeez, Brentwood." Brentwood High School was not usually on the schedule, but this match had been added months earlier.

As team captain, Michael introduced all the players before the match. Then he went off by himself for his pregame ritual. He was crouched over, talking to Ron, when the Brentwood players formed a huddle, clasped hands, and shouted in unison, "Free O. J.!"

Michael could not believe what he had heard. He did not say anything, but he felt dazed. Suddenly he heard his own team respond with a spontaneous cheer of its own, "Kill O. J.!"

SIXTEEN

On the day after Ron and Nicole were murdered, sometime after the killer had returned from Chicago and was speaking with police at his Rockingham estate, his longtime friend Robert Kardashian was seen walking away from the grounds with a garment bag. The prosecution wanted to know what was in that bag, and wanted Judge Ito's permission to call him as a witness.

We viewed Kardashian as an enigmatic and sinister individual. Kim had a clear opinion of the man: "Slimy. Sleazy. Bottom of the barrel." He was a key player in several events during the week following the murders. First, he had spirited away the defendant's garment bag. Later in the week he had driven the murderer back to LAX to retrieve his precious golf clubs. And, it was from Kardashian's home that the defendant and A. C. Cowlings had fled in a white Ford Bronco.

In court Kardashian appeared to be like a dental retainer, simply there to take up space. He played no observable role in contributing to the legal defense, but his presence *in* court was vital to the defense's strategy to keep him *out of* the witness stand. Kardashian had not practiced law in years, but shortly after the murders he had reactivated his status as a lawyer. The "Scheme Team" claimed that he was one of them; therefore, he could cite attorney-client privilege and not be forced to testify.

What was it, we wondered, that Kardashian did not want to tell the jury?

Deputy D.A. Hank Goldberg handled the direct examination of LAPD criminalist Dennis Fung who, along with junior associate Andrea

Mazzola, had collected the physical evidence at both the crime scene and the killer's home. Responding to Hank's gentle, methodical questioning, Dennis described the trails of blood at both locations. He identified the bloody glove found at Rockingham.

The information was vital to the case, but questions and answers came in meticulous detail. Dennis paused frequently to look up information in his notes. Bailiffs had to remove one of the spectators for dozing off in court.

In the D.A.'s office during a break, Kim asked him jokingly, "Dennis, what is your name?"

He replied, "Let me look it up."

The touch of humor was welcome, because Dennis was nervous. Under Judge Ito's rules, objections could be raised only by the lawyer who would conduct the cross-examination. As Hank had taken Dennis through his testimony, it quickly became apparent that Barry Scheck would do the cross-examination. This made Dennis wary, because Scheck had already exhibited an obnoxious, loud, and tenacious style.

The cross-examination commenced during Dennis's second day of testimony. Indeed, Scheck was tough. His voice dripping with sarcasm, he attacked from all sides, sometimes forcing Dennis to admit that not every bit of evidence was collected, or recorded, according to proper procedures. After court that day, Dennis said, "It was grueling." We all knew that Scheck had only begun his assault.

The next morning, as we gathered in the D.A.'s office, Dennis was trying to psych himself up for the confrontation, vowing, "I'm going to make him work for his answers. I'm not going to let him get to me."

Hank Goldberg, who has a great, dry sense of humor, relieved the tension somewhat by doing an outstanding impersonation of Scheck and some of his made-for-TV attempts at courtroom drama.

We knew that we could not give Dennis a visible thumbs-up signal, but we wanted to devise some way to show our support. So we came up with a bit of sign language. We told Dennis that if one of us touched our lower lip, it meant "Way to go, you're doing great."

Dennis tried to hold firm. When Scheck delivered one of his extended questions, Dennis sat with his hands in his lap, pausing long and thinking carefully before he answered. At times he spotted Kim touching her lower lip and he showed a hint of a smile. At other times he seemed to grow weak, withering under the extended attack.

Scheck had an annoying habit of putting words into the witness's mouth; he would make statements and then ask the witness to verify them. He was able to draw reluctant admissions of errors in protocol, suggesting that Dennis had bungled the record-keeping procedures and, in general, attempting to paint a picture of investigators slogging through the crime scene, spraying blood, hair, and fibers everywhere. Defense lawyers such as Scheck are content to try to make an honest witness look like a liar instead of a fallible human being. From our perspective we could see that, yes, some mistakes were made. But they did not alter the big picture, and it was worrisome to look at this jury and wonder what it might consider to be "reasonable doubt."

Day after day, hour after hour, question after question, the defense pounded away at Dennis, pursuing two separate themes, seeking to prove: (1) dozens of investigators conspired to frame the defendant; (2) the investigation was flawed by incompetence. In our opinion, these appeared to be mutually exclusive concepts. The police, the technicians, and the prosecutors would have to be exceptionally competent in order to devise, create, and maintain a phony case. And since the defense argued for both explanations, it was obvious that its actual intent was to (3) confuse the jury.

Dennis's testimony highlighted many of the basic absurdities of this trial. During a lunch break Judge Ito retired to his chambers to review a videotape that showed Dennis as he worked at the crime scene. When court reconvened, the judge had to admit that he had inadvertently hit the RECORD button, erasing about five seconds of evidence in the "trial of the century." At another point Judge Ito squandered ninety minutes of everyone's time while he considered the defense team's contention that, because one page of Dennis's report did not have a staple mark in it, it was evidence of a conspiracy. During a sidebar conference a spectator suddenly began shouting that someone sitting next to him was threatening to hit him; the man, wearing a garish dress and heavy makeup, was a local wacko who called himself "Will B. King." And Robert Shapiro had to issue an apology for a joke he made outside the courthouse; passing out fortune cookies to reporters, he quipped that they came from a Chinese restaurant called "Hang Fung."

This was not a trial. It was theater of the absurd.

Perhaps an even greater absurdity occurred when, after eight days of testimony, Dennis was finished. He left the stand and shook hands with Chris. Then he stopped at the defense table and, with a smile on his face, said goodbye to the group of lawyers who had attacked him without mercy for more than a week. He shook hands with Cochran and Shapiro. Barry Scheck, the architect of Shapiro's "Hang Fung" strategy, actually said, "Thank you." Then, to our utter horror, Dennis reached his hand toward the killer and shook hands with him.

Whose side are you on? Patti wondered. Are you trying to be polite or are you just stupid? It was a royal slap in the face, and done in full view of the jury. Anything Dennis had said in our favor was instantly negated by this sophomoric show of support for the defense.

During a break Patti voiced her disgust and surprise to Chris Darden. He simply shrugged his shoulders in mute embarrassment.

Throughout Dennis's testimony, another disturbing distraction occurred. The jury had consistently been described as expressionless and difficult to read, and that was certainly true. We were, of course, anxious to know how they were reacting to the evidence. With the dismissal of juror Jeanette Harris on April 5, we got a sobering glimpse.

Judge Ito dropped Harris from the jury after he was informed that she had once been a victim of domestic violence, and had failed to report that on her jury questionnaire. She was the latest of several jurors to be dismissed, but she was clearly the most outspoken. On the evening of April 5 she gave an interview to KCAL-TV and stated that she was "quite impressed" with the defendant. "He's gone through a lot," she said. "Whether he did it or not, he presents a picture of someone who's dealing with a lot. . . . He hasn't been allowed to grieve. He's got two minor children at home that he's not allowed to comfort. . . . He sits there, and it totally amazes me that he's able to handle it."

It was difficult not to throw a rock at the television set.

Harris told interviewer Pat Harvey that "from day one I didn't see it as being a fair trial," and that black and white jurors may be under pressure from their peers to cast their votes along racial lines. She also said that she did not believe Detective Fuhrman and when asked if she thought that someone who made racial slurs was also capable of planting evidence, her response was, "Yes, I do." At best, she predicted, the case would result in a hung jury.

Patti said, "There's too much racial bullshit going on here." It was clear that Harris had her mind made up before she ever took a seat in the jury box. She was not about to let the evidence dissuade her. The defendant was not guilty and that was that. How people like this end up on a jury is disturbing. Perhaps she should have tried to put herself in our shoes.

Because Harris made allegations, the judge conducted separate interviews with Harris and with each of the twelve jurors and six remaining alternates.

Some of the jurors complained about toes being stepped on, occasional pushes, shoves, and hurt feelings. At one point someone whined that the black and white jurors did not like the same movies and that when it came time to choose which movies to watch, the white members were frequently outvoted by their black counterparts. The Sheriff's Department responded by providing separate movie-viewing rooms. In an attempt to stave off disaster, Judge Ito directed that the deputies be replaced.

This caused further division. On Friday, April 21, the jurors stamped their collective feet and threw a temper tantrum. It was the 101st day of their sequestration, and they asked Judge Ito to visit them at their hotel so they could explain their anger. Ito refused, and summoned the jurors to the courthouse, where thirteen of them arrived wearing black or dark clothing in an apparent gesture of solidarity. Four others were attired in brightly colored garb in an apparent gesture of defiance. The standoff continued as the offended jurors refused to go back to work.

We appreciated the fact that sequestration is difficult, but from our perspective, the jury was beginning to sound like a bunch of spoiled brats.

The trial was in chaos. Speculation ran rampant that this group would never be able to reach a verdict. We were confused and deeply worried because it seemed that, at the very least, this jury was predisposed to taking sides. They were clearly communicating with one another about some aspects of this case.

We were terrified that a mistrial was in the making. Kim was so nervous that she was sick to her stomach, and she was losing what I thought was a dangerous amount of weight.

It was a real snake pit. Foremost among our concerns was that if Judge Ito excused the entire jury and a higher court disagreed with him about the legal necessity of doing so, prosecutors would be unable to pursue their case because of the constitutional prohibition against double jeopardy. A killer would walk free.

One morning, as Patti was attempting to enter the courtroom, she was stopped by a bailiff whom she knew only by his last name, Jex. He pointed to the water bottle peeking out of her purse. "You're not supposed to have that in there," he said, in a rude, disrespectful tone. "You better watch it, and you better not drink it."

Patti went on the attack. "I can't believe you're telling me this," she said. "I've been carrying a water bottle in my purse since the beginning of this trial and I have never taken it out in the courtroom. I will never take it out in the courtroom. The nerve of you to assume that I would do that!"

Jex stood firm. "Well you're not supposed to have it in there."

"Well, what's the difference if I'm not going to drink it?"

"Well, you better not drink it!"

"Do me a favor," Patti growled. "Don't talk to me. I don't like your tone of voice and for you to think that I would do something I'm not supposed to do in here is insulting to me." She walked away and never looked back.

Kim congratulated her for fighting back. "It's the power of the red hair, Patti!" she quipped. "You've got the power!"

Later, Patti wrote a letter to Judge Ito complaining of the bailiff's treatment, but never received a response. In and of itself, the incident was not a big deal. But it underscored the question: Where were the priorities?

As disheartening as Jeanette Harris's comments were, we took hope in the knowledge that the prosecution had not yet presented the most damning and important part of the case, the physical evidence. So, we tried to be patient.

Now the prosecution had moved to the core of its case. Greg Matheson, a chief forensic chemist and assistant director at the LAPD laboratory, provided the key point to blast the "incompetence" theory out of the water: If blood samples were contaminated, they might fail to yield any results, but they would *not* produce false results that implicated the defendant.

Matheson's testimony began to forge an incontestable link between the killer and his victims. He had conducted basic tests of blood types and enzymes; other experts would follow with the results of more sophisticated DNA testing.

According to this expert, only one out of every two hundred people could have left a specific telltale blood drop at the crime scene; that person was the defendant.

Referring to blood found on a sock in the defendant's bedroom, Matheson testified that it could not have come from the defendant; it could have come from Nicole.

Predictably, the "Scheme Team" spent days attempting to tear down Matheson's testimony. Defense Attorney Robert Blasier's questions insinuated that minuscule amounts of blood had been taken from one sample and used to taint others. He questioned the record-keeping abilities and storage procedures of the lab and, in general, attempted to bolster the contention that a multitude of investigators had conspired to frame the defendant.

Hank Goldberg responded with a touch of sarcasm. On redirect examination, he asked a question that he knew would be disallowed: "Is there any kind of a mechanical device or other device in the evidence processing room that would warn . . . that someone was approaching and about to enter, maybe a device that might yell out: 'Warning, someone is about to enter the evidence processing room! All evidence tampering must cease'?"

Blasier objected and Judge Ito, with a wry shake of his head, sustained the objection, but Hank had made his point.

On May 5, Kim and I filed a wrongful-death lawsuit, charging that the defendant had "brutally murdered" Ron.

This was a difficult decision for us. We did not want anyone to perceive that we were trying to make money off the tragedy. After all, we had bitterly resented Sharon when she filed a similar suit so early on. But it was a question of erring on the side of caution. Nearly eleven months had passed since the murders, and the statute of limitations for a wrongful-death case is one year. We could always drop the suit if we chose to, but after the deadline passed we would be prohibited from filing.

We sought an unspecified amount of "punitive and exemplary" damages "in order to send out a message . . . that such vicious and outrageous savagery inflicted by one human being upon another shall be met with the severest of civil penalties."

We hired attorney Robert Tourtelot, who also represented Detective Mark Fuhrman. Bob is a congenial fellow, and we trusted him.

Bob Tourtelot declared that he was confident he could get a substantial judgment.

Kim spoke for all of us when she said, "It doesn't have anything to do with money. If we can make the killer feel a quarter of the pain we feel, it's worth it."

I vowed publicly to "haunt the halls of justice."

SEVENTEEN

Finally the preliminary bouts were over. It was time for the main event.

Dr. Robin Cotton, director of Cellmark Diagnostics in Germantown, Maryland, the nation's largest private DNA laboratory, took the witness stand. She would be the first of three DNA experts who would testify about the results of three separate rounds of tests. Neatly drawn charts helped illustrate her points.

Deputy D.A. George "Woody" Clarke, who had vast experience prosecuting cases on DNA evidence, led Dr. Cotton through a basic primer of what DNA is and how it can link evidence to a particular human being. She explained that DNA is present in nearly all human cells, and that each person inherits a combination of characteristics from his or her parents. In humans more than 90 percent of all DNA is identical—that is what makes us human. But the remaining 10 percent is unique, and that is what makes each person distinctive. Dr. Cotton said, "If we make the assumption that a blueprint contains all the information for how to build your house, the analogy is that DNA contains all the information on how to build you."

This was certainly the most complex subject the jury would have to consider, yet Dr. Cotton explained it with remarkable clarity. Gazing directly at the jury and speaking in a soft, clear voice, she said, "You can look around even in a very large room . . . and you'll see that, with the exception of identical twins, people are different. Even closely related people, brothers, two brothers, are different. You can always tell them apart. And the exception is identical twins. And identical twins are identical because they have identical DNA."

Aha! Kim thought. Will the defense now try to convince us that the killer's evil twin, Bozo, committed these murders?

Skewering the defense's attack before it was launched, Dr. Cotton told the jurors that even if a sample was contaminated or degraded, it would *never* point falsely toward a suspect. "There is no environmental effect that can work to simply change one type and make it become another," Dr. Cotton testified. "You may lose the type altogether. You may degrade the DNA so much that you can't type it, but you won't just change types from one to another. It doesn't happen."

Due in large measure to the frequent objections of Defense Attorney Peter Neufeld—Barry Scheck's longtime partner—Dr. Cotton was on the stand for two days before she was able to testify about specific results. Near the end of the second day, prosecutors introduced into evidence X rays that portrayed the results of the genetic tests as a series of striking black "bands" arranged in identifiable patterns. As the "Scheme Team" huddled about the defense table, inspecting its own copy of the set of X rays, someone must have offered a quip, for Simpson suddenly burst into laughter. He covered his mouth quickly and worked to regain a serious expression.

We wondered if he would still be smiling when Dr. Cotton finished her testimony.

Over the next few days her testimony became very specific, concentrating on two samples:

• Only one person in 170 million has the genetic characteristics of the blood found near Ron and Nicole's bodies; the defendant's blood matched those characteristics.

• Only one person in 6.8 billion has the genetic characteristics of the blood found on the sock in the defendant's bedroom; Nicole's blood had those characteristics.

Kim worried about whether or not the jury was getting it, but she noticed that Juror 6 seemed very interested in the testimony. He leaned forward in his chair, writing copious notes. Dominick Dunne noted the change in him as well, and offered the opinion that he thought the man was upset and disappointed that it was being proved to him that the "killer" had actually done it.

Another DNA expert followed Dr. Cotton to the stand and, over the course of several days, added more incontrovertible evidence. Gary Sims, a veteran analyst at the California State Department of Justice laboratory in Berkeley, testified that the DNA in four bloodstains on the glove found behind the guest house on the killer's property matched that of either Ron or Nicole. Prosecutors said that at least one stain on the same glove was consistent with the defendant's blood.

Various blood samples collected from inside the defendant's Ford Bronco matched the DNA patterns of the killer, Ron, and Nicole.

Patti and Kim were astonished. Here was the "trail of blood" that led from the crime scene, to the Bronco, to the killer's home, and even into his bedroom. Had there been any shadow of a doubt, it was now permanently washed away. The man sitting at the defense table was indeed the killer who murdered Ron and Nicole.

Kim sat in the front row, weeping silently. The killer stared straight ahead, occasionally whispering to his lawyers. He did not seem to be paying attention to the testimony. Kim wanted to ask: Are we boring you?

Repeatedly leaping out of his chair like some kind of mop-headed jack-in-the-box, Barry Scheck hammered away, using a mixed bag of accusations: He accused police of sloppy procedures; implied that one lab incorrectly interpreted the statistical significance of DNA matches; inferred that police had sprinkled the socks with blood after the fact.

Later Assistant D.A. Lisa Kahn, in a welcome bit of logic, pointed out that some of the blood samples were degraded while others were not. This suggested that they had been subjected to different degrees of exposure to the elements. However, if the drops had been planted or tampered with in the lab, they would have degraded at the same rate. "The evidence shows that neither a lone officer nor a cadre of plotters could have accomplished such a frame-up," she concluded.

Wrapping up his questioning of Sims, Assistant D.A. Rockne Harmon moved to counter Scheck's suggestion that the samples were "cross-contaminated." His voice heavy with sarcasm, Rockne asked, "Can DNA fly?"

"I don't think so," Sims responded, laughing agreeably.

"I mean, there are no scientific studies that have shown that, are there?"

"No. I don't think it has wings."

There was simply no way to deny the dramatic impact of the DNA evidence, so the defense returned to its conspiracy theme. In Scheck's fantasy world, he saw the investigators trading hair and fiber samples and splashing blood about in a grand, felonious conspiracy.

There were apparently no limits to the fertile imaginations of Scheck and his compadres on the "Scheme Team." Way back in September, KNBC-Channel 4 had reported that DNA tests of the defendant's socks had revealed the presence of Nicole's blood. Since the tests had not yet been performed, the report was erroneous. Now that we knew that Nicole's blood was, indeed, on the sock, Scheck found grounds for suspicion. Did KNBC *know* that it was Nicole's blood because they *knew* that detectives had planted it there? Obviously the entire news staff at KNBC had plotted with the police, the D.A.'s office, the coroner, the scientists and—who knows—Saddam Hussein?—to frame the wonderful, caring human being who was paying Scheck's enormous fee.

Scheck had built his career on proclaiming the reliability of DNA evidence in order to win the release of prisoners who had been wrongly convicted. Now, as DNA evidence had proved to the entire world who killed Ron and Nicole, here he was, selling his soul in an attempt to convince the jury of the preposterous notion that—in this case—the evidence had been planted.

Patti had never worn the stepmother label. She was always more of a friend than a parental figure to Ron and Kim. But now, as Patti and Kim spent every day together, driving to court, listening to the hours of testimony, and returning home, they developed a closer, more adult-to-adult, friendship. It was one of the positive developments to come out of this horrendous experience.

During the early-morning hours, negotiating the maddening traffic on the freeway, they shared their feelings about everything. Sometimes that meant tears and frustration, other times anger, and sometimes brief moments of levity. Before long, they were finishing each other's sentences and blurting out the same reactions. "We're spending way too much time together," they joked.

In some respects this was true. Patti checked in by phone with Michael and Lauren several times a day, and tried her best to spend quality time with them. She came to all of Michael's home tennis matches and, whenever possible, drove Lauren to and from special events. But occasionally simmering resentments surfaced and hurt feelings arose.

Michael was the one who tended to turn inward. As far as the trial was concerned, he was optimistic. He thought: This is going great. The DNA evidence was undeniable. You can picture numbers. One in how many billion people? There aren't even that many people on the whole planet. This is cut and dried! You can't argue with these numbers.

But, in fact, Michael also realized that we were living in a complex and crazy world. On one of the few occasions when he was able to come to court, he found himself transfixed by the jury. He was raised not to think in racial terms, but he now found himself worrying about the large contingent of black faces in the jury box. Can they fly in the face of this incredible evidence? he wondered.

As the days stretched into weeks, and the weeks into months, however, he became saturated. At times, it felt as if the family did not think about or care about or talk about anything other than the trial. Michael was in school from 7:30 A.M. to 2:30 P.M. Tennis practice ran from 3:15 until 5:00. Every day, right after tennis practice, he drove to the cemetery to spend a few minutes with Ron. He visited the grave more often than any of the rest of us, keeping his grief private.

But he was a high school junior, an adult-in-the-making. There was a future out there and Michael was busy preparing to face it.

In the evenings at home, when he would try to talk to Patti about something that happened in school, she too often responded with a "Shhh" because she was watching trial coverage or commentary on TV. Michael wanted to shout, "You've been there all day. You've watched the news all night. Enough!" He had other things to tell us and other news to share, but no one had time to listen. By the end of tennis season, he and his doubles partner had amassed a remarkable record of thirty-three victories and only three defeats, but he had difficulty getting us to share his elation. To Michael, it just did not feel like home anymore.

He began to do his homework at his friend Alicia's house. Most evenings, he did not come home until 11:00.

He knew that Patti wanted him around more, and sometimes she grew angry enough to call him, asking him to come home. But they never really talked about it too much. Michael did not want to tell her, or any of us, how he was feeling.

EIGHTEEN

Brian flew to Los Angeles to join us for Memorial Day weekend. On Saturday we faced a task we had all been avoiding. We knew that it was going to be a wrenching experience and we did not want to do it more than once, so we had waited until the entire family was present. With Brian here, it was time.

It was difficult to believe that nearly a year had passed since we had cleaned out Ron's apartment. At that time, we were unable to do much more than pack his belongings into cardboard boxes and plastic bags. Everything was still stored in our garage.

We spent several hours going through the contents of those boxes, deciding what to do with the tangible remainders of Ron's stolen life. We cried softly throughout the day, and often one of us had to leave the room to regain composure.

Here was a volleyball we had given Ron for his birthday. There were a number of softball bats and, of course, his tennis racquets.

Michael came across Ron's tennis shirt from Oak Park High, which brought back memories of the season when Ron coached his team. "I'm not surprised he kept this shirt," Michael said. "It was just like him to do that." He asked if he could keep the shirt in his room.

We found a tie that Ron had worn to Mike Pincus's wedding and decided that it would be nice to give that, along with a red and turquoise pullover, a red jacket, and a bandana, to Mike.

I found the black-and-white houndstooth sport jacket that he wore occasionally, and remembered how incredibly handsome he looked in it.

Here was a sweater that Ron's former girlfriend, Jacqui, had given him. She had asked us if she could have it, and it was fine with us. We found his bowling ball and a few books. There were several Marilyn Monroe posters that he had collected. One of them had been a birthday present from Kim.

We also gave a bandana and a vest to Ron's friend Pete. Kim searched for a contract signed by Ron and Pete. She reminded us that Ron and Pete had joked about becoming the world's biggest gigolos. They had made a pact that the first one to get married would have all his wedding expenses paid by the other, including a lavish honeymoon. They had committed their pledge to writing and, after Kim witnessed it, it had been filed away for posterity.

Kim set aside Ron's cozy down comforter. She wanted to keep it, but was not ready to take it just yet.

We decided to give many items to the people at the cerebral palsy center and to another charitable organization where Patti had worked a few years earlier, the Coalition Against Household Violence.

After separating the items we intended to pass along to Ron's friends, we placed what remained in a trunk. It suddenly occurred to Kim and me that doing this was analogous to Ron himself. All of his belongings were now stored in this one simple place and Ron was an uncomplicated, simple person.

Kim found the bitter letter she had written to Ron in December 1993, when she accused him of taking her for granted. Had life progressed the way it was supposed to the letter would have been long forgotten, but now she agonized over the question: Is that how he remembered me? It bothered her deeply that he had saved the letter, and she wished that she had never written it.

Kim and I came across a folder labeled "Ankh" that we had previously overlooked. As I read through it, I was hit with an amalgam of emotions: surprise, pride, sadness, remorse. The folder showed, in amazing detail, plans for the restaurant or club that Ron had dreamed of opening. Architectural sketches, names of potential vendors, stacks of business cards, projected costs, and menu ideas filled the pages.

The shape of the building was unique, with a top curved portion creating a bar area and dance floor. The seating areas resembled arms, extending out on either side. The entranceway flared downward. The exterior of the club would not have a sign; it would simply have a large symbol on the door, which, in fact, was the very shape of the building, if viewed from above. It was the ankh, the Egyptian symbol for eternal life, the ornament that Ron had worn around his neck; Kim was wearing that necklace now.

She had mentioned these restaurant plans of Ron's during the Barbara Walters interview almost a year earlier, but I had no idea how extensive they actually were. In an instant, I knew why he had not shown them to me.

My primary conflict with Ron was what I had perceived to be his lackadaisical attitude toward a career. After he dropped out of college, I was tough on him, and my fatherly concern deepened over the next several years.

Life was sweet, and Ron loved it. Not so sweet were the bills he accumulated. At one point, he fell hard for a young woman with expensive tastes, and the money he made waiting tables just was not enough. For a time, he took a white-collar position with a headhunting firm, but that job necessitated an expensive wardrobe. His bills continue to mount. Little by little he got in over his head.

By 1992, he was $12,000 in debt and creditors were hounding him. I took a tough-love approach and told him he'd have to handle it himself. We went to a financial counselor, consolidated his debt, and Ron made the effort to get out of the hole. It was way too deep, and ultimately Ron filed for bankruptcy.

Kim disclosed, "Ron and I had a lot of discussions about his relationship with you. You were both so stubborn. You both thought you were right—about everything. You were not the easiest guy to get along with—especially for a kid who was just trying to find his own way. You had very high expectations for both of us, but you were much tougher on Ron. I was always 'Daddy's Angel.' I could do no wrong. That was a problem between Ron and me, so when we talked about you, I found myself siding with him, so that he wouldn't call me 'Daddy's Angel.' But more often than not, I did agree with him. I understood his pain and frustration. Ron really wanted to prove to you that he could succeed, and didn't need to go to college to do it."

Kim knew all about Ron's plans for the "Ankh." However, Ron was not going to share them with me until he felt that they were professional and complete enough to impress me. My pragmatic, skeptical approach to some of his past business ideas had probably helped him make that decision. I had thought that Ron was still struggling to get his act together when, in fact, he knew what he wanted to do, was setting about doing it, and doing it beautifully. How I wished I could tell him how proud I was of what he had accomplished.

On Sunday at 10:30 A.M. we gathered again at Pierce Brothers Valley Oaks Memorial Park in Westlake Village.

The sun was shining. Hundreds of American flags were on display for tomorrow's Memorial Day service, and a light breeze caused them to sway.

Gil Garcetti had assured everyone in the D.A.'s office that it was fine if they attended, and many of them did. Among those who joined us were Marcia Clark, Bill Hodgman, Ron Shipp, and Patty Jo Fairbanks as well as many of the law clerks. Unfortunately, Tom Lange and Phil Vannatter did not attend. They feared that the defense team would use it as an example of bias against the defendant, and they were unwilling to take that risk. Chris Darden was out of town attending a wedding.

Rabbi Johnson was the first to speak:

Ron's family has not been permitted the normal opportunity for mourning, and expressing their grief. The brutal slaying of Ron and the attendant trial and publicity have kept his family away from any form of grieving in a normal way. . . .

If Ron could speak to us now, he would probably be at peace with his own physical death, but he would be in pain knowing the anguish that his family continues to experience as the trial inches along. . . . Ron is lovingly looking down upon you this day and every day, praying for an early resolution, when some semblance of justice is finally brought upon the one guilty for these slayings. . . . Amen.

After the rabbi spoke, some of Ron's friends shared their remembrances. Lauren, Michael, Brian, Kim, Patti's mother, Elayne, and I spoke to Ron while the others listened quietly. Finally the granite grave-stone was uncovered, bearing the heading

Loving Son, Brother and Friend
Ronald Lyle Goldman
July 2, 1968—June 12, 1994

Patti read the additional message we had inscribed:

> Sometimes when we are alone and lost in thought,
> and all the world seems far away,
> you come to us as if in a dream,
> gently taking our hands and filling our hearts
> with the warmth of your presence.
>
> And we smile, knowing that,
> although we cannot be together for now,
> you're always close in our thoughts.
>
> Missing you now,
> Loving you always.

Someone put a small American flag near the marker. Kim placed a bouquet of flowers on the grave, along with a note:

> Ron—I hope the sunflowers bring you warmth. But nothing can ever compare to the warmth of your soul. I love you. Kim

Many people felt that the service would be a way to help us find some closure. However, Kim, in particular, had a difficult time with the concept of "closure" because, as she says, "my brother will always be gone." The unveiling of the headstone was very painful for her. Seeing Ron's name, etched in stone, along with the dates that began and ended his life, forced a sense of permanence that she did not expect.

Kim told a reporter, "It's not a matter of feeling better. It's just more permanent."

Although it had been a beautiful day and a lovely service, Kim found herself wishing that the trial had never been mentioned. "Ron deserved this day to himself," she said, "just the mention of the trial brings unwanted people and intrusive thoughts into what should have been a very private time."

When we were back home, Lauren sought the solitude of her room and wrote a letter:

Ron,
    Where do I begin? The loss of you has become so new to me. It seems like only yesterday that we were talking on the phone about my eighth grade graduation, which was the last time that I ever heard the words, "I love you" out of your mouth again.
    We have shared so much together in what seemed like such a short time. I miss you so much and it is so hard for me to understand how or why someone took you away from us. . . .
    I loved the fact that you were always here to watch out for me. Even though you were not always at home, you still took the time to call and see what was going on in my life. . . .
    Whenever I hear a sad song on the radio, I think of you and the wonderful and promising life that you lost. I wish that I could give your life back to you, but obviously God needed you for something.
    I pray that you did not suffer and that you are out of pain, because I cannot bear the thought of that. . . .
    I know that we have not said good-bye forever because one day we will be reunited again, forever!
    I love you very much and I will miss you always.

    Love Always,
    Squirt

NINETEEN

Assistant D.A. Brian Kelberg asked Dr. Lakshmanan Sathyavagiswaran, "If we call you Dr. Lakshmanan, you will not be offended, will you?"

With a grin, the Los Angeles County coroner replied, "No, I will not."

The chief coroner was on the stand because the man who actually performed the autopsies on Ron and Nicole, Deputy Medical Examiner Irwin Golden, had provided inept testimony during the preliminary hearing. Dr. Lakshmanan acknowledged that Dr. Golden had made some mistakes, but insisted that they were not critical to the case.

Moving slowly toward what promised to be the most graphic evidence of the trial, Kelberg elicited basic verbal descriptions of the two victims.

Dr. Lakshmanan spent only about ninety minutes on the witness stand during this shortened Friday session. It was a prelude to next week, when the jurors—but not the courtroom audience—would be shown the autopsy photographs. Judge Ito warned the jurors, "If at any time during the presentation of this evidence you feel unusually uncomfortable or if you need to take a break, feel free to let me know."

With the exception of the days following Ron's death, we knew that the coming week would be the most difficult of our lives.

During a hearing on Monday, Patti and Kim heard Cochran explain to Judge Ito that when the autopsy photos were displayed for the jury the next day, his client might not be able to remain in the room. He wanted the judge to prepare an instruction to the jury in case the killer found it necessary to flee the courtroom.

The judge was unsure whether he could legally allow the defendant to waive his right to be present during the trial. The prosecution, on this rare occasion, agreed with the defense, but did not want the defendant to leave the courtroom when the jury was present. Deputy D.A. Brian Kelberg opined, "One might argue whether this is a performance by Mr. Simpson, the actor, or truly a reflection of Mr. Simpson's alleged grief for his deceased wife."

Marcia agreed, asking Judge Ito not to "turn this into a circus side-show for maudlin displays by the defendant." Hearing this, the killer rolled his eyes and glared at Marcia.

They were setting the stage for some more two-bit acting for the benefit of the jury. We could just see it coming, the quivering lip and the crocodile tears. Finally Judge Ito ruled that the defendant would either have to leave the courtroom before the photos were shown or remain for the entire session. He decided to stay. Then Cochran insisted that the victims' families be put under the same restriction. We agreed, knowing full well that if we found it necessary to leave, we would do just that.

Both Brian Kelberg and Ken Lynch advised us not to come the next day. The autopsy photographs would be displayed in such a way that only the jurors could view them, but the testimony would be graphic. "You don't want to remember him that way," they insisted. Marcia and Chris also encouraged us not to attend.

We talked about it throughout the evening, weighing the pros and cons.

"I don't know," Kim said. "Maybe what's in my imagination is worse than the reality. Maybe I need to hear what really happened."

We continued to vacillate. Finally, just as earlier when photographs of the murder scene were shown, we concluded that whatever trauma we experienced would pale in comparison to what Ron had endured. We decided that the most important issue was to demonstrate to the jury our support for the prosecution. We hoped that our presence would somehow personalize Ron to the jury. If we had to flee, so be it.

On Tuesday, June 6, Patti and Kim realized there was a change in the defense team's seating arrangements. Up until now, Robert Kardashian had been seated at the back table, in front of the rail. Now he had moved

up to the defense table and seemed to be in a position to block out the
TV camera's view of the murderer.

Brian spent much of the day simply questioning Dr. Lakshmanan,
building toward a dramatic visual conclusion. However, even the testimony, although often dry and technical, provoked vivid images. The
coroner testified that Ron had bled so profusely that there was not
enough blood left in his heart to take a sample.

Now came one of the most abhorrent moments of the trial. A large
easel was set up so that the jury—and no one else—could view the photos. When the first one was displayed, one of the women jurors covered
her mouth in horror. Another began to breathe very deeply.

As the coroner described the photos, the killer reacted. The *Los
Angeles Times* reported that he "worked his jaw slowly and winced." But
that is not what Patti and Kim saw. This man whose lawyers argued that
he was worried that he might have to flee the courtroom, knowing that
the easel blocked him from the jury's sight, bobbed his head to a silent,
up-tempo beat. His fingers tapped out a rhythm on the table in front of
him. Cochran would probably claim that he was simply trying to get the
mental images out of his mind, but we would disagree. Patti and Kim
were there. They saw what Kardashian blocked the TV camera from
showing. This man was dancing!

On the other side of the room the jurors were reacting quite differently. Many of them cried.

Standing a few feet away from the jury and using a pointer to indicate details of the photos, Dr. Lakshmanan traced a gash from the left
side of Nicole's throat to just below her right ear. He noted that there
were no marginal wounds around this cut, indicating that she did not
resist, and that she may have already been unconscious when the lethal
blow was delivered.

When Brian asked the coroner to demonstrate how the final, fatal
blow to Nicole could have been inflicted, Dr. Lakshmanan rose, stood
behind the deputy D.A., grabbed him by the hair, pulled his head back,
and sliced a ruler across his neck.

With each passing day, the testimony grew more ghastly. Dr. Lakshmanan, using the forensic evidence, reconstructed the sequence of events.
He theorized that the killer first confronted Nicole, face to face, and

inflicted four thrusting wounds to her neck. At least one of them would have been fatal without immediate medical attention. Wounds to the back of her left hand indicated that she attempted to ward off the blows, but her defensive wounds were minimal, which showed that the attacker had quickly overwhelmed her. The coroner then suggested that Nicole was knocked unconscious by a blow to the head. She fell to the ground. The killer then apparently paused in his attack. Dr. Lakshmanan testified that the fall caused a bruise on Nicole's head, which took one minute or more to develop, and which would not have appeared if her throat had been slashed then, and her blood pressure had dropped to zero.

This was the minute of Ron's death.

Patti and Kim continually, quietly, asked one another, "Are you okay?"

In Dr. Lakshmanan's scenario, the killer may have been interrupted, and turned his fury upon the interloper. A minute or so later he returned to the unconscious Nicole, grabbed her by the hair, exposed her neck, and administered the vicious, maniacal coup de grâce.

Dr. Lakshmanan testified that, in his opinion, the wounds were administered by a right-handed assailant using a single-edged knife. Hearing this, the killer leaned forward and jotted a note to Carl Douglas.

Patti noted that he wrote with his right hand.

Lou Brown, acting as executor of Nicole's estate, filed a civil suit against his former son-in-law. Now three separate cases were active: Sharon's, ours, and the Browns'.

As we spent the weekend finalizing plans for a candlelight vigil to commemorate the first anniversary of Ron's death, a new issue began to preoccupy us. During the past year we had been astounded by the volume of mail that poured in. Only a few people knew our address, but thousands found creative ways to get mail to us. If a letter was sent to "The Goldman Family" in Los Angeles or Agoura or Westlake Village or even Brentwood, the post office managed to get it to us. All the letters contained messages of sympathy and support. Some people sent monetary contributions to help us with unforeseen expenses, and we appreciated them very much. The most poignant letters came from a legion of people who could sincerely empathize because they, too, had lost family members to senseless acts of brutality and evil. Our anguish was in the national consciousness, but every one of these other stories was just as painful and infuriating.

An idea flickered within us. Could we begin to direct our sorrow to some useful end? We did not know where this concept would take us, but it was comforting.

We expanded the concept of our candlelight vigil to honor the memory of other victims as well. Because Ron loved tennis so much, initially we thought we would conduct the service at the high school tennis courts, but we did not want candle wax to damage the playing surface. Patti contacted Dennis Anderson at the Rancho Simi Parks and Recreation Department, and he graciously allowed us use of the facilities at Oak Canyon Park. He even offered to supply park rangers and police to direct traffic.

The service was set for 8:30 P.M.

Monday, June 12, 1995.

Ron had been gone for one year. Who could believe it?

Dr. Lakshmanan was attending an international scientific conference, and court would not convene until the afternoon.

Judge Ito, seeking to maintain "some final shred of dignity" for Ron and Nicole, had barred journalists from viewing the autopsy photos but, under pressure, he relented. This morning forty-eight reporters filed into the empty courtroom, where eight large charts containing fifty-eight photographs were set up on easels. Judge Ito, in shirtsleeves, sat in the jury box with two prosecutors and a law clerk, observing.

No one spoke above a whisper.

Andrea Ford of the *Los Angeles Times* described what she saw as "ugly, powerfully violent images."

After a time, Dominick Dunne found a seat off by himself, and stared blankly toward the front of the room.

Twenty-eight minutes later a bailiff called out, "Time."

As the journalists filed out, a CNN reporter kept asking them, "Are you all right? Are you all right?"

Kim asked Dominick Dunne if he had seen the autopsy photos. He simply turned his head; he could not look at her.

* * *

That afternoon, Dr. Lakshmanan turned his attention to the one minute that took Ron from us.

Patti, Kim, and I sat as close together as we could, gripping each other for support. One of the prosecutors handed us tissues.

Close-up photos of Ron's head and face were displayed to the jury. One of the older jurors, a man, gagged and choked. He wiped his face with a handkerchief.

Dr. Lakshmanan told the jurors that Ron was stabbed and slashed to death, and that all of the wounds could have been caused by a single knife. Some of the wounds suggested that Ron put up a fight, but a variety of cuts to his throat, lung, and abdomen robbed him of blood pressure and vitality, rendering him helpless.

Two of the cuts appeared to have been made when the killer was holding Ron still, drawing the knife across his throat in a threatening manner. The coroner said, "You can see this type of injury when somebody is immobilized, and you are threatening to do bodily harm to them."

He added, "Without medical treatment . . . " Ron "would have died within five minutes."

I dropped my chin to my chest. Unstoppable tears streamed down my face.

A bailiff approached us, offering three small cups of water, which we accepted gratefully. Incredible, horrible phrases rebounded inside our heads: thirty wounds, five of them could have been fatal; Ron lay there, gasping for breath; he was found with one eye still open. Kim caught Marcia's attention and mouthed the words "I'm out of here."

Marcia, in turn, met Judge Ito's gaze and said the same thing to him. He nodded and we rushed from the room.

All we could do was pace the halls and cry. And cry. And cry.

No family should ever have to endure such a thing.

TWENTY

As twilight faded into night, carloads of people descended on Oak Canyon Park. Police allowed them to park on one side of the narrow, twisting entrance road, but soon the spillover extended onto Kanan Avenue. Hand in hand, families—many with small children—made their way to a secluded amphitheater in a natural dish sculpted into the surrounding hills. Before long, more than a thousand people had assembled. Everyone carried a candle. We were overwhelmed by the turnout.

Kim was the first to speak:

My name is Kimberly Goldman. My brother, my best friend, was brutally murdered one year ago tonight alongside his friend, Nicole Brown Simpson. My brother was only 25 years old, and just on his way to a happy, healthy, prosperous future when he was literally stopped dead in his tracks. He lost his life at the selfish and savage hands of another, a type of hate and rage that was never a part of Ron's life. He was a warm and caring soul, who would do anything for anyone, and the reality here is, he did. He died trying to help his friend.

Ron would tell me not to stand here and be angry, but to remember the good and happy memories, and to keep him alive in all of us. I would tell you that Ron had a zest for life that I was envious of. He had a glow about him that was amazing. He held his head high, all his days. He was beautiful, charming, loving, caring, dedicated, and he wanted nothing but the best for everyone he knew. I miss him so much. I need him and I want him back. I am holding Ron closest to my heart, and I know that anyone I will ever meet in my life will know Ron's life through me. He deserves the best now. I owe him that.

We come together tonight not only to remember Ron and Nicole but others who have lost their lives to violence. Let's extend that to anyone who knows the pain and sorrow of losing a loved one. Please take tonight to give those people the respect, the honor and the love that they deserve. . . .

We have been overwhelmed with the sense of community we have experienced, from people all over the country, strangers, people that have just extended themselves to us, shared their pain with us, and just wanted us to know they cared. Everybody gets really down on the world, and you think there is so much violence but I have come to learn that for every one violent and horrible person there are twenty thousand who are wonderful. That shows up in all of your faces and all of the tears you have shed. I am very honored to be a part of that and very proud to share it with all of you. My brother would be very happy.

Our friend Loren Lathrop sang Eric Clapton's "Tears in Heaven." The poignant words wafted softly through the park. Lauren dissolved into tears. She knew that Clapton had written the song as a tribute to his own lost son.

No one spoke when the sad strains of the song came to an end. Only sniffling sounds could be heard.

Rabbi King's closing words were:

Let us take the hands of our loved ones' souls, and together work to make this world a bit more just and a little safer. In this way, their light will fuse together with our own and shine beyond transient headlines to the very gates of eternity itself. Thank God for the lives of Ron and Nicole, and each of our beloved victims of violent crime. . . .

May their memories be a blessing for us, and for all humanity, and let us all say Amen.

Colleen Campbell, the former mayor of San Juan Capistrano, spoke as a representative of victims and their families everywhere. Her empathy was obvious. Her own son had been murdered when he was about the same age as Ron. The extended justice system took seven years to bring the killer to trial and, during the trial, Ms. Campbell's brother and sister-in-law were also murdered.

Then Dominick Dunne, who earlier in the day had sat dumbstruck in the quiet courtroom where Ron and Nicole's photos were on display, addressed the crowd:

> I am not here this evening as a journalist, I am here because, I, like Fred Goldman, am the father of a murdered child. I am here because I understand as one who has been through what they are currently going through, the pain, grief, and rage of the Goldman family.
>
> Six months ago, on the eve of this trial, Judge Lance Ito assigned me a seat in his courtroom next to the Goldman family. In the months that have followed, I have come to know Fred and Patti and Kim, whom I think of as the conscience of the trial. My admiration for this family has no bounds. Their devotion to each other is simply a beautiful thing to observe. They are that wonderful, old-fashioned, gone out of style word, they are a family.

Dunne was interrupted by heavy applause. Then he continued:

> I have loved watching the love that Fred and Patti feel for each other. I have loved watching the deep affection that exists between Patti and Kim and I have loved watching the loveliest kind of parental love, which is the love of a father and a daughter for each other.
>
> It is difficult to sit there in a courtroom and listen to graphic descriptions of your child's violent death. Yes, it is. Would it have been easier to skip the trial and go out of town until the whole thing was over? Yes, it would have been. But that is not what the Goldmans would ever have done. They are where

the jury can see the devastation that has been caused. They are attending to the last business of Ron Goldman's life. During this past week, horrifying photographs and equally horrifying descriptions and reenactments of the terrible crimes that happened a year ago tonight, they have remained throughout like the thoroughbreds they are. With Fred in the middle, with Patti on his left, with Kim on his right, clinging to each other, I feel honored that they have allowed me a place in their lives.

It has been thirteen years since my daughter's death. From the time the telephone call came, at five in the morning, to tell me the terrible news, my life and the lives of my former wife and our two sons were changed forever, as will the lives of the Goldman family be. I had never been to a trial until I attended the trial of the man who killed my daughter. My eyes were opened by the experience. I learned that the rights of victims do not equate with the lives of the defendant on trial. I learned that the victim becomes the forgotten person in the trial. I learned that days, sometimes weeks, go by and the victim's name is barely or rarely mentioned as attention shifts to the defendant on trial. My life took a new turn after the trial of the man who killed my daughter. I have rarely been out of a courtroom since. . . .

You will go to parties. You will go to the movies, but what has happened is always there. A part of everyday life. But now, when I think of my Dominique, my lovely daughter, I no longer dwell on her dreadful death. I think of her beautiful life and the good times that we had. And that is going to happen to you. The time will come that when you think of Ron, you will hear his laughter.

Several of our friends and friends of Ron spoke, sharing their memories. And then, as the darkness of night enveloped us, it was my turn. Glancing toward Kim, I began:

Kim's a tough act to follow. I have been truly blessed. I had a great deal to be proud of, and I still do. I had a wonderful son who lived life to its fullest, who cared about other human beings, who cared about his family, who cared about everyone he came in touch with.

I have a daughter who blows me away. I don't know where she gets it. She is so incredibly special. I know Ron is as proud of her today as he was yesterday, and will be tomorrow.

I have been blessed with this lady in my life [looking at Patti] who, with Michael and Lauren and Kim and Brian, have made this year almost bearable and without them, I can't imagine doing it. And I have been blessed to have friends who are unbelievably warm and gracious and kind and sensitive, and we owe them an enormous debt.

Colleen mentioned to me the other night that 26,000 or more people are dying every year by violence. Their faces, their names, their voices are never heard. We have a chance to speak because of the person who took my son and Nicole away, because of his notoriety, and it is for all those faceless people that most of us don't know that we light these candles ultimately tonight, so that perhaps people across this nation will see all of you wonderful people, and kind human beings that are in fact a majority of our world, and hopefully, all of us together will send a message that we will no longer tolerate crime and violence, and we will no longer tolerate this ravage in our society, and this taking away of brothers and sisters and mothers and daughters. Thank you all, from the bottom of my heart, for being here in these enormous numbers. It is amazing to me.

You owe yourselves an enormous amount of thanks. You are who this world is all about—not those vicious and violent human beings who prey on us.

As Loren began to play "Dust in the Wind," cigarette lighters snapped and matches scratched. Flames flickered. Within minutes the faces of a thousand respectful, thoughtful, wonderful fathers, mothers, brothers, sisters, sons, and daughters radiated with a brilliance that dispelled the darkness that surrounded us all.

TWENTY-ONE

It was the dawning of a new era, when we began to realize to a far greater degree than before how much support and friendship and plain old human love was out there. Yes, the evil remained, but the good was fighting back.

This was symbolized for us as the crowd at the candlelight vigil began to disperse.

Kim stepped off the sandy platform of the amphitheater onto the grass. Suddenly she heard someone yell, "Kim, Kim!" She turned and looked up—way up—into the kind, smiling, ebony-hued face of a giant. He stood six feet five inches tall, and weighed about three hundred pounds. I am a six-footer, and I know Kim thinks of me as a big man, but to her I was diminutive next to this great big teddy bear of a person. He gave Kim a hug that swept her off her feet and into the air.

He introduced himself as Rosey Brown. He was a police officer in Inglewood who moonlighted as an actor. In addition to his size and his incredibly infectious, toothy grin, we were drawn to him by his baseball cap with big, shiny, orange letters that proclaimed: O. J.'s GUILTY.

Someone commented, "Nice cap."

He smiled from ear to ear and said, "I always say if anyone has a problem with my hat, they can just come on over and try to take it off."

Rosey said that he wanted to meet us and let us know that he supported us. Left unsaid was the notion that not all big, black "tough guy" types condone those who beat their wives—and worse.

Michael's eyes widened at the sight of the man, and he thought: I'm sure glad he's on our side!

*   *   *

And yet the horror continued. The day after the vigil we endured additional graphic testimony from Dr. Lakshmanan. In meticulous detail he described a stab wound to Ron's chest that went through one rib, punctured his right lung, and struck another rib. The coroner said, "You can expect death in a very short time after the injury."

That comment knocked the wind out of me, and one of the younger women jurors had to rush from the courtroom. Judge Ito called for a break.

As I tried to compose myself, the killer shared a few words with his lawyers. When they laughed out loud, Kim tried to stare them down.

Kim asked Mark Arenas, our Victim-Witness Assistance advocate, if she would be allowed to swear during her victim's statement after the killer was found guilty. "Low-life scumbag just doesn't cover it," she pointed out. Mark had assured her that she could say whatever she wished, and no one would wash her mouth out with soap.

Directly in front of Kim, Jonathan Fairtlough, who was in charge of all the prosecution's visual aids, flipped through an album. Kim suddenly caught a brief glimpse of one of the autopsy photos. She gasped, covered her mouth, and dropped her head.

Seeing Kim's discomfort, Phil Vannatter reached over the railing and held her hand.

She was thankful that her vision is so poor.

Both Patti and I had other commitments that made it impossible for us to attend court on June 15. And Mark had to attend a meeting, so Kim was there alone.

The witness was Richard Rubin, former vice president and general manager of Aris, the company that manufactures Isotoner gloves. Chris Darden asked him if a pair of extra-large gloves would fit the defendant's hands. Rubin responded, "At one point in time, those gloves would actually be large, I think, on Mr. Simpson's hand."

When Chris asked for permission to have the killer try on a new pair of extra-large Aris Isotoner gloves, Judge Ito called for a sidebar. During this conference it was the judge himself who suggested "it would be more appropriate" for the defendant to try on the actual gloves in evidence.

Marcia objected, noting that the defendant would have to wear latex surgical gloves underneath, so as not to contaminate the evidence. "They're going to alter the fit," she contended.

But Judge Ito ruled that the demonstration could proceed.

Kim thought that she was going to throw up. The railing that separated the spectators from the courtroom was about three feet high. She hung her arms over it and stared at Judge Ito. He stared back at her. Tears trickled down her cheeks and she hissed in a stage whisper, loud enough for those close by to hear, "He's going to lie. He's going to fake it."

The courtroom grew eerily silent. The killer rose from his chair and sauntered toward the jury. He carefully picked up the pair of cashmere-lined leather gloves and made a show of trying to push his latex-covered hand into one of the shrunken and wrinkled gloves. His lips pouted. He raised his eyebrows.

Kim could see that he was bending his fingers. "He's not putting his hand all the way through," she cried.

The killer raised his hands and displayed them to the jury. He flexed his fingers to show how uncomfortable he was. He shoved his hands in Marcia's face. He turned back to the jury and muttered, "Too tight."

"He's waived his right! He's talking to the jury," Kim said.

As the killer returned to the defense table, he and his lawyers shared their smirking expressions with one another in full view of the jury. Winks and nods abounded. Cochran patted him on the back with an "atta boy, good job" look on his face. The killer leaned back in his chair, looking self-satisfied. He ripped off the latex gloves and tossed them idly onto the table.

Chris tried to counter the murderer's two-bit acting job by eliciting testimony from Rubin that the latex surgical gloves might have made the Isotoners fit snugly, but the damage was done.

Frustration and anger enshrouded Kim. Within a five-minute period, she felt as if ten pounds had dropped from her body.

She called Patti and me as soon as she could. Both of us had been listening to radio reports, but neither of us had seen the absurd piece of theater that the killer had staged.

When Michael watched the seemingly endless press coverage, he could not understand why everyone was making such a big deal about the killer's performance with the gloves. For one thing, he had worn latex gloves underneath. It was obvious that he was faking. "The gloves fit," Michael said. "You stick out his hand and let me shove that glove on it and I guarantee you it will fit!"

FBI expert William J. Bodziak described an international hunt to identify the source of the trail of bloody shoe prints leading away from the murder scene. The prints, found along the walkway where the bodies were discovered, indicated that the killer had turned back at one point. A heel print on the back of Nicole's dress suggested that the killer had his foot on her when she was lying on the ground. This corresponded with previous testimony that the murderer stood over Nicole, pulled her hair, and raised her throat to deliver the final blow.

The pattern on the soles of the shoes was a rare one. Investigators finally matched them to an expensive, Italian-made brand known as Bruno Magli. The defendant could easily have afforded the $160 price tag.

The shoes were European size 46, which corresponds to size 12 in the United States. The defendant wears size 12 shoes.

It was all circumstantial evidence, for Bodziak had no way of knowing if the defendant actually owned a pair of size 12 Bruno Magli shoes. Bodziak told the court that only 299 pairs of the shoes had ever been distributed in the United States, but investigators had been unable to find a store or clerk who remembered selling such a pair to the defendant.

On cross-examination, F. Lee Bailey pooh-poohed the testimony, intimating that it shed little light on the case.

None of us, in fact, had any way of knowing how those bloody shoe prints might come back to haunt the killer.

California State Department of Justice analyst Gary Sims returned to the stand to present additional DNA results. He told the jury that only one person out of fifty-seven billion could have been the source of two particular bloodstains. Only one person out of fifty-seven billion could have left the blood found on a gate near the crime scene. Only one person out of fifty-seven billion could have left the blood on the socks found in the defendant's bedroom, the same ones that also contained stains from Nicole's blood.

That one person who matched the DNA pattern was seated on the left side of the courtroom, surrounded by his defense attorneys.

He was, indeed, special. He was one person out of fifty-seven billion!

July 2 was Ron's twenty-seventh birthday.

Michael and Lauren left for Chicago to visit their dad. We could tell that they were a bit upset. Of all the days that they could fly to Chicago, why did it have to be this one?

Patti, Kim, and I went to the cemetery. We sat next to the headstone, tears streaming down our cheeks. For quite some time, we were silent.

Then I said, "I never know quite what to say when I'm here. What should I say to Ron? There is so much to say. Will he be able to hear me?"

Patti had no answers. Silently, she asked herself: If he knows what we are thinking, feeling, going through, fighting for, does he feel all of our pain as we constantly feel his?

Despite Judge Ito's comment "I would like to finish this case sometime this lifetime," the two sides continued to wrangle, and wasted yet another week in contentious proceedings, often outside the presence of the jury, concerning the hair and fiber evidence. Finally FBI Special Agent Doug Deedrick, head of the hair and fiber unit of the Bureau's famed crime lab, was able to testify.

Deedrick declared that the blue knit cap found near Ron's feet bore numerous hairs that "exhibit the same microscopic characteristics" as the defendant's hair. Another hair resembling the defendant's was found on Ron's shirt. Thirty-five hair samples resembling Nicole's hair were found on Ron's clothing. A twelve-inch hair resembling Nicole's was found on the bloody glove discovered at the defendant's Rockingham estate. When Marcia asked whether the hair had been "naturally shed or forcibly removed," Deedrick replied that it was "cut and torn."

Fibers resembling those of Ron's shirt were found on both gloves—one at the crime scene and one at the defendant's home.

Reddish-beige carpet fibers resembling those from the defendant's 1994 Ford Bronco were found at the crime scene and on the Rockingham glove. Deedrick noted that these could not have come from A. C. Cowlings's similar Bronco, which has blue carpeting. But Judge Ito ruled that the prosecution had been late in apprising the defense that these very unusual fibers could only have come from Ford Broncos built in 1993 or 1994, and he barred Deedrick from making this critical point. Patti thought: This is crucial evidence, one more direct tie-in with the killer. Instead of allowing it, the judge slapped us in the face.

On July 6, after calling fifty-eight witnesses, Marcia declared, "The people rest."

At a news conference, Gil Garcetti praised the job done by his team in presenting a "giant mountain of evidence." He predicted that after the defense presented a perfunctory case, "the arrow is still going to point to only one person."

Over the phone Michael told us that the prosecution had done a great job. "I don't see how the defense can counter any of it," he said.

At dinner Patti was nervous and scared. "It's now time for the defense bullshit," she warned. "There will be plenty of it flying everywhere. There's going to be a lot of smooth talking and slithering movements across that courtroom, and lots of diversions from the hard evidence. They will point blame at anyone and everyone they can come up with. And there will be a slew of racial implications."

TWENTY-TWO

It was family day in court. For the first day of its presentation, the defense would call the defendant's daughter Arnelle, his sister, Carmelita Simpson-Durio, and his mother, Eunice. All three arrived in court dressed in pale yellow.

Johnnie Cochran lost no time in reminding the jury of the defendant's glorious football past, eliciting a response from Arnelle that she "was born the same day my dad won the Heisman Trophy." She recalled that Nicole had been ill—sometime around Mother's Day of 1994—and her father "went over to her house one day to help . . . with the kids and to bring her some soup and medicine."

Arnelle said there was "an ongoing joke within the family" that her father would never prepare for a trip ahead of time. He always hurried around at the last moment.

On the day after the murders, she described her father as "very upset, emotional, confused." That evening he sat on a couch, next to his mother, muttering about the television coverage. "He was numb," she said.

Throughout her testimony, Arnelle frequently locked eyes with her father, who listened with a wide smile on his face.

Carmelita Simpson-Durio echoed this testimony, characterizing her brother as "shocked and dazed" that night.

Finally Carl Douglas helped the ailing Eunice Simpson into the witness chair. She spent only about twenty minutes on the stand, telling the jury how she treated her son's childhood rickets with "tender loving care," detailing the family history of arthritis, and describing her son's behavior on the night following the murders.

When the prosecutors decided not to cross-examine the defendant's mother, Douglas helped her back to her seat. Cochran brought her a cup of water.

In contrast to the plodding pace of the prosecution, the defense sped through numerous early witnesses in their own hectic version of a "rush to judgment." The prosecution argued that the murders occurred about 10:15 or 10:20 P.M. But the defense produced various Brentwood residents who claimed that they heard no barking or wailing dog until after 10:30 P.M. One by one Marcia and Chris wore them down during cross-examination, getting them to admit that they had not really paid attention to the time or had originally told police a different story. One witness was forced to admit that he wanted to peddle his story to a tabloid magazine or talk show.

Robert Heidstra's testimony backfired on the defense. He claimed that he had heard two men arguing that night, near the scene of the crime. One man exclaimed, "Hey, hey, hey!" The other responded, but his words were drowned out by two dogs barking loudly.

When Michael heard this, he knew that it was Ron shouting, "Hey, hey, hey!" It was Ron, trying to save Nicole's life. That was in his character. He stood a little over 6 feet tall and weighed 171 pounds, but he did not hesitate to take on a former pro football player. "Ron was definitely a hero," Michael said. "He is my hero."

Patti agreed. "Ron was not a fighter and he was not a confrontational person, but he would not have shied away from someone in trouble."

Heidstra originally said that he heard the shouts about 10:30 P.M., but under cross-examination, admitted that he had not looked at his watch, and thus could not be sure of the time. Then Chris drew out a damaging admission. The witness testified that he had seen a white sport utility vehicle fleeing the area. He described it as a Jeep or a Chevrolet Blazer, but he conceded that it could have been a Ford Bronco.

Here was curious testimony. Jim Merrill is an employee of the Hertz Corporation. Before dawn on June 13, 1994, he met his company's famous spokesman at Chicago's O'Hare International Airport as his red-eye flight came in from Los Angeles. He described the defendant as relaxed and cordial. Merrill took the defendant's golf clubs, in preparation for the scheduled match.

A few hours later the defendant called Merrill to inform him that he had to return to Los Angeles immediately and that he wanted his golf clubs back. His voice was "cracking," Merrill said. "It sounded like he was crying." Merrill raced to O'Hare in an attempt to return the clubs. But he missed the defendant's departure, and sent the clubs back to Los Angeles on a later flight.

Carl Douglas asked Merrill if he subsequently spoke to the defendant about his clubs.

"Yes," Merrill replied.

"What day was that?"

"That was the following day. Tuesday."

Douglas asked, "Did you call him, or did he call you?"

"He called me," Merrill answered.

Golf clubs? We wondered what kind of man is worried about his golf clubs when his ex-wife has just been butchered? Is he that obsessed with the stupid game? Or was there something about the golf bag and its contents that was of deep concern?

The defense brought Dr. Robert Huizenga to the stand. In the week following the murders, Robert Shapiro had hired Dr. Huizenga to examine his client twice, and to evaluate his "mental status." The doctor, a former team physician of the Los Angeles Raiders, testified that the defendant "looked like Tarzan" but walked like "Tarzan's grandfather," and suffered from a host of football injuries that limited the movement of his knees, ankles, elbows, wrists, and hands. However, the doctor's examination revealed "no evidence of bruises, scrapes, or other injuries" that could have resulted from a struggle. The doctor said that the cuts on the defendant's left hand "appeared" to have been caused by broken glass, but could have been caused by a knife.

On cross-examination Brian Kelberg focused on the key point. He forced Dr. Huizenga to admit that the defendant "certainly could hold a knife." At another point Brian asked if the doctor had discovered anything during his examination that would have prevented the defendant "from murdering two human beings on June 12."

"No," the doctor replied.

When Brian turned his attention to the defendant's mental status during that fateful week, Dr. Huizenga waxed poetic. "The tack I took," he said, "was to address his mental status problems and his insomnia and his difficulty handling this incredible, incredible stress that maybe no other human being short of Job has endured."

Excuse me, Patti thought. You want to talk about stress?

Kim could only mutter, "Waah, give him a tissue."

Brian's voice grew hard. He asked, "If he had murdered two human beings, Nicole Brown Simpson and her friend Ronald Goldman, would that be the kind of thing that would cause a great weight to be on a man's shoulders?"

After Judge Ito overruled Robert Shapiro's objection, Doctor Huizenga replied, "If someone hypothetically killed someone, they certainly would have a great weight on their shoulders."

Brian produced evidence that "someone" literally killed "someone." When he showed the doctor the autopsy photos of Ron, Dr. Huizenga appeared rattled. He had to take a few deep breaths before he could continue. Brian asked him, if Ron had suffered hand injuries while backing away, could that explain why the defendant's body showed no evidence of a struggle.

"Yes," the suddenly subdued doctor answered.

Brian presented the now-famous exercise video that the defendant had recorded about three weeks prior to the murders. It seemed to produce a mixed reaction in the courtroom. We saw a man dancing across the screen, flashing his phony smile, demonstrating aerobic exercises with apparent ease. Others saw a man having difficulty with his knees. The defendant himself laughed and chuckled and pointed to his own image on the screen.

We were not laughing when the tape picked up the killer's sick attempt at humor. As he was shadowboxing, jabbing with his fists, he quipped, "I'm telling you, you just gotta get your space in if you're working out with the wife, if you know what I mean. You could always blame it on working out."

Two horrible events reminded us once again that life is fragile.

Reporter Robin Clark was covering the trial for *The Philadelphia Inquirer*. His colleagues regarded him as a fantastic wordsmith. On those rare occasions when Dominick Dunne could not attend the trial, Robin would take his seat. A genuinely nice guy, he was usually attired in blue jeans and a sport jacket. He was always pleasant to us, and, like Dominick, he seemed to be in our corner.

Robin's cousin Nicole Weaver and her friend Melissa Penn were visiting L.A., and on Friday, August 4, Robin decided to take them for a drive along the Pacific Coast Highway. They were in the Santa Monica area when Robin's Volkswagen van collided with a Volvo, and all three were killed. We were very saddened when we heard about the accident.

Judge Ito recessed the proceedings in Robin's memory, saying, "He was liked and admired and, most importantly, respected by his colleagues. I think that's the highest tribute that anybody can pay in the journalism profession."

And then on Sunday, Dominick Dunne's son Alex was reported missing. Thirty-eight-year-old Alex Dunne was from San Francisco, but he was visiting his ailing mother at her home in Nogales, Arizona. On Saturday morning he borrowed his mother's beige 1980 Toyota Corolla station wagon and drove to a rugged area along the Mexican border to go hiking or bicycle riding in the Santa Rita Mountains. He had not been seen since. On Monday Dominick caught a plane and headed for Arizona to help in the search.

In court Judge Ito kept Robin Clark's seat empty, and a deputy hung his press pass on the back of the seat.

We ached for both families.

Throughout the trial, Dominick, especially, had been a wonderful stabilizing force for us. Every morning he had a sincere smile on his face and would give us a warm "Hello." He was always concerned that we were doing okay. He gave us advance copies of his *Vanity Fair* articles, which we read with rapt attention because he often came up with new pieces of information that invariably turned out to be true. Because he had lost his own daughter to a murderer, we knew that if he lost his son, too, he would be completely destroyed.

We called him several times in Arizona to offer our moral support. There did not seem to be any indication of foul play, but Dominick worried about sunstroke, snake bite, or worse.

On Wednesday Dominick, peering down from a private plane, spotted the car parked near the head of a trail on rugged Madera Canyon in the Coronado National Forest, forty-five miles south of Tucson. Search crews began to concentrate on the area.

On Thursday evening, dehydrated and exhausted, Alex Dunne walked out of the forest and encountered a Nogales police officer who was guarding the station wagon. He explained that a weak ankle had buckled on him and a nasty twenty-five-foot fall had caused a previous back problem to flare up so that he could barely move. Sometime during the past several days he had heard searchers calling for him, but his throat was so parched he could not answer loud enough to be heard. It was an afternoon rain on Thursday that had revived him enough to rise and endure a four-and-a-half-hour trek down the mountain. He was taken to a hospital for observation and X rays on his ankle.

The next day, as he was interviewed by reporters, he acknowledged that his—and his family's—ordeal would undoubtedly be chronicled in his father's book about the Goldman-Brown murders. "I'm now one of the subplots," he quipped.

Of course, we were very relieved for Dominick, and looked forward to seeing him back in court.

The defense continued its case with a series of witnesses designed to bolster their absurd theory that virtually the entire law-enforcement community of Los Angeles was attempting to frame the killer. During direct testimony, each witness seemed to add tidbits to the theory, but the prosecutors did a wonderful job of tearing them down on cross-examination, frequently drawing out bits of damaging testimony.

Phil Vannatter commented publicly, "The police conspiracy theory is the stupidest thing I've ever heard in my life."

As the case plodded on, Judge Ito and the attorneys from both sides grew increasingly short-tempered. In our view, it was the judge's own fault. He had lost control of the courtroom from the very first day, and he seemed clueless how to regain any judicial muscle.

Meanwhile, on the other side of the United States, developments were taking place that would—in some people's minds—render meaningless the weeks and months of technical testimony. These would set the trial completely off course, hand the defense a dubious trump card, and ignite our family's indignation to the point of explosion. Early on, Robert Shapiro had promised that the defense would not play the race card, but when Johnnie Cochran took over, race became one of the key issues.

The defense had discovered that, starting ten years earlier, North Carolina screenwriting professor Laura Hart McKinny had conducted a series of interviews with Detective Mark Fuhrman as part of research she was doing for a screenplay. It was reported that, on the tapes, Fuhrman used the N-word and made other potentially inflammatory comments, contradicting his previously sworn testimony.

Johnnie Cochran fought hard to bring McKinny to California to introduce the tapes into evidence. A judge in Winston-Salem, North Carolina, had ruled against a subpoena, but an appellate court now overruled that decision. Cochran called it the most important ruling of the case. Barry Scheck commented cryptically: "Huge, huge. It could be the case."

The critical factor was that, under California law, the judge instructs the jurors that if they conclude that a witness lied about one fact, they may then decide that he or she has lied about other facts as well. Fuhrman had testified that he had not used the N-word in the past ten years; he also testified that he found a key piece of evidence—the bloody glove—on the grounds of the Brentwood estate. If the tapes revealed that Fuhrman had lied about the N-word then, theoretically, the jury could conclude that he lied about when and where he found the bloody glove. It was a patently ridiculous attempt to connect two unrelated issues, but it played right into the hands of the defense's attempt to convince the jury that the killer was framed by racially biased police officers. Cochran was, indeed, ready to play the race card and move the trial as far as possible from a search for the truth.

Judge Ito had already ruled that McKinny was required to give the defense her material, but he had not yet ruled that the jury should hear the tapes. That would depend on whether prosecutors opposed the admission of the tapes and if so, whether the emotional effect of playing them would, in Ito's judgment, substantially outweigh the value they might have in raising questions about Fuhrman's testimony.

Cochran argued: "In a search for truth, these tapes are imperative. . . . I'm absolutely shocked that the prosecution did not join in our attempt to obtain them, but now the whole world is going to know the truth."

Chris Darden stated that the prosecutors had not yet heard the tapes and had not yet decided whether to fight their admission.

Fuhrman's attorney, Bob Tourtelot, tried to put the best spin on the situation: "This ruling does not mean that the tapes or the witness will be heard by the jury. That will be up to Judge Ito. To allow these tapes to be heard by the jury would not be material and would be highly prejudicial to the prosecution's case."

No one on the prosecution team spoke with us about this, and we watched in frustration from the sidelines. Patti wanted to scream, "What does *race* have to do with this case?"

Judge Ito muttered, "Just when you thought we couldn't have anything crazier happen." It was Tuesday, August 15.

As the prosecution and defense wrangled over whether what was now known as the "Fuhrman tapes" should be played for the jury, we learned that those tapes contained some disparaging references to Captain Margaret York, the highest-ranking woman in the LAPD. She also happened to be Judge Ito's wife.

The prosecution team now argued that Judge Ito should remove himself from the case.

The defense team vowed to fight that, unless it would result in freedom for its client.

Judge Ito took an extended lunch break to consider the options. When court reconvened, the mood was somber. Both sides presented short arguments detailing their position.

Then Judge Ito issued his ruling. His voice broke with emotion when he said, "I love my wife dearly, and I am wounded by criticism of her—" He scratched at a doodle pad, then continued. "—as any spouse would be." Again he paused. Then he proclaimed, "I think it is reasonable to assume that could have some impact." He concluded that another judge should decide whether his wife should be called as a material witness. If so, the judge would have to be replaced.

Suddenly everyone scrambled upstairs. Reporters and spectators pushed and shoved. Elbows flew about and curse words were hurled indiscriminately. Patti and Kim had the luxury of an escort to the courtroom of Superior Court Judge James Basque, presiding judge of the county criminal courts. Judge Basque quickly assigned the case to Superior Court Judge John H. Reid, and the mad dash was on to yet another courtroom.

Judge Reid made it clear that he would not allow Cochran to take control of his courtroom. With dispatch, he announced that he would receive the tapes that afternoon and begin to review them. He would meet with the lawyers on Friday. Just like that, the hearing was over, and everyone returned to Judge Ito's courtroom. We were sure that Cochran was delighted to return to the environment that he controlled.

The "Scheme Team" gloated on the courthouse steps after the day's turbulent session. They accused the prosecution of an unethical and cynical attempt to remove Judge Ito from the case because they knew that they were losing and were desperate to regain momentum. Cochran said, "Today, the wheels came off the wagon of their case. And all America saw it."

Marcia had her own view. "The defense has brought this to a head," she said. "They have played the race card. . . . They have opened Pandora's box."

In other words, all hell was about to break loose.

The three of us, Patti, Kim, and I, were all in court the following day. Everyone's nerves were stretched to the limit. We spent the morning listening to the lawyers wrangle. Marcia backed off from her suggestion that Judge Ito should remove himself from the case. Thus, Judge Reid did not have to make a ruling.

But Shapiro would not let the issue drop. He accused Marcia and her colleagues of resorting to "prosecutorial extortion" in an attempt to pay back Judge Ito for unfavorable rulings.

Then it was Chris's turn to throw a tantrum. Refusing to speak from the same podium that Shapiro used, he raged at the defense team for turning the trial into an extended, ludicrous joke.

Amid all the wrangling, the issue of the Fuhrman tapes smoldered. Would Judge Ito allow them into evidence? Would he surrender to the assault and allow Cochran and Company to turn a straightforward double-murder trial into a referendum on racial issues?

Watching all this, hearing all this, we felt a fire burning inside. Did anyone here—anyone at all—remember the names Ron and Nicole?

When we went upstairs to the seventeenth floor for the lunch break, Mark Arenas said that one of the reporters wanted to know if we were going to say anything. At first I said no, but the more I thought about it, the more agitated I became and the more I realized that *it was time* to do so. Patti tried desperately to dissuade me, but I knew that if I did not speak out, I would explode. I do not believe I have ever been so angry in my life. I could not let them get away with it.

It never made Kim feel good to vent frustrations to the press, because it did not change anything and it did not make any difference. But we had been pushed, prodded, and tested for months. Both Kim and I felt that if we remained quiet now, it might appear that we were not offended by what was going on. From Day One of this trial, Judge Ito should have put a gag order on everyone. But he had not, and we were tired of seeing the self-righteous members of the defense team pontificating on talk shows.

"Mark," I said, "let the press know we're going to speak."

Things happened very quickly. Reporters, many holding walkie-talkies, started running, pushing one another out of the way. Pens flew out of pockets, and there was a general stampede to the courthouse steps.

You could see the fear and the worry on Patti's face. She was terrified that I would have a heart attack or stroke, and she begged me to calm down but knew there was no way she could stop me.

Her fears for my health were compounded by other issues. She worried about the safety of the entire family. Images of riots, burnings, and beatings flew through her head like snapshots. If I spoke out, would it just fuel the flames of hatred that the defense team had ignited?

With her heart racing, Kim spoke through her tears: "We usually don't speak just for the sake of speaking, so obviously something has to happen for us to feel enraged enough to get out there and talk. So excuse me if I ramble, but—I'm fed up."

Waving a hand above her head, she said, "My emotions are up to here. Over and above the loss of my brother I have all this other crap to deal with. These last few days have pushed me to the edge. I have never been more offended by the actions on behalf of the defense. . . .

"Shapiro . . . said that he would never play the race card in this case. Call it whatever you want, race card, perjury card—I don't care what you call it—the issue is still the same. The attorneys are trying to divert the attention from the facts in this case, and the fact is their client is accused of murdering my brother and Nicole Brown, and the evidence against him is overwhelming. They have no other choice but to play the race card, the perjury card. This is called the Fuhrman trial now, and this is ridiculous. They don't have a defense. They don't have any evidence to disprove what the prosecution has so far. The only defense now is to blame it on somebody else, and to be able to say the N-word in open court.

"Cochran said, back in jury selection, that all he needed was one black on this case. How offensive to the human race. To not give them the benefit of the doubt that they would be able to try this case according to the facts and according to the evidence and not have to put in the crap of the racial bias. That's insulting to people's intelligence. I don't care what color you are, what race you are, what religion you practice, that's insulting. They don't think that they could just be able to try this case according to the facts and according to the evidence? I don't even think there is a word to describe what that does to me.

"And to stand up there and say how unethical the prosecution is. Excuse me. When has the prosecution stood out here and slammed the defense and all of their tactics? How ethical, how moral is that? The defense has been doing that from Day One in this case. Chris said it this morning. This is a circus. They created a circus atmosphere.

"And I am sick, sick to my stomach. Okay? And this is embarrassing. This is embarrassing to the judicial system. I've never been a part of this before. This is repulsive to me. . . .

"Try your case according to the evidence, okay? You don't have to bring in all this other crap. You don't have to say that everybody is a racist, and everybody is a liar. If your client is so innocent, the evidence should prove that. You shouldn't have to pull in all this other baloney."

Kim turned away, sobbing.

Now it was my turn. It was difficult to talk because I could not catch my breath. My heart raced and my palms were cold and wet.

I began: "Needless to say, Kim and each of our family is angered, upset. What is so incredibly outrageous is that from Day One, *Day One!*, we all remember Mr. Shapiro making the comment that race would not be an issue in this trial. They have wanted to introduce other issues into this trial from Day One. They have been doing it in bits and pieces, and what is horrendously unfortunate is that one of the witnesses in this case may have said some rather disturbing things. That's not what this trial is about. There is not one *scintilla* of proof that has come from the defense, not one *iota* of evidence from the defense to indicate that there has been planting of evidence or conspiracy. But they have been playing that bull from Day One.

"They now see an opportunity to enrage everyone. Do you honestly believe what their interests are is to prove perjury? Are we all *fools*? Do they take us all for *morons*? We all know what they want is to inflame the emotions of the jury, and to inflame . . . the public's mind with issues that don't relate to this trial."

All the color had drained from Patti's face. Her eyes begged me to stop. She placed a comforting arm on my shoulder, but I shrugged it off.

My voice cracked as I continued. "Ron and Nicole were *butchered* by their client. Do any of you believe otherwise? You have seen the evidence in this trial. It is overwhelming. This is *not* now the Fuhrman trial. This is a trial about the man that murdered my son."

By now, Patti was crying, pulling on me, whispering, "Let's go, let's go," but I would not leave. I could not leave. I had to get it out.

I could see nothing through my tears, but I raged, "How *dare* they take the position that all they want to do is prove perjury? They are *liars!*"

When Michael walked into work at the Oak Tree Deli, the television was on, as usual.

This day the room was strangely quiet. Scott, Michael's boss, beckoned Michael over to him and said, "Fred is speaking." Michael looked up and saw my face filling the screen; Patti and Kim were in the background. Whoa, what's going on? Michael wondered.

He said later, "When it was over, I walked around the room and heard customers commenting on what an amazing man Fred Goldman was. They were all so impressed with his courage and his passion. It felt good to hear all the positive reactions in the room. It filled me with pride. Fred and Kim have done such a remarkable job of keeping Ron's memory alive. It's nice to hear that other people admire them as much as I do."

That evening, the adrenaline still pumped through all of us but we were exhausted. Patti's eyes looked like a deer's caught in the headlights of an oncoming car. "Do you realize," she said, "that we will never, ever, be able to leave our home again without being recognized, approached, and looked at like we are some kind of bugs under a microscope? I want my life back."

Someone from LAPD reported that a gang member had threatened, "We've got to shut that Goldman up." Local police were notified and our house was put under twenty-four-hour surveillance. Fortunately, nothing happened.

All the next day D.A. investigators stayed especially close. They told us not to smile at them, so that they could remain inconspicuous.

Patti and Kim were very shaken. They cautioned me to keep quiet in the future, but I refused to be intimidated. I grumbled, "I'm not about to roll over for that kind of trash."

Despite the fiery rage that I had exhibited in front of the cameras, I had still mentally edited my words. I had not allowed myself the freedom to scream the obscenities that were begging to come out. My choice was to try and stay in control and maintain civility at a time when nothing seemed civil.

In truth, there are probably no expletives strong enough to describe how I view the killer and his swarm of morally decayed attorneys.

TWENTY-THREE

～

Judge Ito warned the jury that there would be "substantial dark time" as the court grappled with difficult issues. But some testimony was heard, in and around the contentious hearings concerning the relevancy of the Fuhrman tapes.

The most significant of these defense witnesses was the celebrated criminalist Henry Lee, director of the Connecticut State Forensics Science Laboratory, who was touted as perhaps the nation's premier guru on the analysis of physical evidence. His testimony covered several days. Lee began with a recitation of his background, numerous awards, and expertise. Although Lee said he almost always testifies for prosecutors, he seemed to enjoy an easy rapport with defense lawyer Barry Scheck. Scheck made one gaffe when he described one of Lee's awards for his work as a "distinguished criminal."

Lee smiled and corrected, "Distinguished criminalist."

In fact, he appeared to be just that. And, although much of his testimony seemed to raise questions about the evidence gathering and testing procedures, he was very careful to couch his conclusions with qualifying words, such as "could have" or "might have."

He criticized LAPD criminalists for placing one of Ron's blood-smeared boots into a brown paper bag while the blood was still wet, declaring that such careless handling could cause "cross-contamination" of blood samples. And, indeed, DNA tests had disclosed that one of those stains was consistent with a mixture of Ron's blood and that of the defendant. Lee did not explain how that could have happened if the defendant was home chipping golf balls, or taking a nap, or in the shower.

Scheck turned Lee's attention to a single drop of evidence, a blood-stain found on a walkway outside Nicole's condominium. DNA tests had pegged the defendant as the likely source of the Bundy blood drops, but Scheck suggested that LAPD investigators had tampered with the blood swatches before sending them to labs for testing. Lee testified that his close examination of four small patches of blood showed that some had leaked onto the paper packet wrapped around the evidence. The blood swatches could have leaked onto the paper only if they were pack-aged while wet, he said, yet LAPD technicians had testified that they left the swatches to dry overnight.

Scheck wanted to know how Lee accounted for the stains on the packaging.

"The only explanation I can give under these circumstances is, something's wrong," Lee answered.

Patti's assessment of Dr. Lee echoed mine. "This guy certainly has a high opinion of himself," she said.

Hank Goldberg was brilliant on cross-examination. He got Lee to acknowledge that evidence handling was a less-than-perfect science that did not necessarily reflect a grand, department-wide conspiracy. Lee admitted that during the early years of his work, he and his analysts occasionally used paper towels to dry samples, rather than special blot-ters. Once, he said, when he was drying a scrap of evidence in his back-yard, a dog ran off with it.

"And despite these kinds of problems," Hank asked, "would it be fair to say that you and your laboratory people . . . have still been doing very high-quality work?"

"We try our best," Lee responded.

The prosecutors had argued passionately that the Mark Fuhrman/Laura McKinny tapes should not be played in open court; to do so would only inflame the jury and serve no other purpose. They acknowledged that Fuhrman had lied when he denied under oath that he had used the racial slur during the past ten years, but they still fiercely contended that there was no evidence that the detective could have planted evidence. Without such evidence, the tapes were irrelevant.

However, Judge Ito's initial ruling favored the defense. He would allow the tapes to be played in court, outside the presence of the jury, before he determined what was admissible.

On August 29, the voice of Mark Fuhrman filled the silent courtroom. "You've got two hundred niggers who are trying to take you prisoner," he said in one interview with the screenwriter ten years earlier. "You just chase this guy, and you beat the shit out of him." In another excerpt, McKinny asked whether he had probable cause to arrest black suspects.

"Probable cause?" Fuhrman responded. "You're God."

In other tapes Fuhrman boasted of fabricating evidence and expressed amazement about the racial makeup of the LAPD's Wilshire Division. "All niggers," he said, "nigger training officers, niggers."

The sickening epithets bounced off the walls, reverberating with hatred. We sat in disbelief at what we were hearing and what the jury might hear. Tears streamed down Kim's face as she cried silently. Patti fought a wave of nausea. She felt nothing but disgust for Detective Fuhrman, but also realized the absurdity of this smoke screen the defense was throwing in front of the world.

During the lunch break I spoke to reporters, complaining angrily, "This is now the Fuhrman trial. . . . I don't understand why the hell we had to listen to two hours of this hate. It's disgusting. My son, Nicole, our families, have a right to a fair trial. And this is not fair."

We were still reeling when Defense Attorney Gerald Uelman began arguing why the jury should be allowed to hear the tapes. In an impassioned voice he said, "After we've read all of these transcripts and listened to all of these tapes and come to the sickening realization of who Mark Fuhrman really is: Los Angeles' worst nightmare, probably the greatest liar since Ananias. But the jury has only seen a very polished and professional performance that was carefully orchestrated, in which Detective Fuhrman sounded more like a choirboy."

Marcia rose slowly and approached the podium. "This may well be the most difficult thing I've ever had to do as a prosecutor," she said. "I don't think that there is anyone in this courtroom . . . who could possibly envy me."

She had one hand placed across her chest as she addressed Judge Ito. "I am Marcia Clark, the prosecutor. And I stand before you today,

Your Honor, not in defense of Mark Fuhrman but in defense of a case of such overwhelming magnitude in terms of the strength of the proof of the defendant's guilt that it would be a travesty to allow such a case to be derailed with a very serious and important but very inflammatory social issue."

The prosecution offered to stipulate that Fuhrman had lied under oath—a move that would allow the defendant's lawyers to suggest that the jury disregard all of his testimony.

Marcia continued, listing all the facts that argued against Fuhrman's ability to plant evidence: Other officers had arrived at the crime scene before Fuhrman and saw only one glove; Kato Kaelin reported hearing three thumps on his wall near where the glove was found, thumps that he heard before police knew of the murders; Fuhrman had no way of knowing whether the defendant would have an alibi for the time the murders occurred; Fuhrman did not even know if eyewitnesses might emerge to testify that they saw the crimes committed by someone else.

Judge Ito interrupted her to add another point bolstering that line of argument: He noted that fibers in the glove were later found to be consistent with those from the inside of Simpson's Bronco—a fact that Fuhrman could not have predicted when he reported finding the glove.

"This is not something I can rule on from the seat of my pants," the judge said finally. "I need to sit down and look at each one of these individual situations and make the appropriate ruling."

We were hopeful. There was simply no legal or plausible reason why the jury should be confronted with these inflammatory, wretched tapes.

On Thursday, August 31, Judge Ito ruled that jurors would be allowed to hear only two short excerpts of Fuhrman using the word "nigger." In rejecting Fuhrman's comments of police misconduct in other cases, the judge said that it would require a "leap in both law and logic" to link those comments to this investigation. The fact that Fuhrman had bragged about lying or fabricating evidence in other cases did not mean that he planted a glove outside this defendant's house, Ito said. "It is a theory without factual support."

Cochran went on the attack, staging a news conference outside of his Wilshire Boulevard office. Flanked by other "Scheme Team" members, he said that the ruling was "perhaps one of the crudest, unfairest decisions ever rendered in a criminal court." Then, in a display of unmitigated gall, he urged residents to remain calm, as if a Godlike signal from him would ignite riots, burnings, and general mayhem. He accused Judge Ito of "doctored, tortured reasoning" and proclaimed: "The cover-up continues."

In an interview after the news conference he ranted, "This inexplicable, indefensible ruling lends credence to all those who say the criminal justice system is corrupt. This is unspeakable."

Peter Neufeld joined the fray. "It is a victory for racism," he said. "It's a green light for a rogue and racist cop to engage in brutality, evidence tampering, and the fabrication of probable cause with impunity."

Gil Garcetti released a statement through a spokeswoman: "While we decry racism, these tapes are for another forum, not this murder trial. The court's ruling will help keep the focus where it should be: on relevant evidence that allows the jury to determine whether Mr. Simpson is responsible for the murders of Ron Goldman and Nicole Brown Simpson. Now let's get on with the trial and get it to the jury."

I was relieved, and hoped that the volatile issue would be put to rest. Speaking to a group of reporters gathered outside our home, I said, "We hope that this is an indication that this trial will be back on track. We all want to thank the judge for his time and effort." And then, referring to Cochran, I added, "I'm sure he is disappointed that he can't turn this trial into a racial horror. He should be ashamed of himself for trying." But Kim believed that conjugal "pillow talk" would spread the word to the jurors. Whether the judge allowed one excerpt or twenty, the damage was done.

Fallout from the Fuhrman interviews continued. In Washington a federal official announced that the Justice Department would review allegations of civil-rights violations arising from the interviews. In Los Angeles Fuhrman's attorney, Robert Tourtelot, announced he was "profoundly disgusted and horrified" by his client's comments and thus could no longer represent him. We respected that decision by Bob, who remained as our attorney for the dormant civil suit.

Saturday night—in an attempt to unwind—we went out to dinner at a Chinese restaurant in Thousand Oaks. We had driven two cars that evening, and Michael was driving me home when we encountered a sobriety checkpoint set up on Thousand Oaks Boulevard. This was not a problem, for we had not been drinking. But as a Ventura County police officer approached the car, he saw Michael's billy club, the O. J. Beater, in plain view in a cavity between the dashboard and the windshield.

"Why do you have that?" the officer asked.

"Just in case I have a problem at night," Michael responded truthfully.

The officer asked him to step out of the car and walked him over to the sidewalk. I tried to follow but was ordered to stay back.

The first officer called over several others. They were pleasant, but informed Michael that possession of the billy club was illegal. "If you had a gun, it would be a misdemeanor," one of the officers said. "But this is a felony." They searched him, and prepared to arrest him, handcuff him, and take him to the station. He was terrified. They said that I could come down to the station and post bond.

Confused and upset, I tried to intervene on his behalf. "This is crazy," I said. "Michael's a good kid. He's just frightened. He wasn't hiding anything. He didn't know he was doing anything wrong."

That failed to impress the officers. With Michael in tears, they prepared to haul him away.

I did not expect any special treatment, but I thought that it would be appropriate to explain who we were, so that they might understand why Michael was frightened enough to carry protection. I said, "I don't know if you recognize who I am, but Ron Goldman was my son, Michael's brother, and—"

"—I don't give a damn who you are," a single officer snapped.

The only thing that saved us from a trip to the police station was that the officers finally checked Michael's driver's license and determined that he was not yet eighteen. Since he was a minor, they issued him a citation.

Right and wrong, good and evil, seemed to be inverted.

Blocked from using most of the inflammatory tapes, the defense decided to call other witnesses who would paint Fuhrman as a racist. As Loyola law school professor Laurie Levenson said, "If they don't get what they want behind door one, try door two."

She was right. On Tuesday, September 5, after cooling its heels for a week, the jury was allowed back into the courtroom. The defense called real estate agent Kathleen Bell to the stand. The plump, blond witness fought back tears while telling the jury that Fuhrman had told her during their first meeting that interracial marriages were disgusting and that African Americans should be "gathered together and burned."

Of course, we had no way of knowing what, if any, information had filtered into the jury from the outside, but this was the first time jurors had been presented with evidence of Fuhrman's alleged racism and willingness to lie under oath.

Michael was in the courtroom that day. Every time he heard the inflammatory word he looked at the jury. He thought: That's it, it's done. It's all these jurors need. You could show them a video of the killer slaughtering Ron and Nicole but, because Mark Fuhrman had used the N-word, nothing else mattered.

Near the end of the day, with McKinny on the stand, the defense played the two allowable tape excerpts. "They don't do anything," Fuhrman said of women police officers. "They don't go out there and initiate a contact with some six-foot five-inch nigger who's been in prison seven years pumping weights."

"That was his voice?" Cochran asked.

"That's his voice," McKinny answered. "No doubt about it."

Kim was devastated. We all were.

The admission of the racial issue was, in our view, completely unwarranted. I tried very hard to look at that and say objectively, "Do I really believe that this had a place?" And I kept coming back to the answer, no. Whether or not this police officer used vile language ten years earlier was of no relevance at this moment in this trial. The judge should have made the defense team show the relevance.

The defendant was not a run-of-the-mill criminal who happened to be black. He was a celebrity who did not function in the black world. To make that leap, Judge Ito had to go beyond reason. Once he let in the issue of race, he opened the floodgates, and justice was in danger of drowning.

Here was the essence of the defense team's argument to the jury:

A. Fuhrman said something disgusting.
B. Therefore, he did not like black people.

C. Therefore, he did not like the defendant.

D. Hence, he planted evidence and engineered a widespread conspiracy, convincing dozens of his colleagues to become accessories to a double homicide, which, if the defendant were convicted and executed, could theoretically make them subject to the death penalty as well.

To that convoluted reasoning I could only add: E. Give me a break.

Clearly it was the Fuhrman trial now, and Patti's reaction to the detective's original testimony proved terribly prophetic. When Fuhrman had denied having used the racial epithet at any time during the past ten years, Patti knew immediately that he had lied and jeopardized the entire case. Now he was to reappear before the court, called by the defense to be asked directly whether or not he had lied. Judge Ito ordered the examination to occur outside the presence of the jury, so that he could consider its admissibility.

It was widely reported that Fuhrman, now retired from LAPD and living in Idaho, would hide behind his Fifth Amendment right against self-incrimination. And the problem was, he could not exercise that right selectively. The Fifth Amendment offers blanket protection; a witness cannot invoke it only for selected questions. Therefore, if Fuhrman answered one single question, he would face a wide range of additional questions.

Kim went to court alone this day, Wednesday, September 6. The investigators who always escorted her from the parking garage to the D.A.'s office knew that she was beside herself with fury. They brought her in through a different hallway than usual, and Kim demanded to know why. When they would not tell her, she knew that they were hiding something from her. Indeed, Fuhrman was sequestered in a room nearby, and the investigators did not want Kim to encounter him.

In court, sitting alone in the front row of the spectators' section, Kim had to endure additional testimony about Fuhrman's obvious biases and his alleged misconduct. Laura Hart McKinny added sexism to the list of Fuhrman's "crimes," reporting his complaint that female police officers do not support "certain cover-ups that some men on the police force are doing."

Then came the testimony of Roderic Hodge, a soft-spoken black man, who said that, after his arrest in January 1987, he was sitting in the back of a police car when Fuhrman said to him, "I told you we'd get you, nigger." Hodge was tried and acquitted on drug charges.

After this, the jury was excused, instructed to wait upstairs in a lounge.

A tension-filled silence spread across the courtroom. Kim turned to see Fuhrman entering, surrounded by several bodyguards, who took up stations by the doorway. Fuhrman's eyes scanned the courtroom for a moment. Then he moved forward, pausing briefly to pat the shoulder of CNN reporter Art Harris.

Marcia and Chris turned their backs. Cochran gloated and shared jubilant high-fives with the defense team. Their behavior was, as usual, inappropriate and disgusting.

Defense Attorney Gerald Uelman asked Fuhrman, "Was the testimony that you gave at the preliminary hearing in this case completely truthful?"

Fuhrman leaned over and whispered to his new attorney, Darryl Mounger. Then he answered, "I wish to assert my Fifth Amendment privilege."

Uelman asked, "Have you ever falsified a police report?"

"I wish to assert my Fifth Amendment privilege."

"Did you plant or manufacture any evidence in this case?"

"I wish to assert my Fifth Amendment privilege."

By invoking his constitutional right, Fuhrman in no way admitted to wrongdoing, but he gave the defense a huge psychological boost. The entire prosecution team appeared demoralized. So were we.

Kim was unaware that by answering even one question Fuhrman would negate the blanket protection of the Fifth Amendment. She was frantic. She wanted to scream: Why can't you just answer NO?

As Fuhrman and his bodyguards left the courtroom through a private doorway, the defendant hunched over the defense table and buried his face in his hands—perhaps so that no one could see if he was crying or laughing.

Brian Hale was the only African American on the team of D.A. investigators, and we were concerned for him. He confided to us that he got "weird vibes" from Fuhrman, and we knew he had to be disturbed by all of this. It was ironic that now, when Fuhrman needed protection to come back in and plead the Fifth, it was the D.A.'s investigators who provided it.

Upstairs in the D.A.'s office, Kim encountered Chris. "Chris, I want to scream at him," she said.

"I'll help you," Chris replied. "Where do you want to go? What do you want to do? Do you want to be alone with him?"

"Yes," Kim said.

Bill Hodgman approached and asked, "What's going on?"

"I want to talk to him," Kim declared again.

"Kim," Bill said softly, "what's that going to prove?"

Hank Goldberg joined the conversation. "Why do you want to, Kim?" he asked.

Kim felt that Chris was encouraging her, egging her on. She thought he knew that she would say the things to Fuhrman that he longed to say. But Bill and Hank cautioned, "Don't sink to that level." It was like being pulled between a devil and an angel—revenge against restraint. Kim felt her characteristic signs of stress. Her stomach was in open revolt. An excruciating pain in her elbow moved up her arm.

Finally Kim made the decision not to confront Fuhrman. "They were right," she told us later. "It wouldn't do any good. The damage had already been done."

Kim sometimes regrets that decision. Her mind replays the speech she would have delivered: I don't understand the kind of arrogance that comes over someone like you. It is your fault that you're a racist. You lied and you knew you were lying. Why did you have to drag everyone else down with you? I trusted you. You are a police officer. You are what I was raised to respect and obey.

You are a despicable human being!

TWENTY-FOUR

The pressure was strangling us.

Each of us dealt with it in our own way. Emotions were more readily brought to the surface, about anything, not just Ron's loss. Tension filled the house to the point where we could almost see it hanging in the air. We either tiptoed around each other or lost our tempers over something that was totally insignificant. Sometimes a chilly silence prevailed when no one spoke at all.

There was a widespread misperception of how often I was actually in the courtroom. Perhaps it arose because of the press coverage we got whenever I chose to speak out. In truth, I had to pay attention to my work, and it was a grinding daily decision. I had been a successful salesman for most of my adult life, but my job felt increasingly irrelevant. Each morning I asked myself: Do I really have to go see that client today? Can I postpone this appointment so that I can slip into the courtroom? Can I go in the morning? Can I go in the afternoon?

Kim had no appetite. Michael saw her in the swimming pool one day and was shocked to realize how emaciated she had become. Her always slight frame now resembled pictures he had seen of girls suffering from anorexia. However, we all knew that it was useless to say anything to Kim about it. I was very concerned about her health, but whenever I encouraged her to eat more, she snapped back at me, "Leave me alone!"

Michael and Lauren were maturing into young adults, experiencing all the new excitements and pains that they wanted and needed to share with the family, but the trial had eclipsed everything.

Lauren still had great difficulty sleeping, and was plagued by night-mares.

For months on end Patti had run through her days at full gallop, with no downtime. She complained, "I feel like a machine." There was simply not enough of her to go around. She wished that she could clone herself. Her commitment to attend the trial had turned out to be far more grueling than she ever imagined. She wanted and needed to be there every day, to represent me and to support Kim. But Michael and Lauren needed her, too. She had always been a very "hands-on" mom, but now she was stretched to the limit.

At times she felt unappreciated and taken for granted, especially if she had to leave the courtroom early to attend one of Michael's tennis matches or to drive Lauren somewhere. If I, or anyone else, made a com-ment that she interpreted as questioning her priorities, she quickly lost her temper and steamed for days. When I suggested that she was doing too much, and should ask the children to chip in more and carry some of the weight, she became defensive and angry, taking it as criticism.

We did not get to bed until very late in the evening and, even as Patti dropped her exhausted head onto the pillow, she knew that morn-ing would arrive far too soon.

Now, as she realized that this miserable trial was finally drawing to a conclusion, Patti felt a compelling need to do something for herself. She told me that she did not want to return to her part-time job at Right Start, sitting in front of a computer, answering telephones. It was not satisfying. She wanted to do something more significant.

"Great!" I said, but I had no idea what thoughts were tumbling around in her head.

Patti looked in the yellow pages for an electrology school and thought that she might enjoy the work. Without telling any of the rest of us, she made some calls, interviewed, and decided that she was inter-ested. Because the courses began at widely spaced intervals, if she did not start now she would have to wait many months. Classes were held Monday, Tuesday, and Wednesday from 8:30 A.M. to 5 P.M., and the schedule would force her to cut back on her attendance at the trial. But Patti decided to go for it.

When she told me, after the fact, I was not as enthusiastic as she would have liked.

"Where did you come up with that?" I asked. "Did you ever think of doing something else?" My attitude and the tone of my voice reminded her of some of my past conversations with Ron about his plans and ambitions. Sometimes my pragmatism can sound like criticism or disapproval, a sort-of unintentional putdown.

"No," she said, curtly.

'Would you like me to sit down and help you think of some other things?" I offered.

"No, I would not," Patti replied. "I'm starting on September eighteenth."

Although the specific decision surprised me, as I thought about it I was very happy for her and pleased that she had finally done something for herself. Patti deserved some time for Patti.

The last few witnesses took the stand amid the usual wrangling among the attorneys. Under pressure to conclude its rebuttal case, the prosecution dropped plans to introduce evidence about the defendant's failure to surrender to police. They also lost a battle to inform the jury that fibers on the bloody glove found at the Rockingham estate probably came from a Bronco resembling the defendant's. To add insult to injury, Judge Ito fined the prosecution team for being late to court.

Prosecutors did, however, win the right to recall State Department of Justice analyst Gary Sims to introduce a new DNA test result concerning three stains found inside the defendant's Bronco. The stains had been subjected to a form of analysis known as RFLP, and Sims testified that the results indicated a mixture of Ron's blood and the defendant's blood. This was a major addition to the prosecution case, since it suggested that the defendant's blood was mixed with that of a murder victim with whom he had absolutely no previous contact. That information, all by itself, should have been enough to convict this man, we thought.

Seeking to counter the ill-fated glove demonstration, the prosecution recalled Richard Rubin, the former general manager of the Aris glove company. After showing a videotape of the defendant broadcasting from the sidelines at a 1991 football game between the Cincinnati Bengals and the Houston Oilers, Chris Darden asked Rubin's opinion about the gloves that the defendant was wearing.

"Based on what I've seen," Rubin responded, "I would say that this is Style 70263, size extra-large, brown."

Chris asked, "How certain are you of that?"

"I'm one hundred percent certain," Rubin declared.

The point was exquisite, for the bloody glove found at the murder scene was Style 70263, size extra-large, brown. And the bloody glove found at the killer's home was Style 70263, size extra-large, brown.

On Friday, September 15, in an effort to undo the damage inflicted by the defense's expert witness Henry Lee, the prosecution re-called FBI Special Agent William Bodziak. He displayed numerous photographs to support his contention that the marks Lee saw as blood imprints were actually artifacts left years ago by the masons who constructed the walk-way. He also testified that another stain Lee photographed on June 25, 1994, more than a week after the murders, was simply not there the night the crimes were committed.

Marcia asked, "Based on your analysis of all the evidence, including Dr. Lee's photographs, is there any evidence that more than one set of bloody shoe prints were left at the scene at the time of the murders?"

"No, there is not," Bodziak replied. "All the bloody shoe imprints were made by size 12 Bruno Magli design shoes."

"Has anything changed your opinion that the defendant cannot be excluded as a wearer of those size 12 Bruno Magli shoes?" Marcia asked.

"No," the agent responded.

This testimony brought an amazing response from Dr. Lee. After court recessed, he spoke to the press, saying that he regretted his involvement in the case and adding that he would resist testifying in any retrial or rebuttal phase of the case. "I'm sorry I ever got involved in the whole thing," he said. "I feel a little bit disappointed about the whole process. . . . This trial has become a game. I don't like to play games."

We certainly agreed.

But the games, indeed, continued. Johnnie Cochran, unhappy with a ruling by Judge Ito that he would not inform the jury that Detective Mark Fuhrman had refused to testify further, choreographed a protest. One morning the entire defense team showed up in court wearing ties made from African kente cloth. This sent an unbelievable message to the jury. Marcia was prohibited from wearing a tiny angel pin on her lapel, but it was apparently perfectly all right for the defense to dress as a team in order to show solidarity with African-American concerns.

Judge Ito should have thrown the entire crew out of court until they were appropriately dressed. But his only comment to Cochran was "Nice tie."

We wondered if they would come in for closing arguments all wearing Buffalo Bills football jerseys with the number 32 on the back.

On Friday, September 22, in the absence of the jury, Cochran requested permission for his client to address the court, to personally waive his right to testify. This was strange. If he spoke to the court, was he not testifying?

Marcia was instantly on her feet. "This is a very obvious defense bid to get material admitted through those conjugal visits that is not admitted in court . . . " she argued. "Please don't do this, Your Honor. I beg you, I beg you."

Cochran shrugged off her objection with a caustic reply. "There seems to be this great fear of the truth in this case," he said. "This is still America. And we can talk. We can speak. Nobody can stop us."

Judge Ito made no formal ruling on the issue. He simply glanced at the defendant and said, "Good morning."

With that, the murderer stood up and began to speak:

"Good morning, Your Honor," he said. "As much as I would like to address some of the misrepresentations made about myself and Nicole concerning our life together, I'm mindful of the mood and the stamina of this jury. I have confidence, a lot more it seems than Ms. Clark has, of their integrity, and that they'll find—as the record stands now—that I did not, would not, and could not have committed this crime. I have four kids—two kids I haven't seen in a year. They ask me every week, 'Dad, how much longer?' "

Judge Ito finally cut him off. "All right," he said.

With that, the defendant concluded, "I want this trial over."

The judge should have shut him up immediately, but once again he allowed the defense to run the show.

"Why's he letting him talk?" Patti asked.

With Dominick Dunne sitting on my left, I hissed under my breath, "Murderer, murderer, murderer."

It was my understanding that the killer had just crossed over a very important line. He had made a statement. He had just put himself in a position to be cross-examined!

Marcia tried to argue the point, but the judge refused her request to cross-examine.

In my opinion, letting the matter drop after a rather weak attempt was the most serious mistake that the prosecution made. I longed for any member of the prosecution to stand up and shout, "Judge, he just testified. Now I have a right to cross-examine him and if you don't get him up there on the witness stand, I'm bringing this issue to the court of appeals tomorrow!"

Everything would have come to a grinding halt at that moment. I believe that the court of appeals would have overturned Judge Ito's ruling, the defendant would have been forced to submit to cross-examination, and he would either have had to lie through his teeth or confess.

Later, at a press conference, I said of the defendant's statement: "It's disturbing, and it's outrageous. If he had a statement to make, he should have gotten on the damn stand and said something and not been a coward."

Kim was in Chicago for the weekend, to attend the wedding of a friend. She was sitting alone in a car, listening to coverage on the radio. Suddenly she heard the killer's voice proclaim "did not, could not, would not . . . " "I went ballistic" is how she described her reaction.

TWENTY-FIVE

L ight rain was falling.

Claiming that he had received death threats, Johnnie Cochran arrived at the courthouse surrounded by six beefy-looking body-guards, all members of the Nation of Islam. Wearing somber suits, and even more somber expressions, sporting their trademark Louis Farra-khan look-alike bow ties and carrying walkie-talkies, they skulked about in the hallway outside the courtroom.

Cochran wore an enamel lapel pin depicting the Statue of Liberty. Explaining the pin, he commented, "That's what we're trying to get—liberty for our client."

It was Tuesday, September 26, one year to the day after jury selection began. In that year the jury had heard 465 hours of formal testi-mony—less than two hours per workday. And now the prosecution was ready to deliver its closing statements. I joined Patti and Kim and Patti's mother in the court.

Marcia Clark, with a hand over her heart, urged the jurors to con-centrate only upon the evidence, despite the fact that "the sideshows may be very interesting."

She spoke for more than six hours, weaving together the time-line and the chain of physical evidence that linked the defendant to the murders and pointing out the "smoke and mirrors" that the defense concocted to obfuscate the truth. She urged the jurors to see past the conspiracy, two killers, evidence planting, theories that she termed an effort to systematically fragment the case.

Marcia looked exhausted; her eyes were shrouded with deep purple circles. Her voice was low and serious as she said, "There were roads raised, created by the defense to lead you away from the core truth and the issue that we are searching for the answer to, which is who murdered Ron and Nicole. These roads, ladies and gentlemen, these are false roads. The false roads were paved with inflammatory distractions but even after all their tireless efforts, the evidence stands strong and powerful to prove to you the defendant's guilt."

For a time, Marcia focused on the demeanor of the accused. "If I were asked to try on the gloves that were worn by the murderer of the father of my children, I would not be laughing," she said. "I would not be mugging. I would not think that was funny at all. Is that the attitude you expect, the laughing and the mugging, putting on the bloody gloves that were used to murder the mother of your children?"

Meticulously, she reminded the panel of the significance of the blood, hair, and fiber evidence.

"That's his blood," she concluded.

As Marcia spoke, Barry Scheck scribbled on a yellow legal pad, then rolled his eyes, raised his eyebrows, and puffed out his cheeks in obvious disgust. The defendant continually muttered under his breath.

Jonathan Fairtlough, the prosecution's electronics expert, had been up all night, working until 4:00 A.M. to complete a unique presentation that Marcia now utilized effectively. As she detailed each significant point of evidence, she announced, "Another piece of the puzzle," and the screen above the witness stand displayed a jigsaw-puzzle piece falling into place. Eventually they formed a picture of the defendant's face.

"There he is," Marcia concluded. "You haven't even heard the why of it, why he did it, and you know he did it."

It was nearly 7:00 P.M. when Chris Darden rose to begin to answer the "Why?" by weaving a tale of violence, abuse, and control. He said that the defendant had lighted a fuse of rage early in his relationship with Nicole, and he eventually exploded. When the defendant beat his wife, humiliated her, and spied on her, he was demonstrating a desperate desire to control her, Chris pointed out. "The fuse is lit, and it's burning," he said, "but it's a slow burn."

As the long day finally drew to a close, Chris reminded the jury that Nicole kept a safety deposit box with a copy of her will and photographs of herself after her husband had beaten her. "She was leaving you a road map to let you know who it is who will eventually kill her," Chris said in his soft-spoken style. "She knew in 1989. She knew it and she wants you to know it. She didn't know when," he added softly, "but whenever that event came, she wanted you to know who did it. Think about that. Just think about that."

A group of investigators, law clerks, and some of the attorneys joined us for drinks at the Los Angeles Athletic Club later that night. For the first and only time, we saw a vulnerable, emotional side to Marcia. Through her tears, she spoke of how much she loved her own brother and how badly she felt for Kim's loss.

Chris continued his closing statement the next day by playing a 911 tape. Once again, the tortured voice of Nicole echoed in our ears, pleading for someone, somewhere to help her. Chris asked the jury to consider several points revealed by the tape. He noted that the defendant's two young children were asleep in the house at this moment. "The fact that the kids are in the house means nothing to this man," Chris said with obvious disdain in his voice. And after that incident, he said, Nicole "knows he's going to kill her at some point."

Chris repeatedly used the phrase, "The fuse was burning." He declared that the knife wounds to the two victims represented the eruption of the defendant's rage, the explosion that resulted when the fuse finally burned down. Each thrust of the knife reduced some of the rage, Chris said, so that by the time the defendant was finished, he was calm again. So calm that "he just walked away."

Throwing the defendant's courtroom statement back in his face, Chris said, "We have shown you that he would have killed, could have killed, and did kill these two people."

Chris pointed directly at the defendant, who shook his head angrily. "He is a murderer," Chris proclaimed. "He was also one hell of a football player, but he is still a murderer."

We all thought that Chris did a wonderful job. He spoke from the heart, not relying on the sophomoric theatrics that had so permeated this courtroom.

That was Johnnie Cochran's job.

* * *

It did not take long to see where Cochran was headed. "Your verdict in this case will go far beyond the walls of the courtroom," he said near the beginning of his argument. "Your verdict talks about justice in America, and it talks about the police and whether they're above the law."

He pooh-poohed the prosecution's contention that "this recognizable person" would don a knit cap and some dark clothes and go kill his wife. In illustration, he pulled a knit cap onto his head and remarked, "If I put this knit cap on, who am I? I'm still Johnnie Cochran with a knit cap. . . . It's no disguise. It makes no sense."

He looked so ludicrous prancing about in the knit cap that Kim could not contain herself. Marcia heard her snickering and turned around. She, too, lost her composure and started to giggle. In fact, we did not understand why everyone simply did not laugh this fool out of the room.

Referring to the glove demonstration, Cochran tried some asinine poetry. Warming to his theme, he intoned his mantra, "It doesn't fit. If it doesn't fit, you must acquit."

When Cochran strutted in front of the court, looked directly at us, and commented condescendingly that "some people couldn't handle the truth," Kim was no longer laughing. She was seething. It took every ounce of her restraint not to stand up and scream at him.

We could not believe that Judge Ito allowed Cochran to say the things he said. Throughout his argument, he was talking down to the jurors, treating and manipulating them as if they were idiots.

Near the end of the day, Cochran turned to the subject of Detective Mark Fuhrman. We knew that he would have much more to say when he concluded his argument tomorrow. But for now, he raged, "Mark Fuhrman is a lying, perjuring, genocidal racist!"

Thursday, September 28. Police were concerned about the expanding crowd that gathered outside the downtown Criminal Courts Building. Bomb scares and death threats were commonplace.

In court Cochran blatantly gave the predominantly African-American jury permission to disregard the evidence. He urged them to take this opportunity to "get even"—in other words, to free a double murderer in retaliation for hundreds of years of white oppression. This was absurd and very disturbing. The law is the law. If there are inequities in the system, you fix the system. But you do not fix the law by breaking the law. Or ignoring it.

Even more preposterous was Judge Ito's tolerance of the statement. He should have silenced Cochran instantly and proclaimed, "The jury will disregard what's been said. Mr. Cochran, meet me in chambers immediately." But as Patti said, "Judge Ito just didn't have the courage to do anything about it."

Then Cochran screamed at the jury: "Stop this cover-up. If you don't stop it, then who? Do you think the police department is going to stop it? Do you think the D.A.'s office is going to stop it? Do you think we can stop it by ourselves? It has to be stopped by you. . . . Who, then, polices the police? *You* police the police. You police them by your verdict. You are the ones to send the message."

Who was the racist here? It was Johnnie Cochran himself who was fanning the flames of racial hatred. Did he not comprehend that if this jury allowed a double murderer to go free, race relations in America would be set back decades?

Apparently not. Returning to the subject of Mark Fuhrman, Cochran made the single most offensive statement of the trial. He said, "There was another man not too long ago in the world who had those same views, who wanted to burn people, who had racist views and ultimately had power over people in his country. People didn't care. People said he is just crazy. He is just a half-baked painter. They didn't do anything about it. This man, this scourge, became one of the worst people in the history of the world, Adolf Hitler, because people didn't care or didn't try to stop him. He had the power over his racism and his anti-religion. Nobody wanted to stop him, and it ended up in World War Two."

We could not believe what we were hearing. Kim bowed her head in disbelief. Patti saw the veins in my neck protrude. The color drained from my face. My fists clenched. I twisted in my seat. I muttered angrily. Worried that I would lose my composure in open court, Patti held me down.

I whispered, "I'm going to have a news conference at the break."

Patti tried to dissuade me, but I would not be silenced.

Cochran continued. "And so Fuhrman, Fuhrman wants to take all black people now and burn them or bomb them. That is genocidal racism."

Patti could not remember feeling such deep hatred for anyone in her entire life as she felt, at this moment, for "Johnnie Cockroach."

I could contain myself no longer. The instant that Judge Ito called for a break, I told Mark Arenas to alert the media that I wanted to talk. "ASAP," I growled. As I bolted from the courtroom, Patti pleaded, "Calm down, calm down." Scared and very upset, Kim retreated to the safety of the D.A.'s office.

Patti followed me into the elevator, and we rode down nine floors to the lobby, where the press had set up its cameras and microphones. It all happened so quickly that only a handful of reporters were there when I began.

Trembling with rage, I yelled, "We have seen a man who perhaps is the worst kind of racist himself." I pointed out that Cochran is "someone who shoves racism in front of everything, someone who compares a person who speaks racist comments to Hitler, a person who murdered millions of people."

I screamed, "This man is the worst kind of human being imaginable. He compares racism of its worst kind in this world to what's going on in this case. He has suggested that racism is the foundation of the Police Department, of our justice system. . . . This man is sick. He is absolutely sick."

I could feel Patti pulling at my arm, willing me to stop.

Upstairs in the D.A.'s office, Kim watched on television and cried hysterically, certain that I was going to collapse before I finished speaking.

Tears blurred my view of the dozens of reporters who were scrambling to hear my words. I heard my voice quiver and crack. But I would not stop.

I continued. "He walks around for the past days screaming his life has been threatened, and who does he choose to walk with? Guards from the Nation of Islam. He's talking about racism, and he talks about hate. Who does he connect himself with?" Everyone knew that Cochran's bodyguards were disciples of Louis Farrakhan, a demagogue notorious for his anti-Semitic views.

"This man is a horror walking around amongst us. And he compares what Mark Fuhrman did to misery from the—the beginnings of history. This man ought to be ashamed of himself to walk among decent human beings. This man is a disgrace to human beings. . . . He is one of the most disgusting human beings I have ever had to listen to in my life.

"He suggests that racism ought to be the most important thing that any one of us ought to listen to in this court, that any one of us in this nation should be listening to and it's because of racism we should put aside all other thought, all other reason, and set his murdering client free. He's a sick man. He ought to be put away."

That evening the phone rang constantly. Friends from all over the country called nonstop to offer their support and to find out if I was okay.

A thousand spectators gathered outside the courthouse. Some chanted, "Free O. J.!" Others responded, "Fry O. J.!" Several tussles broke out.

It was Friday, the day that the prosecution would have the last word. As we waited in the D.A.'s office for court to convene, one of the men in the Brown entourage approached Kim and asked, "Did you get the speech?"

"Excuse me?" Kim replied.

"Did Patty Jo give you the speech yet?"

"Speech about what?"

"About how to behave in the courtroom!"

Before Kim could answer, Judy Brown was at her side, launching into a litany of rules on how to behave in court when the verdict came in.

"Judy, I think I know," Kim said coldly. She thought: What arrogance! I've been here every day for nine months. Have I done anything wrong? No. Have I done anything to embarrass myself or my family? No. Have I been chastised by Judge Ito? No.

Chris Darden, who, more and more, was caught in up in a pivotal moment in this nation's racial history, told the jury in a soft, compelling tone: "You can't send a message to Fuhrman, you can't send a message to the LAPD . . . by delivering a verdict of not guilty in a case like this where it is clear. You know it is clear, you feel it, you know it in your heart. . . . Everybody knows it."

Chris acknowledged the tension that this particular jury had to feel. "You've got a tough job, a very tough job," he said. "I don't envy you in that regard. But let me tell you something, I have had a tough job, too.

The law is a tough thing to enforce in this town. Not everybody . . . wants to live up to the law or follow the law. Not everybody thinks that the law applies to them.

"I have been a prosecutor for almost fifteen years, and if there is one rule that I have lived by, if there is one rule that means a lot to me, it is this one: No one is above the law; not the police, not the rich, no one."

He derided the characterization of the defendant as a hero. "A hero," he said, "is a man that would rush into a life-threatening situation to save a woman without ever thinking about himself first."

Phil Vannatter leaned back over the rail and placed a hand on my knee as Chris added, "There are no heroes in this courtroom today."

We owed the prosecution team so much for all they did. They gave up their lives for a year and a half. Most nights they were up until three in the morning, working on the case. Their families seldom saw them. They were scrutinized, sometimes vilified, and put through an emotional wringer. The law clerks and the investigators always seemed edited out of the thanks and praise they deserved. Kim said of our Victims' Assistance advocate, "I would give Mark my left lung if he asked for it."

And so on this final day, we catered a lunch for the entire team. It was our small way of saying thank you to all the people who gave up so much of their lives to try to see that justice was done.

I spoke for a few minutes, and then it was Kim's turn. Through her tears she told everyone that she had really grown to love and cherish them as a family. She said that she was very grateful for the opportunity to teach them about who her brother was. She singled out Chris for a special thank-you, but the praise made him uncomfortable.

Finally she commented, "But in one second I would give all of you up to have my brother back."

In the afternoon Marcia took the jurors through the case one final time. Where was the defendant on the night of the murders? She reminded the jurors that blood, hair, and fiber evidence inextricably linked the defendant to his two victims. She retraced the trail of blood from the murder scene to the defendant's home. She acknowledged that the defense disputed the quality of some of that evidence, but she displayed a chart showing that the uncontested evidence alone, such as blood drops at the crime scene, the defendant's unexplained whereabouts, and the history of spousal abuse, were sufficient to convict.

She said, "It's very clear, and it's very obvious. Mr. Simpson committed these murders."

The prosecution ended its case with a dramatic audio-visual display. Once again they played the 911 tapes of Nicole pleading desperately for protection from the defendant. At the same time, on the overhead screen, they flashed slides showing Nicole, battered and bruised. Finally they showed, one last time, the murder scene, with Ron and Nicole's bodies soaked in blood.

Marcia paused for a moment. Then she said in a somber voice, "I don't have to say anything else. . . ."

It was 3:57 P.M. Now it was up to the twelve men and women in the jury box.

TWENTY-SIX

We were exhausted, apprehensive, and uptight. We made no plans for the week following closing arguments. We prepared for an anxious and lengthy wait.

Patty Jo had all of our phone numbers, and by now, these were legion. She had our home numbers, cellular numbers for Patti and me, the number of Patti's school and my office, and, finally, our pagers.

I believed that there were only two possible outcomes. The best-case scenario was a guilty verdict. It was simple and logical: one plus one equals two. The worst-case scenario was a hung jury. Was it possible that one dissenter could hang the jury? Yes, of course.

I asked myself: Is it possible that twelve people could have heard all the evidence and agree that he is not guilty?

And I answered: Not a chance.

The jury would begin deliberating on Monday. All weekend we kept asking one another, "How long do you think it will take?"

We decided that it would be at least two weeks before they could sift through the mountain of evidence and reach a decision.

I went to work as usual on Monday morning. Michael, Lauren, and Patti, too, all went to school. Kim manned the home front. A persistent New York reporter, who had been bugging Kim all morning, was camped outside the house.

Kim could not allow herself to expect a guilty verdict because she knew that if it did not happen, it would destroy her. As the jury began its deliberations, she refused to watch television. She was tired, to the point of meltdown, of listening to the pundits offering worthless opinions. Reporters who had never set foot inside the courtroom, law-school graduates who had never tried a case, news anchors who could not put a sentence together without the aid of a TelePrompTer, all espoused opinions as to what those twelve people should and would decide.

So Kim donned a black bathing suit, escaped to the backyard, and lay next to the pool, trying to relax in the sun.

It was around noon when two of her reporter friends called to say that the jury had requested that portions of limousine driver Allan Park's testimony be read back to them.

Kim called Patty Jo at the D.A.'s office and asked, What did this mean? Patty Jo reassured Kim that it was not unusual for a jury to make such a request.

Phone calls flew back and forth. Kim learned that Chris Darden and Bill Hodgman were headed for the courtroom, as was Defense Attorney Carl Douglas, for a 1:00 P.M. session wherein the jury would revisit the testimony of Allan Park.

This was very encouraging because, during her closing statement, Marcia had declared that Park's testimony was "the defining moment of this trial. . . . Because when you understand that the defendant was out that night, when you understand that he lied to Allan Park about being asleep, when you understand that Bronco was moved and that he was out in that Bronco that night . . . then you understand how the defense falls apart. . . . The Bronco was not there. And neither was the defendant."

About 3:00 P.M. Patty Jo called Kim with the astounding news that a verdict had been reached. Kim was frantic, almost immobile. She asked herself: Who do I call? What do I do?

"Calm down," Patty Jo cautioned. "Call your family." She explained that the verdict was sealed and would be read in open court the following morning. Johnnie Cochran had been so certain of a lengthy deliberation that he had gone out of town and would not return until that night. "You won't have to come in till tomorrow morning," Patty Jo said.

Kim's hands were shaking so badly that she had difficulty dialing, but she managed to reach Patti on one phone and me on another. "You guys," she shouted, "they got a verdict!"

"Son of a bitch, they've nailed him," I said. If they had reached a verdict in such an incredibly short period of time, there could be no question. I was one hundred percent certain that the jury had found him guilty. The evidence was overwhelming.

Patti thought: A verdict already? He's guilty, of course. We're going to get him! Twelve sane, thinking people simply could not ignore the evidence, even if it was Santa Claus who was on trial. Shaking nervously, she told everyone at school that the verdict was in. She shared a tight hug with Dolly, the school's owner, and left for home. The short drive seemed to take forever, and her mind twisted and turned. All along, we had been aware of the possibility of a hung jury, but never, in Patti's wildest imagination, did she consider the possibility of a not-guilty verdict. And if the deliberations were over so quickly, a hung jury was out of the question.

Kim knew that Michael had finished school for the day and would already be at work. She called Rob Duben and asked him to meet Michael. "He needs to be with someone," she said. "He might need some moral support." Then she called Scott, Michael's boss at the deli, and asked him to relay the message that the verdict was in, and that Rob would be there shortly to pick up Michael.

Michael thought that this was strange because he had driven himself to work. Why could he not drive himself home? This seemed ominous, and Michael did not feel good about the news. "They'll never get him," he told Scott.

"Yes, they will," Scott replied. "They'll get him. They called for Park's testimony. They're going to get him."

Michael's hopes started to rise.

Cheerleading practice had ended early, and Lauren had arranged a ride home with April, one of the varsity cheerleaders. Her friends Teresa and Colleen rode with her. Soon after Kim finished speaking with Scott on the phone, April's Eagle Talon came to a stop in front of our house. Kim rushed out the front door, still wearing her bathing suit. She yelled, "Hurry, Lauren! Get inside now! The verdict is in!"

"Oh my God!" Lauren cried. Teresa called out something, but Lauren ignored her. She grabbed her books and ran up the driveway babbling, "Oh my God! What are we going to do? What does this mean?"

Lauren ran past Kim and into the house. Instinctively she fled up the staircase and into her room. What am I doing up here? she wondered. Quickly she ran back downstairs. "Let's go get dressed," Lauren said to Kim.

"It's not till tomorrow morning," Kim replied, trying to calm her sister. She wondered why she had told Lauren to hurry into the house.

Then Patti walked in, shouting, "They got him!" Patti, Kim, and Lauren shared a hug.

Michael arrived home to a scene of chaos. He was quickly included in the circle of hugs.

Lauren was certain of the verdict. She knew that the repulsive, contemptible man who sat at the defense table had brutally murdered her brother. She could not imagine how anyone in his right mind could think otherwise.

The same mayhem that we had experienced in the week following the murders descended upon us all over again. The phones rang off their hooks. Friends and neighbors—the Golds, the Zieglers, the Dubens, the Roses, the Berkes—poured into the house and assigned themselves tasks. Maralyn Gold screened our calls. Everyone expressed surprise over the speed of the decision. Everyone offered comfort and support.

Chris Darden called, asking us to be at the courthouse by 8:00 A.M., two hours prior to the session. When we asked Chris about the speed of the verdict, he said, "Nothing about this trial surprises me."

The familiar cadre of reporters and tape crews gathered outside our house, jamming the street, covering the sidewalks, hovering hungrily for any tidbit of information. But we declined to comment.

Jubilant cries echoed through the house: "We nailed him!" "We got him!" "He's guilty!" But Kim was worried about me, and she struck a note of caution. "You've got to be prepared," she warned.

Then she went upstairs and hid.

We ordered pizza; it was the easiest thing to do.

We learned that, once again, there had been some kind of threat made against our family. So two police cars were assigned to watch our house overnight, although the presence of the news teams seemed to make this caution unnecessary.

*　*　*

Michael replayed the events of the day in his mind: Allan Park's testimony was very incriminating. He had no motive to lie. He never sold
his story. He gained nothing from this case. It was good that the jury
wanted to hear his testimony again.

Lauren called her father in Chicago because he is a retired lawyer.
He agreed. "They probably got him."

Once again the television lights glared in through Lauren's bedroom
window. She did not sleep for more than an hour that night.

For all of us, sleep was an impossibility.

Patti was the first one up, worried about staggering the shower schedule
in order to have enough hot water.

Even though they knew that they would not be allowed into the
courtroom, about thirty of our friends decided to come with us. We all
left the house together, and our friends clustered about us, hoping that
the media would not be able to get much footage. Lauren heard the
snapping sounds of camera shutters, but she just kept her eyes down and
moved forward. We all ignored the shouted questions.

Our five-car caravan headed down Lindero Canyon Road, and we
were wordless as we drove past Pierce Brothers Valley Oaks Memorial
Park. Patti sent a thought out to Ron: We're going to get him!

As we rounded the cloverleaf to turn south on the Ventura Freeway,
we saw a huge white sheet hanging over the rail of the Kanan Avenue
overpass. A single word was emblazoned on it in big block letters:

GUILTY!

In the rearview mirror Michael noticed that the same letters had
been written in reverse so that they could be read backward.

The long drive through the early rush-hour traffic seemed to take
forever. Other than the muted sounds from the radio, we rode in complete silence.

Kim thought: All this time, all the pain, all this tension, and it's
going to be over in a matter of minutes.

Patti thought: We're going to get him. This jury will do the right
thing. There will be justice. There is no way he'll be acquitted. We will
all have a chance to speak at the sentencing hearing. What will I say?

We piled out of our cars and went immediately to the D.A.'s office. Kim was astounded when once again the Browns tried to lecture her on how to behave when the verdict was read. She became even angrier. She vowed to herself: I will react however I feel like reacting. Enough is enough.

Kim could not sit still. Mark walked with her as she paced around and around the floor. Bill Hodgman sat in his corner office with the door open. Each time Kim walked past she said, "Hi, Bill." But she could not ask him what he thought was going to happen.

She posed that question only to one person, Ron Phillips, Mark Fuhrman's former partner. She asked, "Well, Puppy, what do you think?"

"Acquittal," Ron answered tersely.

"Excuse me?" Kim said. "Ron, why do you think that?"

"I don't know. I just don't think they're going to get him."

The exchange left Kim feeling so twisted that she fled to the hallway and began to cry. She could not bring herself to ask anyone else for their prediction of the verdict.

The hands on the clock almost seemed to move backward. It was a quarter to ten . . .

Fourteen to ten . . .

Thirteen to ten . . .

Finally, at 9:50, Patty Jo called us all together and launched into a lecture on verdict decorum.

Patti thought: They're treating us like children, as if we don't know how to act in public.

Tension crackled in the air like fireworks.

We huddled together and solemnly headed for the elevator. No one said a word.

The doors opened and we stepped out. A reporter approached Kim, wanting to talk. "Please, just leave me alone," she pleaded.

"How are you feeling?" the reporter pushed.

"I think I'm going to throw up," Kim admitted. "Go away!"

Michael stood next to Kim, adjacent to a water fountain. When the courtroom doors opened and people started piling in, Michael said, "Come on, Kim."

"I'm not going," Kim replied. She just stood in the doorway, staring into the courtroom, trying to stop shaking.

"Kim, you have to go," Michael said.

Some of the investigators encouraged her to enter.

"No," she said.

One of them put his hands on her shoulder and said, "You can do it. Be strong." Gently he pushed her into the room.

Somehow Kim got to her seat. She shared a brief glance with Tom Lange and Phil Vannatter. Her silent tears continued to flow. Next to her, Dominick Dunne kept his eyes toward the front of the courtroom.

Judge Ito was already there.

Michael closed his eyes and prayed.

The killer came in through the side door, a bit more subdued than usual, but smirking and waving at his side of the audience. I put my arms around Kim. I was crying.

The jury filed in, never looking at us.

Michael grabbed Lauren's hand and started kissing it. He said, "Please, Ron, please."

Lauren's heart was pounding. Her knees and hands were shaking. She looked at the killer and saw a blank face.

Michael and Lauren kept repeating the words "Please, please, please."

Patti had her left arm around Michael and Lauren. Her right hand clutched mine. She did not want to look at either the defendant or the jury, so she stared straight ahead.

Judge Ito called for his clerk, Deidre Robertson, to read the verdict.

Patti took several deep breaths.

"Please, Ron, please, please," Lauren whispered to her slain brother. She stared at each juror. None of them showed any expression whatsoever.

Mrs. Robertson began to read: " . . . We the jury find the defendant . . . Orenfal—"

Patti's mind instantly plunged into despair. Oh my God! she thought. Deidre can't even say his name correctly. She's in shock, too. She's horrified by this verdict and in shock, just like us. I can't believe this is really happening. He's going to walk!

Mrs. Robertson continued. "—Orenthal James Simpson not guilty of the crime of murder . . . upon Nicole Brown Simpson, a human being."

A unanimous gasp echoed throughout the room. The killer mouthed the words "Thank you" in the direction of the jury.

"Murderer!" Lauren thought. She bent over, willing herself not to vomit on the floor.

"Breathe, Lauren, breathe," Michael said.

Kim was sobbing uncontrollably, her head hidden in my shirt.

"Oh my God!" Patti said aloud. She felt her neck collapse and buried her head in her lap. Crying hysterically, she asked herself: Is this for real? What in the hell is wrong with this jury?

I was staring straight ahead with a blank, lifeless expression on my face. I was simply, totally, terrifyingly numb. I heard the word "murderer" slip out of my mouth.

Michael's body was shaking, but he maintained his firm grip on Lauren's hand.

Kim was desperate to hear the verdict regarding Ron. She had an irrational hope that it might be different.

But Mrs. Robertson read: "We the jury find the defendant Orenthal James Simpson not guilty of the crime of murder . . . upon Ronald Lyle Goldman, a human being."

"He killed Ron!" Kim cried.

"Bastard!" I spat.

"How could they do this?" Lauren sobbed. She rocked back and forth, holding her stomach, trying to breathe.

Judge Ito ordered the jury polled and we watched in total shock as each juror said yes when asked whether he or she agreed with this damnable verdict.

With each nod of the head, Lauren realized anew that this disgusting man, who had murdered her brother, would be free. He would be free to walk the public streets, eat in public restaurants, and shop the public malls.

Kim's chest was heaving. Tom Lange patted her on the back. Patti had her left arm around Michael and Lauren. She rested her hand on me as I embraced Kim.

Judge Ito appeared dumbfounded, as if he did not know what to do.

The words "not guilty" reverberated through Michael's head. He looked at the killer and saw him grinning from ear to ear. Michael's impulse was to leap across the railing and bash the smirk off his face.

Then came the real message of the verdict. As the jury left the court-room, Michael saw Juror 6 raise his left fist in some kind of salute toward the defense team. He did not know exactly what the gesture was, but he realized immediately that it carried a racial message. He thought: That's what this is all about. We could have had fifty eyewitnesses. We could have had a videotape of the actual murders, and the verdict would have been the same.

Patti saw this gesture also, and recognized it as the black-power salute. You son of a bitch, she thought. How dare you do that in this courtroom in front of these families and these people. How dare you?!

Then the killer looked directly at Kim and smiled. Johnnie Cochran did the same.

"You fucking murderer!" Kim yelled. She felt a strange need to apologize for her language, and turned to those around us. "I'm sorry, I'm sorry," she mumbled.

Judge Ito ordered everyone to stay calm and remain seated.

Defying him, we got up and walked out, with words echoing in our heads that would remain there forever: " . . . not guilty of the crime of murder . . . upon Ronald Lyle Goldman, a human being."

TWENTY-SEVEN

～

We rode the elevator back up to the D.A.'s office. The halls were lined with people of every description. Tears were the common denominator. I wanted to scream out my fury. My hands were balled into fists, and I felt like punching a hole in the wall; I wanted to destroy something. It was as if the wind had been knocked out of all of us. Michael and Lauren were sobbing. Patti was in shock.

Kim walked over to a window and stared out, weeping bitterly. Mark kept a close eye on her.

Judge Ito's clerk, Deidre Robertson, approached and told us that the judge had locked himself inside his chambers and was refusing to speak to anyone. She confirmed Patti's instant realization that the reason she had stumbled on the defendant's name while reading the verdict was because she could not believe it. "I'm so sorry," she said. "The system really let you guys down."

In the background Kim heard the Brown family chattering. "Do you think he'll be able to play golf?" one of them asked. Another chimed in, "Do you think he's going to want to pick up the kids this afternoon?"

I nearly blurted out: The son of a bitch was just found not guilty and you're worried about whether he's going to pick up the kids this afternoon?! But somehow I managed to hold my tongue.

Tanya Brown mused, "I wonder who he'll go out to dinner with now."

Kim felt as if she were trapped in a mental ward, and she could not remain silent. She yelled out, quite loudly, "Shut up, Tanya! Who cares who he's going to party with. There is a murderer walking the streets, folks!"

226

I said quickly, "I need to get out of here. I need to get some air."
Kim ran outside of the room with me and sobbed, "Thank God you said that. I was ready to jump out the window."

That afternoon our house was once again filled with friends and neighbors. Our victim's advocate, Mark, and his wife, Chanele, were the only ones present from the prosecution team.

Kim felt as if she were isolated inside a strange bubble. It was as if a nuclear bomb had exploded and we were the only people left on the face of the earth. Everything was somber and still. Time was suspended.

Kim found herself wishing that she had a vice, something to allow her to blow off steam, to find some release. She thought: I'm not much of a drinker. I don't use drugs and I don't smoke. I don't gamble. I don't run marathons. It's a good thing that I've never tried cocaine, because that type of escape would probably be very attractive to me right now. There's nothing I can do to escape from the pressure cooker I am living in.

She wanted to go to the cemetery, but what would she say to Ron? She had never promised him that we would make the murderer pay for his crimes, because she knew that we did not have the power to do that and she did not want to promise something that she could not deliver. Still, she would have to tell him that the killer got away with it. We all felt as if we had failed Ron.

It was about 4:30 P.M. when Kim slipped away and drove to the cemetery. Some members of the press and a few photographers were there, but they left her alone. She sat on the gentle slope of the hill, beneath the large oak tree, staring at the headstone. She thought: I'll never get used to it, seeing my brother's name etched into hard, cold stone.

As she looked at the dates that marked the beginning and the end of Ron's life she realized, with full force, that now no one would ever be held accountable for his murder.

She cried inconsolable tears. Over and over again she said, "I'm sorry. I'm so sorry. We couldn't do anything. Please, don't be mad at me. We tried our hardest. Everybody fought for you, but we let you down."

TWENTY-EIGHT

As we faced the chilling reality that Ron is gone, that we are never going to see him again, and that his murderer escaped punishment, the sense of permanence was, and is, overwhelming. There is no way to escape it.

Lauren complained, "I have such a hatred for *him*. I have never felt such hatred for someone. I'm afraid someday he will be in the house. I see him on TV and I just scream and curse him. I can't look at him."

Deep emotions caught us all off-guard. Driving alone in his car, Michael heard one of Ron's favorite songs on the radio. It was Chicago's recording of "Inspiration." Michael sobbed so heavily he could barely see the highway.

I came across a collection of old photographs. Leafing through them, I found several that were taken at Halloween, when Kim was about seven and Ron was ten or eleven. I had made the costumes myself. Kim was a sunflower and Ron was Count Dracula. Tears flooded my eyes, and my body began to shake at the sight of the mock coffin that I had fashioned as part of Ron's costume.

Kim came into the room. Wordlessly, I handed her one of the pictures. I did not need to explain myself. She knew exactly why I was crying.

Patti told a friend, "Sometimes I think I can't take this anymore. I'm at my breaking point. It's just—everything is just too overwhelming. I want to pull the covers over my head and hide. All the stress—every single day—strangers approaching us—constantly talking to lawyers—constantly being approached by the media. It's been nonstop since that horrible June twelfth."

Kim was seriously concerned that she would suffer a nervous break-down. She was living in the past and obsessed about her future.

During the criminal trial the killer was locked up, and escorted to and from court by police. Now he walked the streets, drove the freeways, and dined in whatever establishment would have him.

I, too, have imagined walking through a mall and seeing him, or entering a restaurant and realizing that he is there. One part of me would say, "I'm out of here." Yet another part of me would bristle and sneer, "Why should I be the one who is forced to leave?"

Kim said, "Dad, once the civil case is over we will begin the mourning process that we need." But after considering her words, she concluded, "I don't think that's really true. I feel that time, that process, was taken from us. We will never be able to go back in time."

The killer began to mouth off in public, but only on a selective basis. He spoke by phone with Associated Press reporter Linda Deutsch. He tried to negotiate a pay-per-view gala, but no one was interested. He made a surprise call to *Larry King Live.* We were angered, reminded of the dismal fact that if he was in prison, he would not have these opportunities.

He placed a phone call to Bill Carter, a *New York Times* reporter whose beat was television, and who previously interviewed him for a book about *Monday Night Football.* Caught off-guard, Carter scrambled to take notes. Despite the ambush tactics, Carter elicited a few interesting comments. For example, the killer asserted, "Maybe I'm a little cocky, but in my heart I feel I can have a conversation with anyone." He then declared that he would like to debate Marcia Clark, in order to "knock that chip off" her shoulder. We thought that was a poor choice of words for a powerful athlete who had pled no contest to beating up a woman. However, it did conjure a laughable mental picture of this man verbally sparring with the razor-sharp intellect of Marcia Clark.

When Carter asked if he was broke, the killer replied smugly, "I still have my Ferrari. I still have my Bentley. I still have my home in Brentwood and my apartment in New York."

That was an interesting comment in light of the only avenue of justice that remained open to us. Once acquitted of criminal charges, the murderer could never be retried. Even if new evidence surfaced, even if he confessed, the criminal courts could never punish him for murdering Ron and Nicole. However, the double-jeopardy statute does not apply to a civil case. If a drunk driver kills your wife, you can sue to collect damages. If your daughter dies in an airplane crash, you can sue the airline. And if a crazed, knife-wielding maniac slashes the life away from your son and brother, you can ask a civil court to take away his Ferrari, his Bentley, his home in Brentwood, his apartment in New York, and every red cent that he has.

At a post-verdict press conference in the courtroom, as he waited for the authorities to release a double murderer onto the streets, Jason Simpson had read a prepared statement purportedly written by his father: "I will pursue as my primary goal in life the killer or killers who slaughtered Nicole and Mr. Goldman. They're out there somewhere. Whatever it takes to identify them and bring them in, I will provide it somehow."

We have this to say to the killer: We have yet to see you pursue as your "primary goal in life the killer or killers who slaughtered Nicole and Mr. Goldman."

But that *is* our primary goal. And we now set about to pursue you with vigor.

From the very beginning of the case, we wanted to do something for the prosecution team to show our appreciation for their tireless work. We had the utmost respect and admiration for them all. So we hosted a large "thank you" dinner party at La Pasta, a local Italian restaurant, and were gratified that so many attended. It was a chance for us to share some happier moments, outside the courtroom setting, where we could unwind and be ourselves. We knew that it was the last time we would all be together.

After that, however, we moved forward. When we had originally filed our wrongful-death lawsuit, we had not envisioned the need to follow through; rather, it was a safety valve, in case the criminal trial resulted in the unthinkable. The verdicts had devastated us, of course, and we were now extremely grateful that the civil courts gave us one final option.

Not everyone was supportive of our decision to pursue justice for Ron through civil proceedings. Occasionally someone would ask, "Are you sure you want to go through this again?" or "Why not just let it go and get on with your lives?" Patti's dad told her he was concerned about the stress she had been under, the weight she had lost, and how tired she appeared at times. "You're never going to get him," he predicted, "so why put yourself through this?"

We all knew the answer to that: His name is Ron.

Hundreds of people wrote to us or to our attorney, Bob Tourtelot, offering their condolences. Many of them were professionals who offered us legal and technical support.

We had developed the utmost respect for Bob, but even after he resigned as Mark Fuhrman's attorney, we were worried that the taint remained. In addition, everything connected with this case had grown far larger and more complex that we could ever have imagined. The killer hired Robert Baker, an attorney with a tough-as-nails reputation, to represent him in the civil case, and it was clear that Baker would head a new version of the "Scheme Team." We wondered whether Bob's small, two-attorney firm had the ability to handle the mountains of intricate paperwork that the high-powered Baker would surely create.

By now we knew that highly competent attorneys would take our case on a contingency basis, but we also knew that we would somehow have to cover expenses. On the air, the night after the verdict, KABC radio talk-show host Bill Press had pledged $100 to support us in the civil case and challenged others to do the same. Five thousand dollars was quickly raised and additional money followed. The Ron Goldman Justice Fund was born.

Then one day, with no warning, I received a telephone call from the chief executive officer of a well-known corporation. I had never met the man. He told me that he was 100 percent on our side and that it was obvious who had committed the murders. He added, "If you don't mind me sticking my nose in it, I've thought about your attorney and I don't think he's big enough for this. You need a firm that is bigger, stronger, and more well established." It was an echo of what we had been saying to one another. The gentleman recommended Daniel Petrocelli, a partner in the Los Angeles firm of Mitchell, Silberberg & Knupp. Dan is renowned for aggressively pursuing—and winning—tough civil cases.

We met Dan and liked him immediately. Patti characterized him as "full of piss and vinegar." Kim sensed positive energy and optimism flowing from him.

Dan said to us, "I am in this and I am going to fight. Are you in? Are you up for it?"

We responded, "Obviously you don't know us! Absolutely!"

Dan and his associates set to work immediately.

The same corporate CEO who had recommended Dan pointed out that the money we had raised for the Ron Goldman Justice Fund was woefully insufficient. And we knew that the defense would do everything it could to drive our expenses as high as possible.

With our grateful permission, our new friend set up an office inside his corporate headquarters and called it the Ron Goldman Justice Fund Room. He established a toll-free telephone number for contributors to call, placed ads in newspapers across the country, and even allowed some of his employees to act as volunteers during company time.

His enormous generosity—and that of the many thousands of people who responded—was overwhelming to our family.

Sadly, we cannot thank him publicly, for fear that his company might suffer a backlash from people so shortsighted in their view that they would boycott a certain brand name.

The support that we have received from total strangers has given us the ability to continue the fight, and there is no way we can adequately thank everyone who has helped. It reassures us that there are legions of decent people in the world who just want to do the right thing.

Originally our civil suit was filed jointly by Kim and me. However, Ron had died without a will. Since he had no children, a court ruled that his parents were his legal heirs and, under California law, a wrongful-death suit can be filed only by an heir. Thus, Kim's name was dropped from the lawsuit. As far as we were concerned, it was a mere change in the paperwork. Our family was in this together.

Santa Monica Superior Court Judge Alan B. Haber "conjoined" the lawsuits filed by Sharon, the Brown family, and us. For the convenience of the court, the three cases would be tried as one.

The rules for a civil trial are quite different from a criminal trial. Only nine of the twelve jurors must agree on a verdict. And that verdict is based, not upon whether there is a reasonable doubt, but upon a "preponderance of the evidence." The legal definition of the term simply means that if 51 percent of the evidence by volume or weight points to the defendant's guilt, the juror must decide in favor of the plaintiffs.

This time, the murderer could not lateral the ball to his attorneys. He would have to "limp" to the witness stand on his arthritic legs. His left hand, its knuckle healed from the deep cut found there the day after the murders, would rest on a Bible. He would raise his right hand, the one that had dropped the bloody glove behind Kato Kaelin's room, and swear to tell the truth.

Baker managed to delay the day of reckoning, and rumors surfaced that the killer would flee the country to avoid giving us his sworn deposition. Patti and I did not believe this would happen. He had already gotten away with murder, both literally and figuratively, and we were sure that he assumed the same thing would happen this time. "His ego will keep him here," Patti said.

But Kim was beset by doubts and bitter over the turn of events. This was our case, not the state's; we were supposed to be in control, not the murderer.

We did not learn what would happen until a day or two before Monday, January 22, when Dan called and said, "Okay, he's coming."

I made my way to a tenth-floor suite in West Los Angeles, not much more than a mile from the scene of Ron's death. These were the offices of Dan Petrocelli's law firm. We assembled in a long conference room. The witness would sit at one end of the table as he gave his pretrial deposition under oath.

Kim asked to be allowed in. But since she was no longer a legal party to the wrongful-death suit, the killer could refuse the request, and he did so. "I'm all of one hundred pounds," Kim complained. "What can I do?" Asked by a reporter why he had refused, Kim snapped, "Because he knows that we know he murdered my brother. Would you face me?"

The killer swaggered in. He schmoozed his way around the room, jokingly reliving his latest golf game with his attorneys. He had a big, all's-right-with-the-world grin plastered across his face, and his movements were extremely animated. He conveyed the sense that these proceedings were no big deal. He was just a happy-go-lucky guy.

I fixed my gaze on him. He looked at me, but quickly averted his glance. I continued to stare, but after a while I determined that I was not going to accomplish anything by looking at him except to give myself a splitting headache. He was not worth it.

A reporter asked me later how it felt to sit at the same table with the man I had openly called a coward and a murderer. "Necessary, but difficult," I replied. "Let's just say, you know what my feelings are and it would be difficult to be in the same room."

A pattern emerged immediately. Whenever Dan asked a benign question, the killer looked him right in the eye and answered directly. Conversely, when the questions were of substance to the case, he appeared spacey and his gaze slipped past Dan. He took many deep, labored breaths. He fidgeted constantly. At key moments, his lead attorney, Robert Baker, asked for a short recess.

His testimony ran counter to both the physical evidence and the eyewitness accounts of scores of individuals. He contradicted himself. This is a man who so loves the sound of his own voice that he frequently volunteered information in defiance of his attorney's advice, once prompting Baker to ask rhetorically, "Am I a potted plant?"

The tedious process took a total of nine days and produced a 2,582-page transcript. Dan would revisit this murky territory during the civil trial, and there were a few notable statements that were sure to cause the murderer serious discomfort.

I was not able to be present during every day of the deposition. Once, when I had to leave early, we asked if Kim could take my place for the afternoon.

"Absolutely not!" was the response, and the door was slammed shut.

"It's very unusual," Dan said. "Normally a family member is allowed in, if only for moral support."

"You know," Kim observed, "it's always women who speak out that he attacks. Faye Resnick, Denise Brown, Marcia Clark—now me. There's a pattern here."

If she was not to be allowed inside, Kim vowed to haunt the halls. Every day she stood near the closed door, as close as she could get without coming inside. Before and after the sessions, and during breaks, she availed herself of every opportunity to glare at the killer.

Suddenly she found herself face-to-face with him, so close that she could smell his breath.

He looked her up and down and flashed his insulting half-smile.

"Don't do that!" Kim thundered.

He chuckled.

Later, Kim moaned, "Of all the things I have longed to say, all I could come up with is, 'Don't do that!'"

The Browns' attorney, John Q. Kelly, described a disturbing scene to me. Everyone was taking a break. The videotape was not running. The court reporter was not transcribing. The killer and his attorneys were, once again, discussing their golf games. It seemed to be all they could ever talk about, and Kelly bowed out of the conversation. He was lost in his own thoughts when the killer said something directly to him. Kelly did not bother to answer. Unaccustomed to being ignored, the killer became agitated and kicked at Kelly's chair. Then, when he still did not respond, the killer walked over and slapped him on the back.

I asked Kelly to be more specific, to reenact exactly what had happened. He kicked my chair with such force that I almost tipped over, and when he slapped me on the back, he knocked the breath out of me.

"Are you sure you aren't exaggerating this?" I asked. Kelly swore that he was not. Sharon's attorney, Michael Brewer, was also in the room at the time and verified what had happened.

Clearly this is a man who must always be the center of attention. And if he senses that he is being ignored, he reacts with force.

TWENTY-NINE

Early on we had formed a negative impression of Faye Resnick. Her book about her friendship with Nicole, proclaimed as sordid and opportunistic, and her admitted drug use left her open to criticism and ridicule. We had not read her memoir and had been angered that she chose that route rather than protecting her credibility as a witness, which might have helped us in court.

As time passed, however, Resnick became more of a central figure. The defendant claimed that Resnick, not Nicole, was the real target that night, set up for a "hit" by drug dealers. The two were in agreement on only one major point: In the months preceding the murders, Resnick and the defendant had spoken frequently. The killer claimed that he was upset with Resnick and her drug-using friends, and was worried about Nicole being drawn into her world. Resnick had a very different story to tell when the attorneys traveled to New York to take her deposition.

It quickly became clear why she had been so certain, from the very beginning, who the killer was.

Referring to the defendant, Dan asked, "You have seen him fly off the handle?"

"Yes, I have," Resnick answered.

"Now, during those occasions when you saw Mr. Simpson get very angry toward Nicole, describe what his face would look like when he would get angry. And for that matter—you can describe, like, his whole body. You know what I mean?"

"Yes, I know," she responded. "O. J. would get very—his facial structure, his jaw would protrude, his teeth would clench, sweat would come pouring from his head. You could see that his body, that he would perspire through his clothing. His eyes would get narrow and black. He became—and the only way to describe it is animalistic when he would become angry at Nicole."

"And that would happen suddenly?" Dan asked.

"It would happen within minutes."

"You could see changes in his face?"

"Yes."

"What about his body? Was there any body language that also changed?"

"He just became bigger than life. He just got big."

"Dominant?"

"Very—it was very aggressive, just, you—"

"Did it frighten you?"

"Absolutely."

Much of Resnick's testimony consisted of conversations with Nicole that would probably be considered as hearsay evidence, inadmissible in court, so we were particularly interested in her encounters with the defendant himself. According to Resnick, in the month preceding the murders, he telephoned her numerous times, threatening to kill Nicole because he could not bear the shame and humiliation that he felt she inflicted on him by breaking off their relationship. She quoted the defendant from a May 1994 conversation: "I know she is seeing another man, and if I catch her with another man . . . I will kill her."

One evening we played a game called "What If?" One of the questions was "What if I only had an hour left to live?"

I responded, "For the first five minutes, I would do the obvious, then I would do something else for the remaining fifty-five."

Kim was not so charitable. "I would beat him, take him into a corner, and torture him until he was dead, and I would take the full hour to do it."

In my wildest fantasy I see myself alone with the killer. No one sees me come into the room and no one sees me leave. I put a gun to his head and I say, "You have one chance to tell the truth. If you tell the truth, you will live. If you lie to me, you will die. The question is this: Did you murder my son?" And if he says, "Yes," I say, "I lied, you piece of trash, and you're out of here."

I recognize this as the fantasy of a father in agony. In reality, I could never do this. It is not who I am or who we are.

However, sometimes fantasy and reality come too close for comfort. I had just completed a business meeting in a pleasant, modern office complex in L.A., and as I walked through the parking lot, I heard someone call out, "Mr. Goldman?"

I turned and saw a man walking toward me. He introduced himself and said, "I just wanted to tell you how sorry I am about your loss. How are you doing?" Before I could answer, he continued. "I have an office right up there." He pointed to the second floor of the building I had just left and kept talking. "Look, if you ever decide you want to kill that son of a bitch, just let me know. I can get you a high-powered rifle and scope that will never be able to be traced and you can take care of him."

"No, no, no," I stammered quickly. "I don't have any interest in anything like that." I desperately wanted to exit myself from this conversation.

"Yeah, well, I understand," the man said. "If you don't want to be the one to do it, I'll find you somebody who can do it for you."

My mouth was agape. I could not believe what I was hearing. A total stranger was standing here, in the middle of a parking lot, in the bright California sunshine, offering to commit, or arrange for, cold-blooded murder. And he was deadly serious. "Thanks, but no thanks," did not seem quite strong enough, but that was all I could muster.

As I walked away he called out, "If you ever change your mind you know where to find me."

I was deeply shaken. A whole family of things came to mind as I drove home after this freakish encounter. For an instant I wondered if this could be a setup, a sting of some kind designed to get me into trouble, but upon reflection, I doubted it. You only have to pick up the newspaper or watch the news on television to realize that there are many people who perceive violence as a legitimate solution to their grievances.

A long-suppressed memory returned to me.

My mind transported me back to Army basic training at Fort Leonard Wood, Missouri. We were there for one reason. We were being taught to kill.

The instructors "armed" us with a rifle-bayonet mock-up—little more than a stick, padded at both ends. We looked like hockey goalies, wearing helmets, padding on our chests, and crotch protectors. Two by two, young soldiers entered a sandpit.

The training sergeant grew frustrated with the ineptitude of the combatants. None of the men were mastering the techniques to his satisfaction. He looked at me; I was a squad leader. "Get in there, Goldman," he ordered. "You show 'em how it's done."

So I suited up and entered the pit. Instantly my opponent whacked me on the side of my head.

I went berserk. Survival instinct took over, and I flew through the motions I had been taught. After I knocked my opponent on his butt, the sergeant sent in another, and I dispatched him quickly. The sergeant continued to throw men into the pit and, one after another, I crushed them into submission. The illusion was very powerful; I truly felt as if I were fighting for my life.

Not until later that night did the emotional impact of the training exercise descend on me. I realized that if I was placed in a kill-or-be-killed situation, I was capable of violence. If I had to, I would fight for my life. If I had to, I could kill. But I would be left with a dismal sense of remorse. I wondered: How can someone consciously decide to kill someone else and not think twice about it? It is beyond my understanding.

Now, many years later, as I drove home on the Ventura Freeway, I recalled other memories from my military training. A young soldier learns to kill in a multitude of ways. The belt that holds up your pants can be used to strangle an enemy. If you put a lemon-sized rock into your sock, it can crush a skull with one powerful swing.

But the most troublesome techniques then, and especially now, were the uses of knives and bayonets. They can slash a windpipe or pierce a heart with chilling speed and efficiency.

I believe that we learn things throughout our lives that never leave us. Those things come to the surface when we need them. We surprise ourselves, often, with bits of information and pieces of knowledge that we had not thought of, consciously, in years. They are there, etched into some hidden corner of the mind. And I believe that phenomenon came into vicious play on the night of June 12, 1994.

During the fifth day of the killer's deposition, Dan had asked about the time he was in Puerto Rico to play the role of a character named Bullfrog in an action-adventure movie entitled *Frogman*.

There was one scene where he wielded a serrated knife. Dan asked, "Did anybody show you in connection with that particular scene how to perform the physical actions?"

The killer replied, "How they wanted it to be done, yes."

Dan produced excerpts from the *Frogman* script and read them aloud:

Without a sound, Bullfrog has entered the dive show shop. Doesn't turn on the lights. Doesn't have to. . . . Bullfrog comes up with a lethal, serrated dive knife. . . . Bullfrog cases the area. All clear. . . . Looking toward the back of the shop. Through the mazes of counters and gear, he sees a shadow. . . . Bullfrog steals past. Silent. Bullfrog's made a circle. He's behind the shadow. He lunges and, in one swift move, has the intruder on the floor, one arm twisted back in a punishing hold.

That scene was filmed two months prior to Ron's murder.

THIRTY

~

W e joined three other couples for dinner one evening. I had not seen one of the men there in several weeks. He asked me a few questions about the trial, and we ended up sitting at the end of the table, ignoring the others, and discussing the criminal and civil cases for hours. On the drive home, Patti was very frustrated with me. "This cannot be the focus of everything we do," she said.

"Well, he asked me," I countered. "He wanted to know."

"Well, next time it happens, could you just say you appreciate their interest but you don't want to spend the majority of the evening discussing it? Tell them you're trying to focus on other things during the weekends. It's so consuming."

Patti busied herself building a clientele for her electrology business and was finally able to rejoin her tennis league. Michael and Lauren were immersed in high school activities and their respective social scenes. I tried to attend to the details of the civil case and, in the meantime, sell point-of-purchase displays.

But Kim's life had been on hold since she had dropped out of school and moved back home. After the criminal trial she was in limbo. She signed up for some additional college courses to, as she put it, get her brain functioning again, but she no longer wanted to major in psychology.

None of us had ever sought the limelight, but bits and pieces of our lives continued to be on display. Ron's picture—and sometimes ours— regularly appeared on the covers of various tabloids, alongside screaming headlines that often reported erroneous information. So many people, all over the world, were so hungry for scandal that we never knew what would surface next. Kim, especially, felt naked.

Tricia Argyropoulis, a cousin of Ron's friend Pete Argyris, was one of the many who had left a message on Ron's answering machine the weekend that he died. She and Kim grew close. Tricia is an up-front, in-your-face kind of woman. Once, she and Kim visited a club called Roxbury that Ron used to frequent. They were enjoying themselves, dancing, when a woman intentionally pushed Kim. Kim just stood there, frozen. Tricia saw what had happened and immediately told the woman off. After her tirade, Kim said, "Gosh, you're tough!"

Later, they joked about the incident. "Oh, God," Kim said, "I can just see the headlines in the tabloids: 'Goldman Brawl in Bar: Lesbian Lover to Rescue!' " It was a facetious comment, but the tabloids were always a concern.

Kim remained close to Chris Darden as well as several of the trial reporters, including Dominick Dunne, Cynthia McFadden, Shoreen Maghame, and Dan Abrams. The tabloids exploited this, reporting that Kim and Dan were "an item." This was not true, and it underscored the difficulty of filtering friendships through such a public funnel.

Thanks to a recommendation from one of her reporter friends, Kim accepted a job with the TV production company that produces *The Larry Sanders Show.* She was nervous about going back to work full time. After so much public exposure, she worried about preconceptions that people might have about her. "Fate must have been smiling on me," she said later, "because as soon as I arrived, I met Joanne Geller, and within an hour, it felt as though we'd been friends for years. My moods can change from upbeat to sadness to fiery anger very quickly, and Joanne rides those waves with me—never complaining, always supportive."

Although she never knew Ron, Joanne quickly pinned one of our Remember Ron buttons to her purse. She says that she talks to him sometimes, and feels a connection.

Kim shared with Joanne a realization that haunts her. If it had not been for Ron's death, she would never have landed this job, and she would never have met Joanne. As much as she values the friendship, she would give it up in a heartbeat just to have her brother back. Joanne understood completely.

There is one other special friend who has remained in contact. Sometimes when we come home after a long day, we press the PLAY button on our answering machine and hear Barbara Walters's distinctive voice say, "Just wanted you to know I'm thinking about you."

During an unscheduled early-morning call to radio station KJLH-FM on February 29, the killer uttered the absurd statement that he knew that I felt "the same way" as he did about the murders.

We were in court that day. During a brief hearing, both sets of attorneys informed Santa Monica Superior Court Judge David D. Perez that they would not be ready by the previously scheduled trial date of April 2. Our lawyers sought a new date in mid-July, but Robert Baker claimed that previously scheduled trials in other cases would make him unavailable until autumn.

There was another hitch. Baker told the judge that he had been informed this morning that co-counsel F. Lee Bailey "may not be available for some time." Evidently, earlier in the day, a federal judge in Florida had ordered Bailey to begin serving a six-month jail sentence for contempt of court. This was for failing to comply with the judge's order to turn over millions of dollars in cash and stocks that federal prosecutors said he took without permission from the assets of a former client, confessed drug smuggler Claude Duboc.

I chuckled when I heard the news; it warmed my heart. I loved the thought of him in jail. I just wished that his client could share the cell with him.

The upshot of all this was that Judge Perez postponed the civil suit for more than five months, ordering that it would begin at 8:30 A.M. on September 9.

I was very upset. At a news conference on the courtroom lawn I declared: "I am disappointed that it has been moved back. . . . My family, and I'm sure the Brown family, would like to get this as much behind us as we can. This just makes for additional pain."

Privately I asked Dan, "Can't we get this thing rolling?"

He took a deep breath and replied, "It's okay." He knew that our case would benefit from the extended preparation time.

Then someone asked me how I felt about the killer's radio remarks earlier in the morning, that he and I felt the same way about the murders.

"My answer is bullshit," I said. "He's got a lot of nerve saying we feel the same. He didn't lose a son.'"

As the parade of pretrial depositions and procedural hearings continued, the *Los Angeles Times* reported that the Internal Revenue Service filed a tax lien with Los Angeles County, warning that it might seize the murderer's home if he failed to pay $685,248 in back taxes from income earned in 1994—the year of the murders.

This raised the ugly issue of money. Some experts estimated that the killer had spent between $5 million and $6 million on his criminal defense, and of course our civil case was adding to his legal fees. Just how much money did he have left?

Dan explained to reporters, "The Goldmans never have expressed concern about whether funds will be available for them at the end of the trial. They're concerned about getting justice in this case, about getting a jury to declare Mr. Simpson responsible for the death of their son. It's not about money."

In other words, it was not about *us* receiving money; it was about *him* being forced to pay for his murderous rage. Kim said, "Money is what he thrives on. If he has to write a check to us, even for a dollar, he will know it's because a jury decided he's the killer."

Even if we realized a substantial judgment, my guess was that we would never see much of his money. First, we assumed that, even during the criminal trial, he and his attorneys had been making efforts to squirrel away what money he had, perhaps burying it in foreign accounts. Second, he claimed that his earning power had been thwarted, although we had financial experts ready to testify that there were still some people who are willing to "buy" anything that he has to "sell." Third, there were rumors and other indications that some of his legal bills from the criminal trial remained unpaid. Robert Shapiro claimed that he was owed $500,000.

We conjectured that it might be a constant struggle to try to get money out of him. I said, "That's okay with me. If he is hiding money, he runs the risk of getting his ass in a wringer with the IRS."

I told a friend: "I don't know how much money the killer has or where he has it buried. It will likely always be a struggle to get him to honor whatever judgment there might be against him, but the judgment lasts for ten years and can be renewed. I intend to put a hook in him that will last for the rest of his life, and I will drag him into court again and again if necessary. There is not enough that I can do to him to make his life miserable, a living hell.

"If that sounds vicious or vindictive, so be it."

Even during the worst of times we are constantly amazed at the thoughtfulness of people and surprised at the impact Ron's murder has had on individuals who had never even met him. The second week in June, when we visited his grave, we discovered a blue notebook and a gold pen resting on Ron's headstone. The pen had a small angel attached to it. On the cover of the notebook was a message that suggested, "Use this angel pen if you wish to express for Ron, words, on the second anniversary of his passing. This book is offered to the Goldman family in hopes to ease and comfort your pain." We had no idea who left it there.

Kim wrote a lovely note of appreciation inside the front cover, and we left the book there for a few days.

On the evening of June 12, the second anniversary of Ron's death, we gathered at the cemetery with our circle of friends. We retrieved the notebook and found it filled with the most amazing messages—written not only by friends but by strangers who feel a connection to Ron and to us. There were notes from people whose lives have been shattered by violence and domestic abuse. There were letters that share memories and tell us how Ron touched lives in one way or another. Many people recalled Ron's numerous small acts of kindness.

Kim read all the messages aloud.

One woman wrote: " . . . You had some kind of magic about you that just seemed to make anyone who came in contact with you smile. After bumping into you somewhere or coming to the shop to just talk, I'd leave feeling all was right with the world and I was a beautiful person. You could make an ugly troll with warts feel beautiful."

That was the Ron we knew and loved.

Late that night Kim lay on her bed, thinking: Two years ago, right now, our fate was sealed. Our lives will never be the same. She knew that *Larry King Live* had scheduled a rerun of an interview with Chris Darden, and decided to watch the late telecast. She came downstairs. All the lights were off. A memorial candle flickered on the kitchen counter. Kim turned on the television. After watching a few minutes of the interview, she felt an overwhelming need to speak with Chris, so she called him.

"I'm watching you on *Larry King,*" she said.

"I never watch myself," he replied.

They spoke at length about the sadness that they shared, about Kim losing Ron and about Chris losing his own brother to AIDS. The quiet conversation helped them both.

It is very sad that our youth have so few heroes outside of the sports arena. Our heroes and heroines should be teachers, scientists, policemen, and firefighters. And people like Chris Darden.

Father's Day was four days later.

I was still tired all the time. I tended to go to bed very late, feeling that if I got good and tired I would fall asleep more quickly. Still I tossed and turned. Still I woke at 2 A.M. or 3 A.M., and it took some time before I could fall asleep once more. Sometimes I just had to get up. This had been one of those nights.

Michael and Lauren prepared a bagel, some juice, cottage cheese, and fruit and presented me with breakfast in bed. It was part of a family tradition that includes cards and gifts later in the day, and an evening dinner out. But everyone sensed that I was vulnerable. No one knew whether or not to mention Ron, or Father's Day. Would it help or hurt? There was no correct answer, of course. The family kept a low profile.

As the morning progressed, I found myself wound tighter and tighter.

Sometime later I happened to glance into the backyard. I saw Lauren in the Jacuzzi and Michael, Patti, and Kim lying on lawn chairs, getting some sun. For no discernible reason the tranquil scene set me off, and I stormed outside. I could feel that red-hot anger was etched on my face as I exploded into a tirade the likes of which they had never experienced. I screamed, "I appreciate the fact that you brought me breakfast this morning, but no one has given me any gifts. You don't care about me. You didn't take any time to give me a card. None of you give a shit. The hell with all of you. I'm getting the hell out of here, goodbye. I don't give a goddamn." Without giving anyone time to respond to my outburst, I turned and ran for my car.

Kim ran after me, begging me to stop. But I sped away.

Kim knew that tangible gifts are not, and never have been, important to me. What was going on was far deeper than that. She wanted to be compassionate and understanding, but she was furious with me. She felt that the lion's share of my anger was directed at her and that she had failed me in some way. At the same time she was weighed down by the unfairness of it all. With Ron gone, she often feels that she is all that I have left, and that is a constant source of anxiety for her.

I drove aimlessly, and much too fast. Kim and Patti called me several times on the car phone, but I did not want to talk and I did not want to come home.

As my anger slowly subsided I remembered that cards and gifts were always given out later in the day—much later. I began to realize what this was all about. Even though I had not awakened angry, desolation was still chewing me up inside.

Michael's high school graduation was on June 20. Earlier in the day he went by himself to the cemetery to talk to Ron for about a half hour.

That evening, as Michael was sitting with the other members of his senior class, ready to line up for the processional, he slipped off by himself and sat in a corner for a time, wishing Ron was there. Then he marched in with the rest of his class, forcing a smile on his face.

When the valedictorian said something about how all of the family and friends of the class of '96 were here, Michael said to himself: No, not everyone is here with me. He closed his eyes to hide the gathering tears. He knew that Ron would have been so proud of him. Ron's words came back to Michael: "Never give up. Always do your best because you won't have a second chance. Make things memorable and always make an impact."

The last time Kim had attended an event at the school was at her own graduation in 1990, and she could not shake the mental image of Ron hugging her after the ceremony. She did not want to ruin the evening for Michael, or to inflict her tears on everyone, so she slipped away and sat by herself for a while at the side of the building. She relived every moment of her graduation night.

She remembered when I aimed a camera and asked Ron to pose for a photo with his sister. Ron had his arms around her. They were hugging, and he had a quirky little smile on his face. After I had snapped the picture, Ron had said, "Okay, let go."

"No, I don't want to let go," Kim had replied. "I love you and I don't want to let go."

Michael was accepted by the University of Arizona. He confided to a friend: "Things are better around here, but tempers are still flaring and Kim's mood swings are getting harder and harder for me to take. Sometimes she will seem really up and happy and the next minute I'll say something to her and she'll blow completely. And it feels like, no matter what happens, Fred is always on her side.

"Lauren is growing up and going through a lot of changes, too. I think we've gotten closer in the past year or so.

"I love everyone in my family with all my heart, but I am very anxious to go away to college and start a life of my own. I think that once I'm away, my family will have more respect for me and listen to my opinions. It's going to be hard, though, because I'm a real momma's boy, and I'll miss her very much. She hugs me and tells me how much she's going to miss me, and I'm going to miss her, too. But I can't help but be excited about getting away."

Kim knew that it was time for her to leave also. She and Dakota found an apartment with Sarah Kupper. "Sarah is such a wonderful friend," Kim remarked. "She is never judgmental, accepts my mood swings, and always understands."

Just as happened to me on Father's Day, unexpected emotions continued to ambush Kim. Her friend Paul Geller took her to the beach on a lovely afternoon. As Paul was surfing, Kim looked out at the seemingly endless vista of water and found herself consumed by sadness. Methodically, she started picking up rocks, remembering all the times that she and Ron had done the same thing. They used to have a contest about trying to find the ugliest rock on the beach. Now doing this by herself brought an ache that was physical in its intensity. She missed her brother so much, and realized that there was nothing she could do about it. "It overwhelmed me," she said. "I never know when these waves of emptiness will encompass me, but I have learned to expect them."

THIRTY-ONE

❦

We were surprised that, even with the passage of time, the public's passion did not seem to have changed one iota. Everyone still seemed to have a very strong opinion about the case. Total strangers continued to approach us, choked with emotion, to offer their support.

Of the thousands of letters we received, perhaps only one out of a hundred was negative. A few came from some who thought we should give up our quest for justice, either because they believed in the defendant's innocence or felt that our actions were futile. Some people advised that we should put this all behind us and get on with our lives. I do not believe this is possible. Ron's death left an incredible, gaping hole in our hearts, and we can never fill it.

Judge Alan Haber faced a gargantuan task. By now the paperwork surrounding the civil case dwarfed that of the entire criminal trial. Dan had slapped the killer with several phonebook-thick motions demanding that he respond to 480 oral queries, turn over scores of pieces of potential evidence, vouch for the authenticity of more than 500 items, and answer a lengthy written questionnaire.

Over the course of time the judge issued several important rulings. We won some and lost some, but one of our most critical victories was the judge's decree that, in order for the defense to employ its "conspiracy" theory, it would first have to explain to the court precisely how it believed that evidence was planted, fabricated, or contaminated. He ruled that the defense attorneys had to review all the exhibits introduced as evidence in the criminal trial—from bloodstained socks to autopsy photos—and either admit the authenticity of each item or explain their reasons for challenging them. For example, the defense was required to show some tangible evidence that Ron's blood was planted in the defendant's Bronco or that DNA analysts had botched their tests. The defense could not simply present innuendo or inference to the jury. One of our attorneys declared, "O. J. Simpson can no longer hide behind unsubstantiated assertions."

Under California's civil trial procedures, each side has one—and only one—opportunity to recuse a judge. We were not certain that we wanted to keep Judge Haber on the case, but we did not know how the defense felt about him either. It was an interesting chess match. Without question, we preferred that the defense use up its recusal privilege first.

Judge Haber's ruling on the "conspiracy" defense proved to be the final straw for Baker and Company. On July 17, the defense exercised its right to challenge one judge. Haber was removed from the case, and sixty-year-old Santa Monica Superior Court Judge Hiroshi Fujisaki was named to preside over the civil trial. The *Los Angeles Times* described him as "a gruff, tough jurist with a passion for motorcycles and an empathy for victims."

Dan was very pleased. He had argued two previous cases in front of Judge Fujisaki, and he declared, "He will put up with no nonsense, no shenanigans in his courtroom."

During his nearly twenty years on the bench, Fujisaki had earned a reputation as a crack-the-whip judge with little tolerance for chitchat. He ran his courtroom in such a way that no one forgot who was in charge. Unlike Judge Ito, he refused to reconsider rulings, did not banter with attorneys, and made it very clear that he took his job and the court extremely seriously.

One of Judge Fujisaki's colleagues commented, "He does not suffer fools lightly."

However, I found one of the judge's early rulings to be a problem.

"No counsel may discuss anything connected with this trial with the media or in public places. This order encompasses all parties, attorneys, and witnesses under the control of counsel."

The twenty-nine words of that gag order, uttered by Judge Fujisaki on Tuesday, August 13, silenced parties to the lawsuit and all of the attorneys for the duration of the trial. This time there were to be no press conferences on the courtroom steps; this time it would be tried in the courtroom.

I quickly learned that holding my tongue can be more exhausting than speaking out.

A gaggle of media attendants, protesters, and just plain paparazzi descended on Santa Monica. In downtown L.A. during the criminal trial the area around the courtroom was known as "Camp O. J." In Santa Monica it was now being referred to as "O. J. by the Sea." It was Tuesday, September 17, 1996. How ironic that two years and one day ago we were beginning the criminal case.

An artist displayed a mural depicting two bodies and a knife. Excerpts of speeches by the Reverend Martin Luther King, Jr., blared over a loudspeaker. A spectator shouted insults about the killer to anyone who would listen. Another arrived in his aqua Cadillac Coupe de Ville, plastered with pictures of Ron and Nicole. "If O. J.'s a celebrity, why can't Nicole be a celebrity?" he asked. "We need to focus on victims."

Since the gag order had muzzled all the principals, reporters were reduced to interviewing each other. One of them quipped to a colleague, "We're fascinating."

Inside the courtroom, Judge Fujisaki raced through a stack of pretrial motions several feet thick in two hours, issuing thirty-nine rulings. Once again the defense wanted permission to attack the LAPD as a group of inept bunglers who contaminated the evidence and/or corrupt, racist officers who planted evidence.

Patti thought: Uh-oh. Here we go again.

Judge Fujisaki apparently agreed. "The point to be addressed to the jury is whether the evidence that was collected tends to prove Mr. Simpson's culpability or not," he said. "This is not a case about did the LAPD commit malpractice." He pointed out that "Mr. Simpson is not suing the LAPD."

He further ruled that the defense would not be allowed to swerve into topics he deemed irrelevant or speculative. They would not be allowed to argue to jurors that the LAPD failed to examine all the blood from the crime scene, or that Colombian drug lords could have been behind the killings. Most important, the judge blocked them from introducing evidence about Detective Mark Fuhrman's allegedly racist attitudes, and his use of Fifth Amendment protection when asked whether he had planted evidence—a linchpin of the conspiracy theory.

We finally got to the task of jury selection, a process that would continue for a full month. No one ever told us that we had a right to be present at jury selection in the criminal case until the trial was well underway, so we were determined to be involved in that process for our civil litigation. None of us was prepared for the effect that would have on us. It was an exercise in maneuvering, manipulation, and second-guessing—on both sides.

As prospective jurors were questioned, we found ourselves looking beyond their answers and into their motivations and possible agendas, asking ourselves: Is she lying? Why does he want to serve on this jury? She'd be good for our side. I hope he isn't chosen, he's likely to be pro-defense. It was troubling and exhausting.

We are not racists. Nor are the many black people who have approached us to express their disdain for the criminal verdict. Sadly, most add the disclaimer "But I can't say this in public."

As the criminal trial progressed, Johnnie Cochran had increasingly turned the focus away from the murders and into a false struggle over nonexistent racial issues. Now we could see the killer expanding upon the theme. He attempted to rally the support of the black community, and we believed deeply that he was trying to influence potential black jurors.

"This is a twisted process," Kim said. "I wasn't brought up to judge people this way—relying on stereotypes. It makes me feel like a hypocrite."

Each day the killer limped into the courtroom for another round of charm-the-public. Whenever there was a lull in the proceedings, he joked and bantered with the press until he was finally reprimanded for doing so in front of prospective jurors. It was very disturbing that so many of the attorneys, reporters, and spectators were concerned over the racial makeup of the jury. There was no guarantee that a white person would vote for us or that a black person would vote against us, but the jury consultants warned us that there was no way to escape the issue in this extraordinary case.

Thank you, Johnnie Cochran.

* * *

During the weekend of Yom Kippur, I made a decision that would alter the remainder of my life.

As a boy, I walked a mile to and from school and there was never anybody saying, "Don't talk to strangers. Be careful of this. Be careful of that." After school I went outside and played. My mother did not hover over me, afraid that some pedophile would snatch me. My friends and I stayed outside until dark. Today there is a security system on our house, and alarms on our cars. People are not safe on the freeways or at the neighborhood park—nor even in their homes. Did the situation change because we are tough on criminals? Of course not. It changed because we started treating criminals as if they are really just damaged human beings. When someone commits a violent crime, we slap them on the wrist. They may or may not serve some prison time, but they are back on the streets again before long. Instead of blaming them, we blame society. We give them reasons for what they did. We understand. We say to them, "Aw, you had a rough childhood. Your daddy ignored you. Your mommy wasn't home enough. It is society's fault that you are a mass murderer. We understand your pain."

We need to change the situation, so that good, decent, law-abiding people can feel safe.

During the criminal trial I began to question my focus, my purpose in life. In the past I had always enjoyed my job, but the passion was not there anymore; it was replaced by matters of greater importance. That issue grew more troubling. I faced the same daily struggle, trying to eke out a few hours of my day to attend the trial.

I had been exploring career opportunities. My passion now was to somehow make Ron's life and death more meaningful by working for reforms in our judicial system. We had considered starting a nonprofit organization to lobby for judicial reform and victims' rights, but realized that governmental rules and legal restrictions would make this very difficult. Then I was introduced to Jim Whooten, the director of Safe Streets Alliance, a nonprofit organization based in Washington, D.C., that actively works for judicial reform.

Jim and I spoke on the phone, then he flew to California to meet with me. He shared my concerns, and it was interesting to note that he came to his viewpoints from a different background. He was not a victim; rather, he is an attorney who has seen the problems from within the system.

And so, after nearly thirty years in the sales and packaging business, I decided to switch occupations, accepting Jim's offer to become the public affairs director and chief spokesman for Safe Streets Alliance. During the course of the civil trial I would make some appearances on behalf of the organization, but I would not commence my primary duties until the trial was over.

I was excited and impassioned with the potential to help bring about changes within the system that currently tolerates absurd inequities. I hoped, for Ron's sake, that I could make a difference.

However, my euphoria was short-lived. I learned that on Thursday night, September 26, *Larry King Live* would be guest-hosted by CNN legal analyst Greta Van Susteren. She was scheduled to interview Donald Freed, co-author of a book entitled *Killing Time*. The book purported to use "scientific research" to prove that the defendant did not have time enough to commit the murders and that Ron may have been the target.

I called the show and said that I did not want to speak on the air just for the sake of being on—I had the gag order to consider. But if Freed said anything to demean Ron, I wanted to respond—and to hell with the gag order. I was placed on hold.

Eventually Freed did put forth his absurd suggestion about Ron. He was the cause of his own death.

I could hold my tongue no longer. Over and over again, I have said that if anyone attacked Ron's good name, no gag order on the face of the earth was going to shut me up.

As the show progressed, Patti heard me muttering, "Who does he think he is? Where does he get this crap?" Then I raged, "This guy is a fraud. It's all theory. There's no proof. He doesn't authenticate anything. He's there to hawk his book."

I went on the air and berated the man, suggesting that the only reason he was proposing his ridiculous theories was to capitalize on this horror.

Freed immediately turned defensive. He suggested that my grief made it impossible to view the topic with logic.

That set me off further. As I said to Dan the next day, "I can't remember my exact words, but I think I ripped this man a new one."

Things got worse. By Friday morning I was aware that there had been numerous news reports suggesting that the Ron Goldman Justice Fund was, in fact, a fraud perpetrated by someone other than our family.

During the noon break in the jury-selection process, I held an impromptu press conference to explain the fund-raising activities. I declared that the Ron Goldman Justice Fund was legitimate. There was no fraud or subterfuge, and we could only assume that the attacks were somehow orchestrated by the opposition.

A reporter noted my comments the previous night on *Larry King Live* and asked me if I had violated the gag order. I smiled politely, shrugged, and answered, "Maybe. But I'm not going to stand by and have someone demean Ron."

I did not return to court that day. Instead, I headed to my office to attend to some of the details I had to clear up before officially changing jobs.

When court resumed, the defense complained that my statements the previous night, and again this day, were violations of the gag order and might taint potential jurors.

Dan defended my actions, noting that the author was "on television in effect trashing my client's murdered son, and my client called in to express his outrage."

Judge Fujisaki snapped, "If the parties are going to violate the order, I don't think monetary sanctions are going to be sufficient. It's my intention to seek an appropriate remedy to the situation, which I think is going to be somewhat draconian—and that's an understatement." He had the option to find me in contempt of court, which carried a maximum penalty of five days in jail and a $1,000 fine.

We waited to see whether or not the defense would move to have me punished. Our attorneys checked my statements. They agreed that portions of the gag order were vague. I may have pushed the envelope a bit, but it was unclear whether I had really violated the order.

It was not until some time after the criminal trial verdict that we came to realize just how alienated and abandoned Michael and Lauren had felt, at times, during the long, long months of the criminal trial. Patti knew that she could not rewrite history, but she determined that she would do things differently in the future.

Someone needed to be there at the end of the school day. Someone had to throw a ball for Lucy, scratch Pitzel behind her ears, and give Riley an occasional cuddle. Someone needed to make our house a home again, and that was her priority. As the civil trial loomed, Patti announced that she would attend the proceedings only one day a week unless something extraordinary was scheduled. She settled on Mondays because her business was closed that day. Her decision made a remarkable difference. Very quickly, she and Lauren and Michael rediscovered their close and loving relationship, and much of the previous tension evaporated.

Even during jury selection I was eager to give Patti a blow-by-blow description of what I had heard and seen. "Please, just give me the big picture," she said, "not all the details." She now suggested a "gag rule" of her own, asking that, especially when Lauren was present, we would not discuss the day's proceedings during dinner. She and Lauren wanted to talk about other things. Whenever I slipped, Patti shot me a look that pleaded: Not now. Later.

By Monday, October 21, we had a jury and eight alternates.

In an ideal world the press would have reported that the jury consisted of twelve human beings sworn to serve the cause of justice. But the bean counting continued. For the record, the seven-man, five-woman panel comprised nine whites, two blacks, and one mixed-race individual. We did not care one whit about gender or ethnicity; we wanted honesty and fairness. We did not want to win this case on the basis of the jurors' skin color. The *evidence* was black and white.

That was all that should matter.

This time around, both sides were assigned eight seats in the crowded courtroom. So the killer got eight, but we had to divide ours among three plaintiffs. After some maneuvering, we got three seats, the Browns got three, and Sharon got two. We were willing to share and make accommodations, depending on who could attend on a given day, but it would be a continual scramble.

We all wanted to attend as much as possible, but this time things would be a bit different. Patti would be there every Monday, and would also attend when critical events were scheduled. Kim found it nearly impossible to be in close proximity to the killer, to see him walking freely among the public. "I don't want to breathe the same air," she said. She would come to court when she could, but she knew that her attendance might be intermittent. But my new career gave me the freedom to be present at almost every moment.

I said to Patti, "It is an eerie situation to suddenly discover that we are only a day or two away from beginning this nightmare again."

Our mood deepened as we drove north on the Ventura Freeway. On our left, the hills were ablaze. Wildfires, fed by the Santa Ana winds, consumed the dry brush that lay between us and the Pacific Ocean. The farther we drove, the more we were enshrouded by dark, acrid smoke.

It felt as if we were driving through hell.

THIRTY-TWO

O ur attorneys booked a suite at the Doubletree Hotel, directly
across the street from the courtroom. They set up a "war
room," complete with computers, phone banks, copiers, and
fax machines. We would assemble there each morning to discuss the
coming events of the day. Our family would be much more involved
than we had been in the criminal trial. This was our case. Patti and Kim,
because of their constant attendance at the criminal trial, knew the evidence better than some of the lawyers.

The problem with this arrangement was that we would walk a gauntlet as we made our way to the courthouse. On Wednesday, October 23,
the crowd of spectators, aware that the infamous defendant would probably make an appearance, were both numerous and vocal. Kim was apprehensive as we emerged from the hotel. Comments were shouted at us
from all sides. Reporters sought to get us to violate the gag order. Many
onlookers expressed their support; others hurled insults. At this time
there was no team of investigators from the D.A.'s office to protect us.

Kim thought: Some of these people might be capable of violence.
She kept her head down and cried, "I can't deal with it!"

"Just pick your head up," I advised. But she started to lag behind. "If
you fall back you're only drawing attention," I said. "Safety in numbers."

As we passed through a metal detector and entered the courtroom,
we found ourselves in close proximity to the killer, who was seated on
the defense side, calmly leafing through a newspaper.

Many members of the killer's family were present. His grown children, Arnelle and Jason, were notably absent. Before the proceedings

began, the killer's clan huddled around him to pray. As they implored God to aid their cause, the murderer perused the sports section.

Finally, at 10:15 A.M., the jury filed into the courtroom. At that instant Patti's entire body began to tremble. She thought: We're going to have to go through all of this again!

I felt an enormous flood of apprehension. I asked myself: Would these twelve people see things more clearly than the other twelve who were so willing to ignore the evidence? God, are we going to be able to do it this time?

Dan rose to present his opening statement. In a low-keyed delivery, he promised the jurors that we would reveal "the lies and deceptions of Mr. Simpson."

As he previewed the case, it became clear that these jurors would see and hear evidence that had never made it into the criminal case. Fibers found at the crime scene did not merely match the fibers of a Ford Bronco; they matched the somewhat unique fabric of the killer's Bronco. His taped interview with police the day after the murders raised numerous questions and conflicted with later statements. One of the most dramatic pieces of brand-new evidence was a photograph showing the defendant wearing the "ugly ass" Bruno Magli shoes that he swore he would never own.

Dan indicated that we would rely upon a different timeline than the criminal prosecutors. He contended that the murders occurred around 10:35 P.M., several minutes later than Marcia and Chris had calculated. Some observers considered Dan's new scenario risky, because it gave the killer less time to drive home and dispose of the murder weapon and the clothes he was wearing. But we felt that we had credible testimony to establish this timeline, and we had forensic experts ready to inform the jury that the assault happened so quickly that the killer had ample time to make his escape.

Dan's new timeline made a good deal of sense. A dog will bark at almost anything, but now we had a real person who would say, "This is what I heard at the moment." It narrowed the window of time for the killer to flee, but it gave us more credibility.

The murderer stared straight ahead during most of Dan's statement, but occasionally he clenched his jaw, smiled in mock disbelief, or shook his head in protest. Rarely did he look at the jurors. Some members of his family busied themselves with "Word-Find" puzzles. His sister, Shirley Baker, and her husband, Benny, played "Hangman."

As Dan neared his conclusion, we listened to his clinical, graphic description of how Ron died. We all held hands and tried to get through it. But we were unprepared when he concluded with a chilling fact.

"Ronald Goldman died with his eyes open," Dan said. "In the last few moments of his life, he saw the person who killed his friend Nicole. The last person he saw through his open eyes was the man who ended his young life, the man who now sits in this courtroom, the defendant." That image will always haunt us.

Patti and I left court at noon on Thursday to fly to Arizona. We would miss Robert Baker's opening statement for the defense, and we would miss the first day of testimony, but there was no way that we would miss Parents' Weekend during Michael's freshman year.

Kim was able to attend.

Baker spoke without notes, sometimes seemed disjointed, and frequently backtracked. Kim concluded: He's trying to cover his ass on everything.

Baker tried to convince the jury that Nicole's own reckless and immoral behavior put her in harm's way. He also attempted to show that some of the killer's past frustrations with his wife were justified. Kim was repulsed by his depiction of Nicole as a heavy-drinking, promiscuous woman who kept company with a variety of low-life friends. In fact, he said, the defense would prove that Ron had gone to Nicole's apartment for a prearranged "date." He tried to paint his client as a man who was simply concerned for his children, and told the jury that he was the one who had been stalked, not the other way around. According to Baker, after the breakup of their marriage, Nicole had the audacity to send her ex-husband cookies and even showed up at his country club.

No wonder he had to slit her throat, Kim thought.

Going as far as the judge's restrictions allowed, Baker tried to raise the old, tired issues of contamination and corruption of evidence. Although prohibited by the judge from mentioning Mark Fuhrman's perjury plea, he managed to interject the controversial ex-detective's name into his statement whenever possible.

Then Baker made a key mistake. He mentioned that the killer had once offered to take a lie-detector test, but the prosecutors had refused. This was a good news/bad news situation. It left the jury with the impression that he had not taken the test, but it opened the door for us to revisit the topic later.

Baker said one thing with which we heartily agreed. Above all, he told the jury, "listen to the testimony of O. J."

With Kim as our only family member in attendance, the mind games began in earnest. She described the scene vividly in her journal:

Having to be in close proximity to the killer is much worse than even I expected. I knew it would be uncomfortable, but it's nearly impossible to take. He stares at me, often running his tongue across his upper lip, with a smirking leer on his face. I stare back, willing the daggers in my eyes to pierce straight through him. It's become a sick game of one-upmanship. I heard him whine to a reporter, nodding in my direction, "Look what I have to deal with. She does this 24 hours a day." Then I was confronted by a woman, who is the killer's self-proclaimed best friend. She walked over to him. He motioned towards me. She walked over and stood in front of me to block my view. I moved to the left. She followed. I moved to the right. She followed. I tilted my head, as did she. I looked at her and said, "Do you think what you are doing is effective? I could just move around you." And I did. She turned to me and said, "He is pretty good looking to stare at, isn't he?"

The killer and his idiot bodyguard were laughing. They knew exactly what she was doing and saying.

This is the beast whom I believe butchered my brother and left him to die. His ex-wife, the mother of his children, met the same horrible fate. Yet, he saunters around the legal system, mocking us, laughing at us, it's like pouring salt into an open, oozing wound.

We are constantly warned to maintain decorum and dignity, to turn the other cheek and simply take it.

But I am ready to rumble.

I can feel it coming. I can feel it brewing inside me. I cannot maintain this much longer. An explosion is in the offing. And there is precious little I can do to stop it.

* * *

And then there was Sharon. Until now, we had ignored her, and she had returned the favor. But on this day, after court, she came up behind Kim and whispered, "Do you want to reconsider talking to me? You are making this obvious."

"Sharon, walk away from me," Kim replied.

"It's 'Mom' to you," Sharon said.

Kim turned to leave, aware that reporters and lawyers hovered everywhere. "You are a little bitch," Sharon hissed in her ear. "Who do you think you are? You have an attitude. That is my son and you have no right to sit here. I don't know who you are. You are not my daughter, and you can tell your father that, too. How dare you both make shit out of me on TV. I'll get you back."

"Stop talking to me!" Kim growled.

Kim was rattled, and very angry. She reported the incident to Dan, and he suggested that Kim just politely tell Sharon that this was not an appropriate time to be discussing such matters. For the sake of the trial, we did not need to air our dirty laundry.

But Kim had had enough. "No way," she told Dan, "just tell her to stay the hell away from me."

Once again Kim heard a witness recall Ron's final words.

As testimony began on Friday, our "ear witness" Robert Heidstra told the jurors that he was walking his dog in an alley behind Nicole's condominium at about 10:34 on the night of the murders when he heard the sounds of two men arguing. "I heard a clear voice yelling, 'Hey! Hey! Hey!,' " he said. "It was a male, no doubt about it." Then he said he heard "another voice, a deeper voice, talking very fast—it sounded like an argument. . . . Then I heard a gate clanging, bang." Five minutes later he saw a white Jeep-like vehicle with tinted windows, come "out of the dark" and speed from the area.

In a surprisingly brief cross-examination, Baker got Heidstra to stress that the white vehicle turned south, speeding away in the opposite direction from the Rockingham estate. But Baker spent little time attacking Heidstra's testimony because he, too, was satisfied with the later timeline.

Stewart Tanner, the Mezzaluna bartender, testified that Ron did not have a "date" with Nicole that evening, that he was, indeed, merely returning Juditha Brown's eyeglasses; in fact, he said, he and Ron had had plans to meet another friend at Marina del Rey later that evening.

Other witnesses set the grisly scene. Brentwood resident Sukru Boztepe recounted how he tried to calm the frantic, bloodstained Akita that he found on Bundy Drive at about 10:55 P.M., and described how the dog dragged him to Nicole's condominium, where he saw a bloody body.

As Boztepe testified, jurors leaned forward to stare at a crime-scene photo. There before them was the grisly sight of a bloody walkway, with Nicole's body visible at the far end.

It soon appeared that testimony would speed along much more quickly than it had during the criminal trial. By midafternoon Dan told Judge Fujisaki that, because he had anticipated more rigorous cross-examination, he had run out of witnesses for the day.

Patti and I were back in court on Monday; Kim was back at work. Things continued to move along briskly. Our side called the first three LAPD officers who had arrived at the crime scene. Officers Robert Riske and Miguel Terrazas and Sergeant David Rossi described the crime scene and identified where they had found various pieces of evidence.

Dan used Riske's testimony to introduce photographs of the crime scene. It was the first time since the criminal trial that Patti and I had seen the chilling pictures of the bloody, horrible place where Ron had died. This viewing was even more painful than before. We were closer to the television screen, and this was *our* case. Patti and I were reduced to tears.

The officers testified that blood drops on both the walkway and the back gate appeared fresh and moist. Additional officers, who had responded a few hours later, said that the stains were bright red, not the brown color of blood that has been exposed to the elements for a long time. This early testimony was very important. The officers clearly established that there was blood all over the place about midnight. At midnight, there was blood on the back gate. The officers testified that they saw only *one* bloody glove at the crime scene. At midnight. Long before the detectives—including the maligned Mark Fuhrman—arrived on the scene.

The killer himself did not show up in court until the afternoon, and we noted his own reaction to the crime-scene photographs. At first, he did not wince or shed a tear or display an iota of remorse. But after he consulted with his lawyers during a short recess, whenever the photographs were shown, he turned his head away quickly.

"What a joke!" Patti murmured.

Kim met us at court on Thursday. It happened to be Halloween, but Kim was tired of wearing a mask. She said, "You know, Dad, we are not behaving normally. People commend us on our ability to remain calm and dignified under these terrible circumstances and it just isn't right. We should be screaming, yelling, and clawing at him."

Our attorneys cautioned her to stay calm, and not to say or do anything that might jeopardize our case. "People watch every single move we make," she complained. "If they catch us smiling, they want to know why. If we look upset, they assume the worst. Why don't I have the right to just be myself and permission to say the things that are churning inside me all the time?"

We wished the cameras were there to catch the derisive expression the killer developed for Kim. His eyebrows would arch, one side of his mouth would turn upward, and his eyes scanned her body from head to toe.

This proved to be a ghoulish day that left us all limp with anger and despair. Former Detective Tom Lange testified about the passport, revolver, money, underwear, socks, and the fake moustache and goatee that the killer had brought along with him while fleeing arrest five days after the murders. Prosecutors in the criminal case chose not to deal with this evidence, but we contended that he was carrying supplies to enable him to escape the country. To us, it was clear evidence of "consciousness of guilt."

However, it was Tom's duty to portray the horror of the crime scene for the jury, and this entailed the presentation of photographs that were larger and far more vivid than the ones displayed previously.

As the court viewed Nicole, slumped in a fetal position, surrounded by her own blood, the killer looked away, just as he had done in the criminal trial. He mouthed words to himself and seemed to be breathing rapidly. A few jurors audibly gasped, but listened attentively as Tom pointed out the positions of the bodies, and the bloody trail of footprints and drops on the walkway.

Kim glared at the murderer. It was her way of saying: You're not going to get any more of me. I'm going to make sure you know I hate your guts.

Then photos of Ron were on display. Kim and I hung our heads and struggled to maintain composure. As many times as we had heard this testimony, as many times as we had seen the photos, it did not get any easier. Kim whispered, "I can't even close my eyes, because the pictures are already in my mind." As she listened to Tom describe Ron's wounds in a clinical, professional manner, she thought: He tried so hard to ward off the knife. What were his last thoughts? Was he scared? Did he know what was happening? Did he think about us? Did he know he was dying? Did he know how much we loved him?

A part of us wished that the public could see these ghastly photographs. People would have to say, "Oh my God, this is real!"

I could only glance at the photos briefly before I had to look away. I wanted to see Ron. But I did not want to see Ron this way. I stayed in court longer than I wanted to, to support Kim. Finally, knowing that I was close to hysteria, my daughter sent me out.

By day's end, our nerves were shot and our emotions were raw. Court was adjourned and the room was almost empty. We were still inside, with our attorneys. I happened to turn and see that the killer was near the closed courtroom door. He was staring in our direction with his face contorted into a sneer. As he opened the door and was confronted by reporters, I shouted, "Don't give me any of your goddamn dirty looks!"

Appearing indignant, he raised his voice to respond, "I wasn't looking at you. I was looking at your daughter, who was staring at me. She plays staring games."

Later, Patti had to listen to my rage: "That scumbag lying son of a bitch who first murders my son and then has the colossal gall to stare at my daughter and give me a snotty look. He's trash, that's all there is to it!"

THIRTY-THREE

On our way home from court one day, Patti pulled into the shopping center at Kanan Avenue and Lindero Canyon Boulevard. She stayed in the car while I went into Ralphs to pick up a few groceries. As I was going through the checkout line, my gaze fell upon the cover of *Globe* magazine. In the lower left-hand side of the page was the caption: RON DIED WITH HIS EYES OPEN. Underneath was a close-up of Ron's eyes.

Somehow I made it out of the supermarket and back to the car. Patti started to shift into drive, but I reached out my hand and said, "Stop."

Patti hesitated. When she saw tears pouring from my eyes, she shoved the gearshift back into park. "What is it?" she asked.

I told her what I had just seen.

Patti slipped her arm around my shoulder and asked, "Do you want me to go in to see it?"

"It's up to you," I said.

Patti consoled me for a few moments. Then she slipped out of the driver's seat and disappeared into Ralphs. When she returned she, too, was shaking. "Why did they have to print that?" she asked.

We sat in the parking lot for several minutes, hugging one another.

"It never ends," I said.

We had heard it in court, but we were unprepared to see the photograph on a tabloid cover.

Yet events were racing toward a conclusion. Many of the same witnesses who had testified at the criminal trial took the stand. They generally presented similar testimony, but there was a refreshing crispness to the proceedings. Dan stuck to business, asking the key questions and refusing to get bogged down in nit-picking details. In the process, he stymied the defense team, which could only address issues that we raised during direct examination.

This tactic left Baker almost in shock, seething with questions that Judge Fujisaki would not allow him to ask. By the time the relatively brief testimony of Detectives Tom Lange and Phil Vannatter ended, Baker seemed, as I said to Patti, "confused and dazed." He frequently took out his frustrations by demeaning his son in open court. Philip Baker was a young associate counsel on the defense team, clearly there as his father's whipping boy. Kim referred to him as "Little Baby Baker."

During the criminal trial, LAPD chemist Gregory Matheson spent five days on the witness stand. Now, when he testified that the defendant was one of about 550 individuals in the population who could have left a blood drop on the front walk at the murder scene, he was on and off the witness stand in a matter of hours.

Criminalist Dennis Fung testified that he had found possible traces of blood in the killer's shower, in his bathroom sink, and on a wire dangling in an alleyway on the killer's Rockingham estate, near the site where Fuhrman found the bloody glove. The stains were so tiny that Dennis could perform only a basic chemical test, but those results indicated the possible presence of human blood.

This was critical new evidence, disallowed into the criminal trial record. If there was blood on a wire in the alleyway, it strengthened our assertion that the defendant was bleeding when he vaulted the fence behind Kato Kaelin's room—and it refuted the theory that the glove was planted. The relevance of the shower and sink stains was obvious.

Cross-examination was conducted by Robert Blasier, a holdover attorney from the criminal trial, who tried to mount a blistering attack. Dennis acknowledged that he could have done some things differently, but contended that his procedures overall were correct. During the criminal trial, Dennis had endured a nine-day ordeal on the witness stand; now he was finished in little more than an hour.

Richard Rubin, the former president and general manager of Aris Glove Company, once more testified that the bloody gloves fit the defendant. He acknowledged that the fit was of "poor quality," but he said that was because they had shrunk by about 10 percent. Judge Fujisaki allowed the defense to show a video from the criminal trial, reprising the murderer's infamous "attempt" to force his hands into the gloves. The judge, however, would not allow the jury to hear the audio portion of the performance. It was quite remarkable to watch this scene without sound. There was the image of the killer holding his hands up in front of the jury with an insolent look of amused victory on his face. But without the distraction of his dubious comments, the gloves did, indeed, appear to fit.

Turning to the subject of the cuts on the killer's hands, Dan and his team had a barrage of interesting information to present to the jury. The public seemed to remember only the one dramatic cut on the middle finger of his left hand, but Dr. Robert Huizenga testified that when he examined the defendant days after the murders, he found three lacerations and seven abrasions on his left hand. The cuts measured from ⅛ inch to ½ inch, and were all fresh.

In one of the versions of his story, the defendant had said that he first cut himself at his home the day of the murders, and then reopened the wound in Chicago when he broke a drinking glass in his hotel bathroom. But our attorneys now read from the deposition of Detective Kenneth Berris of the Chicago police, one of the investigators who had examined the killer's hotel room. There was not one drop of blood in the bathroom. There was a broken glass in the sink, but no blood was found on it. And there were no chips of glass on the vanity or on the floor, as one would expect to find if the defendant had backhanded the glass with his left hand. Berris said that he found blood on the bedsheets, and we displayed photos for the jury. Would the killer have to change his story, claiming that he crawled back into bed for a nap after learning of Nicole's murder?

It was difficult to know at this point, for the killer left court early that day, claiming that he was ill. However, he was seen playing golf.

"Sometimes when I read the paper or listen to the news, I can't believe that the reporters were in the same courtroom, listening and watching the same testimony I was," Patti said. "If the criminal trial had to be televised, I think this one should have been, too."

The press walked a tightrope. ABC TV's Cynthia McFadden and Shoreen Maghame, and Court TV's Dan Abrams had become close to us, especially to Kim, but their jobs required objective, nonbiased reporting and, just as in the criminal trial, their public accounts were sometimes difficult for us to listen to.

Shoreen told Kim that the killer had approached her and commented on the brace she was wearing to counter a carpal-tunnel problem. He had touched her arm and commented about arthritis. "Kim," she said, "I was paralyzed. All I could see were the scars on his hands!"

The killer seemed to develop a crush on one of Dan Abrams's colleagues, a tall, attractive redhead. He constantly made suggestive comments to her, winked, whistled, and flirted. The woman was repulsed, and attempted to avoid him.

Another reporter told us, "The day my editor says I have to interview him is the day I quit."

Patti and I were sitting in court one morning, waiting for the judge, when we realized that Lawrence Schiller was sitting directly behind us. He was the writer who collaborated with the killer on his offensive book *I Want to Tell You.* He had also helped produce the killer's videotape. Now Schiller had written his own account of the defense team's antics, wherein he disclosed that the murderer had failed a lie-detector test, and reported that Robert Kardashian had developed doubts about the innocence of his longtime friend.

We had never spoken to Schiller, but Patti could not resist the opportunity now. She turned to him and commented, "You're sitting on a different side this time."

Schiller smiled and said of the defense, "They're probably ready to kill me."

"Oh, well—" Patti responded, and then turned her back on him.

Friday, November 8, was a dramatic day, when once more we had to steel ourselves to listen to gruesome autopsy testimony. The Browns chose not to come; once again we decided to tough it out. The murderer did not attend and everyone assumed that he was still feeling poorly. It was only later that we heard a report that he played golf this day also.

One of our talented co-attorneys, Ed Medvene, called upon an expert witness with an animated, friendly style. Dr. Werner Spitz, the author of *the* definitive pathology textbook, was without question our most interesting witness thus far.

An enlargement of the killer's wounded left hand was flashed on a television monitor. Dr. Spitz pointed out the jagged edges of three curved wounds. "These are not caused by glass, and these are not caused by a knife," he declared, explaining that broken glass or a knife blade would produce smooth-edged cuts. What, then, caused the lacerations? Dr. Spitz declared, "These are fingernail marks." He testified that the gouges could have been inflicted by either Ron or Nicole during a struggle with the killer.

As the jury viewed a series of fourteen autopsy photographs and Dr. Spitz maintained a running commentary, we slumped forward and sobbed. Several times I had to flee the courtroom, but I forced myself to return. Kim remained throughout.

Dr. Spitz presented the jury with his own theory of how the murders occurred. He suggested that Nicole was slain in one furious knife assault. He described in detail the depth of the fatal slash across her throat, which went all the way back to the vertebrae and severed her carotid arteries. Using his hands to demonstrate, he showed how all of Nicole's wounds could have been inflicted in fifteen seconds or less.

It was during this brief, terrible moment in time that Ron must have arrived and shouted, "Hey! Hey! Hey!" Dr. Spitz described everything that happened to Ron—stab wounds to his chest, the stab wound to his left back that punctured the aorta and was likely the fatal blow, the slash to his left leg, the cuts and abrasions on his hands. In total, Ron suffered about thirty stab wounds. Dr. Spitz estimated that Ron struggled with his assailant for one minute or less.

From his examination of the evidence, this renowned pathologist concluded that one person, wielding one knife, could have committed the murders and escaped with few bloodstains on him.

Baker went on the attack during cross-examination, prompting numerous angry exchanges. Dr. Spitz held his ground and drew diagrams to explain his conclusions. Nicole's blood had spurted forward and down, away from the killer standing behind her. Ron suffered massive internal injuries, but did not bleed very much outside his body until he had slumped to the ground.

During his contentious cross-examination, Baker made an unbelievable mistake. In an arrogant tone of voice, he asked, "Dr. Spitz, do you
believe that Nicole Brown could have pulled the glove off Mr. Simps—
uh, the assailant's hand?"

Remarkably, he repeated this gaffe two or three more times. On one
occasion he spoke the defendant's complete last name and then added
quickly, "—if he were the assailant."

These were very telling Freudian slips. I said to Patti, "I guess the
truth always comes out."

When the trial resumed after a break for Veteran Day, Dr. Spitz was still
under cross-examination. Baker must have had a bad weekend, for he
was on a short tether. He sought yes-or-no answers to his questions, but
Dr. Spitz felt the need to explain his points. Again and again Baker lost
his temper. Once he shouted, "No, no, no, no, no . . . we're not here to
have you make speeches."

Baker challenged the witness's contention that the cuts on the defendant's hand were caused by fingernails. He said in a derisive tone, "You
don't mean to tell me" that Nicole's fingernails made the gouges?

Dr. Spitz answered, "I don't know who made them."

Baker observed that Ron had very short fingernails. Did Dr. Spitz
think that Ron could have caused the gouges?

"Yes," Dr. Spitz replied. He pointed out that his own fingernails
were as short as Ron's, and asked, "Would you like me to show you how
this works?"

Baker moved quickly toward the witness stand. Pulling off his suit
jacket, he challenged: "Go ahead. Gouge me!"

"You want me to scoop tissue out?" Dr. Spitz asked.

Judge Fujisaki jumped into the fray, warning, "I'm not going to have
any gouging of flesh in my courtroom."

Dr. Spitz said, "Then I'll do it to myself." He took off his jacket,
rolled up his sleeve, and dug the four fingernails of his right hand into
the skin of his left arm. He raised his arm for the jury to see. The marks
were clearly visible. "You see? It can be done," he declared. "When you
fight for your life and you dig in deep, you push back the flesh so your
fingernail suddenly becomes longer."

A short time later, during a break in the testimony, I was standing near Dr. Spitz when a reporter asked to see his arm. The witness rolled up his sleeve and displayed the marks. All four of his short fingernails had broken the skin and drawn blood.

Dominick Dunne visited court on a few occasions. In reminiscing about the trial of his daughter's murderer, he mentioned an effective tactic. To illustrate the time it took to commit the crime, prosecutors had stopped the court proceedings for a full five minutes. It had seemed like hours. "I will never, ever forget those five minutes," Dominick said. "Everyone in the courtroom was crawling out of his skin."

Kim passed this suggestion on to Dan, and we decided to try it to dramatize the sixty seconds we believed took Ron from us.

On redirect examination, Ed Medvene called for the courtroom to remain silent for one minute, and asked Dr. Spitz to mark the time. The witness checked his watch and tapped a pen against the edge of the witness stand to signal the start of the minute.

No one spoke.

No one moved.

We stared straight ahead.

We kept waiting to hear the tap of Dr. Spitz's pen, but the silence remained, and seemed to deepen.

Still the second hand ticked slowly.

It is amazing how long one minute is.

A dark depression engulfed me as I realized that in one minute such as this, Ron's life had been snuffed out.

It was continually curious to watch the behavior of the killer and his lawyers before and after court and during breaks. Whenever the jurors were out of the room, they joked and backslapped one another, constantly discussing their golf games. They did not appear to take this matter seriously. Clearly this team of defense lawyers was spawned from the same garbage bin as the original "Scheme Team."

FBI Special Agent Douglas W. Deedrick presented the results of his analysis of hair fragments and carpet fibers linking Ron and Nicole to the killer's Ford Bronco, once more tightening the circumstantial case against the defendant.

Deedrick was cross-examined by defense attorney Daniel Leonard. One of his main lines of attack was to show that Deedrick was a biased witness. He got the FBI agent to acknowledge that he displayed in his office a photograph of himself posing with Kim and me. This was a surprise to us, and we discovered that the photo had been taken during Phil Vannatter's retirement party, which we all attended.

Later, we learned Deedrick's theory as to how the defense discovered the existence of the photo. Someone claiming to be a writer had come to his Washington office and asked for an interview. Deedrick became suspicious when the "writer" nosed about his office and specifically commented about the photo.

We cut to the chase. Under direct examination by Tom Lambert, our three DNA experts, Dr. Robin Cotton of Cellmark Diagnostic Laboratory and Renee Montgomery and Gary Sims, both from the California Department of Justice DNA laboratory, presented the evidence in a "user friendly" manner.

The statistics were familiar to us, and as damning as ever: The probability that blood leading away from the crime scene came from someone other than the defendant was as low as 1 in 170 million and as high as 1 in 1.2 billion. The chance that blood on the socks found in the killer's bedroom came from someone other than Nicole was 1 in 6.8 billion people. The probability that blood found on the back gate at Bundy came from someone other than the defendant ranged from 1 in 57 billion to 1 in 150 billion.

It was the task of defense attorney Robert Blasier to counter these incredible probabilities. Despite the fact that the defense, prior to the trial, had agreed to accept the DNA results, Blasier fired question after question in an effort to confuse and confound the jury.

When I tried to summarize what Blasier was trying to say, I wound up with a mishmash of thoughts: *There are an enormous number of cells in the body; if you took all of the DNA in someone's body and you took each DNA marker and separated them by half an inch, they would stretch twice around the earth; and, of course, you have to consider how many nanograms of blood were tested in this case; by the way, a nanogram is a billionth of something; and don't forget that the computer has to calculate an error factor; blah blah blah.*

I said to Dan, "I think it would be fair to say that Blasier is a bit anal."

Neither Blasier nor any of the other defense attorneys addressed the issue that, considering the volume of the evidence, it was outrageous to contend that there was a conspiracy and contamination. Ron's blood, Nicole's blood, and the defendant's blood was all over the crime scene. It led away from the bodies, crawled into the defendant's Bronco, spattered onto the glove found behind his home, dripped into his foyer, and came to rest on the socks in his bedroom. If *any* of this blood had been planted, it *all* had to be planted. If *any* of it was contaminated, it *all* had to be contaminated. The killer would have to be the unluckiest man on the face of the earth to be the victim of such an incredible set of coincidences.

Dan explored the defendant's well-known penchant for beating Nicole. LAPD Sergeant Mark Day described the 1984 incident, before the couple was married, when the defendant had used a baseball bat to smash the windshield of Nicole's Mercedes.

Then Detective John Edwards testified about his investigation of the couple's vicious fight on New Year's Day, 1989. In his deposition the killer had explained away this brutal fight by claiming that he and Nicole were "rassling." Patti thought: That is not exactly the word I would use if I suffered the bruises and cuts that I saw on the pictures of Nicole's face and arms.

Finally Dan played a tape recorded by an LAPD officer when he responded to Nicole's 911 call on October 25, 1993. Nicole's description of her ex-husband echoed that of Faye Resnick. "He gets very animalistic-looking," Nicole said. "All his veins pop out and his eyes get black, black and cold, like an animal."

Like it or not, our family was increasingly visible. I was involved almost daily with early-morning and late-night interviews for Safe Streets—primarily on radio—but even on the Internet. I had to be careful not to comment on the trial; rather, my job was to promote a book entitled *Freed to Kill.* Offered at no cost, it chronicled the life histories of eight violent criminals and their journeys through the revolving doors of our broken criminal-justice system.

It was a rewarding feeling to be able to speak out in public about much-needed reforms. But it did raise our profile.

Walking to and from court was a constant concern for Kim and Patti. During the criminal trial, the D.A.'s investigators escorted us. Now we were unprotected. We tried to stay in a tight group with the attorneys and walk briskly, avoiding eye contact with the throngs of people who gathered.

After court one day, as we walked across the street, a stranger infiltrated our circle and accompanied us right into the lobby of the Doubletree. Afterward, Kim berated me for speaking to him. I shrugged my shoulders and commented, "He didn't look shifty."

"These people are capable of surrounding us and yelling at us," Kim pointed out. "How do we know one of them doesn't have a knife or a gun? There are lunatics out there."

One of Dan's interns, Steve Foster, took Kim's fears seriously and arranged for three Santa Monica police officers to escort us. But as soon as they were spotted, the questions started flowing: "What's the matter, Goldmans? Did you guys get a death threat?" It seems we're damned if we do and damned if we don't.

Dan confided, "I went into the men's room the other day, and *he* was there. He looked at me and said, 'You're not going to beat me up, are you?'"

The encounter disturbed Kim. "Dan, do you realize that could have happened to my dad?" she asked. "Anytime he's out of the room, I'm terrified for him."

During the killer's deposition, Dan had elicited comments concerning the Bruno Magli shoes that had left bloody shoe prints at the crime scene. Dan had asked, "Did you ever buy shoes that you knew were Bruno Magli shoes?"

"No," the killer had answered. He did not say that he could not recall owning a pair of Bruno Magli shoes. He used no qualifying words, such as "perhaps" or "maybe." His response was unequivocal, and he was stupid enough to embellish it.

"How do you know that?" Dan asked.

The witness replied, under oath, "Because I know, if Bruno Magli makes shoes that look like the shoes they had in court that's involved in this case, I would never have owned those ugly-ass shoes."

Those words came back to haunt him. Earlier in the trial, photographer Harry Scull, Jr., in a videotaped deposition, described how he took a picture of the killer at a Buffalo Bills football game on September 26, 1993, in which he was sporting Bruno Magli shoes. We displayed the complete contact sheet for the entire roll of film, proving that the specific shot showing the shoes was part of the photographer's work on the day in question.

Now FBI Special Agent William Bodziak compared the bloody crime-scene shoeprints to the pattern of the soles of the shoes in the photo. He detailed the angled heel, the waffle-pattern sole, the deep stitching groove—eighteen features in all—that matched exactly.

"He nailed the son of a bitch," I muttered.

Even after our best days in court, Kim found herself unable to maintain optimism, and she sometimes voiced those sentiments to Dan.

"Don't rain on my parade," Dan pleaded.

Kim shot back: "Dan, please hear me. I trust you. But we got hit in every possible way the first time around. I don't have any faith in the system. Why should I? I can't get my hopes up. I can't let myself get that way. I will not allow myself to trust the system again. Ever."

THIRTY-FOUR

~

The sky was overcast, somber, providing a fitting backdrop. It was Friday, November 22.

Rob and Barb Duben were with us. "This is what we've all been waiting for," Patti said to Barb, "ever since the criminal trial—when the bastard didn't have the nerve to take the stand."

As we emerged from the Doubletree Hotel, we saw that today's crowd was two or three times larger than usual. Cameras and microphones were shoved in our faces, and the normal barrage of questions rang out: "How are you feeling?" "Are you nervous?" and, one reporter's particular favorite, "What did you have for breakfast?" If she had been willing to respond Patti would have replied in sequence: "Sick to my stomach," "Cool as a cucumber, of course," and, "A banana, what else!" But mum was the operative word.

A cacophony of cheers and jeers assaulted our ears. Some shouted, "Goldmans, we love you!" "Don't give up, O. J.'s a murderer!" and "We're on your side!" Other demonstrators yelled, "Free O. J." and "We love you, Juice!"

One man shouted, "Golddigger!"

Rob said jokingly, "He probably meant to say, 'Goldman'!"

Patti found it difficult to swallow. She took several deep breaths as Dan intoned, "Pursuant to California Evidence Code Section 776, we call to the stand the defendant, Orenthal James Simpson."

Patti felt her heart race, and her hands began to shake. She thought: This piece of human refuse is finally going to testify—to tell all of his lies—to be on his very best behavior—to do the most incredible acting job of his entire career.

The killer was asked to stand and raise his right hand. Maybe he should raise his left hand, Patti thought, so it would be easier for him to lie.

The clerk asked: "You do solemnly swear that the testimony you may give in the cause now pending before this court shall be the truth, the whole truth, and nothing but the truth, so help you God?"

The witness replied, "I do." Then he began to tell one lie after another.

He seemed to have difficulty knowing where to focus his eyes. If he looked straight ahead, he would be staring at Patti, Kim, and me, and he chose not to do that. Neither did he turn his gaze toward the jury. So he glanced at Dan, or toward the ceiling, or around the edges of the room. He looked very nervous. Several times early in his testimony he began to breathe heavily; we had learned during his deposition that this was a sign that he was at his most evasive.

He pushed the microphone away from his face. The bailiff moved it back into position. The moment she turned her back, he defiantly pushed it away again, muttering, "They can hear my breathing." Kim told the bailiff what he had done, and shortly thereafter Judge Fujisaki ordered him to keep it in front of him—no matter what.

A few minutes into the questioning, Patti realized that the defendant's children were nowhere in sight. She never expected Sydney or Justin to be there, but she thought that Arnelle and Jason might show some support for their ever-so-innocent father.

The killer admitted that there had been some problems in his relationship with Nicole, and that she had hit him numerous times. Dan asked, "And how many times . . . did you hit Nicole?"

"Never."

"How many times did you strike Nicole?"

"Never."

"How many times did you slap Nicole?"

"Never."

"How many times did you kick her?"

"Never."

"How many times did you beat her, sir?"

"Never."

Dan said, "Let's talk about 1989, okay . . . tell this jury exactly how you caused all those injuries on Nicole's face."

The killer responded, "I don't know exactly how it happened, but I felt totally responsible." When Dan displayed the famous photo of Nicole's battered face, the witness explained: "A lot of this redness would normally be there most nights, once she picked and cleaned her face." He admitted that he "wrestled her out of the room," but he claimed not to know how she sustained a split lip and a welt over her right eye. He said, "Maybe my hand hit—hit or was on her face. I certainly didn't punch her or slap her . . . I had her in a headlock at one point, in trying to get her out of the door, so I would assume that my hand was somewhere around her—her face."

He said this in a rather nonchalant manner, as if there were nothing unusual about putting your wife in a headlock.

At the defense table, we heard one of the killer's own attorneys mumble, "This is sad."

Judge Fujisaki looked on with raised eyebrows; it seemed as if he, too, found the killer's denials implausible.

In the World According to the Killer, this "altercation" was Nicole's fault. She had run into the room, "jumped on me, on the bed, and with her knees and arms—and then I kind of grabbed her and we kind of fell over on the floor."

Dan pointed out that as the witness was answering the question, he had balled his right hand into a fist. He asked, "Is that what you did that night when you grabbed her?"

"Quite possibly when I grabbed her arm, quite possibly I did." As he answered this question, the killer put both hands into fists.

Dan quoted from a book the murderer had published early in his football career, wherein he boasted, "I think I lie pretty effectively."

The killer blamed that passage on his ghostwriter.

He even lies about lying, I thought. He doesn't know how to tell the truth.

Dan then quoted the killer's words during an ESPN interview following the "altercation." He told sports reporter Roy Firestone, "We were both guilty. No one was hurt, it was no big deal, and we both got on with our lives."

The witness explained: "It was a sport show, and yes, I most definitely on this sport show minimized what—minimized what happened in my personal life, yes. . . . To me and Nicole it was a big deal. To America—I didn't think it was any of their business."

Dan took the witness through a series of incidents. The killer denied slapping Nicole's face and knocking off her glasses during an argument in the parking lot of a veterinarian's office. He denied slapping Nicole to the ground during an argument at the beach.

He denied stalking his ex-wife. After the divorce, he said, it was Nicole who pursued him. He complained, "She showed up at the golf course where I was, she followed me to Mexico, she made me cookies and . . . she called my home and my office incessantly." He was "a thousand percent sure" that Nicole was pursuing him.

It was around Mother's Day, 1993—little more than one year prior to the murders—when the couple decided to attempt a reconciliation. The killer testified that he was not sure things would work out, so, he said, "I gave her a year."

During the incident of October 25, 1993, when a 911 tape caught the sound of the killer's voice raging in the background as a terrified Nicole called for help, he admitted, "I was pretty upset, yes." But he denied that Nicole showed any signs of fear, and, a few minutes later, he challenged: "I will debate forever that she was not frightened of me that night."

Dan asked, "You heard that 911 tape, sir, did you not?"

"Yes."

" . . . So you think she just lied to the 911 operator?"

"Yes," the killer stonewalled. " . . . I think she was trying to control—"

Referring to the tape the police had made when they responded to the 911 call, Dan asked, "And it's true, sir, that when you did get mad and angry, you would acquire a very animal-like look, right?"

The witness answered, "Yeah," then he equivocated, adding, " . . . I can never recall being mad and looking in a mirror."

Thanks to a new law that we had encouraged the legislature to pass and had urged Governor Pete Wilson to sign, Judge Fujisaki ruled that we could introduce excerpts from Nicole's diaries in order to show her state of mind.

By the spring of 1994 the attempted reconciliation had come to an end. The murderer had resumed a relationship with Paula Barbieri, but he still had plenty of interaction with Nicole.

Referring to an argument with her ex-husband on June 3, 1994—nine days prior to the murders—Nicole wrote that the killer had said to her, "You hung up on me last night. You're going to pay for this, bitch." He also called her a "fucking cunt." But the killer denied the statements.

Dan asked, "Nicole just made all this up?"

"Absolutely. And this is not true."

The defendant's social life was in a shambles. According to Paula Barbieri, they argued on Saturday night because he would not let her come to Sydney's dance recital the next day. At 7 A.M., the day of the murders, Barbieri left an eight-minute message for him, declaring that she did not want to have anything more to do with him. Despite the fact that telephone records showed that he called his message manager at 6:56 P.M., and despite the fact that Paula's message was the only one that had been left there all day, the killer claimed that he never heard the message.

We supposed that the defense would charge that the phone company had joined the multilayered conspiracy.

To preclude such an absurd contention, Dan read from the statement that the defendant had given to Detectives Lange and Vannatter the afternoon following the murders: "And then I checked my messages. She had left me a message that she wasn't there, that she had to leave town."

Dan orchestrated the day beautifully, so that he would leave the jury plenty to think about over the weekend, before the defendant's testimony resumed on Monday. Like the second hand on the clock that ticked steadily toward 4 P.M., Dan moved the subject matter to the key issue. He asked, "Now, between 9:35 P.M. and 10:55 P.M. on Sunday, June 12, there is not a single living human being who you can identify that saw or spoke to you; is that true?"

The killer acknowledged: "That's absolutely true."

"You had gloves; you had a hat; you were wearing a dark sweat outfit, and you had a knife. And you went to Nicole Brown's condominium at 875 South Bundy, did you not, sir?"

The killer was well rehearsed. The defense team, of course, expected that Dan would ask such questions sooner or later. Until this moment, the defendant had never addressed the jury directly. Now, as if on cue, he turned his face and fixed a rather blind stare upon the jurors. He said firmly, "That's absolutely not true."

"And you confronted Nicole Brown Simpson and you killed her, didn't you?"

"That is absolutely not true." The answer came out devoid of any sense of pain or passion.

"And you killed Ronald Goldman, sir, did you or did you not?"

"That's absolutely not true."

Kim confided to a friend, "You almost expect to see his face on television or on the covers of magazines, but it never really hit me how close, physically close, he is to us until one of the law clerks told me she walked into a sushi bar and there he was. I realized at that moment that the same thing could happen to me, anytime, anyplace. He's free to roam. Free to prowl. Free to walk wherever he chooses."

Kim's fear of encountering him continued to grow when Dominick Dunne told her a third-hand story. Dominick said that Lawrence Schiller had recounted a conversation he had with the killer: The murderer had bragged about donning his disguise and driving along Sunset Boulevard. He said that he pulled up to a stoplight and found himself directly next to Kim. It was a great joke! He was proud of himself because Kim had not recognized him. Kim thought: This is the kind of sicko who probably spends his spare time pulling the wings off flies.

Kim found herself constantly checking her rearview mirror. She spotted his car outside the Doubletree Hotel and wrote down his license plate number, 3RJE923. The knowledge that he could be behind any tree or under any rock haunted her.

Kim's friend Paul Geller came to court with us on Monday to hear the second day of the killer's testimony. As they walked the gauntlet across the street, and Paul realized what Kim was going through day after day, he asked a simple question: "How do you do this?"

"I just do it," Kim responded.

We will never understand that segment of the public that seeks a glimpse, a smile, an autograph from this man. After spending a day in the same room with him, we just wanted to go home, take a shower, and wash off the stench.

Before court convened, Harvey Levin from Channel 2, the local CBS affiliate, told us about an incident that had occurred at the killer's house the previous night. A security guard thought he had seen a prowler. The LAPD was called to investigate. As it turned out, the suspected prowler was simply another security guard. How ironic, we thought, that the murderer would call for help from the inept, corrupt, and racist organization that had spawned the "twin devils of deception."

Dan began the day with further questions concerning the defendant's statement, the day after the murders, to Detectives Lange and Vannatter. The killer had since, in various forums, changed details of his story, but he refused to admit that he had lied to the police. He explained the discrepancies by claiming that his story was just "more accurate now," or that the transcript of the police interview was wrong.

For example, in trying to explain why there was blood in his Ford Bronco, he had told the detectives that he cut his hand Sunday evening. He had said, "I recall bleeding at my house and then I went to the Bronco. The last thing I did before I left, when I was rushing, was went and got my phone out of the Bronco."

Only later did he learn that his cellular phone records showed that he tried once more to reach Paula Barbieri at 10:03 P.M., and he did not want anyone to place him in the Bronco shortly before the murders. So his "more accurate" story was that he was standing in his yard when he made the 10:03 P.M. call and, later, as he was rushing about getting ready to go to the airport, he ran to his Bronco and retrieved, not the phone, but the accessories for it.

Dan asked the killer to explain at length what he did after returning from McDonald's with Kato Kaelin. The witness said that he went to his garage to look for his old, favorite sand wedge to take along on his business/golfing trip to Chicago. "And I also needed some balls that I play with, a ball called a Maxflite 100HT," he said. "Unless you play golf, you don't understand how important that is to a golfer, the type of ball that they play with."

As the subject turned to golf, his entire demeanor changed. He seemed relaxed and confident. We found this incredible. During his trial testimony for the vicious murder of his ex-wife and Ron, he was giving golfing tips!

After hitting a few chip shots on his lawn and allowing his dog, Chachi, to do "her business" in the yard of his neighbor, Mr. Sheinbaum, he went inside, "turned off the lights downstairs, except for my lamps that I normally keep on, and I went upstairs."

Dan forced the murderer to admit that he had not told Lange and Vannatter anything about chipping golf balls or walking his dog or turning off lights. This, in fact, was the killer's well-rehearsed version, designed to fit in and around the details supplied by other witnesses—details that he did not know when he gave his initial statement to the detectives.

The witness continued: "I went upstairs. I recall having a little time before the limo driver would call me.

"My limo drivers always call me fifteen minutes before the call time, and that historically is when I go into gear, doing my final preparations to leave, and I knew I had time to sit on my bed, which I did when I went back in the house."

It was about 10:35 or 10:40 P.M. when, he said, he glanced at the clock and realized that he was running late. He jumped into the shower. Over the sound of the water, he may have heard the phone ringing, announcing the arrival of the limo driver.

Minutes later, half-dressed, he brought a suit bag downstairs. He stepped outside briefly to look in his golf bag to make sure he had his black golfing shoes. That, he claimed, was the moment when Allan Park said that he saw a man entering the house.

To us, the entire story sounded absurd, and it was certainly memorized. Dan commented to us that if he asked the killer to repeat his story, he would get it back verbatim.

A series of questions brought a series of denials.

Dan asked, "You have no explanation for how your blood was found in that Bronco?"

The witness answered, "That's correct."

"And you have no explanation, sir, for how blood of Nicole's was found on the carpet of the driver side, do you?"

"No."

"And you have no explanation for how Ron Goldman's blood got in your car that night, do you?"

"Me personally, no."

Then who? we thought.

The killer acknowledged that he had told Detectives Lange and Vannatter that he cut his finger sometime between 10 P.M. and 11 P.M. that night, and may have reopened the cut in Chicago. He now said, "I didn't see that or any mark on my hand between ten and eleven on June 12," and explained the contradiction by saying that, earlier, he must have assumed that he cut his hand the night before.

He denied that he had any other injuries to his fingers when he returned from Chicago. He really did not know how he sustained other cuts by the time he was examined on June 15. If they were fingernail gougings, they must have been inflicted by his seven-year-old son, Justin, as they were roughhousing.

Paul looked at Kim in amazement and said, "Did he just say Justin?!"

"Sickening, huh?" she replied.

Dan exhibited close-up photos of the defendant's hand, taken by the police on June 13. Although there were clearly other cuts depicted in the photos, the killer was evasive, first denying that he could see them; then, when Dan asked where he had sustained the injuries, he replied, "Who knows?"

We had not seen these particular photos before, and they made Patti squeamish. She realized that these cuts might have been made by Ron as he struggled to save himself.

Watching the killer on the witness stand, lying through his teeth, brought us a certain amount of relief. His arrogance was sickening, but until now we had been unable to have the satisfaction of knowing that he was under pressure, that the world could now know him for who he is. Without question, it was unfortunate that this trial was not being broadcast on live TV.

Over the lunch break, numerous reporters told us they were astonished at the level to which he had sunk; he was not responsible for anything; he could not explain anything. The only thing he could say with certainty was that no one in the whole wide world knew where he was between 9:35 P.M. and 10:55 P.M. on the night of the murders.

Dan returned to the subject of the killer's actions after he was informed of Nicole's death. The witness sighed and took a deep breath. Kim passed Patti a note saying that she could not believe his lack of emotion. She wrote: "Every time I think about you and Dad calling me to tell me the horrific news, I get choked up, and I always will. And when HE relives that event, the call? ABSOLUTELY NOTHING."

We knew that from that moment until his arrival back in L.A. he was on the phone almost constantly. He used the phone in his hotel room. On the way to O'Hare Airport, he used his cell phone. He used the Airfone during the flight back to L.A. He spoke several times with his assistant, Cathy Randa, and his business attorney, Skip Taft. He spoke with his daughter Arnelle, and others. He arranged to have criminal attorney Howard Weitzman on hand when he returned to Rockingham. But he was also frantic to contact Kato Kaelin. Kaelin was the last person he tried to call from his cell phone while on the ground, and the first person he tried to reach from the Airfone. He tried at least two more times during the flight, but he was unable to get Kaelin on the phone.

Now Dan forced the killer to admit that he had never before called Kaelin from out of town; they simply were not close friends at all. But he denied that he was trying to find out what Kaelin had told the police.

During the flight, the killer said that it was "more than likely" that he was crying and displaying signs of distress. His left hand was bleeding. At one point he vomited. Yet he still signed autographs.

Dan asked, "You are perfectly able, even when you are feeling very low and devastated . . . to act normal in public and give autographs?"

"Yes."

During the killer's June 13 interview with Lange and Vannatter, the detectives had raised the possibility of his taking a lie-detector test. The murderer had said, "Wait a minute. I've got some weird thoughts, you know, about Nicole."

When Dan asked what he had meant by that, the witness explained: "I think my biggest concern was, I was really tired, I didn't understand what a polygraph was, and I just wanted to make sure that it focused on what it was, this particular crime, and not on other things that may be in your mind. . . . I think what my process was is that I had a lot of weird thoughts about those type of things, I wanted to know just how true-blue it was, and eventually I told them I would—I would do one after I had got some sleep and stuff."

Dan now seized upon the opportunity Baker had given him during his opening statement. We knew from Schiller's book that the defendant had taken a lie-detector test on June 15 at the office of Dr. Howard Gelb. F. Lee Bailey confirmed this during an appearance on *Larry King Live.* Dan asked, "And you did take the test, and you failed it, didn't you? . . . You got a minus 22?"

Even as the killer denied failing a lie-detector test, Baker objected. A heated bench conference followed before Judge Fujisaki allowed Dan to pursue the subject further. He asked, "You went to the office of some person on Wilshire Boulevard and sat down and were wired up for a lie-detector test, true?"

"That's not true," the witness lied. Then he added. "I mean that's not true in totality. . . . What I was asking him is how did it work, and I wanted to understand it. And he sort of gave me an example how it—"

"And he hooked you up to the process and started asking you questions about Nicole, and Nicole's death and whether you were responsible for it, true?"

"I don't know if he went that far with it."

"Okay. At the end of that process, you scored a minus 22, true?"

Once more the killer lied, claiming, "I don't know what the score was."

Dan pointed out that minus 22 indicated "extreme deception," but Baker lodged an extreme objection and the judge sustained him.

So he was hooked up to this intricate machine, Kim thought, was asked questions, but didn't know what was going on. He must be dumber than I thought.

Dan took the defendant through a chronicle of the infamous Bronco ride. The killer tried his best to feign an emotional reaction, but in our opinion he failed miserably. "Whatever acting career he had just went down the tubes," Patti said.

Dan quoted from the killer's cell phone conversation with Detective Lange. The killer had said: "Just tell them all I'm sorry. You can tell them later on today and tomorrow that I was sorry and that I'm sorry that I did this to the police department."

Lange had said, " . . . nobody's going to get hurt."

And the killer replied, "I'm the only one that deserves it."

Now, under oath, he said that he did not recall making that statement, even though it was on tape. However, he admitted that he had been contemplating suicide.

Dan seized on that admission to bring his direct examination to a dramatic conclusion. He asked, "And that is why you were going to kill yourself, because you knew you were going to spend the rest of your life in jail, correct?"

The witness answered, "That's incorrect."

"And you knew that you dropped the blood at Bundy, correct?"

"That's incorrect."

"And knew, sir, that you went there that night and you confronted Nicole and you killed her—"

" . . . No, Mr. Petrocelli. That's totally, absolutely incorrect."

" . . . And Ronald Goldman got into a fight with you as he tried to stop you, and you cut him and you slashed him until he died, collapsed in your arms. True or untrue?"

"Untrue."

"And you left him there to die, Mr. Simpson, with his eyes open, looking right at you. True or untrue?"

"That's untrue."

Dan said, "I have no further questions."

THIRTY-FIVE

We planned to host our usual large Thanksgiving dinner for some of our friends: the Zieglers, Zabners, Shannons, and Golds. Patti's mother also joined us to make her incredible homemade stuffing and sweet potatoes. Patti always handles the lion's share of the work, but the holiday bird is my task.

That morning I picked up the fresh turkey we had ordered from Pavilions, and brought it home to prepare for roasting. I held the bird over the sink, cut open the sealed bag, and slid my hand into the cavity. Blood gushed out, covering my right arm. I pulled my hand out quickly and realized that I was clutching the bird's bloody neck. My body felt cold and numb, and I began to shake uncontrollably. My knees buckled. I was light-headed and nauseated. Afraid that I might actually pass out, I dropped the bird into the sink and staggered to the family room.

Patti found me a few minutes later, sitting quietly in a chair. She could see immediately that I was in shock. "What's wrong?" she asked.

I heard my voice quiver as I explained: "I was cleaning the turkey, and all that I saw was blood spurting out—I can't ever remember that happening before."

"Why didn't you tell me? I would have helped you," Patti said. She rubbed my shoulders.

"The first thing I pulled out was the neck bone," I said. "And it just put me over the edge."

If I know I am going to encounter violence in a movie or some atrocity on the news, I am somewhat prepared for these reactions. But it is at moments like these, when I become aware how deeply such everyday things can devastate me, that I wonder if I will ever be whole again.

On Tuesday, December 3, after the extended holiday break, our plaintiffs' team was unleashed. A wave of witnesses rolled over the shifting sands of the murderer's testimony. He was finally on record in open court and, over the course of several days, Dan and his associates launched a vigorous assault, calling numerous witnesses—some friendly, some hostile—to impeach the killer.

In the spring of 1983 a woman named India Allen saw the murderer with Nicole in the parking lot of the veterinarian's office where she worked. Nicole was wearing a fur coat when she came to pick up her dogs from the groomer. The murderer drove up in his car. " . . . And he was very angry," Allen testified. "When he got out of the car, he came kind of around the car very quickly and started yelling at her about wearing the coat out during the day. And he was very upset; he told her that he—I don't know if I can say this or not, out loud."

Baker said that he was going to object on hearsay grounds, but Judge Fujisaki overruled him.

Allen continued: "He said, 'I didn't buy this fur coat for you to go fuck somebody else,' is what he said. And then he said, 'I want the coat back,' and he grabbed her by the back of the coat and started trying to pull the coat off of her."

When asked to describe the killer's appearance that day, she testified: "Well, he got out of the car, and he was mad. I mean he looked like he was gritting his teeth, and his fists were clenched, and it was—it was kind of intimidating. I stayed where I was. It was enough to keep me where I was with the dogs, and they were a little agitated, so it was difficult to hold on to them . . .

"He hit her in the face, and knocked off her sunglasses and headband. When she came up, it was the only time I saw her without her sunglasses, and she had a sort of fading bruise under her eye." Allen also noticed a redness on Nicole's cheek, where she had been slapped. "I was shocked," she said, "because they were two beautiful, famous people who looked like they were getting ready to have a knockdown, drag-out fight right in front of me."

Pharmacist Albert Aguilera testified that he saw the defendant slap Nicole across the face on July 1, 1986, knocking her down onto the sands of Laguna Beach. "He swung his right hand, hit her across the face, and she went down," he recalled. Aguilera said he could hear Nicole crying, "No, no!"

The Browns' attorney, John Kelly, asked, "When you say he slapped her, what exactly did you observe Mr. Simpson do at that time?"

"He swung his right hand and hit her across the face. And she went down."

"When you saw her go down," Kelly asked, "did she fall to the side, or how did she exactly fall?"

"Almost straight down."

"Okay. And she was—when she was on the ground, what position was she in on the ground at this time?"

"She was on her knees . . . He was crouching over her."

Several witnesses were brought forward—friends of the defendant—who testified that he had talked sadly and repeatedly about his breakup with Nicole in the weeks before the murders. This was in stark contradiction to the killer's assertion that the breakup was no big deal and that he had been the one to initiate it.

A. C. Cowlings, clearly a reluctant witness, was questioned about the brawl on New Year's Day, 1989. Several times he contradicted the defendant's sworn statements. The killer had insisted that he never climbed a neighbor's fence as he fled the scene that day. But Cowlings testified that the defendant had told him he jumped the fence while fleeing with car keys and a bag of Nicole's jewelry. The killer had testified that he was not aware that the police were looking for him after the fight, but Cowlings said that later in the day, when he drove back to the house, the defendant ordered him to take a circuitous route, to see whether a patrol car was waiting. Finally Cowlings said that Nicole told him her husband had pulled her hair and hit her during the fight. Cowlings showed more emotion when the photos were shown than the killer ever did.

The killer had testified that, on the night of the murders, he did not answer the limo driver's repeated buzzes because he was afraid his dog, Chachi, would run out if he opened the gate. However, his housekeeper and his regular limo driver both testified that Chachi never left the property.

The killer had testified that he returned a black sweat suit to the production company after filming an exercise video, but wardrobe stylist Leslie Gardner said that she gave him the sweat suit as a gift. "He never returned anything to me," she declared.

Throughout this assault on his sworn testimony, the defendant stared off into space. He appeared almost bored. He displayed no passion. I thought: He perceives that once again he is going to get away with it. He's the classic sociopath.

I studied the jury carefully. The weight of the evidence was so clear. Under oath, the killer had told one whopper after another. Was this jury getting the message? Reluctantly I concluded: I have no clue.

Nancy N. Ney, a volunteer counselor for Sojourn House, a shelter for battered women, described a twenty-minute hot-line call she received on June 7, 1994, five days prior to the murders. The call came from someone who identified herself as a white woman named Nicole, in her mid-thirties, who lived in West Los Angeles, had a son and a daughter under ten, and had been married to a high-profile man for eight years. This woman named Nicole, according to Ney, "said that her ex-husband had been calling her on the phone . . . begging her to please come back to him. She said he was stalking her. She would be in a restaurant, and he'd be sitting at the next table, staring at her. She'd be in the market, he'd be there in the next aisle, looking at her. She'd be driving down the street and look in the rearview mirror, and he'd be there." According to Ney, this woman named Nicole said that her ex-husband had told her on several occasions that if he ever caught her with another man, he would kill her.

Dr. Ronald Fischman, a close friend of the defendant, testified that the killer was unusually withdrawn, subdued, and tired at his daughter's dance recital, hours before the murders. Sharon's attorney, Michael Brewer, asked, "In all the years that you knew O. J. Simpson, he never appeared the way he appeared at that recital, true?"

"It's true," Fischman responded.

Although the killer had repeatedly denied that he ever received Paula Barbieri's "Dear John" call on the morning of the murders, her testimony indicated otherwise. Barbieri assumed that he did get the message because he left three messages for her later that day, asking her what had gone wrong.

The killer had sworn that he did not deliberately pack his passport in the black travel bag he took with him while fleeing arrest; it just happened to be in the bag. Barbieri, however, reported seeing the passport on the nightstand next to the bed at Kardashian's house, where the killer had slept the night before.

In his pretrial deposition, the killer had described his futile efforts to learn what had happened to Nicole. He called Denise Brown, but she yelled at him and hung up. His daughter Arnelle did not know anything and was somewhat hysterical. He could not reach Kato Kaelin. Although he talked repeatedly to his lawyer and secretary, he claimed that they did not discuss what the police knew or what information had been uncovered. Now, hearing a deposition taken from Mark Partridge, a Chicago attorney who had sat next to the defendant on the flight back to L.A., the jury learned that the killer told Partridge that his ex-wife had died as a result of a crime and that her body had been found near her house. He also mentioned that there was a second victim, whom he identified as male.

He was either lying when he testified that no one had told him these details, or had firsthand knowledge of them.

Friday, December 6, was my fifty-sixth birthday.

This day we planned to finish the presentation of our case. The final two witnesses would be Juditha Brown and me. After nearly two and one half years, I would finally get the chance to speak out, under oath, about how the killer's unspeakable acts had devastated our lives.

We had supplied Dan with numerous family photographs and videotapes, but I did not know how he planned to use them. Many people had offered me the same advice: "Stay calm." I had responded, "At some point, that may be impossible."

We were up early in anticipation. We left home about 7:15 A.M. and picked up Maralyn Gold. Traffic was fairly light on the Pacific Coast Highway, and we arrived at the Doubletree about ten past eight. Kim was running late. She phoned from her car and begged us to wait for her. She did not want to walk across the street alone. None of us did. Kim arrived with fifteen minutes to spare, but she was extremely nervous.

The mood inside the courtroom was electric. Everyone speculated whether Baker would risk cross-examining Judy and me. We believed that the classy thing for him to do would be to refrain from questioning the victims' parents but, as Patti said, "He is incapable of that."

First, Dan had a few details to handle. He asked the defendant's longtime friend and business attorney, Leroy "Skip" Taft, how many cuts he had noticed on the killer's left hand the day after the murders.

"As I sit here today," Taft replied, "I recall one cut."

The answer infuriated Dan. It was *not* what Taft had said during his deposition. And when Dan asked Taft to refer to a certain page of his deposition, the witness snapped, "No, let *me* tell *you* what page to look at."

Judge Fujisaki flashed an animated, puzzled look, as if to ask the witness: "What did you just say?"

His voice thundering, Dan read aloud from the deposition, when Taft testified that he saw "for sure two" cuts and possibly a third when he sat with Simpson in police headquarters on June 13, 1994.

For many minutes Dan and the witness screamed at one another. Taft insisted that he had confused his observations of June 13 with the subsequent viewing of photographs. His testimony was so full of contradictions that reporters watched with their mouths open in astonishment. Finally Judge Fujisaki angrily directed Taft to answer Dan's questions as they were asked, and not try to change the subject. Taft was forced to acknowledge that he had told a different story during his deposition.

Patti said, "I loved watching that liar squirm."

During a break I said to Dan, "This guy just committed perjury."

"Without question," Dan answered.

"What can we do to make sure he gets disbarred?" I asked.

Dan explained that we had two courses of action. We could lodge a formal complaint with the California Bar Association, and we could turn over evidence of perjury to the L.A. district attorney's office. Once the trial was over, we resolved to do just that.

We had to work hard to persuade Sharon not to testify in person, because it was likely she would embellish the description of her relationship with Ron. "We're opening a huge can of worms," Dan cautioned Sharon's attorney. "It would be a sideshow."

The problem was that Baker was sure to launch a contentious cross-examination. The issue of the trial was not whether Sharon had a horrible relationship with Ron; it was whether the defendant murdered two people, and we did not want the focus to shift from that question.

So Sharon told her story via a videotape of her own pretrial deposition. Kim had not seen Sharon's taped deposition and became very upset while watching it now. "Once again, she is talking about Ron as if she knew him. She's making things up and embellishing everything," Kim said. "All I've ever gotten from her is lies, lies, lies." But Sharon admitted that she saw Ron and Kim only sporadically after our 1974 divorce. When our family had moved to California, she lost contact with the children altogether, and there were only tentative attempts to reestablish communication.

After the lunch break, Juditha Brown was called to the witness stand.

We heard something fall behind us. Glancing back, we were stunned to see that Judy had dropped her sunglasses. Patti and Kim stared at each other in astonishment as they watched Denise Brown pick them up. Judy's sunglasses were the genesis of our nightmare.

Clutching a tissue, Judy trembled as she described the defendant's demeanor at Sydney's dance recital, hours before the murders. She characterized him as nervous, upset, and so angry that he stared right through her. His facial expression unsettled her, leaving her with a nervous feeling that lingered even after he drove away.

"Had you ever seen that look on Mr. Simpson?" John Kelly asked.

"Never," she answered emphatically.

From his seat at the defense table, the killer smiled broadly and raised his eyebrows.

Continuing with her anguished testimony, Judy told the jury that at her daughter's wake, the defendant pushed her aside, knelt over the coffin, kissed Nicole on the lips, and said, "I'm so sorry, Nic, I'm so sorry." She then asked him whether he had anything to do with her daughter's death. Judy testified that the defendant refused to answer the question directly, saying only, "I loved your daughter."

During Baker's cross-examination, however, he played a tape of Judy's earlier response to that same question during an interview on *Primetime Live.* Then she had said that when she asked him whether he had anything to do with Nicole's death, he replied, "No, I loved your daughter." All of us were upset, particularly with Kelly. He should have prepared her better for this question.

But all in all we thought that Judy did an outstanding job.

She was excused from the stand at 3:45 P.M. We expected Dan to call me immediately, but when instead he requested a sidebar conference, Patti realized that he was asking to postpone my testimony until Monday. She knew how anxious I was to get this over with, but Dan thought it was too late in the day and he did not want to split my testimony with a weekend. All of us exited the courtroom feeling disappointed.

That evening we met Kim at the Cosmos restaurant in Calabasas for my birthday dinner. During the evening several patrons came to our table to offer support. When a chocolate cake—my favorite—arrived at our table, the restaurant staff gathered around to sing "Happy Birthday." To my surprise, the other patrons joined the chorus. Applause filled the room.

Tears glistened in our eyes. Left unspoken was the thought: Ron should be here with us.

On Saturday morning Patti set out a spread of assorted bagels, coffee, sliced apples, tomatoes, and cream cheese. Dan came over for about an hour to talk about my testimony.

We still did not go over specific points; rather, Dan merely wanted to reinforce what everyone else had been telling me. "Try not to lash out at Baker," he advised. "You've remained dignified since Day One. Don't stoop to his level now."

But I warned, "If he presses a particular couple of buttons, I'm going to bite back." I explained that if he in any way attempted to demean Ron I would not sit there quietly. "And if he insinuates that our family pursued the civil trial merely as a means to gain money or celebrity, I will launch an attack." In fact, I had written responses for those two issues, and I hoped—deeply—that Baker would give me the openings I needed to use them.

Lauren was up at 4:30 on Monday morning. Patti awoke at 5:15. Managing the shower schedule, she got her mother up at 5:30, and roused me at 5:45. We rushed about, but few words were spoken. I knew that everyone was wondering how I must be feeling. In fact, I was a bit more apprehensive than I had been on Friday. I wanted to be done with it.

Jim Ziegler and Barb Duben accompanied us.

A chill ran down Patti's spine as she heard Dan call "Fred Goldman" as the plaintiffs' sixty-fifth and final witness. She felt the color drain from her face. Her trembling hands were cold.

The courtroom was eerily, unnaturally quiet as I raised my right hand to take the oath.

As I answered Dan's questions, I sometimes glanced at my family and, whenever I did, my voice cracked. I broke down several times as I reminisced about Ron and related memories that any parent could understand—from Ron's habit of missing the school bus to his days in the Indian Guides youth program. I acknowledged that Ron was no angel and told the jury about his traffic tickets and subsequent arrest, and the problems that led him to file for bankruptcy.

Patti saw dark anger in my eyes as I stared holes through the defendant. I told of Ron's dream of opening a restaurant and described the ankh. "It stands for eternal life." I sobbed.

I spoke about the ankh necklace that Ron wore and shot another venomous glance at the killer. "He doesn't wear it anymore," I said.

Sniffles and muffled sobs came from various corners of the room. Behind her, Patti heard a man weeping. It was Jim Ziegler. We had never seen him that emotional, even at Ron's funeral.

Dan displayed photos of our family—on vacation, at a wedding, clowning around on the sofa, and at Lauren's Bat Mitzvah, which had concluded with Ron, full of life and energy, looking into the camera and saying, "God knows where I will be in a year."

Lauren broke down. Patti slipped an arm around her.

"Did you love your son?" Dan asked gently.

"Oh God, yes," I answered, gripping a tissue.

"Do you miss him?" Dan asked.

My response was barely audible. "More than you can imagine," I whispered. "There isn't a day goes by that I don't think of him. My life will never, ever be the same."

I was ready, willing, and able to face Baker's cross-examination. I hoped that he would question me with the same hostile, condescending attitude that he displayed in front of most of our witnesses. Come on, I urged silently, say something derogatory about Ron. Try to paint me as a money-grubbing celebrity seeker. I had my written answers memorized.

To my dismay, Baker's early questions were fairly mild and innocuous. He clearly did not want to alienate the jury by being harsh on Ron's dad.

Finally he asked about the book—this book—that our family was writing. Aha, I thought, he's going to open up the subject of money and celebrity. I acknowledged that we had negotiated a book contract some time earlier, and I awaited his next, sneering question about fame and fortune.

But Baker said, "No further questions."

For the remainder of the day Patti sensed that I was in a "weird mood." She was correct. I was deeply disappointed that Baker had not opened the door further.

If he had charged that I was trying to profit from Ron's death I would have responded, as calmly as I could, "You're wrong, Mr. Baker, I'm in it for justice, and if you'd care to change places with me, I want you to remember that you have a son and I don't."

And if he had attempted to suggest that Ron was, for whatever reason, the killer's real target, I would have declared: "For you to suggest in any way that my son was responsible for his own death is an outrage." Then I would have pointed a finger directly at the defendant and continued: "Your client, that butcher, that murderer is, in fact, the only one to blame for this!"

THIRTY-SIX

None of us wanted to do or say anything that would reflect badly on our case. Reporters continually tried to get us to answer questions. We remained silent, but we worried that our facial expressions and body language might convey the wrong message. The constant pressure to "stay calm and do the right thing" drove us to the brink. "It's so unnatural," Kim complained. "How long must I keep my chin up and my mouth shut?"

One day Kim reached her limit. On our way into court a black GMC Suburban drove by, with windows tinted so heavily that no one could see inside. But we knew that the killer was arriving, driven by his bodyguard. Succumbing to an overwhelming temptation, Kim surreptitiously lifted the middle finger of her right hand in his direction.

"Did something set you off?" a reporter yelled.

She longed to respond: "Yeah, how about thirty stab wounds?" but bit her tongue instead.

Later, during a break in the proceedings, Dan Abrams of Court TV said to Kim, "Caught ya'." He informed her that their camera had videotaped her silent salutation. "But don't worry," he added quickly, "we're not going to use it."

After lunch, however, other reporters told her that their networks were going to run the clip. Kim was frantic that her impulsive gesture might somehow affect the outcome of the trial, but she felt better sometime later when we discovered that there was a "legal precedent" for her gesture. It occurred during the second day of the killer's testimony, and is recorded in the thick *Reporter's Daily Transcript* labeled November 25,

1996. There, in Volume 22 of the official trial record, on pages 99 and 100, is the passage:

> Q. Now, the cut on your middle finger is one that still bears a scar, does it not?
> (Witness reviews finger.)
> A. Yes.
> Q. Left hand middle finger, right?
> A. Yes.
> (Witness displays finger to Mr. Petrocelli.)

As the trial neared its conclusion, Dan often stayed overnight at the Doubletree, where he could work twenty-four hours a day if necessary. When Kim expressed her appreciation for his devotion to the case, he explained, "I'm proud to be part of it. It was the right thing to do."

The hours of preparation paid off in the courtroom. Dan seemed to have a photographic memory. At times he had to argue motions on an instant's notice, yet he cited case law and facts as if he had spent the night cramming for that particular topic.

Tom Lambert, Peter Gelblum, Ed Medvene, and Yvette Molinaro handled their areas of expertise with the same fire and brilliance as Dan. Peter commented to me, "It's easy to get up and go to work when you know what you're doing is right." This team was a well-oiled machine that presented our case so forcefully that the defense sometimes seemed bewildered. In fact, the entire defense case was unremarkable. Robert Baker attempted to play the same tired song, searching for any way to suggest that the killer was an innocent victim of a grand conspiracy. But Judge Fujisaki refused to allow him to put the LAPD on trial.

It was not until we saw Judge Fujisaki in action that we came to realize just how ineffectively Judge Ito had conducted the criminal trial. Judge Fujisaki acted quickly, firmly, and brooked no nonsense from either side. We concluded, more decisively than ever, that one of the major reasons that the defendant got away with murder was because Judge Ito was starstruck, bullied, and never in control of his courtroom.

This time, prevented by Judge Fujisaki from spitting out vague tirades and forced to confine themselves to specifics, the defense sputtered.

Many of the witnesses were holdovers from the criminal trial. Baker called former detectives Tom Lange and Phil Vannatter, as well as criminalists Dennis Fung and Andrea Mazzola—and others who had conducted the initial investigation. Except for an occasional lapse (Dennis Fung was noticeably shaky) these witnesses told a generally uniform story of a professional investigation, and the results pointed inexorably toward the killer.

In the criminal trial, molecular biologist Dr. John Gerdes had harmed the prosecution with his assertion that the LAPD was a "cesspool of contamination." But now he could cite only three DNA tests that showed signs of contamination. Under a tight cross-examination by Tom Lambert, he conceded that he could find "no direct evidence" of contamination of any evidence.

Pathologist Dr. Michael Baden attempted to counter the testimony of our expert pathologist, Dr. Werner Spitz, who had told the jury that he believed the murders were committed by one person in a very short period of time. Dr. Baden suggested that Ron might have remained on his feet for five minutes or longer, struggling with his assailant. One of the reasons for this conclusion, he said, was that blood from Ron's neck wound saturated the left side of his shirt and pants, and he would have had to be standing for this to occur.

But under cross-examination, Dr. Baden grew frustrated when Ed Medvene displayed a photo of Ron's shirt and pants. Yes, the left pants leg was saturated with blood from a wound to his leg. But the shirt was stained on the right side, not the left. Ron was found lying on his right side, and the blood had obviously collected after he had fallen. Dr. Baden tried to recover, explaining that he really did not mean to use the word "saturated." He finally admitted that Ron's wounds were so severe that he may well have lost consciousness within seconds.

A chief concern for the defense attorney was the dramatic Harry Scull photograph showing the killer wearing Bruno Magli shoes. In a desperate attempt to restore their client's credibility, they called their most absurd "expert," photo analyst Robert Groden. Dan had learned that Groden was the defense team's third choice. We knew for certain that one of their other experts had declared the photo to be authentic, and we assumed that the second expert had agreed because, to find Groden, they had to reach beneath the bottom of the barrel.

No one can simply take the witness stand, declare himself an "expert," and issue pronouncements. First, he must present his qualifications to the court, and the judge decides whether to certify him as an expert witness. The slightly built, fifty-one-year-old Groden admitted that he was a high school dropout who had never taken a course in photography. But he claimed an early interest in snapping photos, and this set him on his way to becoming an "expert." Two decades ago, he said, he had worked as an optical technician for a film company, and he also held a job with a company that duplicated slides. From 1976 to 1978 he was a photo consultant to the congressional committee that was investigating the assassination of President John F. Kennedy. He claimed to have testified four times before congressional committees; in fact, his most recent appearance was to answer charges that he had stolen photos of the Kennedy assassination and sold them to *Globe* magazine. In the past twenty years he had been paid twice—once by the *National Inquirer* and once by a Korean political party—to analyze photos purportedly showing ghosts.

Peter Gelblum argued, "The fact that he simply sits around his house looking at photos and deciding whether he thinks a picture is fake or not does not qualify him as an expert."

Judge Fujisaki appeared quizzical, as if to ask the defense: Is this the best you can do? In fact, it was, so the judge declared, "His credibility will be determined on cross-examination."

Cleared to testify, Groden immediately began to attack the authenticity of Harry Scull's photograph. He explained that he had taken the picture to a Kinko's Copy Center, made a photocopy, and enlarged it to eight times its normal size. Working with this, he pointed out a dozen "anomalies" that, according to him, indicated that the photo had been altered.

In a brutal cross-examination, Peter ridiculed Groden's qualifications and proved some of his conclusions patently false. For example, one of Groden's anomalies was a thin blue line between the edge of the negative and the film sprockets. Groden said that line appeared only on the one negative in question. But Peter showed at least two other negatives from the same roll that displayed the same line, and forced Groden to admit that the lines "could be" scratches caused by the camera mechanism.

Peter had much more to cover, but an event now occurred that, in retrospect, would loom as one of the key strokes of luck in the entire trial. The court was getting ready to adjourn for a two-week holiday recess, and the defense wanted to call forensic toxicologist Dr. Frederic Rieders, so that he could return home to Philadelphia.

Peter agreed. And that meant he would have an opportunity to resume his cross-examination of Groden after the holidays. Little did we know how important that would be.

As we were driving home, Patti asked, "Can you believe that in a month this will finally be over? I want so much to believe we are going to win this. The evidence is so obvious, so cut-and-dried. But the evidence was there in the criminal case, too, and look what happened."

That evening we learned that Orange County Superior Court Judge Nancy Wieben Stock had awarded the killer custody of his children Sydney and Justin. We were not surprised. California law made any other ruling highly unlikely. But we were very dismayed that the judge did not defer her decision. Patti said, "The timing is terrible. The judge had ninety days to rule on the custody issue. Why did she have to do it in the midst of the civil case?"

Would our jury be influenced by the ruling? There was no way to tell.

Somehow we had to make it through this torturous two-week hiatus. We were so close to bringing the case to a conclusion that it was difficult to accept the concept of a vacation. Celebration was out of the question.

Sleep became even more of a stranger. I lay in bed, late into the night, mulling every possible scenario: What are we going to do if they do *this*? What are we going to do if they do *that*?

One night Patti found me with a flashlight in my hands, searching a bathroom cupboard for a sleeping pill. "I didn't want to turn on the light and disturb you," I explained. I finally found a light sedative that had once been prescribed for Lauren and took that. Sleep came, but it was all too brief.

Paul Geller joined Kim for a late coffee. Although he had never met Ron, he said to her, "You know, Kim, I feel like your brother is sitting here with us. I really miss him. Through you, I feel like I know him."

Kim's mind flashed back to a conversation with her friend Jana Robertson. After Kim and Joe had broken up, Jana had expressed her sorrow that Ron would never know the man she would marry. That realization had inspired Kim to do her best to keep Ron alive, so that the new people in her life would know and love him, too.

Now, she said to Paul quietly, "Good, that means I did my job."

In fact, Ron was with us always. On Christmas night Kim and Paul sat in a darkened theater watching *Ghosts of Mississippi,* a film about the murder of civil rights leader Medgar Evers and his family's subsequent quest for justice. "The similarities to our situation are amazing," Kim whispered to Paul. "His family—the trials—it's eerie to watch." At one point in the film the camera panned to a close-up of Evers's tombstone. Kim gasped: Medgar Evers was born on July 2—Ron's birthday—and he was murdered on June 12—the date of Ron's death.

The following day was Kim's twenty-fifth birthday. All she could think about was that Ron was only twenty-five when he died. "No one should die this young," she raged. "At twenty-five you haven't lived enough, experienced enough, accomplished enough." She wondered if Ron had those same thoughts in the moments before he died.

I was in the reception area, waiting for Patti as she underwent her routine mammogram screening. After the procedure, the technician escorted her down the hallway. Recognizing me, she suddenly realized who Patti was. She said, "I feel bad for you guys. It makes me so angry to know he's walking the streets a free man. Someone's going to kill him. I'm sure of it. Someone's going to do it."

It was just one more incident when a stranger vented her frustration to us and we continued to be amazed that people's passion had not abated with the passage of time.

Patti said, "I do not think I will ever get used to being recognized that way. I cannot count the number of people who have said to me, 'He'll answer to a higher authority one day' or 'His time will come,' and I always think the same thing: Yes, but will we live long enough to see it?"

Michael's first semester of college went well. It was refreshing for him to get away from the tension that surrounded our lives, yet he was still vitally interested in the case. Several of his term papers concerned the conduct of the criminal trial, and the manner in which the press reported it.

Although we had spoken on the phone several times a week and tried to keep Michael informed of developments in the civil trial, it was always difficult to give him the full picture. Now, after he had spent the first portion of his holiday break with his father in Chicago, we had a wonderful, all-too-brief visit with him. When he discussed the highlights of the trial with Patti, he commented, "Mom, how can we *not* get him?"

I raced into our suite at the Doubletree on Monday, January 6, and said immediately, "Let me see those photos!"

Peering through a magnifying glass, I studied a contact sheet with thirty small prints, all snapped by part-time photographer E. J. Flammer at the September 26, 1993, Buffalo Bills football game, the same day that Harry Scull's camera had captured an image of the killer wearing Bruno Magli shoes. Flammer had delved into his files and discovered these shots. Over the holidays his attorney had contacted our team and provided this dramatic new evidence. Flammer had the negatives, and he would testify to their authenticity.

Dan had four of the photos printed to full size and had three of those enlarged further to show details of the shoes. The murderer was dressed exactly as he appeared in the Scull photo, from the top of his sports coat to the tips of his Bruno Magli shoes.

"This is major," Patti said. "I think that's the case. It's the frosting on the cake that we needed."

We all had the same reaction: GOTCHA!

The Browns' attorney, John Kelly, wanted to save the damning new evidence until our rebuttal case, but Dan argued for immediate action. "If we wait for our rebuttal case and the judge does not allow us to raise the issue of the photos, we've lost our chance," he reasoned. "We've got to try to get them in *now*." Fortunately for us, Peter was ready to resume his cross-examination of defense photo "expert" Robert Groden.

Before the jury was seated, the two sides argued bitterly over the admissibility of the Flammer photographs. Baker and company were apoplectic.

Dan cited testimony from the killer, who had labeled the previously shown Scull photo a fraud. The killer had said, under oath, "I wasn't wearing Bruno Magli shoes." And pointing to the Scull photo, he testified, "Those shoes are not my shoes."

Now Dan argued that we should be allowed to show jurors the new photos to impeach the defendant's credibility. "If you're going to go in front of the jury and make those kinds of representations, you have to suffer the risk that you may be caught red-handed—and that's what happened here," he said.

Defense attorney Daniel Leonard countered that it was unfair to introduce these photos at the last minute and pleaded with Judge Fujisaki to halt the trial for two weeks to give them time to prove that the photos were either irrelevant or fake. "It's a total sandbag," he whined.

Judge Fujisaki's response was immediate. "That's usually what impeachment amounts to, Counsel," he said.

If the Fuhrman tapes had bushwhacked the prosecutors in the criminal case, these new photos did the same to the defense team now. As the jurors filed into the courtroom, the defense team huddled, obviously in panic, trying to spot something in the photos that would allow them to question their authenticity.

Peter showed Groden one of the new enlargements and asked, "Does this change your mind" about the authenticity of the Scull photo?

Groden glanced at the enlargement and declared that he remained convinced, "to an overwhelming degree of certainty," that the Scull photo was phony.

Peter asked that the Flammer photo be handed to the jury. As the jurors began to examine it, Peter produced a second enlargement and asked Groden, "Does this change your mind?"

"No."

Peter methodically presented the additional prints and blowups, asking the same question and eliciting the same denial, even as the jurors passed the evidence to one another. Finally Peter asked a hypothetical question: Assume that experts studied the negatives—assume that you studied the negatives—and everyone agreed that these thirty photos were authentic, "Would that change your mind?"

The squirming witness had to admit that it "probably would."

At times some of Groden's ludicrous testimony brought muffled laughter from the spectators. During one such moment, Patti happened to glance at the killer's sister Shirley Baker. One seat from where Shirley was sitting, a woman, one of the spectators, was snickering at the witness. Shirley took umbrage with that. She reached across the person next to her and dug her nails into the woman's sweater-covered arm.

Patti concluded: Violence must run in the family.

During a break, the spectator approached us. She pointed to her arm and told Patti there were visible gouges. She asked, "Do you believe what she did?"

Patti rose to the woman's defense. "Tell her to keep her hands off you," she said. "Tell her she has no right to lay a hand on you that way!"

"I can't do that," the woman said. "They'll kick me out."

"No, they won't," Patti vowed. "I saw what she did to you."

We were jubilant as we ate our lunch, until a touchy subject arose: Would the jurors get it? Would they understand that the photos—like the other evidence—proved that the defendant had lied under oath, blatantly and with detached arrogance? Would they be able to peer through the veneer of this man's public persona and see him for what he really was?

Someone on our team idly mentioned the possibility of a hung jury.

"What do you mean?" Patti asked sharply. "I thought it's either we win or they win."

No, one of our lawyers explained, in a civil case a minimum of nine jurors must decide one way or the other. "Eight-four is a hung jury," he said. "Seven-five is a hung jury."

Patti looked as though the wind had been knocked out of her. "I don't know if I could go through this again," she said.

"It's zoo time," I commented as we walked to the courthouse after lunch on Friday, January 10. The killer was once more going to take the witness stand, and the crowd was predictably larger and more vocal than usual. Michael had come to court today. It was his final day on holiday break, and he was eager for a chance to hear the killer's testimony in person.

For three and a half hours a warm and fuzzy Robert Baker took the killer through a meticulously rehearsed litany of his past achievements and *Ozzie and Harriet* lifestyle. The performance was so saccharine that Baker several times addressed the witness as "Juice."

Foreign-sounding, comical words tumbled out of his mouth. According to the killer, he and Nicole lived an almost idyllic life, surrounded by a "cornucopia" of friends. Hearing this, we glanced at one another, wondering who had coached him to use that word.

Baker asked if he had ever lied about anything; the defendant replied, "No, I don't lie."

Throughout the afternoon, Dan lodged few objections. He wanted the killer to ramble, letting his ego—and his big mouth—get him into trouble. The killer admitted that one source of tension in the marriage was that he wanted to go places and do things, but Nicole preferred to stay home with their daughter, Sydney. The "devoted" father slipped away from his prepared script when he commented, "And when Justin came around, it almost went to a new level."

To hear the killer tell it, the New Year's Day 1989 incident was merely a family argument, and Nicole's hideous injuries must have occurred when she attacked him and he wrestled her out of *his* bedroom. Our mouths dropped open in amazement when we heard his proof that he had not hit Nicole. If he had, he almost boasted, "She would have looked a little different."

He painted Nicole with a sordid brush, expressing his concern that she had fallen into a society of heavy drinkers, drug users, and promiscuous friends. In the past he had raged at Denise Brown and Faye Resnick for broaching such subjects, protesting the effects on Sydney and Justin. But now, desperate to reclaim whatever reputation he thought he had left, clearly worried about his dwindling fortune—and determined to win at all costs—he was willing to trash his ex-wife.

"Those poor kids," Kim said. "How can he say those things about their mother? Doesn't he realize they will hear all of this someday?"

Later, I summed up his testimony: "I'm a handsome, well-dressed, generous, former Heisman trophy winner with tons of friends—incapable of any kind of violence—who, unfortunately, was beaten and stalked by my ex-wife, who had morphed into a sex-crazy, drug-taking lush. And, oh yes, I *never* lie."

Prior to Dan's cross-examination of the killer on Monday, a contentious argument ensued over the admissibility of an eight-page, undated letter written by Nicole. The defense made its usual "it's prejudicial" rant, but Judge Fujisaki ruled that we could use it to show Nicole's state of mind.

Dan read portions of the letter aloud, over Baker's repeated objections, but opted not to include an inflammatory paragraph that disclosed, "You beat the holy hell out of me and we lied at the X-ray lab and said I fell off the bike, remember?" In any event, the letter was now in evidence, and the jury would have the opportunity to read every vivid word during its deliberations.

Dan asked the killer, "Isn't it true you've lied repeatedly to this jury . . . isn't it true you've lied repeatedly throughout your entire life?"

"No," he replied.

A few minutes later Dan asked, "There were times when you were married to Nicole that you were unfaithful to her, isn't that correct?"

"From time to time, yes."

"And that was dishonest on your part, wasn't it?" Dan continued.

"I think, morally, yes."

"That was a lie, wasn't it, sir?"

The defendant responded, "I think morally it was dishonest of me, yes. I don't know if I would characterize it as a lie."

As we ate lunch on Tuesday we had a chance to meet our next witness. He was Gerald Richards, the former head of the FBI's photo-analysis division. He smiled at Kim and said, "The defense is not going to be happy with me."

That proved to be a gross understatement, for Peter Gelblum took Richards through some of the most gripping moments of the entire trial. Peter set up an easel in the courtroom and positioned a large chart listing the dozen "anomalies" that Groden had cited to indicate that the Scull photo had been altered. One by one, Peter asked Richards to explain these "anomalies" to the jury.

Richards responded in an animated, easy-to-comprehend manner. And he blew the defense case to smithereens.

For example, Groden had found what he characterized as suspicious scratch marks on the negative that did not align with scratches on other negatives. But Richards produced a Canon F1, the same model that Scull used, strode over to the jury, opened the back of the camera, and demonstrated how the film wavers as it is advanced. The Canon F1 is notorious for producing these variances in scratch marks, he said, and added pointedly that any first-year photography student would know it. Peter then stepped over to the chart and scratched a large "X" over this particular anomaly.

Groden had used the enlargements he made at Kinko's to declare that there were microscopic differences in the size of the Scull negative and other negatives on the roll. Richards demonstrated on the overhead projector how a photocopy machine itself distorts the size of a copy. Then he donned a sophisticated piece of headgear, demonstrated the proper way to measure size, and showed the jury that there was no anomaly. Peter drew another "X" on the chart.

Groden had noted that the Scull photo had a reddish tint, whereas other shots on the roll had a greenish tint. Richards pointed out the obvious. The photo in question showed the killer walking through the end zone, which was painted with the red Buffalo Bills insignia; the other photos were taken on the green football field. Peter drew another "X" on the chart.

Jurors leaned over the railing of the jury box, scribbling notes.

Kim thought: This man is like the science teacher who finally makes physics exciting! The spectators were mesmerized. Judge Fujisaki's jaw sometimes dropped open in amazement. On and on it went until all twelve of Groden's "anomalies" were crossed off the chart.

I said to myself: We kicked their butts. We're going to beat them!

The force of that thought surprised me. Until now I had been unwilling to voice that opinion to anyone—even to myself. Now I truly believed that we would gain the measure of justice that we so achingly desired.

When I arrived in court on Thursday I noticed the killer was wearing a garish pair of green and black loafers. Catching a reporter's eye, I asked, "Did you see—"

"—You mean *those* ugly-ass shoes?" the reporter said, chuckling.

Our next witness was Dr. Brad Popovich, a brilliant young man and a member of the board that certifies the work of DNA labs. Under direct examination by Tom Lambert, he reviewed the results of the three DNA labs that had worked on the case and arrived, independently, at the same conclusion. He declared definitively, "My opinion is, there is absolutely no evidence of any contamination whatsoever."

Gerald Richards returned to testify—once again clearly and convincingly—that he had examined the thirty Flammer photos and found them to be authentic.

As we neared the end of our witness list, the killer disappeared. We speculated that he was afraid we would try to recall him to the witness stand to ask him about Nicole's letter. I chalked it up to one last act of cowardice.

Our final witness was FBI agent William Bodziak. He held in his hand a size 12 Bruno Magli shoe and compared it to eight enlargements of the Flammer photographs. He pointed out the similarities: "The sole is unique to Bruno Magli shoes . . . the upper portion of the shoe is unique to Bruno Magli shoes." And finally, "My opinion is the shoes depicted in those eight exhibits are Bruno Magli . . . shoes."

At 3:25 P.M. Dan said, "We rest our case."

I found myself suddenly, strangely choked up. The activity in the courtroom blurred before my eyes. Baker rested the defense case. Judge Fujisaki announced that closing arguments would begin next Tuesday, and the jury could expect to have the case by Thursday.

The words spun past my consciousness. Once again I thought: We're going to beat them. Then I commanded myself, Don't think that.

Court was adjourned.

It's all over, I thought. Period.

I was overwhelmed by the sense of finality.

As we walked across the street to the Doubletree, Dan put his arm around my shoulder. "Fred," he said quietly, "there's no doubt. We proved to everyone that he killed your son. Do you know that?"

"Yes."

THIRTY-SEVEN

Dan was like a thoroughbred horse, ready to burst through the starting gate. "I'm anxious to give them hell," he said. "I'm going to slam them with everything that is so incredibly obvious."

It was Tuesday morning, January 21. We were at the Doubletree, awaiting the beginning of closing arguments. "I don't want to know what you're going to say," I declared. "I want to hear it fresh in the courtroom."

Patti was a cheerleader. "Go get him, Dan," she encouraged.

After we crossed the street and entered the courtroom, I took a seat alongside our attorneys. Patti, her mother Elayne, Kim, and Kim's friend and co-worker Joanne Geller sat directly behind me. The killer took his position at the far end of the defense table, about a dozen feet to my left.

Prior to the session, Baker asked the judge for a favor. Later in the week, Robert Blasier would present a portion of the defense's closing argument. But he was recovering from back surgery and was confined to a wheelchair. Baker wanted Judge Fujisaki to allow Blasier's wife, Charlotte, into the courtroom because, he explained, "She is really his attendant." But a few weeks earlier, Judge Fujisaki had banned Charlotte from the courtroom because she had been caught with an electronic device. Baker attempted to belittle this breach of security, labeling it "inadvertent, minor." He said, "We would be most appreciative if she could be in the courtroom for the remaining days while Mr. Blasier is here and gives his final summation . . . and there is no objection from the plaintiff's counsel."

Judge Fujisaki had a stern response. His decision to ban Charlotte Blasier had nothing to do with the plaintiffs. "It has to do with maintenance of order in the courtroom," he said, "and the court will not change its ruling. Bring the jury in."

Blasier jumped into the fray, requesting an opportunity to bring the matter before another judge. But Judge Fujisaki snapped, "It's *my* courtroom, Mr. Blasier." Once again, our respect for this judge increased.

Dan began his presentation by displaying, on the large overhead screen, a photograph of Ron, grinning as he held a baseball bat; I started to cry immediately. "By now, today," Dan said, "Ron Goldman would have been twenty-eight years old, and I think he would have had that restaurant that he wanted to open."

Next, Dan showed Nicole, smiling over her shoulder as she walked through a crowd. "Nicole Brown Simpson would have been thirty-seven years old," he said, then added softly, "Nicole . . . will never see her children grow up."

Suddenly Dan contrasted those glowing, vibrant pictures of life with the stark reality of death: There was Ron's body, crumpled around a tree stump; there was Nicole, curled in a pool of blood at the foot of her front stairs.

I doubled over, sobbing. I felt one of Patti's hands on my shoulder, offering me a Kleenex. I reached back to clutch her other hand.

Joanne broke down completely. This was her first exposure to these photographs. Elayne, her eyes rimmed with tears, rubbed Patti's and Kim's shoulders.

Kim's reaction was the same as it had always been: extreme anger. She glanced toward the killer and was sickened to see that he showed no emotion whatsoever. She thought: He has never acknowledged any sorrow over the fact that two human beings were brutally murdered.

Dan noted that neither Ron nor Nicole was able to take the witness stand. But, he declared, in "their last struggling moments" they "provided us the key evidence necessary to identify their killer."

"They managed to get a glove pulled off, a hat to drop off; they managed to dig nails into the left hand of this man, cause other injuries to his hand, forcing him to drop his blood next to their bodies as he tried to get away.

"And by their blood, they forced him to step, step, step as he walked to the back, leaving shoe prints that are just like fingerprints in this case that tell us who did this . . . unspeakable tragedy.

"So these crucial pieces of evidence after all are the voices of Ron and Nicole speaking to us from their graves, telling us, telling all of you"—Dan pointed directly at the defendant and continued—"that there is a killer in this courtroom."

The killer responded with an insolent stare.

We knew that Dan was good, but even we were not prepared for the passion and the brilliance of his closing argument. The courtroom was hushed. Jurors and spectators alike were riveted on every word he uttered, every move he made.

In a blistering series of rhetorical questions, Dan asked the jurors whether the defendant ever explained why his blood was at the crime scene, in his driveway, in his bathroom, or in his Bronco. Did he ever explain how the victims' blood got into his car or on a glove discovered at his home? Did he tell them why his hairs were entwined in the knit cap that lay by the bodies? Why were the victims' hairs found on the blood-caked Rockingham glove? What about the rare carpet fibers found at the crime scene, matching those from the defendant's Bronco? Did he explain why there were now thirty-one photographs showing him wearing the "ugly-ass" Bruno Magli shoes that he swore he had never owned?

Dan reminded the jury that one week earlier the defendant had had his chance to answer these questions. But, confronted with such conclusive evidence, what did he choose to address? He talked about breaking football records, winning awards, and playing golf.

Dan asked, "What kind of man . . . confronted with this bruised and battered picture of Nicole, says . . . I was just defending myself? . . . What kind of man takes a baseball bat to his wife's car . . . and then says he was not upset? . . . What kind of man says his deceased wife is lying when you heard her voice trembling on that tape? . . . What kind of man says cheating on your wife isn't a lie?"

In a strong, confident voice, Dan proclaimed, "Well, let me tell you what kind of man says those things. . . . A guilty man. A man with no remorse. A man with no conscience. This man is so obsessed with trying to salvage his image and protect himself that he'll come into this courtroom, knowing the whole world is watching, and he will smear the name and reputation of the mother of his children while she rests in her grave.

"This is a man, ladies and gentlemen, who I submit to you has lied and lied and lied to you about every important fact in this case.

"Every one."

As Dan spoke, Baker and the killer muttered comments to each other. At times their voices were loud enough to carry across the courtroom. They appeared to be making a conscious effort to disrupt Dan's rhythm. Their obvious arrogance and disrespect showed a clear contempt for anyone who would dare to oppose them.

In the spectators' section, some of the killer's family members once more busied themselves with word puzzles, even as Dan presented a riveting oration that he characterized as "a few sort of obvious observations."

He said, "Bundy is the home of Nicole Brown Simpson. These murders didn't occur at—in a dark alley or parking lot or convenience store; they occurred right at her home, not far from her front door, which was left wide open, with the lights on inside. . . . There's no evidence of a burglary here, robbery, vandalism, or rape, or any kind of sexual assault. We're not dealing with that here. . . .

"The children were upstairs, asleep in their bedrooms, unharmed. . . .

"Ron Goldman went there at the very last minute, when he was asked by Nicole, right before ten o'clock, to drop off a pair of glasses.

"Nobody knew Ron Goldman was going to Nicole's condominium on his way to meet some friends. . . .

"So it is very clear that Nicole Brown Simpson was the target of this attack. By someone who knew she would be home and someone who knew where she lived.

"It's not a gunshot killing. We're talking about a killing by a knife, up close, by a person—obviously from these wounds—in a state of rage. . . .

"And all these signs, ladies and gentlemen, point directly to a person who knew Nicole, knew where to find her, and had no reason to go to her house that night except to confront her, and had no reason to expect Ron Goldman, who showed up unexpectedly.

"There's no such person other than O. J. Simpson, ladies and gentlemen."

Dan turned to a systematic review of the evidence. He placed a three-ring binder on the podium, holding an outline of the points he planned to cover. Each time he finished a point, he flipped a page over with a loud, almost popping flourish, as if to say: That's one more piece of the damning, compelling, *complete* trail of physical material that has been before the public for two and one half years and proves conclusively that the defendant and the killer are one and the same.

Dan assured the jury that the defense, in its closing argument, would once again cry "Contamination!" and "Conspiracy!" He predicted, "You're going to hear all that stuff, okay. None of it is true. . . .

"But I'll tell you one thing. They can't make that argument, even that lame argument . . . about these shoe prints.

"They can't argue that the shoe prints are planted. . . . This is one of the single most crucial pieces of evidence in this case. . . .

"If that photo is real, O. J. Simpson is the killer. That's it. It's the end of the ball game."

During the lunch break, one reporter—a veteran who had been covering criminal cases for years—commented to me, "It's the finest closing argument I've ever witnessed."

I thought: Everything that Dan laid out so passionately was so incredibly clear. There was a volume of evidence, all pointing to one person. It was unbelievable to hear all of that condensed into a three-hour period.

But Dan was not satisfied. "I've got more to do," he declared. With a sandwich in one hand, he spent much of the break going over his notes, discussing with his associates what he wanted to cover during the afternoon session.

Throughout the afternoon Dan pounded away. What was at the Bundy crime scene? Ron's blood, Nicole's blood, the defendant's blood, Bruno Magli shoe prints, an Aris Isotoner glove, a watch cap, hair from the defendant, and fibers from his car. What was in the defendant's Bronco? Ron's blood, Nicole's blood, the defendant's blood, and more shoe prints.

What was at the defendant's Rockingham estate? Ron's blood, Nicole's blood, the defendant's blood, a matching Aris Isotoner glove with blood, hair, and fibers all over it, and a pair of bloody socks.

It was exhilarating. These were the words I longed to shout from the rooftops. The killer's mask of affability was ripped from his face, exposing him for the lying, vicious, egomaniac we knew him to be.

Kim thought: I know we've got all the facts on our side in this case, but Dan's making it sound so sensible, so reasonable. This is amazing.

Several times during the presentation I caught myself trying to read the faces of the jurors. Each time I lectured myself: Cut this out. You've done this before and it didn't work.

Dan mused, "You know when someone leaves their blood at the scene of a murder, that's usually the end of the ball game, and that person did it.

"Now, if Mr. Simpson did it, as we believe the proof shows, and if he left blood there, which we believe the proof shows, then one would expect there to be some injury to Mr. Simpson, something cut, something abraded, gouged, whatever, but someplace where that blood came from.

"And, in fact, when Mr. Simpson returned from Chicago the next day and went down to talk to the police, he had cuts or marks or gouges, whatever you want to call them, but he had injuries. Where? Left hand. Left hand. That's where the blood was dropped, to the left of various shoe prints. He had injuries to his left hand.

"Do you know what kind of an extraordinary coincidence it would be for O. J. Simpson's ex-wife to be murdered by a killer who bled from the left hand and he has a cut on the left hand and he didn't do it? And he got that cut that night, at the time she's being murdered.

"So when he came back from Chicago, he had a big problem."

In sum, Dan said, "It all points to him and no one else. Nobody else. Just him. Just him. Because he did it."

Afterward, in our war room at the Doubletree, Kim said to Dan, "I love it when you use words like 'liar.' You told it like it is."

There was much discussion about the killer's reaction to Dan's closing. He had spent most of the day with his head down, scribbling notes. Even when Dan pointed at him and called him a liar and a killer, he had little response. Instead, it was the little, inconsequential things, that seemed to irritate him. For example, at one point Dan declared that the defendant had played one of the most violent of all sports. The killer's head shot up and he mouthed the words, "Football's not violent!"

It was very strange. We would never be able to get inside the mind of this man. But it was a place we did not want to go.

That evening at home we were consumed with conflicting passions. We were in awe of what Dan had accomplished in the courtroom. There were pieces of evidence that we had almost forgotten, but Dan did not miss an iota of it.

All indications were that our plaintiffs' team would finish its presentation in the morning. We had no idea how long the defense would take for its closing statement, but what could Baker and his associates possibly say?

I quipped, "I see only two possibilities. One, he could say, 'Everybody's lying.' Two, he could say, 'Ladies and gentlemen of the jury, this is a Heisman trophy winner. How can you imagine that he could do such a thing?' "

On Wednesday morning, Dan summarized. "In the end, it all comes down to this: There's blood, there's hair, there's fibers, there's cuts, there's sweatsuits, there's hats, there's no alibi, there's plenty of time, and there's motive.

"And that's on our side of the scale.

"What's on his side?

"His word that he didn't do it, his credibility, his truth telling."

Dan reminded the jurors of an instruction they would receive: "'A witness willfully false in one part of his or her testimony is to be distrusted in others'. . . . What that means is that if you believe O. J. Simpson lied to you on just one important point . . . you can reject his entire testimony."

Suddenly Dan said, "Can you bring out the board, Joe?" His assistant, Joe Lester, displayed a huge chart on an easel, depicting fifty-seven witnesses and documents that contradicted the defendant's sworn testimony:

Either: Simpson Is Lying
Or: All of These Witnesses and Documents Are Lying,
Mistaken, or Faked

Nicole Brown Simpson
Writings by Nicole Brown
  Simpson
India Allen
Albert Aguillera
Mark Day
John Edwards
Sharyn Gilbert
Al Cowlings
Lenore Walker
Medical records from 1989
  beating
Photographs of Nicole's face
  after 1989 beating
Frank Olson
Robert Lerner
Donna Estes
Jackie Cooper
Nancy Ney
GTE telephone records
Paula Barbieri
Craig Baumgarten
Ronald Fischman
Juditha Brown
Kato Kaelin
Allan Park
Charles Cale
Dale St. John
Gigi Guarin
Robert Riske
Michael Terrazas

David Rossi
Donald Thompson
Ron Phillips
Tom Lange
Daniel Gonzales
Leslie Gardiner
Frank Spangler
Richard Aston
Thano Peratis
Willie Ford
Angelica Guzman
Dennis Fung
Andrea Mazzolla
Collin Yamauchi
Jim Merrill
Raymond Kilduff
Mark Partridge
Skip Taft
Michael Baden
Photograph of left hand on June 13
Phillip Vannatter
Robert Kardashian
Kelly Mulldorfer
Harry Scull
Photograph of Simpson taken by
  Harry Scull
E. J. Flammer
30 photographs of Simpson,
  taken by E. J. Flammer
Buffalo Bills Report, 11/93
Orenthal James Simpson

"For him to be innocent and for him to be believed," Dan declared, waving his hand at the chart, "you have to disbelieve all of them. . . . All these people, all these writings, all these photographs, they either have to be fraudulent, lying, altered, mistaken. Bottom line, they all have to be wrong, and only he is right. . . .

"These photos all have to be false; police all have to be liars, mistaken about everything they did.

"Medical records of Nicole's '89 beating, wrong.

"People who witnessed domestic violence incidents, wrong.

"GTE telephone records showing he picked up the message, wrong. . . .

"His lawyer, Skip Taft, who saw the cut on his fourth finger the day when he came back from Chicago, wrong.

"His lawyer friend of, what, twenty, thirty years, Robert Kardashian, wrong. Lied. He lied. He lied when he said Simpson asked him to get the golf clubs. That was a lie."

Dan was on a roll.

"And Orenthal James Simpson, I guess he's got to be a liar, too, because he told us how mistaken he was when he told the police all those things that he now wants to recant. . . . I was wrong. I was assuming.

"When he said he was driving over to Paula's after the recital. I was wrong, that wasn't Sunday, that was Saturday.

"When he said he picked up Paula's message. Oh, I was wrong about that, too, I didn't pick it up.

"So I guess he's a liar."

Without missing a beat, Dan requested, "Can you bring out the next board?" Joe set up a huge display showing all thirty-one color photographs of the killer wearing Bruno Magli shoes. In the center of the board was a plastic pocket holding a copy of the *Buffalo Bills Report* from November 1993.

Dan said, "This is just a good illustration of how a liar gets trapped in his lies." He reminded the jury of the killer's statement during his deposition that he would never wear those "ugly-ass" shoes. Then, a few months later, the Harry Scull photograph surfaced. The defendant's only option was to claim that the photo was fake. But suddenly he was confronted with thirty additional photos.

"Understand something," Dan said, "he took this witness stand in his own defense, with his whole case riding on this one point. . . . Did his lawyer ask him a single question about these photographs . . . ?

"No. I had to ask him. . . . And maybe for the first time in his life, I guess he realized he was out of room to run."

Dan paraphrased the killer's response: "Yeah, I was there. . . . Those are my clothes, not my shoes."

Gesturing to Joe, Dan said, "Can you reach that for me."

Joe pulled the four-page *Buffalo Bills Report* from its plastic pocket and handed it over. Turning to page 3, Dan displayed for the jurors a large photograph of the killer wearing Bruno Magli shoes. It was frame 7-A of the Flammer photos. "Well, wait a minute," Dan said. "This came out in the newspaper, November 1993." That was eight months prior to the murders. Dan asked caustically, "How could this be a fake?"

We had never seen anything like this—either in real life or in courtroom dramas. The room was stone-cold silent.

I knew that Dan was nearing the end of his presentation, and I had a gut sense of what was coming next.

"We're going to talk very, very briefly about my client, Fred Goldman, my client's loss, the loss of his son," Dan said. "There can never be true justice for Fred Goldman. . . . True justice would be to see Ron Goldman walk through those doors right now—"

Hearing those words, Kim broke down. She had a vision of Ron, striding into the courtroom, his eyes shining with pride and appreciation for what all of us—his family and these dedicated professionals—were doing for him. She had an overwhelming desire to go to the cemetery and share this with him.

Dan was now talking about both Ron and Nicole. "There's nothing I can do," he said. "There's nothing you can do; there's nothing this good judge can do; and there's nothing that man"—Dan pointed at the killer—"can do to bring these people back.

"All you have in your power to do is to bring about some small measure of justice by recognizing the incalculable loss my client has suffered, and to require the man who is responsible for this to pay for this, to pay for the loss he caused this man. . . .

"I think we would agree . . . there isn't any loss greater than a parent losing a child."

Glancing toward Baker and his son, Philip, Dan said, "We don't have to look beyond this courtroom. In fact, we don't have to look beyond counsel's table to see the love and the pride that a father has for his grown man—for his grown child, his grown son. You've seen that right here in this courtroom.

"And that is the love and pride that Fred Goldman will have only in memory. In memory, in his heart, and his soul.

"He will never see the beaming look of satisfaction on Ron's face as Ron might have ushered him through his restaurant.

"He will never sit down with Ron at a Fourth of July barbecue or Passover Seder, or a birthday party.

"He will never share the joy of running off to the hospital to see his grandchild, perhaps his first grandchild, a baby that Ron wanted to name Dakota, if you remember.

"He will never see again the smile on his son's face. . . . Fred has lost all of that and infinitely more forever, and his life will never be the same. . . .

"I'd like to play for you, one more time, one of Fred Goldman's last treasures that he has, he will always have, to remember his son by." The overhead screen showed the videotape of Lauren's Bat Mitzvah. There was Ron, dancing with Melanie Duben and Lauren Cohen, supremely enjoying the moment as all of us joined in an impromptu hora.

Then, there I was onstage with Ron, hamming it up as we lip-synched to Bob Seger's "Old Time Rock 'n' Roll." I had viewed the tape many times, and each time it choked me up. But this time I noticed as never before how often Ron and I glanced at each other as we pretended to sing. I noticed how we moved our inflatable plastic guitars together. We were *in synch* as we laughed our way through the unplanned performance.

Standing only a few feet away, Dan turned and looked directly at me, staring deeply into my eyes. I felt Patti's hand, reaching out toward me, and I grasped her palm. Dan said, "There was a sixteenth-century poet named Guillaume du Bartas, who best expressed a relationship between a father and son in a few simple words. Let me read them to you:

"'My lovely, living boy,

"My hope, my happiness,

"My love, my life, my joy.'"

And then he added, quietly, "Fred Goldman's lovely, living boy is no more."

If Judge Fujisaki had not called a recess our collective tears would have flooded the courtroom. After the jury left, we all hugged Dan. Tom Lambert's eyes were very red. Peter, Ed, and Yvette were crying also. Someone said that even the most hard-bitten reporters—both those in the courtroom and those in the auxiliary room who were listening to the audio feed—were awash in tears.

Patti was stunned by Dan's presentation. "He was incredible, stupendous, brilliant, articulate, dignified, passionate, firm, and convincing," she said. "And that's an understatement."

She told him how impressed she was, and he responded, modestly, "That's what you hired me for."

"We didn't know how great you'd be," Patti said. "We didn't know one another. We were taking a chance on you and you were taking a chance on us. I just want you to know how proud I am to have you pursuing justice for Ron."

The Browns' attorney John Kelly followed Dan, and he, too, confronted the killer directly. Lou, Juditha, and Tanya Brown watched intently as Kelly attacked their former in-law. He quoted the killer's own words:

Fame is a vapor, popularity is an accident, money takes wings, but only one thing endures, and that's character.

"And we agree that character endures," Kelly said. "Whether it's good character or bad character, it endures.

"And we've learned a lot about Mr. Simpson's character; we know it was formidable; we know it was complex; and we also know it was frightening.

"And we've seen occasions when a sick, twisted mind would trigger the fury of an animal and the actions of a coward.

"And Mr. Simpson is a coward.

"You've heard about the public Mr. Simpson, the polished veneer. I mean, how many times are you going to hear about the fact he won a Heisman trophy, he shattered professional football rushing records, he was a spokesman for corporate America, and a commentator for the networks?

"But, ladies and gentlemen, winning the Heisman trophy doesn't give you a license to kill."

Kelly spoke of the defendant's willingness to cheapen Nicole, the mother of his children, in front of the jury, and of the way he viewed women in general, as possessions. "Nicole was precious," Kelly said. "She was a gem. She was a total package. And to Mr. Simpson, she was the Heisman trophy of women. But just like that trophy, an object to him."

Quite effectively, we thought, Kelly was able to bring Nicole into the courtroom.

Nicole's battered face appeared on the screen, and Kelly said, "I want her in her own words to tell you people whether she was frightened, whether she was scared, that night of October 25, 1993."

A portion of the 911 call was played. The operator asked, "You're scared of him?"

In a shaky voice that sent eerie shivers through us all, Nicole replied, "Yes."

Kelly asked the jury, "What more would you want? She tells you right there, from as close as we can get to her, that she was scared that night."

Kelly's style was more low-keyed than Dan's but very moving as he described the killer's actions on the night of June 12, 1994: "He put on soft-soled shoes to move quietly—rare designer soft-soled shoes—to move quietly that night.

"He wore a ski cap to avoid identification.

"He wore rare designer gloves so he wouldn't leave fingerprints.

"And he used a knife so he could kill quietly."

The defense had tried to depict the killings as a lengthy struggle. But Kelly said, "I think struggle is one of the biggest misnomers of this case. . . . Nicole received a blow to the brain with such velocity . . . a blow to the brain that bruised it. And Ron Goldman, relaxed, unsuspecting, finished with work, off to meet his friends, dropping off glasses, was ambushed in a pitch-black area, pitch-black. . . . It wasn't a struggle; it was a slaughter."

Kelly's conclusion was forceful.

"And you have to make this man understand—understand things; that when you do things like—you hop fences, you hide things in trash cans, or you run from the cops, or you peep in your wife's window late at night without her knowing, you're a sneak. And when you look at a photograph of you in the killing shoes, and you say it's a fake, you're a liar.

"And when you are unfaithful to your wife, you're a cheater.

"And when you kick her, and when you hit her and you pull her hair, you're a batterer.

"And when you slaughter two people in the primes of their lives, you're a killer.

"And all Nicole and all Ron are asking you people to do is to assign that responsibility to a man who refuses to accept it."

After lunch, the defense got its turn. Prior to beginning his presentation, Baker indicated to Judge Fujisaki that his argument would carry over into Thursday morning. That would still give Dan time for his rebuttal, and the jury would likely begin its deliberations by the afternoon.

Before the jury came in, Dan had an issue to address. He said to the judge, "Yesterday, I saw Mr. Baker with Mr. Simpson working with the gloves. I see the gloves up there, and I don't know what Mr. Baker has in mind, but I would absolutely object to any attempt during closing to put any gloves on Mr. Simpson. That's testimonial. It's evidentiary. I don't want to object in front of the jury."

Ignoring Baker's sputtering, Judge Fujisaki said quickly, "Sustain the objection."

The jury took its seats, and Baker rose to present what was supposed to be the definitive exoneration of his client.

In contrast to Dan's tightly woven, brilliantly delivered argument, Baker seemed disjointed and off his stride. With all the irrefutable evidence on our side, he did not have much to work with. He claimed to be suffering from some sort of virus, and perhaps he wanted the jury to believe this to be the reason that he was erratic and disorganized. To us, it was clear that he was neither as prepared nor as polished as Dan. And perhaps he did not spend much time in preparation, for much of his script appeared to be a plagiarized version of Johnnie Cochran's closing argument during the criminal trial.

I was astounded to realize that, in fact, he was going to argue the issues I had mentioned the night before. Everyone was lying—except for his wonderful, marvelous, Heisman trophy–winning client.

As usual, Baker was rude, cold, and, we thought, ineffective. Early on, he sought to portray the case as some sort of frivolous lawsuit. He lectured, "Now, any one of us, all the people in the gallery, can go down to the first floor of this building and, for about $200, file a lawsuit, and they can charge somebody else, another human being, or a corporation, with malfeasance, doing something wrong, and seek to collect hundreds of thousands of dollars, or millions of dollars. . . . But with that enormous and awesome privilege that is granted to us comes the burden of proof."

He chastised Dan for supposedly ignoring that burden and instead, playing on the jury's emotions. He complained that, because our side would have the final word in rebuttal, Dan had a chance to "sand-bag" the defense. He attempted to point the finger of blame at every-body, everywhere, except where it belonged—at his client. In the World According to Baker there was a long list of despicable people whose sole purpose in life was to trash his client: the plaintiffs, our attorneys, the police, the FBI, our expert witnesses, and even the media. "I'm including the media," he said, "because, ladies and gentlemen, if, in fact, you find him not responsible, the gravy train is over. The case is over. It's not in the news every day. It is gone."

He trained his guns directly on us, telling the jury, "You know, I was kind of amazed that Mr. Petrocelli had to bring up myself and my son. I was kind of amazed that he had to do that.

"I can tell you this, ladies and gentlemen, I would have a terrible time if I lost him. But I wouldn't take $450,000 for a book. I wouldn't prosecute an innocent man. That would never happen."

I felt my pulse quicken and I saw Dan's jaw tighten.

Baker opined that this case was about law enforcement versus his client. "There's no doubt about it. They're linked at the hip, or any other place you want to join them."

He questioned the objectivity of some of our expert witnesses. Referring to FBI agent Douglas Deedrick, who happened to have a photograph in his office of him with Kim and me, he said that Deedrick had testified, "'But I'm independent, you know. I flew out here from Washington, paying my bill. You, the taxpayers, are paying my bill, but I'm unbiased.'"

Then Baker attempted a ridiculous analogy, "Well, you can call a stallion a cow, but you can't get milk from it. He can call himself unbiased, but it isn't so."

Baker's droning attempts at logic were very difficult to follow. Spectators nodded off. Throughout the presentation, Judge Fujisaki often looked surprised at the issues being raised; at other times he appeared simply bored.

Baker derided the theory that his client would use a highly visible vehicle to drive over to Nicole's condo, calling the Ford Bronco "the biggest white elephant that's been made."

He spent about two hours on the subject of motive—attempting to convince the jury that his client did not have a motive to kill Ron and Nicole. We found this quite interesting, because under the rules of this civil litigation, we did not even have to prove motive!

"There was no obsession," Baker said. "Certainly it's a stretch, a quantum leap, but it's part of the effort by the plaintiffs to demonize and to manufacture a motive. You can't get your arms around it because it doesn't fit."

During a break in the proceedings, when few people were in the courtroom, I happened to notice that Baker had strolled over to the plaintiffs' table. He was glancing intently at something. "He's looking at Dan's notes," I muttered. Hearing this, Baker walked away. I stepped over to the table and turned Dan's notes upside down.

Late in the day, Baker was still babbling in a somewhat incoherent, dispassionate way when, in a lame attempt to mimic Johnnie Cochran's "doesn't fit—must acquit" rhyme, he embarrassed himself by saying: "I'm no poet, obviously, but if you don't have time, you most certainly could not commit the crime."

If I did not detest the man so much, I might have felt sorry for him.

Finally, Baker tried an unsubtle ploy. Thwarted in his attempt to have the killer try on the gloves, he found another way to make his point that, in his opinion, the gloves were too small to fit his client. He referred to testimony from some witnesses who failed to see cuts on the killer's hands the night of the murders. Then he turned to the defendant and said, "Look at the size of this man's hands. Hold up your hand, O. J." The killer raised a paw. "His hand's about an inch and a half bigger than mine," Baker commented. "Big hand."

After court, some of the reporters told Kim they did not know whether to laugh or cry at Baker's absurd "gravy train" comment. Many of these people had lived away from their families, in cramped apartments, for months on end. They worked eighty-hour weeks without overtime pay and did not feel as if they were riding a "gravy train."

Patti's stomach was upset over the cheap shot that Baker had taken, insinuating that our primary objective in this case was money. "Dan," she said, "you've got to do something, say something, in your rebuttal so that the jury understands it's not about money. It's never been about money. The jury has to realize that this was the only avenue open to us. It was the one and only way we could seek justice."

"You wait," Dan said to us. "I'm gonna nail that son of a bitch for what he said. I know what I'm going to say."

Baker angered Judge Fujisaki on Thursday morning by declaring that the defense had changed its plans and "probably will go all day long today." The judge reminded Baker that because of the defense team's previous, shorter estimate, he had not changed his plans to attend a judicial conference on Friday—so that meant that Dan's rebuttal could not begin until Monday. Baker was clearly upset that court would be dark on Friday; he did not want Dan to have three days to prepare his rebuttal.

Judge Fujisaki grumbled, "I think that you're not in the position to be too complaining under those circumstances. Okay. Bring in the jury."

I thought: Dan's been ready for months. This delay probably will only make him even more impassioned.

Baker's performance of yesterday was almost universally panned in the press, so it was not surprising that he passed the baton to Robert Blasier this morning. Balsier once more implored the judge to allow his wife back inside in order to witness the "crowning glory" of his career, and the judge relented.

Just as Baker's argument mimicked Johnnie Cochran's, Blasier paraphrased Barry Scheck. Rolling back and forth in his wheelchair, repeatedly butting up against Dan's seat at our table, Blasier used folksy metaphors in an attempt to convince the jury that his client had been framed. He made the incredible assertion: "They proved nothing. We proved everything to a certainty."

But then he contradicted himself, acknowledging, "I'm not going to prove anything to you to an absolute certainty. . . . Nobody can do that."

He reasoned that if the defense could prove that bits of the evidence were unreliable, the jury could disregard all of it, and he illustrated his point with a tasteless analogy: "If you have a plate of spaghetti and you find a cockroach in it, you don't have to really go and look for a second one to know that you can discard the plate of spaghetti."

Blasier repeatedly referred to the murders as an "event," and I was offended beyond measure. The butchering of my son was not an "event."

The defense attorney constantly made the gigantic leap from stating a proposition to assuming that it was a fact. The defense had provided *no* evidence to prove contamination or conspiracy, yet the words were once more thrown about as if they meant something. What he is doing is criminal, I thought.

Blasier complained to the jury that a piece of paper at the murder scene was never collected, and insinuated that it could have led us to the real killer. He opined, "Maybe what's written on the back, if there is something written on the back, had something to do with why these killings occurred. Who knows?"

Kim and I both thought we knew. I scribbled a note and passed it to Kim: "O. J. was here?"

She wrote back: "Follow me to 360 Rockingham?"

Blasier acknowledged that the defense could not explain who allegedly tampered with the evidence—or, for that matter when, how, or why this massive conspiracy unfolded. Still, he insisted that the defense had proved enough anomalies to make it clear the evidence was not, in his words, "hunky-dory." Then he added, "I mean, c'mon folks. . . . Good heavens."

The presentation reached the height of absurdity when he commanded an assistant, "Bring me my Tinkertoys." He was provided with a large plastic bag. Reaching inside, he produced a cumbersome, multi-colored replica of a DNA ladder, fashioned from Tinkertoys. He noted proudly, "My wife and I, my lovely wife, who is in the courtroom, spent last night painting these." He tried to make the ponderous point that a DNA molecule contains some 6 billion "Tinkertoy" modules and to make a positive match one would have to compare all 6 billion—ignoring the simple truth that DNA tests comparing only a few molecules have proved utterly reliable. To Blasier, it seemed, the search for justice was child's play.

Judge Fujisaki's expressive face sported raised eyebrows and a puzzled half-smirk, as if he were silently saying to Blasier: Give me a break. Do you really expect to sell this load of manure to the jury?

As the courtroom filled following the lunch break, the killer stood, inches away, as Charlotte Blasier struggled to maneuver her husband's wheelchair through the swinging gate that separated the spectators from the attorneys. Not once did the killer offer to help. He simply shrugged his shoulders and turned his back on them.

We were told during lunch that the defense had complained about Judge Fujisaki's facial expressions. For the remainder of the afternoon session, he kept his eyes downcast.

Blasier's afternoon performance continued to be dull and full of dubious detail, without passion or conviction. At one point, I glanced back at his "lovely" wife, Charlotte, and realized that, during the "crowning glory" of her husband's career, she had nodded off. I noticed that Baker's eyes were also shut.

At times, Dan and the rest of our attorneys could not hide their reactions to the preposterous things Blasier was saying. Once, Dan simply shook his head in amazement.

Blasier turned to him and asked, "Is there something funny?"

Dan responded, "You don't want me to answer that."

Finally, it was Dan Leonard's turn to speak. Throughout the trial, we had found him to be one of the most offensive members of the defense, and we groaned inwardly as he began: "Did you really think Coach Baker was going to keep me out of the lineup?"

Another sports analogy, Patti thought, how insulting.

Leonard presented himself as a "hardheaded Irishman," and said that he used "common sense" to analyze the thirty-one photographs of the defendant wearing Bruno Magli shoes. "Common sense will tell you," he said, "that these are photographs that come too late and cost too much."

Why, he asked, did these photographs not surface earlier? "There's a reason for that," he declared. "Money. Dough. There's money to be made in those photographs; that's what it's all about." There was the money theme again. Everybody in the world was out for a fast, easy buck—with the notable exceptions of the defendant and his attorneys, who were obviously working pro bono.

He spent some time detailing Groden's dozen supposed "anomalies" in the Scull photo, and dismissed the dramatic rebuttal of former FBI photo analyst Gerald Richards. But his major point had nothing to do with scientific objectivity. He said, "I would suggest to you that there's another very important factor here, and that would be factor 13."

Leonard displayed his "factor 13" on the video screen. It was a price list for publication rights to the Scull and Flammer photographs. He derided this iron-clad, expert-documented evidence, as "store-bought . . . evidence with a price list."

What about "factor 14?" I thought. What about the fact that one of Flammer's photos was published eight months before the murders?

For his finale, Leonard strolled over to the killer, placed a hand on the shoulder of the Heisman trophy winner, turned to face the jury, and asked, "What this comes down to is, Are you going to be able to come back, based on this evidence, and tell my client that he killed the mother of his children?"

Damn straight, I thought.

That evening, Patti, Kim, and I joined several of the attorneys and reporters for Happy Hour at the Doubletree bar. For the others, this was a regular early-evening routine, but we found them somewhat on guard. Michelle Caruso, a reporter for the New York *Daily News,* explained to Kim that, two nights ago, they had noticed a man sitting alone at a nearby table. This stranger seemed to have his head cocked in a "what are they saying" posture. Yesterday in court Philip Baker had made a few comments about things he would have known only had he been privy to this group's conversation the previous evening. And then last night another man—another outsider—had appeared. He, too, sat alone, but fairly close to the group, cocking his head to one side. Michelle and plaintiffs' assistant Steve Foster had decided to call his bluff. Standing close enough to be overheard, one of them said, "Gee, I wonder how much Baker and Company would pay to have someone sit in a bar all evening and listen to our conversations."

The man fled from the bar, never looking back.

Kim wondered if the defense had hired a few KGB spies; she was glad that our war room at the Doubletree was complete with a sophisticated security system that included even a motion detector.

Dan was concerned about the three-day hiatus before the arguments concluded and the jury got the case. Some people speculated that the defense was desperate and would try to lure jurors into discussing the case prematurely. Rumors of jury tampering were whispered.

That led us to a discussion of whether the criminal defense team or the civil defense team was the most despicable. Both, in their own loathsome styles, had manipulated facts, lied repeatedly, and used every cheap trick in the book to exonerate a murderer.

Finally, we concluded, "It's a draw."

Patti looked around and realized what a tremendous impact there would be once this case was finally over. She knew it would be a big load off our shoulders, but we would also suffer withdrawal. We had grown so close to these people. We respected, admired, and cared for each of them. She vowed that we would never lose contact. These friendships had become too important.

Much of our discussion centered around Dan's rebuttal statement on Monday, and how he would counter the defense's absurd presentation. Kim was full of ideas. Referring to Baker's blatant reference to the defendant's large hands, she urged Dan, "Take that and run with it. Show them how easy it would be for those huge hands to overpower Ron or yank a woman's hair back and slit her throat." She also suggested throwing Blasier's "cockroach in the spaghetti" comment back into his face. She said, "Point at the killer and shout, 'There's a cockroach in this courtroom!' " Finally, she commented, "Dan, if you're sort of tired, I'll get up and do the rebuttal for you."

The funny thing was, she probably could have.

A sheriff wrote down our addresses for security purposes and told us they were putting their force on tactical alert prior to the verdict. We were also told that we would have four hours, rather than the usual one, to get to court. Patti's fear of reprisal was rekindled. "Will you protect us going to and from court?" she asked.

"Anything you want," the sheriff responded.

Implicit in all this security was the unspoken prediction of a verdict that the killer was culpable and that protests, or worse, could erupt. We remained angered, and saddened, that the issue of race had ever surfaced. Once again, we said, "Thank you, Johnnie Cochran."

Tension crackled through our house like fireworks. The littlest thing was capable of setting Patti, Lauren, or me off. We snapped at one another, apologized, and snapped again. Volatile mood swings were becoming the norm.

Michelle Caruso said to Kim, "You know, I just have to tell you that I am so happy your Dad and Patti have stayed together. Usually in situations like this, one person ends up leaving."

Remembering all the highs and all the lows, Kim smiled and told the truth. "We're a pretty healthy dysfunctional family," she said.

Tom Lambert called late Sunday night to assure us that the team had worked nonstop over the weekend. They had no way of knowing how long Baker would take the next morning or what points he would cover. But they had made educated guesses. Dan had two rebuttal arguments prepared. One was three or four hours long, the other, a shortened version.

But even after the call, our anxiety level was at a maximum. "Say what you will about Baker," Patti warned, "but he's got a tough reputation and he's not going to roll over and play dead. He's had three days to shore up his attack, and I'm expecting something bad to happen tomorrow morning."

"I'm counting on Dan," I told her.

The first thing that Baker said to the jury on Monday morning was, "I apologize to you because this flu hangs on a long time and I still have it. But we'll get through this."

Before long, Baker was deriding the possibility that only one person could have committed the murders. He asked, "How can you keep Ron Goldman off of a single assailant? If it's O. J. Simpson or the biggest football player who played in the Super Bowl yesterday?"

Kim had the answer to that. She wanted to stand up and scream: How about if you catch him off guard while you're wielding a six-inch knife? She whispered to Patti, "I don't know if I can sit here and listen to this."

Referring to our time line for the murders, Baker said, "So they've got to make them virtually instantly occur. . . . The more you make them quick, the more I would suggest to you it would appear it would have to be a professional killer or professional killers. Not somebody who's in an uninitiated blind rage as they want you to believe."

He once again railed at the LAPD for its so-called rush to judgment. "They had their man," he said. " . . . They had the big fish. O. J. Simpson." Because the LAPD and the District Attorney's office had failed to win other recent, high-profile cases, he charged, "This case they were going to win."

Baker moved easily from dubious to forbidden territory. He declared, "There's one man that wants to be, more than anybody, the linchpin of that case, and that's somebody who you've, I'm sure, now felt there has been an effort to keep out of this trial. Mark Fuhrman."

Dan objected immediately, and Judge Fujisaki sustained him. The court had ordered that there would be no references to the failure of Fuhrman to testify.

But that did not stop Baker from mentioning his name at every opportunity. Now he told a whopper: "And what happens from two-forty-five to four o'clock? Nobody seems to know the whereabouts of Mark Fuhrman." The implication, of course, was that the detective was hopping between Rockingham and Bundy, sprinkling blood, hair, and fibers about with abandon and, of course, planting an Aris Isotoner glove behind Kato Kaelin's room. Why? Because "the big fish was O. J. Simpson. . . . And anybody who doesn't believe that believes in the Easter bunny and the tooth fairy," Baker declared.

More clearly than any member of the original "Scheme Team" ever dared, Baker said, concerning the glove, "That's planted evidence; there's no question about it. . . . And it's done by Fuhrman. And there's no question about it."

At the 10 o'clock break, I said to Patti, "I have probably ground my teeth down to the roots already."

After the break, Baker continued with his lies until he told one so blatant that it got him into immediate trouble. The subject was the killer's call to Paula Barbieri's answering machine at 10:03 P.M. on the night of the murders. We contended that he made it from his Bronco; he said he was standing in his yard. Baker said, "And you and I know that if he had been in the car when that call was made at 10:03, there would have been somebody on this witness stand who would have said, I analyzed the sound from the tape that was on Paula's answering machine when he left the message. . . ."

Dan objected, noting, "There is no such tape, and he knows it. . . . Make him point to the evidence where there's such a tape. Make him point to it."

"Approach the bench," Judge Fujisaki instructed.

An angry, loud sidebar ensued. Philip Baker raged, "There was a tape made by Paula Barbieri's answering machine. It was analyzed by the LAPD, and they couldn't identify whether there's a Bronco."

Dan admonished, "Shhh. Keep your voice down."

"You're the one!" Philip Baker almost shouted, pointing a finger at Dan.

Dan asked the judge, "Can you control this guy? He's trying to make an argument to the jury."

Judge Fujisaki drew laughter when he turned to the jury and said in a folksy voice, "Excuse me, folks. Would you step out in the hallway?"

Then the bickering resumed until Philip Baker made a mistake, arguing that the tape "should be in front of the jury."

"Should be?" Dan asked. And that was the point. Dan did not believe that such a tape existed. But even if it did, it had not been placed into evidence. Therefore, Baker could not—should not—refer to it. Judge Fujisaki called the jury back in and told them to disregard Baker's comments.

But before long, Baker issued yet another bald-faced lie: "Is there a second glove near Ron's body? You bet."

Finding another opportunity to remind the jury that Mark Fuhrman had not testified, he said, "Ladies and gentlemen, the evidence in this case is simply not trustworthy. . . . If you can't trust the messenger—and believe me, the messenger in this case—we have one messenger that came to testify. We have one messenger that didn't."

Kim said to Michelle Caruso, "It's taking everything I've got to keep it inside. I want to scream and run out of the room."

Patti studied the jury. Some were taking notes. She thought: Do they really believe this stuff—these lies? She wanted to shake Baker. She wanted to get up and scream, "What is wrong with you? How can you call yourself an officer of the court?"

Baker moved toward his finale. "Now, I want to, just for a moment, talk about reality, and it may seem somewhat harsh to do this, but this is a lawsuit. I just want to talk a little bit about the parties in this lawsuit.

"And Mr. Petrocelli got up here and told you in a very emotional appeal that Ron Goldman would probably be opening his restaurant now and he would be going into his restaurant.

"Let's examine reality.

"Fred Goldman, for reasons that he called tough love, didn't help his son go through bankruptcy, and he had to go through bankruptcy.

"Ron Goldman wouldn't have a restaurant now.

"He'd be lucky to have a credit card."

Kim was crawling out of her skin. Inwardly she yelled: How dare you try to paint Ron as a loser.

I ground my teeth and glared. My fists were clenched so tightly they went numb. I wanted to leap forward and punch this liar in the face.

Baker concluded, "You can't give him his son back. You can't give Ron Goldman's life back. But you can give back Mr. Simpson his life . . . and give Justin and Sydney their dad back."

I thought I might vomit.

During the lunch break, I said to Patti, "I feel so much—hate? I don't like to use that word—but what he did is so despicable. He might just as well have been there and helped the son of a bitch commit murder."

Dan tried to calm me, promising that, in rebuttal, he and Tom Lambert would throw all the lies back in the defense team's collective face.

Kim implored Dan, "Can you just clean up this point? Can you fix it? About the money. Dad offered. Ron didn't want his help. He wanted to handle the bankruptcy thing by himself."

Dan told her not to worry. "I'm going to get Baker for what he said," he promised.

Kim said to a friend, "It's a damn good thing there's a gag order."

When we started this journey two and one half years earlier, a courtroom was the last place I expected to find blatant fraud, deception, and lies. Many defense attorneys continue to mystify me. Because of the knowledge he gains through the attorney-client privilege, not to mention the evidence, a lawyer often knows that his client is guilty. And still, he does his best to help him walk free. Never for a moment would I suggest that the accused should not have representation, but when the concept was developed, it was to protect an individual's rights and produce evidence in his favor. Today, these so-called officers of the court, who are supposed to be part of the search for truth, are willing to win at any cost. They must sit around and carefully plan what lies they will tell in open court.

In both the criminal and civil "Trials of the Century," there never was any shared responsibility to find the truth about who killed Ron and Nicole. "Scheme Teams" I and II sought to hide or misrepresent the truth whenever it pointed to their client.

I wondered: How do these people get up in the morning and look in the mirror, knowing they are putting food on the table with blood money? How can they smile and laugh and joke, and pat the back of a man they *know* viciously murdered two innocent people?

They are part and parcel of what allows guilty, violent predators to walk free. Forty percent of murders are committed by people who have previously committed violent acts. We are haunted by the knowledge that if the killer had been dealt with severely the first time he laid a hand on his wife, Ron might still be with us.

After lunch, Dan told the jury, "What you have heard in this courtroom, ladies and gentlemen, from the defense over the last four months, and from these lawyers over the last two days, is what a guilty man has to say in response to all this evidence.

"It was all planted.

"It's all contaminated.

"All of the photos are fake.

"All the law enforcement people are corrupt or incompetent.

"Every witness who gets on that stand and testifies against me is lying or mistaken.

"There's a conspiracy the likes of which has never before been witnessed, all to get me.

"That's what a guilty man does."

He pointed out some of Baker's more obvious lies: "Mr. Baker came up here and told you straight-faced that there was a second glove near Ron Goldman's body. . . . He just made it up.

"You know why he made it up?

"He's desperate."

Noting that Mark Fuhrman was still at home, asleep in his bed, when other officers were gathering the evidence at Bundy, Dan reminded the jurors, "Mr. Baker told you earlier today, Mark Fuhrman found all the evidence in the case. That's just false. What trial has he been attending?

"He said Mark Fuhrman was unaccounted for during an hour and a half at Bundy. That's an absolutely false statement." Dan read from the testimony of several witnesses who accounted for Fuhrman's where-abouts during the time in question.

Just as in the criminal trial, the defense had attempted to character-ize any minor discrepancy as evidence of a grand conspiracy. Dan con-ceded, "There's no such thing as a perfect investigation, just like there's no such thing as a perfect crime." Bundy, he said, "is a crime scene; it's not a museum.

"Things move. People walk. Photographs are taken. Bodies are moved. Folks are working. An envelope get moved. What does that mean?

"There's a piece of paper missing. Oh, what are we going to do? A piece of paper was missing. That's another point they made: A little white piece of paper is missing.

"Big deal. What about his blood? That's not missing. And his hair, that's not missing. And his shoe prints, that's not missing. And his hat and his glove, that's not missing."

Now it was Tom Lambert's turn. Point by point, in a lengthy but effective manner, he went over the evidence-gathering procedures and the volumes of incriminating material that it produced. He stressed the big issue that the defense never wanted to mention: Contamina-tion can produce an unusable result, but it does not—cannot—produce a false result. Instead of contamination and corruption, Tom declared, the defense position should start with the letter D: "It's desperation. It's deception. It's dishonesty."

I woke up Tuesday morning with my jaws throbbing from grinding my teeth all night long. Over coffee, I said to Patti, "The way Dan and Tom laid it out—addressed all the manipulations and lies and explained the hoax they tried to perpetrate—how could anyone *not* believe that he's the S.O.B. who murdered two people?"

Patti nodded her agreement as I continued to vent my feelings. "If we pile all our evidence on one side of the scale of justice, and the defense has no credible evidence on their side, what does that tell you? Do they have anyone else's blood, hair, shoe prints—any shred of evidence that points to anyone else? No!"

"It's so disturbing to look at the jury and wonder what they're going to do," Patti said. "They have heard lies and they have heard the truth. Now, they have to choose between the two."

"I know," I said, "there is no assurance. Last time, we had a jury say 12–0 that the truth didn't matter."

This was the day. Tom and Dan would need an hour or two to finish our rebuttal statement. Then the case would go to the jury.

The crowds outside the courthouse were larger and more vicious than ever. Many demonstrators had bullhorns. We heard shouting voices accusing, "Golddiggers!" and rabid, anti-Semitic chants such as, "You Jews just want money, money, money!" We also heard shouts, "Goldman, we love you—go get 'em!" We tried to keep our heads down and walk quickly.

As we sat in court awaiting the beginning of the proceedings, Kim thought: In two hours we put our trust in twelve strangers, again.

But Judge Fujisaki did not appear at the bench. Instead, he summoned the principal lawyers into his chambers. Something was wrong. We could feel it. Suddenly the audience was dismissed. Dan reappeared, grim-faced, and huddled with his colleagues. Patti and Kim raced forward to join us at the plaintiffs' table.

Dan explained that two of the jurors had reported to the judge that someone had attempted to contact them at home. Patti gasped, "Dan was right! Someone tried to tamper with the jury. How can this happen at the eleventh hour?"

How could anyone find out who was on the jury? Our attorneys had no names—only juror numbers. Each day the jury was bussed to and from a parking lot at a location unknown to us. We learned that Channel 9, KCAL-TV, had been bounced from the courtroom for following the jury bus, and we wondered what other sinister forces may have attempted a similar ploy.

Amid all this turmoil, the killer sat at the defense table with some of his cronies, laughing, talking about movies as if he did not have a care in the world.

We listened intently to the plan. Judge Fujisaki would interview each of the twelve jurors and four remaining alternates separately to assess the damage. We had no answers, only questions. It was good that the two jurors had reported the contacts to the judge, but what if he found that others were contacted and did not report the fact? If we lost more than four jurors, would we have a mistrial?

Patti and Kim fled for the hallway. Kim was numb. She said, "Two hours ago, I thought this would all be over. Now this. I cannot believe this."

The press circled. Everyone wanted to know what the delay was all about. Patti and Kim, of course, could say nothing. They paced the hallway, wondering: Is the defense responsible for this? Are they that desperate? That evil? It was possible!

After interviewing the jurors, Judge Fujisaki concluded that there was no misconduct on their part and he allowed the trial to conclude.

Tom Lambert began the day with a final primer on DNA. "Those DNA test results are extremely significant evidence," he said, " . . . establishing the guilt of Mr. Simpson."

He reminded the jury of Robert Blasier's attempt to illustrate his contention that DNA test results are not as significant as they seem. Step by logical step he figuratively tore apart Blasier's Tinkertoy defense: Dr. Robin Cotton noted that DNA testing is a well-established method used to match donors and recipients for bone marrow and organ transplants; Dr. Brad Popovich uses the same technology day in and day out to make life-and-death diagnostic decisions; the defense's own witness, Dr. Henry Lee, did not challenge the DNA test results; another defense witness, Dr. John Gerdes, never said there was any contamination, merely a "risk" of contamination.

"This DNA evidence is reliable evidence," Tom proclaimed. "The experts told you so. Even their expert told you so."

Patti thought: Tom is making it so clear. Does the jury get it like I do?

Dan followed on Tom's heels without a break in the proceedings, and he hammered away relentlessly at the legion of lies told by the defendant and his attorneys. "Mr. Baker actually wanted you folks to believe this was a professional hit," Dan said with a hint of amazement in his voice. "Can you imagine that?

"And he said two professional assassins. . . . That's what he wanted you to believe. Thirty stab wounds. Two professional assassins.

"[If] this was a professional assassin, it would have taken a single bullet in about three seconds. Gone. Not a shred of evidence.

"Is a professional assassin, let alone two, going to stab people over and over and over again? You going to leave all the evidence behind?

"Does that make sense to anybody?"

Instead, Dan said, it was an amateur assassin. "There was only one person the evidence in this case showed had any problem, any hostility, any antagonism, any enmity, any animosity toward Nicole, and that was O. J. Simpson.

"Is it just a coincidence that near the very end of her life these two were at war with one another? . . .

"And then she's just found dead?"

Time after time Dan pointed out the killer's lies and pleaded for the jurors to use their common sense in evaluating what that meant. "Why didn't he just say, You know what, Mr. Petrocelli, I did hit her? I did hit her. I battered my wife that night.

"You know why he didn't tell you?

"Because he knows how damning that is. He knows that if you believe he's the kind of man who could hit his wife in anger, who could lash out and strike her, then you can understand that he did the same thing on the evening of June 12, except this time he had a knife in his hand."

Dan had specific rebuttal points to cover. "You know," he said, "I got a kick when Mr. Baker . . . said that this Bronco was a white elephant. He called it a white elephant. He said, Why would Mr. Simpson go commit a murder in a white elephant?

"You know what Mr. Simpson's other choices were: a Bentley and . . . a Testa Rosa Ferrari, a red one, no less, a fire-engine red."

Dan continued. "Mr. Simpson says he is an innocent man because he didn't act like a guilty man after the murders. . . . An innocent man doesn't put a gun to his head, forty-seven years old, four children, two small, their having just lost their mother—an innocent man doesn't do that. . . ."

Dan effectively used sarcasm to mock the grand conspiracy theory. He referred to the chart that he had presented during the earlier phase of his argument, the chart entitled:

Either: Simpson Is Lying
Or: All of These Witnesses and Documents
Are Lying, Mistaken, or Faked

Dan said, "I did this list before I heard Mr. Baker's argument and Mr. Blasier's and Mr. Leonard's arguments. And frankly, I left a lot of names off. . . . I should have put on all the FBI agents, because he says they're all . . . out to get Mr. Simpson. So I've got to put Bill Bodziak's name and Gerry Richards's name and Doug Deedrick's name on there."

The defense had accused the plaintiffs' team of intimidating its witnesses to testify properly. "You know, we call that fondly, the Doubletree Defense," Dan said.

"I guess we have the ability to pick up the phone and call people up, and hey, you know, we don't know each other, but I'd like you to testify in this case. Meet me at the Doubletree Hotel; meet me in my room, and I'm going to try to get you to commit perjury, a felony, risk your life, maybe go to jail for many, many years, just to help me out.

"Maybe I should—my name should go up there as a criminal. I'm suborning perjury. That's against the law. That's what they say we're doing. I would go to jail for many years, suborning perjury. All my partners, too. Put their names up there.

"We're all begging people to commit perjury.

"I guess we may even have to put Mr. Baker's name up there, because Mr. Simpson says he has a different opinion than Mr. Baker on some very important facts. I guess Mr. Baker's wrong, too.

"I don't know.

"Did I leave anybody off?"

Dan was through with humor now. His jaw tightened. His eyes glared. As he turned to the most distasteful portions of the defense team's closing argument, his temper burst forth. He said, "And Mr. Baker got up here—in one of the lowest moments of this trial—he mocked this young man who lies in his grave.

"Now what I want you to think about this is: If O. J. Simpson were innocent, truly innocent, would he let his lawyer mock this young man? This young man tried to save the life of the mother of his children. He is a hero to O. J. Simpson.

" . . . And Mr. Baker has the nerve to tell you it only cost $200 to file a lawsuit. Can you imagine that?

"And in their zeal to get your verdict, have they become so insensitive to the greatest of human tragedies, the loss of life, that they want to speak about these two dead people in terms of $200?

"My stomach turned when I heard that."

Dan pulled a wad of twenty-dollar bills out of his pocket and shook them in the direction of the killer. He raged, "You know, Mr. Simpson, here's $200. You want it? Give me back my client's son."

Baker yelled out, "Give it up."

But Dan would not be silenced. In one, final burst he roared, "They want this verdict that bad, take it. Give my client back his son, and we will march out of here in a heartbeat."

Court recessed for lunch. As we rose and turned, we saw five uniformed officers lined up at the back of the courtroom, waiting for us. They were standing, rigid, hands behind their backs. Seeing the crowds in the morning, Dan had called the Santa Monica Police Department and requested protection for us all.

And we needed it. Once we stepped outside, throngs of people surged toward us, yelling, pushing, threatening. This was the worst it had ever been. Cameras and microphones were everywhere. The short walk across the street seemed endless. I had my arms around Patti and Kim, trying to shield them. "Get out of our face," I yelled. "Let us go!"

After lunch, Judge Fujisaki, reading in a monotone, gave the jury its instructions. Then, at about 2:30 P.M., the jury left to deliberate.

Leaving the courthouse after the jury instructions was, again, unbelievably scary. Our initial contingent of police officers was augmented by several more on motorcycles. They formed a line and tried to keep the media and the crowd—swarming like killer bees—away from us. Two police cars were positioned to stop traffic as we crossed the street. Sirens wailed in the distance.

Patti could only imagine what it would be like when the verdict came in. "I am dreading that day," she said, "and at the same time, I can't wait for this to be over."

I was somewhat morose, because I realized that even if we got a verdict of "liable," the killer would still be a free man. He would still be able to get up in the morning, have breakfast, play golf, visit with his family and what few friends he may have left. He would still breathe the fresh air and feel the sunshine. There would still be no justice. He belonged in a cell, awaiting the day he is hauled into a chamber and put to death.

In the war room at the Doubletree, Dan checked his watch. The jury had been deliberating for fifteen minutes. He quipped nervously, "You mean they haven't reached a verdict yet?"

"I don't want an instant verdict," I said. "And I don't want 9–3, 10–2, 11–1. I want a 12–0 ruling. I want there to be no hint of racial division. I want twelve people to say, based on the evidence, they all agree that this man killed two people."

THIRTY-EIGHT

The wait began.

Michael prepared to fly home on a moment's notice. Our house was a bizarre mixture of fevered anticipation and somber reflections on the devastation we had experienced after the criminal verdict. We knew that truth was on our side, but we could not allow ourselves to count on that to carry us through. We all tried to protect ourselves from expecting a favorable decision from the jury. We had been sucked in before, and we could not allow that to happen again, but it was difficult.

Kim told Dan how proud and grateful Ron would have been for everything he and our other attorneys had done on his behalf. "Thank you," Dan said. "I needed to hear that right now."

Dan was optimistic, but, as Patti said, "He has to be; he can't allow himself to get down."

We drove one another crazy with our analyses of what had happened and what might occur at any moment.

"Regardless of the outcome," Patti said, "everything that could have been done was done. It's out of our hands, now." I agreed, but it did not make the waiting any easier.

I said to Patti, "As of now the criminal trial was 225 percent longer than the civil case. It is amazing to me. We had all the same evidence as before, plus we had the killer's testimony, new witnesses who contradicted his testimony, the Bronco chase, the disguise, the suicide note, the Bruno Magli photographs, new experts, and still Dan was able to condense it all into a concise, understandable, logical package. It's been almost four months to the day. The criminal trial dragged on for nine."

"We also had Judge Fujisaki instead of Judge Ito," Patti reminded me. "This time the defense was not permitted to put the LAPD on trial and to sidetrack the jury with racial issues."

Kim said, "You know, it drives me nuts when people ask me to compare the two trials and insinuate that Marcia and Chris were not up to the job. I'm not taking anything away from Dan—he was incredible, all our attorneys were—but the criminal trial lawyers had their hands tied behind their backs, thanks to Judge Ito. It's not fair to compare them."

Words were inadequate to express the appreciation I felt for what Dan, Ed, Tom, Peter, and Yvette had done. If, for some incomprehensible reason, this jury had not been convinced of the killer's culpability, I would never be able to understand it.

People constantly asked, "How long do you think the jury will be out?" Patti's answer was always the same. "More than four hours." We were all sure that this jury would take more time than the criminal trial jury. They would surely want to avoid criticism that they had not examined the evidence thoroughly.

Some people also asked, crassly, "How much do you think you'll get?" Our response was: "It doesn't matter. It's never been about money."

Kim said, "All I want is to hear them say he's liable, so I can go to the cemetery and tell my brother."

The jurors had been deliberating for six hours when, on Wednesday, they requested a magnifier and a photograph of a purple top test tube, similar to the one used for the reference sample of the killer's blood. Judge Fujisaki provided them with a magnifying glass but not the photograph, reminding them that they had an actual test tube available to them in the jury room. Like everyone else, we asked ourselves, What does this mean? There was no way to know, and we did not want to torture ourselves with unanswerable questions.

We tried to maintain some sense of order, some structure in our lives. Patti and Kim went to work. Lauren went to school. We talked to Michael and Brian frequently. I tended to some business responsibilities for Safe Streets, but my main task was to stay close to the telephone. Each of us pledged to help the others keep calm once the verdict came in. We knew that we would have four hours to reach the courtroom, and we vowed to maintain our self-control.

Our attorneys called frequently to keep us informed. Each time the phone rang, the hairs on the back of my neck bristled and my throat tightened, making me wonder whether I could keep my composure once the moment arrived.

Some harasser managed to obtain our phone number and pro-grammed a computer to dial at five-minute intervals and then hang up, causing additional stress on our already crackling nerves.

On Thursday, Judge Fujisaki ordered an investigation regarding the incident that had disrupted court two mornings earlier. We now knew that two of the civil case jurors had received letters from two of the criminal trial jurors, ostensibly offering moral support but, at the same time, making reference to an agent who might help them peddle their story once the trial was over.

Kim saw news coverage of the police storming into the home of Brenda Moran, one of the two criminal jurors who had signed the let-ters. She was an employee of the court system and was suspected of pro-viding the names and addresses of the civil trial jurors. Police seized a computer and other possible evidence. "This is unreal," Kim said. "This is totally tripping me out. This stuff happens in drug busts, jewel heists, kidnappings—but it doesn't happen to ex-jurors!"

Then on Friday, Juror 7, Rosemary Caraway, was dismissed at the defense's request when it was learned that her daughter worked in the District Attorney's office. She had failed to disclose this fact on her orig-inal questionnaire.

Rumors flew that the trial was in danger of unraveling.

Judge Fujisaki called the remaining jurors into court and said, "A juror has been excused for legal cause. You are not to speculate as to the reason why." He added that he was relying on their integrity to bring the case to a close. He told them that they must not let themselves be tainted by the relentless publicity churning around the trial. He ordered them to stop watching television, listening to the radio, or reading newspapers—entirely. He asked that they have someone screen their calls and open their mail to guard against unexpected pressure.

"It's unfortunate we have come to this pass," the judge said, "but sometimes in a long trial, because it's so long and because of the inordinate amount of interest that apparently exists, things unravel. I am trusting you to make sure this case does not unravel and we reach, if we can, a completion."

We hoped that he might sequester the jurors for the remainder of their deliberations, but that did not happen.

The defense, of course, argued for a mistrial. Baker claimed that the dismissed juror may already have done his client irreparable damage, but Judge Fujisaki denied his request.

A new juror was chosen by lot from the four remaining alternates. He was an Asian man, a computer specialist in his mid-thirties who, throughout the trial, was one of the most conscientious note takers. Judge Fujisaki ordered the jury to begin deliberations anew.

The forty-eight-hour weekend seemed endless. Kim's anxiety level skyrocketed. "I can't eat. I can't sleep. I can't think straight," she said. "I don't know if I can get through this."

She speculated that, since the jury had been ordered to disregard its previous deliberations and go back to square one, it would take at least as much time as before. The original jury had deliberated for two and a half days. By Kim's calculations, therefore, this new group would not reach a verdict until Tuesday, at the earliest.

On Monday, Baker was at it again, filing a formal, written request for a mistrial. He claimed that research over the weekend revealed that the dismissed juror had scratched out an answer on her questionnaire that would have divulged her daughter's ties to the prosecutor's office. Baker railed, "This is a direct, deliberate attempt to mislead, and I think it's an outrage. It's not inadvertent, and we are entitled to a mistrial. This is misconduct."

Dan insisted that the juror was an honest and conscientious woman who had simply overlooked a question. He noted that, elsewhere on her form, she had disclosed that her daughter was a legal secretary. "They'll do anything, Your Honor, to get a mistrial,' Dan warned. "They'll do anything."

Judge Fujisaki once again denied the motion.

We had spent more than two and one half years watching the machinations of these defense lawyers, and we had reached the saturation point. Kim was terrified. She said, "I feel like someone is screwing with us. Majorly."

Tuesday, February 4, 1997. I drove downtown to meet with Jim Wooten, the president of Safe Streets, to plan my schedule for the coming months, when I could finally devote my energies to my new job. Patti had some shopping to do and had clients scheduled. Lauren was at school. Michael was at his fraternity house in Tucson. Kim, at her office, was covering the phone.

Throughout the day the jury listened again to various portions of testimony that it had requested: Allan Park, A. C. Cowlings, and the killer himself. All of the testimony seemed to pertain to the killer's credibility. We tried not to analyze the message, reminding ourselves that the criminal trial jury had listened to Park's testimony shortly before it set a double murderer free.

As the day wore on, we resigned ourselves to a continuation of the tension. After all the read-backs in court today, we did not expect a verdict. Our best guess was tomorrow. It was about 4 P.M. when, finished with our meetings, Jim and I drove back to his room at, of course, the Doubletree in Santa Monica. On the way, I placed a call to Kim. She was not answering, so I left a message.

At that very moment Kim was on another call. Dan's assistant Carolyn Walker shouted, "Kim, we have a verdict! Dan wants everybody here now!"

Kim's mind spun. Judge Fujisaki had apparently changed his plans to give us four hours' notice. All Kim could think was: Now? Now? NOW!!!

Our careful plans to help one another remain calm evaporated in an instant. Several hours of chaos ensued. Kim checked her messages and heard my voice saying, "Hi, honey, how's it going? Just checking in."

Kim called me immediately and screamed, "There's a verdict. Go now!"

The words did not register in my consciousness; she might as well have been speaking a foreign language. How could this be?

Kim repeated, "They have a verdict. We have to get there now!"

Finally I managed to babble, "I'm almost there. I'm five minutes away."

Nearing the end of her workday, Patti was exhausted. She munched on a small chocolate and peanut butter candy bar, hoping for instant energy. Suddenly, her phone rang. "They have a verdict," Kim shouted, "and we have to get there ASAP! They're going to read it at five o'clock."

Patti immediately called Lauren at home and told her to meet her at a parking lot near an entrance ramp to the Ventura Freeway. Then she gathered her appointment book and water bottle and shoved them into her purse. She called Maralyn Gold to put our phone chain in motion.

"Do you want me to drive you to the courthouse?" Maralyn asked.

Patti told her no, but said that if she wanted to come with her, to meet at the parking lot.

Just as Patti was leaving work, her pager alerted her to a message from her friend Fern Rosenberg, in Chicago. Jumping into her car with the RUNGODO license plates, she grabbed her car phone. As she drove, she returned Fern's call. Then she tried to call Michael but could not reach him at the moment. She also called her mother and father, Brian, her sister Joyce, and several other close friends.

Kim's hands were shaking as she tried to pump enough gas into her car to get her to Santa Monica, and she realized that our plan to keep everyone calm was out the window.

Meanwhile, I arrived at the Doubletree to find it surrounded by police. The street was closed off and so was the hotel. Security guards would admit no one without a room key or a special pass.

I hurried into Room 205 and joined Dan and the other attorneys.

When Patti pulled into the parking lot where Maralyn and Lauren waited, she noticed that Barb Duben had driven in behind her. It was mere coincidence. Barb had not heard that there was a verdict, but when Patti told her, she, too, jumped into the car.

"What would we do without car phones?" Patti said as she answered a call from Kim.

In the backseat of Patti's car, Lauren was tearful and nauseous. Patti had one hand on the wheel, while the other continually punched in numbers on her car phone. Every time she spoke to someone, she started to cry. The tension and anticipation in the car were overwhelming. She tried to call Michael repeatedly. When she finally reached him and told him that the verdict was in, he said, "I want to come home."

"There's no time; it's impossible," Patti said.

Although he did not verbalize it, Patti could tell from his voice that he was deeply disappointed that he could not be here with us.

Minutes later, Patti called Kim for directions. She had missed her regular ramp to the Pacific Coast Highway and was frantic about being late.

I was worried about Patti and Kim having to negotiate through the crowds outside. I called them both and suggested, "When you get five minutes away, call me and I'll come downstairs."

They both said no, I should stay where I was.

When Kim ran into Room 205, she found the mood somber. Conflicting reports flew about. We were told that Judge Fujisaki had delayed the proceedings until 5:30 to give the Browns time to arrive from their home in Orange County. Someone else said that the killer had not yet left home. Apparently, he was determined to be fashionably late.

Lauren continued to shake and cry. She felt as if she were jumping out of her skin. Patti tried to embrace her several times, but she pushed her away; she did not want to be babied or fussed over. Finally, she allowed Patti to place her hands on her face, pull her close, and comfort her with a kiss.

The moment was caught by television cameras, peering in through the hotel windows. Patti's friend Fern called from Chicago. "I saw you kiss Lauren," she said. "I could tell you were saying, 'I love you.'"

Several times police officers came to our room to talk about how we would get across the street. At first the plan was to put us into cars and actually drive us across, but we finally concluded that the police protection was sufficient for us to make the walk.

It was 5:15 P.M. when we left the hotel. As we stepped outside the lobby, cameras were shoved in our faces, but the police were out in full force. Cruisers blocked traffic. Rows of motorcycles kept the crowd back and, for good measure, the sirens wailed. I had my arms around Patti and Kim, holding tight. Dan walked in front of us, holding Lauren's hand. Out of one corner of my eye I saw someone from a camera crew, attempting to follow our progress, lose his balance and fall into a shrub.

"My heart is beating so fast," Patti said. "I cannot believe this day is finally here."

Gradually, as we moved forward, we became aware of a glorious reality. The crowd of spectators was cheering us with shouts of encouragement. A few of the killer's "fans" were in evidence, but their catcalls were drowned in a warm, wonderful wave of support.

Inside the courthouse we paced the halls, shared numerous hugs, and waited.

"How far away are the Browns?" someone asked.

No one was sure, but we heard yet another report that the killer was still at his house. Dan said, "I don't think he's going to be in the courtroom when the verdict is read." Then someone else reported that he was definitely not coming.

Coward! I thought.

Kim was incensed. She did not want to hear the verdict if *he* was not there. "He was laughing at me when he was acquitted," she said. "Now it's my turn."

We literally sweated it out. Since it was after normal business hours, the air conditioning was turned off, and the interior of the building gradually became more oppressive; before long the temperature felt as if it was nearing one hundred degrees.

Three times a sheriff allowed Patti, Kim, and Lauren to use the men's room. They did not want to go out into the adjacent hallway where the ladies' room was located, and where a crowd of reporters waited.

By 6 P.M. we were informed that Judge Fujisaki wanted to wait just a bit longer for the Brown family to arrive.

By 6:30 we heard that the killer was coming after all.

And at 6:55 a deputy told us to go inside the courtroom. The Dubens, Zieglers, and Golds—as well as Jim Wooten and our Victim-Witness advocate, Mark Arenas—all managed to get in with us, although the men had to stand in the back. I took my seat at the second tier of the plaintiffs' table, next to Peter Gelblum. Patti, Kim, and Lauren sat behind me.

The killer arrived. His sister Shirley, her husband, and a niece were the only other members of his family in attendance.

Lauren muttered "murderer" under her breath until Patti warned her to be quiet.

The entire Brown family arrived.

This is really weird, Kim thought. Her body felt numb. Events seemed to move in slow motion; sights and sounds came at her as if from the far end of a tunnel.

The bailiff called out, "Jury is walking."

Patti, Kim, and Lauren were visibly shaking. Tears streamed down their faces. Patti glanced down at her hands. They were absolutely white and her fingernails were digging into Lauren's jeans so deeply that she thought she might tear them. They kept looking at one another, silently begging for support.

The jurors filed in with expressionless faces. What did that mean? I wondered.

As we waited for Judge Fujisaki to appear, I reached my left arm over the railing behind me. Instantly my fingers were entwined with those of Patti, Kim, and Lauren.

Finally the judge came in. He expressed his appreciation to the jury for its work and asked the foreman, "Have you reached a verdict?"

"Yes."

The bailiff took a large manila envelope over to the jury foreman and asked him to verify that these were, indeed, the proper verdict forms. The foreman removed numerous pages from the envelope and read them one by one. The soft rustle of the turning pages could be heard throughout the otherwise silent courtroom. A few reporters craned their necks, trying to read.

Please, please, please, Kim thought. Just do it.

The jury foreman verified the verdict forms, returned them to the manila envelope, and handed it to the bailiff. The bailiff then gave the envelope to Judge Fujisaki, who also read the pages slowly, silently, meticulously. We searched his face for clues, but he remained expressionless.

Finally the papers were given to the clerk and, after a legal preamble, she intoned:

"Question number one, do you find by a preponderance of the evidence that defendant Simpson willfully and wrongly caused the death of Ronald Goldman, write the answer yes or no below."

The clerk continued, "Answer: Yes."

Spectators issued a collective gasp of excitement.

Behind me, Kim shouted, "Yes!"

Next to me, Peter also shouted, "Yes!" He turned and hugged me.

Judge Fujisaki said, "Excuse me. Hold it. If there's any display, I am going to clear the courtroom. Everybody understand that?"

The courtroom once again turned utterly, eerily silent.

The clerk continued reading the sometimes ponderously worded verdict forms. The process took some time, but we now knew what the remaining answers would be.

Did the defendant commit battery against Ronald Goldman? Did he commit oppression against Ronald Goldman? Did he commit battery against Nicole Brown Simpson? Did he commit oppression against Nicole Brown Simpson? Did he commit malice against Nicole Brown Simpson? To each question the clerk intoned, "Answer: Yes."

Kim thought: It's right. It's just right.

Dan, seated in front of me, turned slightly. Keeping his arm low, so that the judge could not see, he gave me a clenched fist signal of victory.

When the final question was answered, Kim looked at the killer. He was staring at the ceiling, expressionless.

Throughout the reading of the verdicts, Robert Baker had his chin in his hands. Now, he said, "Poll the jury."

Judge Fujisaki said, "Ladies and gentlemen, we are going to poll you. The clerk will instruct you how to answer."

The clerk explained, "I'm going to ask each of you individually as to each question whether this is your personal verdict. If you agreed with the answer to the question, answer yes. If you disagreed with it, answer no." She repeated question number one and the answer, "Yes." Then, using the official jury panel numbers, she asked, "Is this also your verdict, Juror 199?"

Juror 199 replied, "Yes."

"Juror 341? Is this your verdict?"

"Yes."

Kim let go of my hand so that she could count on her fingers.

"Juror 186?"

"Yes."

"Juror 294?"

"Yes."

Patti silently counted: One, two, three, four. She made a conscious attempt to make eye contact with each and every juror. She whispered to each of us, "Look at them. It's the only way we'll ever have to thank them. Look at them." The silent tally continued:

"Juror 266?"

"Yes."

"Juror 257?"

"Yes."

"Juror 369?"

"Yes."

I kept hoping and praying that we were going to get all twelve to say "Yes."

"Juror 290?"

"Yes."

"Juror 326?"

"Yes."

They sat up straight in their chairs as they answered. Kim and Patti sensed a firm, indignant tone in their voices.

"Juror 400?"

"Yes."

"Juror 88?"

"Yes."

"Juror 227?"

"Yes."

Finally the clerk declared, "Twelve to zero."

We nailed him, Patti thought. We didn't just beat him, we nailed him!

The process continued for many minutes as the clerk polled every juror on each of the eight questions. Only with supreme effort did we maintain the necessary silence; our emotions bubbled toward the surface.

Finally the last juror intoned the last "Yes." Judge Fujisaki thanked the jurors and dismissed them for the day.

We jumped to our feet. Patti, Lauren, and Kim ran in front of the railing. Our friends and attorneys encircled us. We wept and smiled and embraced one another. The communal hugs held an intensity none of us had ever experienced before. The room seemed to swirl around us.

The bailiff yelled out, "The jury's still here!"

We did not care. We had been silenced at the conclusion of the criminal trial and muffled for months by Judge Fujisaki's frustrating gag order. This was our time. This was our moment.

I wrapped my arms tightly around Kim, and she hugged back, more tightly than she had in a long time. We both said, "We did it. We did it for Ron!"

*   *   *

The killer and his attorneys slipped out of the room quickly, like thieves in the night.

We stepped outside the courtroom to find ourselves engulfed by cheers from a crowd that seemed to have grown even larger. As we began the walk across the street, still holding hands, we raised our arms in the air. "This is your time, Fred," Dan encouraged.

The scene reminded Kim of the throngs who had come to Ron's funeral. For a few moments, all Kim could see was her brother's smile, captured on the photograph of him holding a baseball bat.

We were smiling, crying, shaking, completely overwhelmed by the crowds and their shouts of support. Patti's hands were numb from squeezing Kim's and Lauren's so hard, for so long.

Our group spilled into the hotel lobby and we managed to cram inside an elevator. Away from the media and the spectators, we let loose with shrieks of joy and relief.

Up in Room 205 Dan ran about yelling, "Twelve-zip! Twelve-zip!"

Bottles of champagne appeared.

It was a strange, intoxicating feeling. Our relief and gratitude, our excitement and euphoria were tempered by the knowledge of what had brought this all about. Yes, we had won. But Ron was still gone.

I offered a toast: "Today marks two and a half years and we finally have justice. Our family is grateful for the verdict."

Dan said, "Ron would be proud."

Kim corrected, "Ron *is* proud."

My voice cracked as I proclaimed, "Thank God! Thank God for some justice for Ron and Nicole."

I turned to my family and said, "Twelve-zero. It is just what we wanted. The only thing that could have been sweeter was to see Ron walk through that door."

The comment reminded Kim of the image that Dan had evoked during his closing argument, of Ron striding through the courtroom door. She said to all of us, "Do you know how honored and grateful Ron would be to Dan, to everybody here, for what they've done? I can see the look in his eyes, the expression on his face. Remember how he looked when he watched Jimmy Connors or Andre Agassi play flawless tennis? That's how he would have looked watching Dan demand justice for him. He always recognized and appreciated excellence."

She could see the firm handshakes, the pats on the back, the exuberant high-fives he would share with everyone. She could feel the heat of his infectious, radiant smile and hear him bellow, "Way to go!" Then she could hear his voice soften and see his brown eyes, flecked with green, widen as he said, "Thanks, guys, you did me proud!"

If the killer had been convicted at the criminal trial, we would have presented our victims' statements prior to sentencing. But we never had the opportunity, until now.

We have composed our statements independently, choosing not to share them with each other until they appeared in print.

Lauren

I wish I could have said this directly to you, but I wasn't given the chance.

You won't hear me refer to you as "Mr. Simpson," or "O. J.," because our family refers to you as the "killer" who took our wonderful Ronny away from us.

When I stepped in that courtroom for the first time, I expected to see a man in a blue jail uniform. Instead I saw a coward. A man with a grin on his face wearing a newly pressed suit.

I shuddered at your size—I almost vomited when I realized that your big hands murdered my innocent brother.

Your psychopathic mind has probably convinced you that you didn't commit these murders. You have probably placed the blame on your battered wife or better yet, Ron. You held the knife that lunged into my brother's body so many times.

Did you ever think of Ron and the family that he was leaving behind? Did you ever realize that there were many other people who love Ron and would miss him? Did you ever stop and wonder if Ron might have dreams and aspirations? Did you even care, for that matter?

My life has fallen apart. I have lost my faith in the justice system. My oldest brother was ripped away from me, and you are still alive to talk about it.

Ron will never have the opportunity to watch me grow up. There are things that I want to share with him on a day-to-day basis. I'm sure that you know what that's like with your children. I want to ask him advice, I want to make sure that I'm taking the right path. Now I can't!

My brother wanted to have children; he wanted to settle down and get married. He had dreams to live and to fulfill, and you stopped him dead in his tracks.

A hero is someone we all look up to, someone to admire, someone who would do anything for anyone. Ron was a hero. He risked his life to stop your malicious hand from striking violence on your ex-wife one last time, but unfortunately, he was unsuccessful.

My life has a huge gap which I will feel forever. I often get emotional at the drop of a pin, and I sometimes have dreams about Ron and what his future would have been like. These dreams should be a reality.

When I thought of Ron's death, I thought car accident or some sort of everyday accident. I never thought about a murderer—with a knife. You took a knife and stabbed it into Ron. You took two wonderful human beings off this earth—and everyone is suffering now except you.

I was brought up not to use the word "hate," but I have made an exception. I HATE YOU!!! I hate the fact that you are able to breathe. I hate the fact that you are able to function as a human being. I hate the fact that you are alive. I hate the fact that you ruined my life. I hate the fact that another murderer is loose in our society.

Was Ron afraid? Do his pleas haunt you every night before you go to sleep? Do you realize that Ron will never get to do anything that you are doing? Ron suffered because of your ignorance and your disgusting, jealous behavior.

I would love to have you in a room and pound on you until you told me—How? Why? There are no answers. Murder is final.

Is it fair that all that I have left are videotapes, memories, and pictures? I deserve to have Ron as a part of my life. Ron deserved to live. It should be your useless body six feet under, not Ron's!

When I sat in the courtroom and made eye contact with you, I had to restrain myself from jumping over the railing. I wanted to put you through torture. I wanted you to suffer like Ron suffered. Unfortunately, this was only a daydream.

Not only did you break the hearts of millions of people across the country, but you broke my heart. You broke the circle of love that once knit my family together. You took a huge piece of me when you took Ron.

Ron was the type of person whom I could always count on. He would listen to me for hours on end, comforting me and telling me that everything would turn out for the better. Well, nothing is better. My life is a mess. I had to teach myself to be happy again. I had to try to stop thinking about the murder scene. I had to try to find some kind of normalcy. Do you know what it's like to have a huge chunk of your life missing because of one ignorant human being?

Ron didn't even get a chance to see me off on my first date, to lecture me about guys, to guide me with my dreams. He was always waiting for that chance. He wanted to protect me from everything and make sure that no one would ever hurt me. I didn't get a chance to protect Ron. I didn't think I would need to.

As I sit here with tears rolling down my cheeks, all that I feel is hatred toward you—a murderer!

You will never get to see our Ronny again because you are going to burn in hell with all of the murderers, drug dealers, and robbers of this world, while Ronny rests peacefully in heaven!

Michael

༶

I have spent countless numbers of hours thinking about what I would say to the man who killed my brother if I had the chance. Now that chance is mine. The hate that I feel toward you cannot be paralleled. I think about what you did to my brother—on a day-to-day basis. To think that a human being was capable of that kind of brutality makes me sick. The way you pranced into the courtroom with your "Scheme Team" made me sick. When it was all said and done, and you heard the verdict, I hated you for the way you stared at Kim when she was in tears. Then it happened. Juror 6 decided to throw up a black power sign. That summed it all up. It was not about you killing my brother and Nicole. It was about racism. I bet you felt great when you walked on the streets as a free man—something my brother will never have the chance to do. I have a little news for you, Mr. Killer: You are not a free man. Life just can't be the same for you anymore. You used to be an athlete, but now all you are is a coward and a murderer. You took something from me that I can never replace. Ron was a caring person who gave up his life to save a friend. I really do not know what your fate holds, but I do know that one day you will have to answer to a much higher justice. A justice that does not see color and does not hear racism. What are you going to do then? Think really hard, because life has a strange way of giving things back to people. I have gone over what happened that night thousands of times in my head. All I see is a HERO running in to save a friend, and a coward stabbing him to death. When you took Ron away, it was not only my family's loss, it was the world's loss, because that's the kind of person Ron was. All I can tell you is, you are lucky that I was not there the night of June 12, 1994, because you would be the one who was six feet under now. You say that you feel like the victim; what about Ron and Nicole. What about their families and loved ones? They are the true victims. Like I said before, What goes around, comes around. I believe that yours is on the way. To look at the emptiness in Kim's and Fred's eyes is enough to make me want to kill you. I understand that killing is not a way to fix a problem, but the thought has crossed my mind many times. You killed my brother, and with him a piece of me. I hate you, and there will be a day when you will have nowhere to run. One more thing. Ron and Nicole know when you are coming, but you will be in a place where the heat will be scorching your corrupt soul. You were never a football hero, a hero is my brother, not someone who murders. I hope your life is miserable. I hate you.

Patti

~

A
s I sit here today to express my feelings, I am filled with raw emotions—anger, frustration, sadness, deception, fear, and hatred. I was raised with morals, values, to tell the truth and to be respectful to and of others, whatever their race. I have tried to live up to and by those standards and have instilled the same in my own children. I ask myself almost every day, What is happening in our society? What has happened to our justice system? Why is there more violence and racism than ever before? What message are we giving our children? If you have money and/or you are a celebrity, you can get away with LYING . . . you can get away with CHEATING . . . you can get away with VIOLENCE . . . you can get away with RAPE . . . you can get away with a BRUTAL MURDER! You are treated differently from others. There has not been a day since I felt you were responsible for Ron's death that I have not hoped you would experience the pain—emotionally, mentally, and physically—that you inflicted upon Ron and Nicole. You never shed a tear, you never expressed sorrow, you never showed the slightest bit of remorse. As I watched you in court every day of the criminal trial and for several days of the civil trial, I am convinced that you are not capable of feeling any pain or remorse for the heinous crime that you committed. You took Ron's life from him and from others whom he befriended. You also took away a major part of our lives. As a parent, I can't imagine anything worse than losing a child due to an illness, an accident, or to a natural cause. But to lose a child caused by the brutality of another human being is beyond comprehension and acceptance. I experience an overwhelming sadness each and every day for the pain and suffering I see

in Kim and Fred especially, not to mention the pain experienced by my children, Brian, Michael, and Lauren, and by me. I wish that something could and would bring Ron back from this horrendous nightmare, but you have made such a miracle impossible. We were a normal, blended family who wanted to live life to its fullest—quietly and peacefully. Our lives will never be the same. There will always be a void—that being the loss of Ron's love, his affection, his warmth, his laughter, his smile . . . his everyday presence. Our family will always be associated with the "Trial of the Century" and we will always be remembered as a family who honored Ron and gave him a name—an identity. We searched and fought for justice, with all of our strength, determination, and love. Ron was and still is a real "hero." He made a choice to help his friend Nicole, the mother of your children. In the process, he sacrificed his own life. I will forever hold you responsible for Ron's brutal, savage, and untimely murder. You will be recognized, despised, branded, ostracized, and, someday, hopefully punished for being the "killer"—who got away with murder. For this, my hatred for you is and always will be indelibly etched in my mind.

Kim

I have thought long and hard about how and what to say. I think I got caught up in trying in some way to say something that would affect you . . . but then again, what could I possibly say that would affect a beast who slits his wife's throat and leaves her for his children to find? And a beast who traps his victim in a corner, brutally stabbing him over and over, thirty times over? A beast who has no remorse for the pain, grief, and anguish he has left behind? How could I possibly affect a beast who beats "his" wife in "his" house and blames her? A beast who, while in jail, signs autographs and writes a "poor me" book during the trial of his murdered wife? A beast who walks around chatting and telling jokes while the victims' families sit a few feet away? A beast who cares nothing about finding the true killer because he knows he wouldn't have far to search?

What could I possibly say that would inflict as much pain on you as you have left with me? What could I do to you that would leave you feeling as empty as I am? The answer is nothing. There will never be anything that would reach my level of sadness, which will forever be a part of my life. All I can do is tell you that, while you were so enraged, wielding a six-inch blade, stabbing Ron in the heart and lungs, that while you were viciously and maliciously cutting Ron down, you single-handedly, in one minute's time, destroyed all of our lives.

You took my best friend, my confidant, my only sibling. You took my hero. You stripped society of a gift: Ron. You took his dreams, his hopes, his future. You took a wife and a family that will never be. You took his entire life. A human life. What gave you the right to take all of that? Did you know that each time you sliced my brother you were cutting me, too? With each stab you were taking pieces of me. You have killed a huge part of me. So, while you may have thought that you were physically hurting only Ron, you were simultaneously taking away my life. What gave you the right to my life?

My life was to be shared with my only brother. We depended on each other completely. We knew each other better than anyone. We were to share our successes and our failures together. We were going to raise our children together. We were supposed to share our adulthood together. We were going to be together forever. We were inseparable. What gave you the right to destroy that?

I will never again see his smile, hear his voice, or listen to his laughter. I will never again hold his hand, touch his face, feel his arms around me, or give him a kiss. I will never again be able to tell Ron how much I love and adore him. I will never again be able to express my pride for his accomplishments. I will never be able to sit in Ron's restaurant, the Ankh. I will never again have my big brother to comfort me in sadness and celebrate with me in good times. I will never play with his son or daughter. I will never have him to walk me down the aisle. I will never be able to see if my children look like their Uncle Ron. We will never again share memories. My photo album will be empty. I will never again have someone say how much we look alike and how similar we are. I will never again hear the words, "You are my best friend, Munchkin, and I love you." I will never again be whole.

I will forever be asking myself the what-ifs, the what should have beens . . . the could have beens and the what will never bes. . . . I will forever be tormented with the desire to have Ron by my side. And what will you, a double butcher, be tormented with? I have a few wishes:

I wish that, for the rest of the days that you walk on this earth, you are shadowed with guilt, and that it slowly and quietly engulfs you until you wither up and disappear. And, until that happens, I wish that society ostracizes and harasses you and labels you the Butcher of Brentwood that we proved that you are. I wish you misery and a never-ending nightmare. I wish that Ron's eyes, the same eyes that watched you slaughter Nicole and then watched as you plunged the knife deeper into his body, the same big brown eyes that watched as you left him to die . . . that they always follow you, wherever you go. I wish that Ron's face is what you wake up to, in a cold sweat, in the middle of the night: the image of a beautiful young man, a bigger man than you will ever be.

Ron is a hero. You savagely butchered a hero.

I will never let you forget.

Fred

～

To the sociopathic coward who murdered my son:
      The desire to confront you, to tell you exactly what I think of you, has simmered and burned in me since it because so obvious that you were guilty of taking away from me, forever, the opportunity to hug my son and share his life and laughter. Now that I have the chance to confront you, I realize, with breathtaking certainty, that there is no dictionary, not thesaurus on earth that contains the words I need.

You took from Ron his entire future.

You took from Ron his dreams, his future successes.

You took from Ron the opportunity to laugh, to feel the sun and the wind and the rain.

You took from Ron the opportunity to marry a woman he loved and who would love him.

You took from Ron the opportunity to have children and to be the most unbelievably wonderful father this world could imagine.

You took from Ron the love of his family.

You took from Ron the joy of watching Brian, Michael, and Lauren grow into fine young people.

You took from Ron the opportunity to share the rest of his life with Kim, his sister, his best friend, the other half of his soul.

You took from Ron the love of Patti—more of a mother to him than he ever had before.

You took from Ron the love of a father whose love and respect for him was deeper than he could have ever known.

You took from this earth the kind of man you never were, never have been, and never could be. Nothing can change that. No amount of anger I could vent, or tears I could shed, will alter the one, heartbreaking fact that my son is gone forever. There can be no words that will ever bring him back.

In a just world, you would have been found guilty of savagely murdering two human beings. You would have been sentenced to death. You would have spent the past year sitting in a sunless cell, awaiting the day justice would be carried out.

I believe that this world would be a better place without you.

There is nothing more to say.

You are not worth any more of my words. You are not worth any more of my energy. You are not worth any more of my passion.

You are not worthy to walk in Ron's shadow.

ACKNOWLEDGMENTS

It is impossible for us to express our appreciation to all those individuals who have offered their emotional, professional, spiritual, and financial support during the past two and one half years. Their numbers are legion. There are some we must single out.

To the prosecution team: Marcia Clark, Chris Darden, Bill Hodgman, Hank Goldberg, George "Woody" Clarke, Cheri Lewis, Lisa Kahn, Brian Kelberg, Ken Lynch, Rochne Harmon, Scott Gordon, Alan Yochelson, David Wooden, Diana Martinez, Darrell Mavis, Dana Escobar, Jonathan Fairtlough, Patty Jo Fairbanks, Gil Garcetti, Suzanne Childs—you gave up so much of your lives in the fight for justice for Ron and Nicole. We have the deepest respect, admiration, and affection for each and every one of you.

Let us not forget the numerous law clerks, now D.A.'s—you worked so diligently behind the scenes and still had smiles on your faces every morning before we left for court. Natalie Agajanian, Melissa Decker, Kathy Behfarin, Susan "DJ" Dozier, Lisa Fox, Matthew Gibbs, Tracy Miller, Michael Price, and Tom Ratanavaraha.

Special thanks to former LAPD Detectives Tom Lange and Phil Vannatter, and to Detective Ron Phillips. You are three amazing, honest, caring men who never deserved the mud that was slung in your direction.

To the team of investigators from the D.A.'s office who escorted and protected us throughout the criminal trial: No matter how dismal the day, you had bright smiles and warm greetings for us. Over time, we became very close to each of you—Lieutenant Gary Schram, Bill

Guidas, Wil Abrams, Ken Godinez, Mike Stevens, Dana Thompson, Jack Gonterman, Brian Hale, George Mueller, Pat McPherson, Gene Salvino, Steve Oppler, Mike Armstrong. Thanks for taking such good care of "the package." We will never forget you.

To the Santa Monica and Los Angeles Police Departments and the Ventura County Sherriffs Department: Thank you for going beyond the "call of duty."

To Mark Arenas—our support, our confidant, our friend, our rock, our Victim-Witness Advocate: Without your kindness, knowledge, strength, support, and love, we would not have been able to get through this horrible fiasco every day. You lived it, as we did. Thank you is hardly enough to express the gratitude and the respect we have for you.

To Randy Moss of Ram Video Productions and to Ira R. Ellis of Ira Ellis Photography: Thank you for the endless time you devoted to bringing Ron's memory to life. You are truly special to our family.

To Nancy Claiborne, Ron Zito, Annie Leibovitz, Bob Nagai, Karen Dean Fritt, Bobbi Berg, Joanne Miraglia, Dolly Norris, and Wil Waterman, Très Chique, Brian and Phyllis Harvey, Terry Murphy and Brian Timsit, Colleen Campbell, Rabbi Bernie King, Rosey Brown: You reached out with warmth and gave your sincere support. Thank you.

To the Browns: We know your pain, your frustration, and your deep loss is immeasurable. May your futures be filled with peace, comfort, and happiness.

To members of the media who sacrificed so much of their time to cover this tragedy, especially Shoreen Maghame, Harvey Levin, Michelle Caruso, John North, Dominick Dunne, Cynthia McFadden, Dan Abrams, Geraldo Rivera, and Barbara Walters: We respect and value your difficult job and, most of all, thank you for your friendship and warmth.

To Elayne Rice, Alecia and Edgar Jacobs, and Joyce and Jay Friedrichs and family: You are truly what "family" is all about. Your constant support, comfort, encouragement, and unconditional love have given us strength. What would we have done without *all* of you? Lots of Love, "All of Us."

You treated Ron and me as if we were always part of your family. You took us in, no questions asked. And when tragedy struck, you stayed. You may never understand how much that means to both of us.

From the bottom of my heart, and Ron's, please know how important you are and how much we love you. Love, Kim.

To Brian: Just wanted to let you know that you are important to us and that we love you. Love, Mom and Fred.

Going through this tragedy together, supporting one another and helping each other has definitely brought us all closer. We love you. Lauren and Michael.

To Dad: Your understanding, your love, your support, your ability to stop everything in order to be there as a shoulder to cry on, and just being you, have helped us get through this horrible time in our lives. We love you. Michael and Lauren.

To Charlotte Prochnow, Annette and Izzy Katov, Babe and Irv Rubel, and Irene and Bernie Goldman: The past several years have been a constant reminder of the importance of "family." Thanks for all the calls, the caring, and for being there for all of us.

To Rabbi Gary Johnson: Thank you for all of your encouraging prayers, your phone calls, and your comforting words.

Ron's close friends: Pete Argyris and Mike Pincus, for sharing your memories of Ron with us and for helping us to relive the vital, vibrant, good times that so characterized Ron's short life. Lauren Cohen, you and Ron will be "eternally" connected. Jacqui Bell, for being such an important part of Ron's life. He truly loved you. Each of you has given new meaning to the word "loyal." And to all of Ron's friends, too numerous to mention, thank you for making the word "friendship" so important in Ron's life.

Lauren's friends: Jenny: Your support, guidance, incredible friendship, caring ways, and love have made it easier. I don't know what I would have done without you. Jamie, Julie, Lindsey: thanks for your endless hugs, your hours of company, and for your support. Breann: Our late-night talks and cries got me through a lot of sleepless nights. Theresa: Your compassion and friendship were an incredible help. Vicky: Your hugs, words, and presence made my days easier. Megan: Your support helped me get through this horrible time. John: Your warm hugs and friendly smile made my dreary days brighter.

Michael's friends: You encircled me with love and support. Alexa: Our friendship has helped me through one of the most difficult times in my life. Alisha, Melanie, Teresa, Josh, Chris, Eric, Vaughn, Brian,

Shawn, Mike, the Duben, Gold, Ziegler, Morse, Jensen, and Nacassio families: What would I have done without your support and encouragement? To several of my teachers at Oak Park High School who supported me and listened to what I had to say—Kim Galbreath, Rob Hall, Jeff Chancer, Tess Wilcoff, and Mike McDermitt.

To Kim's friends: Tricia Argyropoulis, for sharing stories of Ron. It truly helped to connect me to him and you. Joe Casciana, for being there in my darkest hours. Rich Davis, for being a loyal and tremendous friend, even in spite of your own tragedy. Stacy Fohrman: No matter how we got to this point, I am fortunate to have you in my life. Joanne and Paul Geller, for always knowing when crying, ranting, or just a hug was necessary. Lisa Hurley: Few people are as capable of offering so much strength, support, and unconditional love. Erika Johnson Iacopetti, for eighteen years of "sisterhood." Ron loved you as his own and so do I. Sarah Kupper, for being my dearest friend and always standing by my side. Amy Levine, for keeping me close every day. Jode Mann, for your insight. You truly get it, and thanks for the "sweater guy." Jana Robertson, for years of friendship to both Ron and me. You will always be cherished. Brian Swislow, for years of friendship, enabling complete trust and understanding. Denise Nilson Woodgerd, who has come through on the deepest levels. Brillstein-Grey and John Ziffren, for giving me an opportunity as well as the space and flexibility to balance a job and fight for justice. Joel Adelman, for giving me the space to live again. And to Bruce Grayson, Carla Whalen, Rae Gelbart, Michelle Fetro, Michele Azenzer, Ron Woodward, Jr., Leslie Wilcox, Mike Hahn, Sharon Simon, Patricia Russell, Linda Robertson, the Jaffe and Kupper families: To all of you for possessing gifts of loyalty, compassion, unconditional love, and unwavering support. Thank you will never be enough.

To our dearest friends Barb and Rob Duben and family, Maralyn and Jerrold Gold and family, Andrea and Jim Ziegler and family: In the past we have shared the best of times, and you were with us throughout the worst of times. Your unconditional love and support has given us incredible strength. We could not have gotten through this nightmare without each of you. Neal and Jill Rose: Thanks for your trips from Phoenix to share your love and overwhelming support. Fern Rosenberg: Thank you for coming here from Chicago. As in the past, our close friendship has brought unconditional comfort, love, and support. Also, many thanks to other friends: Fran and Paul Kaufman, Sheri and Steve Karp, Sherri and Stephan Berke, Sherri and Arnie Friedman, Marilyn Glassman, Judi and Rob Howard, Hilary and Jon Matthew, Jeff and Cindee Zabner, Barb and Dave Shannon, Marcia and Richard Bliss, Arlene and Doug Braun, Barry and Charlene Davis, Ruth and Glen Rose, Pat and Elliot Schutzer, Joan and Barry Otelsberg, Ann and Phil Altman, Pauline and Milt Zablow, Margaret and Barry Pollack, Toni and Bob Liebman, Ernie Wish, Andi and Gary Sherwin, Julie Wish, Cheryl and Mike Dispaltro, Christie Banks, Joyce and Eddie Dolin, Cindy and Steve Pollack, Betsy and Bruce Bender. Each of you holds a special place in our hearts.

To Paul Marciano, CEO, Guess, Inc.: For introducing us to Dan Petrocelli—what a gift. We will never be able to thank you enough for all of your overwhelming support.

To our incredible team of attorneys: Dan Petrocelli, Tom Lambert, Peter Gelblum, Edward Medvene, and Yvette Molinaro of Mitchell, Silberberg and Knupp. Words can hardly express the respect, admiration, bond, and love that we have grown to feel for each of you over this past year. You not only did a phenomenal job to bring justice to Ron and to our family, but you did it with honesty and such dignity. We were proud to be part of your team and we will always hold a special place in our hearts for each of you. To Steve Foster, Carolyn Walker, and Maria Johnson, who worked behind the scenes to make sure that everything was on track. Your dedication and thoroughness were immeasurable. Additionally, Dan, thank you for believing in us, the truth, and the need for justice. Your passion, devotion, and dedication were the driving force of our case.

And, finally, to the thousands of strangers who have written to us, approached us, phoned us, and prayed for us: You will never know how much your kind words have meant to each of us. When you said, "I never knew Ron, but I feel as if I know him now," we know we've accomplished what we set out to do.

Many people have contributed unselfishly to the production of this book and several must be singled out for special thanks.

To our editor, Claire Wachtel: Even though we resisted the process, we respect and admire your tough-love approach and your expertise. To Paul Fedorko, Tracy Quinn, Kim Lewis, Sharyn Rosenblum, Jacqueline Deval, and everyone else at William Morrow. It was worth it, even through all the sweat and tears.

To our agent, Pam Bernstein and Associates. Pam, could you ever have imagined what you were getting yourself into during your brief layover in Los Angeles (on your way back from visiting your son in Colorado)? With warmth and understanding, you gracefully led us through unfamiliar territory. Thank you for your guidance, compassion, and for introducing us to the Hoffers. And to Donna Dever, Pam's assistant, who provided professional and personal support throughout the course of this project.

—The family of Ron Goldman

WITH SPECIAL THANKS

Our task of finding a co-author to understand our pain, sadness, and outrage was one we thought would be impossible. That task was accomplished within minutes of meeting not one but two authors. This husband-and-wife team made the difference and they made it work.

Marilyn and Bill, you each possess warmth, intuitiveness, compassion, sincerity, and understanding. You provided an environment that was safe and trusting in which we could share some of the most precious, painful, and personal events in our lives. You opened your arms and surrounded us as if we were all part of a big family. You masterfully gathered enormous amounts of information and coupled it with our entire family's feelings and emotions. It was major therapy every time we sat down with you. Marilyn and Bill, you have not only become our counterparts, but also our confidants and friends. You became an integral part of our everyday lives and we will forever be in awe and admiration of your skill and art of writing. You are beautiful and loving people. Thank you for helping us to let others know—*His Name Is Ron.*

—With love,
Patti, Fred, Kim, Michael, and Lauren

We add our thanks to the William Morrow team and to our agent, Mel Berger, of the William Morris Agency.

This book would not be a reality without the aid of three of our close associates and friends. Our editorial associate Caroline Frye worked tirelessly. Without her editing, transcribing, organizational, and language skills, the manuscript would still be spinning on our hard disk. Our friend Jean Souza frequently kept the home fires burning.

Thanks to Nancy Grant Heston for her daily messages of encouragement—it's true, we couldn't have done it without you.

And, finally, to Fred, Patti, Kim, Michael, and Lauren: Thank you for giving us an opportunity to know and love Ron, and for reminding us of the true definitions of family, loyalty, and justice. We are honored to know you.

—William and Marilyn Hoffer

ABOUT THE AUTHORS

RON GOLDMAN'S FAMILY lives in southern California.

MARILYN and WILLIAM HOFFER are the authors
of twenty nonfiction books, including *Not Without My
Daughter* and *Midnight Express*. They live in Virginia.

To learn more about Ron, visit www.rongoldman.com.

Made in the USA
Middletown, DE
23 September 2021